Chemistry—a new course for CSE

Secondary Science Series

Chemistry: Consulting Editor
Dr R C Whitfield
University Department of Education,
Cambridge

General Science: Consulting Editor
R G Gough
Senior Lecturer in Education and
Teachers Centre Warden,
Rachael MacMillan College of Education

Titles in the Secondary Science Series:

Pre-13

Explore and Discover—science for the middle years
    J Darke and G Hughes   *Publication date Spring 1973*

CSE

Chemistry—a new course for CSE
    M Bowker   *Publication date Spring 1972*

GCE Ordinary Level

Chemistry by Experiment and Understanding
    J Gerrish and D Mansfield   *Publication date Spring 1972*

GCE Advanced Level

Patterns in Physics
    W Bolton   *Publication date Spring 1973*

Question Books for the 13–16-year Age Group

Structured Questions in Chemistry
    A D Gazard and E Wilkins   *Publication date Summer 1972*

Objective Questions in Chemistry
    K Valentine   *Publication date Spring 1973*

Biology Question Book
    P Holway   *Publication date Spring 1972*

Chemistry— a new course for CSE

Michael K. Bowker BSc
Senior Lecturer in Science,
Worcester College of Education,
(formerly Head of Science Department,
Wythenshawe Technical High School for Boys,
Manchester)

London · New York · St Louis · San Francisco · Düsseldorf
Johannesburg · Kuala Lumpur · Mexico · Montreal · New Delhi
Panama · Paris · Rio de Janeiro · Singapore · Sydney · Toronto

Published by

McGraw-Hill Book Company (UK) Limited

McGraw-Hill House, Maidenhead, Berkshire, England

---

07 094384 2 (Pupil's edition)
07 094385 0 (Teacher's edition)

Copyright © 1972 McGraw-Hill Book Company (UK) Limited
All rights reserved. No part of this publication may be reproduced, stored in a retrieval system, or transmitted, in any form or by any means, electronic, mechanical, photocopying, recording or otherwise, without the prior permission of McGraw-Hill Book Company (UK) Limited.

PRINTED AND BOUND IN GREAT BRITAIN

Contents

CHAPTER		PAGE
	Preface	vii
1	How chemists work	1
2	Water	18
3	Oxygen and burning	38
4	The simplest atom—hydrogen—and others	55
5	Carbon, fuels, flames, and energy	79
6	Acids, bases, and salts	104
7	Metals old and new	130
8	Detergents	172
9	Plastics	186
10	Nitrogen, sulphur, and chlorine	203
11	Chemistry all around us	223
	Appendix 1 Common and chemical names	238
	Appendix 2 Qualitative analysis	239
	Appendix 3 Revision notes	243
	Appendix 4 Ionic interpretation of reactions	245
	Appendix 5 Data sheets	248
	Index	249

Preface

The purpose of this book is to supply CSE candidates with amplification, clarification, and revision of work done in class, to provide some relief from the tasks of note-making and drawing, and to act as a laboratory manual. I hope the book will also prove useful for the early years of a GCE course, and for students working alone. The links between chemistry and everyday life have been emphasized throughout the book, and I have tried to remember that the subject is studied by girls as well as boys.

The language has been kept simple and direct, and frequent summaries of important points, both in diagram and textual form, are included. These should help to fix the ideas in pupils' minds, for, notwithstanding modern developments in science teaching, much chemistry must still be **learned** if progress is to be made. Many important facts are presented more than once, both for reinforcement and because pupils do not always recognize information in a new context; a pupil who, for instance, knows the reaction between zinc and sulphuric acid as a preparation of hydrogen might not otherwise think of it as a way of making a salt. Additionally, this duplication makes it easier to work through the book in various ways, e.g., metals before acids, or acids before metals. Important terms are defined and emphasized as they are introduced or re-introduced. The Stock notation is used after valency has been taught, and SI units (with the variations for elementary work recommended in the ASE report) are used.

The experiments are an integral part of the book. Although pupils enjoy and learn from practical work, shortage of time, apparatus, laboratory space, and assistance means that they cannot always do or see all the experiments, so each experiment is followed by a brief description of the results. Direct questions are asked after the early experiments, but later in the book, when pupils have had more experience of investigational methods, these are replaced by the instruction, 'Observe . . .'. There are review questions at the end of each chapter, and some more general questions requiring reference to various parts of the book appear at the end.

For the sake of clarity, all experimental details are printed in a different colour from the main body of the text, and questions are marked by a coloured bar on the left-hand side of the page.

Every teacher must decide how far to omit, simplify, or suppress difficult

PREFACE

topics and I do not expect my choices to meet with universal approval. Writing with the **average** CSE candidate in mind I have not hesitated to select the chemistry to fit the pupil; formula weight, for example, is used instead of relative molecular mass, gas volume correction does not appear, and ionic equations are used very sparingly. The important ideas of particulate nature, which lead to equations and the bonding between atoms, are introduced gradually over five chapters rather than in one large mass. Similarly electrolysis is not treated as a topic, but is mentioned in many sections, and summarized in the appendix on ionic interpretation of reactions. I have tried to build theoretical work on a firm foundation of experimentally observed facts, so that, for example, the important but difficult work on the general properties of metals follows the work on individual metals, and a detailed examination of the properties of polythene precedes a theoretical section on polymerization. Although the opposite view has many adherents, and its use enables economies of teaching time to be made, I believe it is less appropriate to CSE work than the arrangement I have adopted.

The Teacher's Notes contain further explanations, discussions, experimental and teaching hints, suggestions for projects and alternative experimental work, and notes on the simplifications introduced in the text. I apologize to those reading material with which they are familiar but hope everyone will find something of value.

I am indebted to many for help in the production of the book. Useful information was received from:

British Steel Corporation, Griffin & George, S. J. Moreland and Sons, The Permutit Company, Proctor & Gamble, Mr D. Rees, Shell Chemicals UK, Spicers (Builders) Ltd., Unilever, and the West Midlands Gas Board. I am grateful for photographs supplied by the British Oxygen Company and Ford Motor Company.

I am happy to acknowledge the many valuable suggestions and corrections made by friends and colleagues who read the manuscript in whole or part. These included Mr E. Howard and Mr M. Taylor of the Worcester College of Education, Mr W. Briggs of the Christopher Whitehead Boys School, Worcester, Mr F. B. Cook, Ellowes Hall School, Dudley, and Mr R. G. Gough and Dr R. C. Whitfield, Consultants for the Series. I am especially grateful to Mr H. S. Finlay of the Beaufoy School, London, for his detailed and painstaking work.

Lastly, I wish to record my thanks to the staff of Messrs McGraw-Hill for their helpfulness and promptness in their dealings with me, and to my wife, who not only put up with me while I wrote the book, but typed and retyped the manuscript and corrected my spelling and English in the process.

Michael K. Bowker

1

How chemists work

On their way to school your grandparents usually saw horse-drawn traffic. They would have been amazed and probably frightened if they had seen and heard *Concorde*. A supersonic aeroplane is only one of the things which you take for granted, but which would have surprised your grandfather and grandmother when they were at school. Which of the things in Fig. 1.1 do you think existed seventy years ago when your grandparents were young?

When they were at school your grandparents might have seen and used the steel screw, the cotton tablecloth, the rubber bicycle tyre, and the carbolic soap. **Steel** and **cotton** have been known and used for hundreds of years although both became very much cheaper between a hundred and two hundred years ago when large-scale industrial methods of making them became possible. The rubber **bicycle tyre** was invented by a Scotsman called John Dunlop, who wanted to improve his son's tricycle. Other inventors had previously tried to make rubber tyres but no one had had much success. Dunlop, a veterinary surgeon when he made the invention, sold the rights of the idea and eventually became a draper, while the company based on his invention grew large and prospered. The **carbolic acid** present in carbolic soap was first successfully used to kill germs by Joseph Lister. When he used carbolic acid solution to kill germs on his surgical instruments, and as a spray in the air of the operating theatre, he found that the terrible death rate following operations about a hundred years ago decreased rapidly. Lister, whose ideas were at first ridiculed by other doctors, gradually convinced them that he was right, and he was made Baron Lister, the first doctor to be raised to the peerage for services to medicine. It is possible that your grandparents might have seen an **aluminium pan**, but about the time when they were at school aluminium was rather expensive and most people were still using steel pans.

The remaining seven things have only become available for general use during the last half century. **Terylene** was made by two British scientists, Whinfield and Dixon, in 1941. They worked in laboratories in Manchester but ICI later bought the rights to the invention. **Nylon** was first made by the American chemist Carothers working between 1935 and 1937. Although we usually think of nylon as a fibre from which fabrics are made, it is a plastic.

Figure 1.1 Which could your grandparents have used?

This means it can be moulded when it is hot, to make such things as combs, small quiet-running gear wheels, curtain runners, and similar articles. **Penicillin** is made from a mould, similar to those which grow on old bread. Its useful properties were first noticed by Alexander Fleming, a British professor working in London in 1927. He was unable to produce penicillin in a form suitable for general medical use, but during the second world war two other scientists made large-scale production possible. Although there was a long delay between his discovery and its common application, he eventually received ample public recognition. He was knighted, becoming Sir Alexander Fleming in 1944, and he shared a Nobel Prize with the other two scientists in 1945. **High octane petrol**, which is suitable for fast, powerful cars, was developed quite recently. Engine designs only recently became advanced enough for ordinary cars to need it, although racing cars have used high octane fuels for a longer time. **Stainless steel**, which does not rust, and is not affected by acids or alkalis, was patented by the English metallurgist, Harry Brearley, in 1916. Brearley was trying to make a material from which better rifle barrels could be manufactured. One of his test samples was unsuitable and was put on a scrap heap with many others. Months later he noticed that one sample had not rusted; from this single observation grew the immense stainless steel industry. A **ball-point pen**, which came into use just over twenty years ago, has a very small steel ball which revolves at the tip of the pen, becoming covered in jelly-like ink which is left on the paper. This type of pen was invented by a Hungarian, Lazslo Biro. Many people call a ball-point pen 'a biro' today, although this is really the name of pens made by one company. **DDT**, which is an abbreviation for the chemical name **D**ichloro **D**iphenyl **T**richloroethane, is a very effective insect killer. It was first discovered in 1873, but nobody used it as an insecticide until a Swiss chemist tried it in 1942. It was an immediate success, partly because it remains active for many months after it has been sprayed. Scientists now think that it remains active for too long, and poisons birds and fish as well as insects.

Scientists at work

All the seven new discoveries are made of substances such as Terylene, DDT, nylon, and stainless steel, which depend on research done by a group of scientists called chemists. What does a chemist do?

Pharmaceutical Chemist	Industrial and Analytical Chemist	Research Chemist
Mixes and sells medicines	Makes things in large quantities and checks the purities of products and raw materials	Invents new substances and investigates their properties

Figure 1.2 Chemists at work

CHEMISTRY

The chemistry you do at school will not be like the work done by a pharmaceutical chemist or pharmacist. It is not usually safe even to taste any chemical in a laboratory, much less to eat the sort of quantity used in medicine. Nor are you likely to make new discoveries. (All the simple things have now been discovered probably, and research is usually done by large teams using expensive apparatus.) Sometimes, however, you will use methods similar to those used by a research chemist. Most of the practical work you will do will consist of making samples of various substances and examining their properties, or purifying substances. You will also use chemical theory, as a professional chemist does, and you will use scientific methods, which involve finding out by doing experiments for yourself.

Experiment 1.1 *Heating ammonium dichromate*

Use a bunsen burner to heat a small pile of ammonium dichromate on a tin lid or sand tray supported on a tripod. When you see something happening to the ammonium dichromate take away the bunsen.

How do you know a change is taking place? Was the substance left after the experiment the same as the substance you started with? What evidence have you for your answer to the last question?

Experiment 1.2 *Heating lead oxide together with charcoal*

Mix approximately equal volumes of red lead oxide and powdered charcoal. On a tin lid make a pile of this mixture about 1 cm in diameter. Put the lid on a tripod, and heat it strongly, using two bunsen burners. Watch the material when it is red hot, and look for changes in its appearance. After about five minutes' heating, remove the burners and wait until the mixture left is quite cool.

Does it look the same as it did before heating? Do you think anything new has been made? What evidence have you for your answer to the last question?

In these two experiments it is obvious from the appearance of the materials used that new substances have been made, and you have looked at some of the properties (for example, colour and texture) of the new substances. Making new substances and investigating their properties is one of the jobs a chemist does.

Purification

Upsetting a sewing-box might produce a mixture of pins and needles. The sorting of this mixture into its two parts is similar to chemical purification,

HOW CHEMISTS WORK

in which the purified substance corresponds to a box containing pins only, or needles only, rather than pins and needles. We shall now consider some of the methods a chemist uses to purify substances.

Experiment 1.3   *Can inky water be purified?*

Figure 1.3   Can inky water be purified?

Using laboratory apparatus as in Fig. 1.3 (a), (b), and (c), or using a pan, a large plate, and a saucer, as in (d), the question can be answered. These pieces of apparatus are all used similarly; the inky water is boiled gently and then the resulting water vapour is cooled by a cold test-tube (a), flask of cold water (b) and (c), or plate (d).

What do you see in the cold region? Is this substance coloured or colourless? Has the water been purified?

CHEMISTRY

The usual laboratory apparatus for this experiment is shown below.

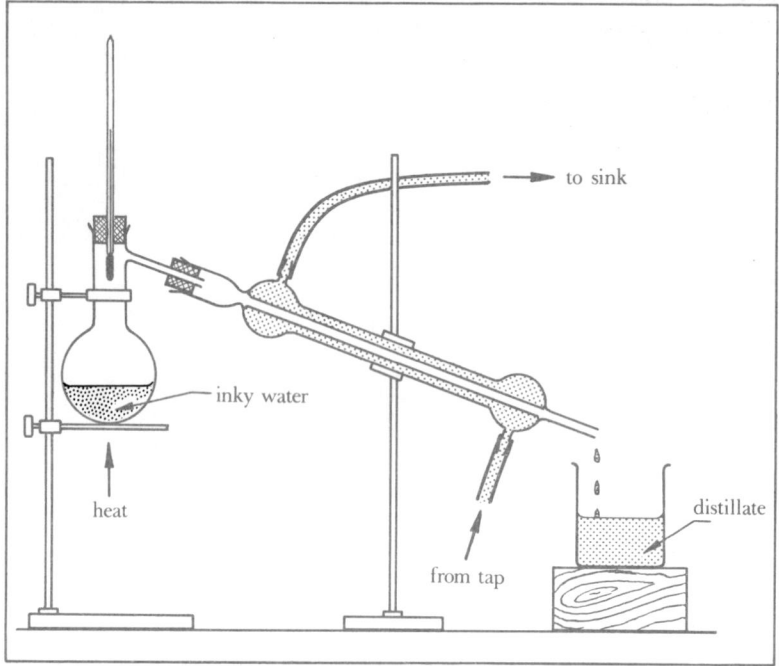

Figure 1.4 **Simple distillation**

This is a **simple distillation apparatus**, and will convert inky water to pure, distilled water. The water in the distillation flask boils, turns into water vapour, and passes into the condenser. The cooling water in the outer jacket cools the water vapour, which is changed back to water. As the dyes in the ink do not boil into the condenser, pure water collects in the beaker. It works because the water changes more readily to a gas (that is, it is more **volatile**) than does the ink. Distillation is sometimes used on ships when drinking water in the tanks is getting low, and ships' lifeboats often have solar stills which use the heat from the sun's rays to produce drinking water from seawater.

If the two substances to be separated are a solid and a liquid (for example, dyes and water, or salt and water), simple distillation works well. If they are both liquids a fractional distillation apparatus must be used.

Experiment 1.4 *Fractional distillation*

A mixture of alcohol and water may be distilled using the apparatus shown in Fig. 1.5. Heat a mixture of alcohol (industrial spirit) and water in the flask.

HOW CHEMISTS WORK

Look for vapour rising into the fractional distillation column. When the vapour reaches the thermometer note the temperature. If the temperature rises more than 10° above this value, put the second receiver under the condenser. When nearly all the liquid has gone from the flask, stop heating. Examine the liquids in the receivers.

> Which is the alcohol?
> Which distilled first, water or alcohol?

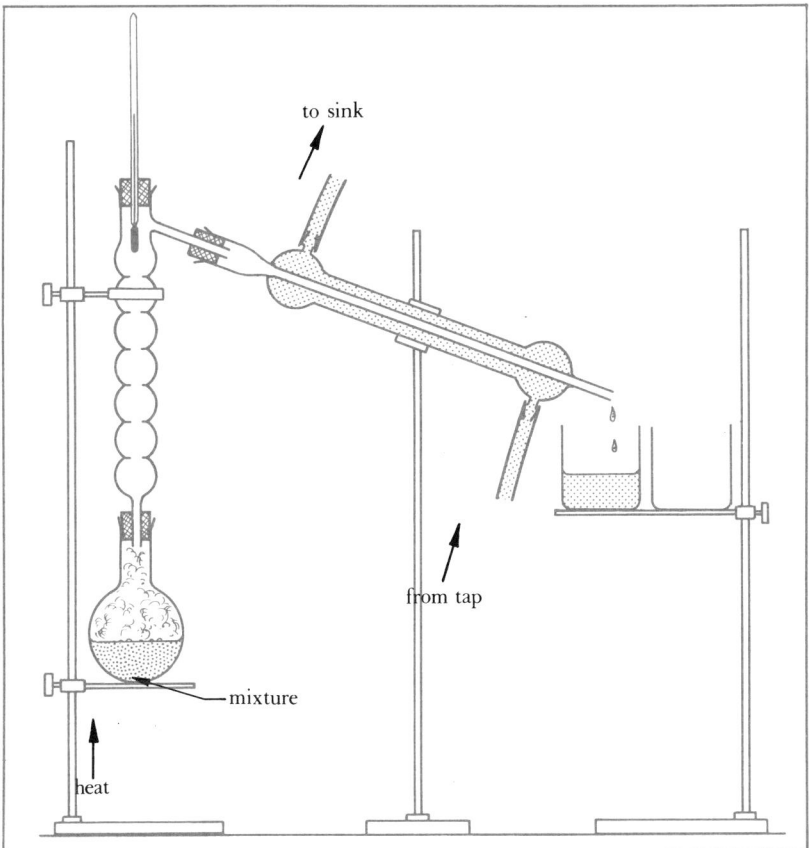

Figure 1.5 Fractional distillation

In experiment 1.4 the mixture was distilled into two parts or fractions. Alcohol and water boil into the column and warm it. The boiling point of alcohol is 78°C, so when the column reaches this temperature the alcohol continues through, but the water, which turns back to a liquid at temperatures below 100°C, condenses and falls down the column back into the flask. Thus the alcohol is separated from the water, and as it distils the boiling point is

7

shown by the thermometer. When all the alcohol has gone from the flask, water boils into the column, the temperature rises to 100°C, and the receiver should be changed as water starts to drip from the condenser.

Fractional distillation is much used in industry. A spirit distillery distils alcoholic liquors, making them stronger by leaving behind some of the water. An oil refinery distils crude oil, separating it into petrol, paraffin, lubricating oil, fuel oil, petroleum jelly, paraffin wax, bitumen, and other substances (see Fig. 5.14). Coal tar from a gasworks is distilled, giving many useful products, and liquid air is distilled into oxygen and nitrogen.

| How would you separate mud from muddy water, which is a suspension of a solid in a liquid?

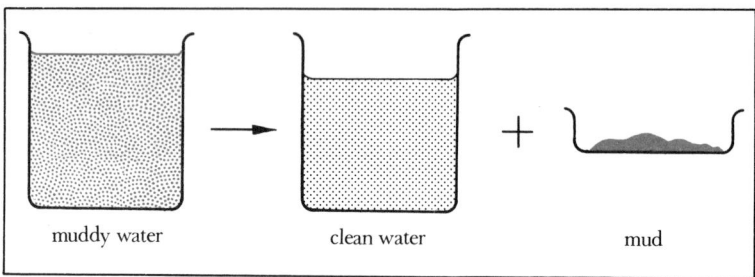

Figure 1.6 **How would you separate mud from muddy water?**

You might have suggested distillation. This would work, but there are easier, cheaper ways to do the job. It would be possible to leave the muddy water until the particles of mud fell to the bottom of the beaker, forming a sediment. The disadvantage of this method is that it is very slow. It can be hastened by whirling a tube full of the mixture in a centrifuge, when the solid

HOW CHEMISTS WORK

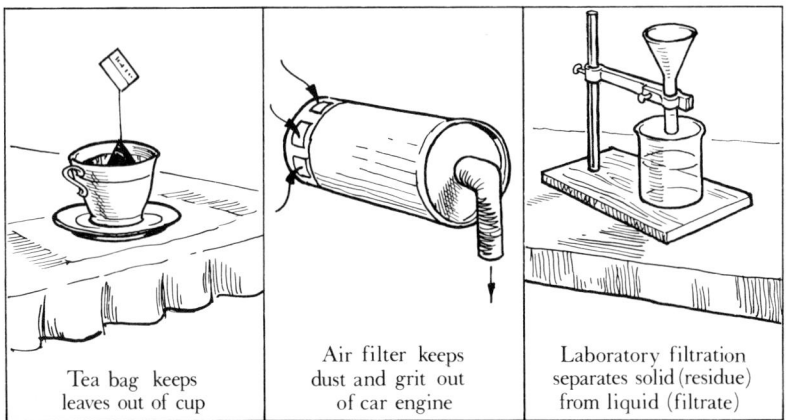

Figure 1.7 Filtration in everyday life

particles are flung to the outside wall of the tube. A spin drier is similar to a centrifuge but it is the water which escapes through holes in the walls, and the solid clothes which are held back. A third approach is to **filter** the mixture of mud and water. Filtration is a common procedure, as the diagrams show.

Filtration works by a sieving mechanism: the liquid **filtrate** flows through tiny holes (e.g., the coffee through the strainer), but the solid particles are too big to go through and remain as the **residue** (e.g., the coffee grounds in the strainer).

Experiment 1.5 *Sublimation*

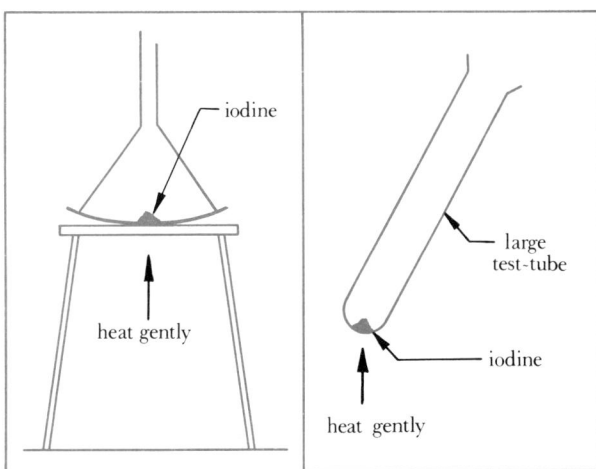

Figure 1.8 Sublimation of iodine

9

CHEMISTRY

Take two or three small crystals of iodine and heat them gently using one of the methods shown in Fig. 1.8.

What do you see above the iodine? What do you see on the cool parts of the apparatus? Look carefully at the iodine to see if it melts.

Safety note: the vapour is unpleasant and should not be breathed in.

Iodine is a substance which **sublimes** when it is heated gently. This means that it turns directly from a solid to a vapour without melting. On cooling the vapour the process reverses and a solid forms. The iodine vapour, which is easy to see because it is a magnificent purple colour, condenses to a sublimate of very dark brown flakes when it is cooled.

Moth-balls and the air fresheners sometimes put near lavatories sublime slowly, releasing small amounts of vapour into the air. Other compounds which sublime are ammonium chloride and solid carbon dioxide.

So far in this chapter we have been talking about three of the jobs of a chemist—making new substances, separating, and purifying. Now let us look at

Building up and breaking down

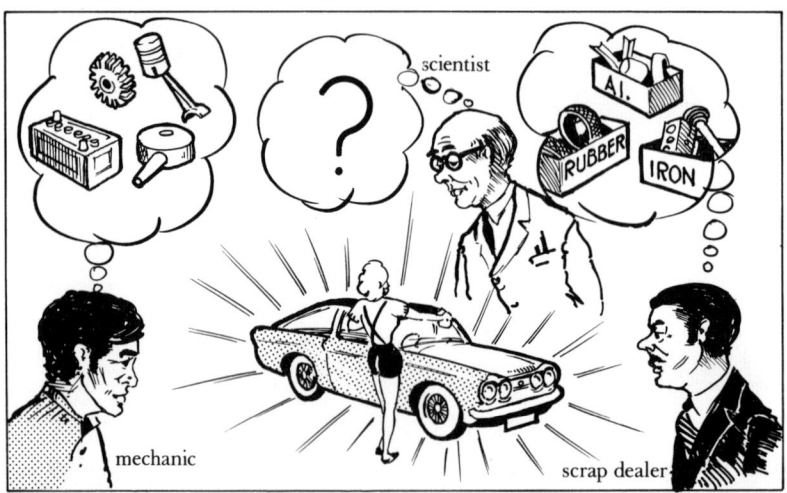

Figure 1.9 What is her car made of?

The owner sees a shiny new car. The mechanic imagines it as a lot of separate parts, while the scrap dealer thinks in terms of the metals and other materials in it. What does a scientist think? Just how far can we go in breaking down a

HOW CHEMISTS WORK

car into its many components? Here are three experiments which can help us to decide.

Experiments on particles

Experiment 1.6

(a) Take five beakers or jars containing marbles or small stones, dried peas, dry sand, lycopodium powder, and water. Tilt each jar slowly and see what happens to the particles, and to the top surface of the material in the jar.

(b) Pour the marbles or stones into a coarse garden sieve, the peas into the same sieve, the sand into a finer sieve, the lycopodium powder into a flour sieve, and the water into a folded filter paper in a funnel.

> Why do the stones, sand, etc., pass through the sieves? Can you see any holes in the filter paper? What does this suggest about the water?

Experiment 1.7

Take a large test-tube of hydrogen sulphide (used in making stink-bombs, when it is known as 'rotten egg gas'), and uncork it in the middle of the laboratory. Keep windows and doors shut, and put observers all round the laboratory.

> How far does the smell travel? Does it fill the room? What volume did the gas occupy before it escaped?

Experiment 1.8

Use a smoke-cell and microscope to look at very small particles of smoke floating about in the air. You will see the smoke particles as very small points of light.

> Do the smoke particles stand still in the cell, or are they moving?

Experiments 1.6(a) and 1.6(b) suggest that water is made of very small particles. Experiment 1.7 shows that hydrogen sulphide can be 'stretched' from filling a test-tube to filling a room. This is easy to understand if we imagine the hydrogen sulphide as very small particles, which get farther and farther apart as they drift through the room. Experiment 1.8 shows that the smoke particles move jerkily all the time. The most probable interpretation is that the smoke particles are being hit by other, smaller particles, too small to see with the microscope. These other particles must be particles of air, which is the only substance in the cell apart from the smoke.

CHEMISTRY

These experiments help to convince us that matter is composed of millions and millions of tiny particles. There is no one final and conclusive experiment which will prove this for us, but over the last 130 years scientists have gradually built up more and more evidence indicating that all matter, solids, liquids, and gases, is composed of particles. This is not very strange really. You can compare the situation to a detective story, where nobody actually sees the crime committed, but the detectives gather more and more evidence which in the end shows without doubt who is guilty. As a result of much painstaking experimenting by many scientists, we now believe that all substances—starch, DDT, salt, natural gas, sulphuric acid, oxygen, water, diamonds, and many others—are composed of individual particles which can be atoms, molecules, or ions. Experiment 1.1 showed the breaking down of ammonium dichromate into a green powder, chromium oxide, and experiment 1.2 showed the breaking down of lead oxide into lead. Molecules and ions in these and other substances are made of atoms. We can now answer the query in Fig. 1.9: the scientist would think of the car as being made of atoms of various types.

Atoms

For many years scientists believed that there were ninety-two types of atom. Some of these atoms have names which are familiar to everyone.

Table 1.1 **Atoms and symbols**

	Type of atom	Symbol	Common occurrence
	aluminium	Al	Many pans are made of aluminium
	carbon	C	Diamonds are made of carbon
	chlorine	Cl	Household bleaches often contain chlorine
	copper	Cu	Electric wires contain copper
	hydrogen	H	Balloons which float in the air usually contain hydrogen
	oxygen	O	An oxygen cylinder contains compressed oxygen

When the names of the ninety-two known atoms were arranged in order of weight, with the lightest atom (hydrogen) first, the last atom was uranium, the heaviest atom known. Uranium and some of the other atoms just before it in the series were known to be **radioactive**. This means that atoms of uranium break down by themselves giving off heat, radiation, and particles of various types. The radiation is harmful in large amounts, and scientists working with radioactive substances wear badges which tell them whether they have received large doses of radiation or not.

Scientists have recently made new artificial atoms, heavier than uranium. There are thirteen of these so far, so that the total number of types of atom known is now one hundred and five. All the artificial atoms are radioactive. People tend to think of nuclear scientists as being dedicated solely to the production of bigger and better bombs, but this is only a small part of their work. Such things as better food preservation, cancer cures, and detection of dangerous flaws in metal structures are only a few of the applications developed by these men and women.

Each type of atom has its own **symbol**. Since there are one hundred and five types of atom, and only twenty-six letters in our alphabet, the symbols usually consist of two letters. The first is a capital letter, the second is a small letter, often the second letter of the name of the atom, e.g., N is the symbol for nitrogen, so neon has to be Ne (not NE). Sometimes the symbol comes from a Latin name; iron is Fe from ferrum. Some atoms are named after famous scientists, (Es for einsteinium), or a place (Fr for francium). The ending -ium usually means that the atom is an atom of a metal (e.g., aluminium, sodium, magnesium). There is a list of types of atom, with their symbols, at the back of the book. **A substance which is made entirely of one sort of atom is called an element**, so we could correctly say that one hundred and five elements are known.

Molecules

Some atoms exist singly, but most atoms join together in groups. After this building-up or joining-up process, the joined-up group of atoms is called a molecule.* Atoms sometimes join with other atoms of their own kind. The air you are breathing contains oxygen atoms joined in pairs to make oxygen molecules which have the formula O_2. (There are two small points to note here: the figure two is dropped slightly below the O, and O_2 is the **formula** for oxygen. An atom has a symbol, a molecule has a formula.)

Atoms can also join with other atoms of different types, building molecules containing two or more sorts of atom. Water is made of atoms of hydrogen and oxygen, and a molecule of water has the formula H_2O. Soda-water contains carbonic acid whose formula is H_2CO_3. It is much quicker

* Some groups of joined-up atoms are called ions, but this need not trouble us at the moment.

CHEMISTRY

to write HCl than to write hydrochloric acid, so these symbols and formulae are used as a convenient type of shorthand. They are also international; a French, German, or Spanish scientist would understand any chemical symbols or formulae you wrote even though he could not speak English.

Summary

There are ninety-two natural elements. These are made of ninety-two types of atom, each of which has a symbol (e.g., aluminium—Al). Some atoms exist alone, but others join in groups to form molecules, each of which has a formula. Atoms may join with other atoms of their own kind (as in oxygen—O_2), or with atoms of another kind (as in water—H_2O).

Experiment 1.9 *Mixtures and compounds*

Make two heaps on a piece of paper. One should contain two measures of powdered sulphur (e.g., flowers of sulphur), and the other one measure of fine iron filings. Any convenient object, such as a teaspoon, a spatula, or a wooden splint, may be used as a measure.

Divide each heap into four approximately equal parts.

Thoroughly mix one-quarter of the iron with three-quarters of the sulphur and examine the mixture. Take a little of this pile and set it aside, labelling it C.

To the main heap, add two more quarters of iron, so that you have a pile containing three-quarters of the iron and three-quarters of the sulphur, and stir this thoroughly. Examine the mixture, then set some aside and label it D. Label the remaining iron A and the sulphur B.

Take the larger pile of iron and sulphur, put it on a tin lid on a tripod, or in some other suitable container, and heat the mixture until it is red-hot. Let the heated mass cool, then tip it on to the paper and examine it closely. Label it E.

Can you see any sulphur? Is the substance still a powder?

Look carefully at the five heaps you have, and think what substances you have in them, and what atoms there are present.

You could have written your results in a table like Table 1.2.

Heap A contains the element iron, which is made of atoms of iron. Similarly heap B contains the element sulphur, which is made of atoms of sulphur. Heaps C and D contain mixtures of iron and sulphur atoms, and the two mixtures contain different proportions of the two elements. You can make a mixture of iron and sulphur in any proportions you choose. This experiment illustrates just two of the many possible mixtures.

What is there in heap E, the mixture after heating? Here, a new substance,

HOW CHEMISTS WORK

iron sulphide (also called ferrous sulphide), has been made. It consists of molecules which have been built up from iron and sulphur atoms. Experiments to analyse the compound show that it always contains 63·6 per cent iron by weight, and 36·4 per cent sulphur. (This applies to all compounds—any specimens of a compound always contain the same elements combined in the same proportions by weight. This is known as the **Law of Constant Composition**.)

Table 1.2 Results of experiment 1.9

Heap	Substances in heap	Appearance	What atoms are present
A	iron	grey powder	iron atoms
B	sulphur	yellow powder	sulphur atoms
C	mixture of S and a little Fe	some grey powder mixed with much yellow powder	iron and sulphur atoms
D	mixture of equal volumes of S and Fe	grey powder mixed with yellow powder	iron and sulphur atoms
E	? (mixture after heating)	grey solid, no yellow visible	?

Many similar experiments could be done with other substances, and they would all show that a **mixture** can be made in differing proportions, but that a **compound**, which always contains two or more types of atom joined together, is always made in one definite, fixed proportion. If, in experiment 1.9, we had had, say 90 per cent iron by weight in the mixture, some of the iron would have been left, unchanged, mixed with the iron sulphide. Another difference between a mixture and a compound is that because a compound is a new substance it is made by a chemical change, but a chemical change is not needed when a mixture is made. The chemical change in our experiment can be summarized by:

$$\text{iron} + \text{sulphur} \longrightarrow \text{iron sulphide}$$

This is an example of a building-up experiment. In it the molecules of iron sulphide are built-up from atoms of iron and atoms of sulphur.

Conservation of matter

A lump of the element uranium would be a hard, heavy grey metal. It would be expensive and also dangerous to go near because it is, as we said earlier in the chapter, radioactive. This means that the atoms of the uranium do not last for ever, but one by one turn into other atoms. They would become atoms of radium, and, after many years, atoms of lead. Only certain atoms are radioactive; most atoms are stable and remain essentially unchanged for millions of years. An iron atom stays an iron atom, an oxygen atom stays an oxygen atom, a sulphur atom stays a sulphur atom, and so on. Atoms might join together in chemical changes, but many experiments show that the total weight of the substances before the joining is equal to the total weight of the substances after joining. Careful weighing of substances in experiments like that illustrated in Fig. 1.10 proved this.

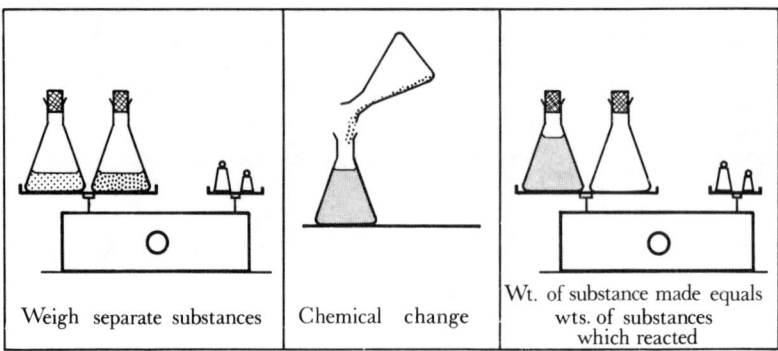

Figure 1.10 An experiment on the conservation of matter

So many experiments of this type were done that chemists put forward the **Law of Conservation of Matter**, which states that in a chemical change matter is neither created nor destroyed. This implies that atoms are neither created nor destroyed in a chemical change, so the Law of Conservation of Matter is really a law about the conservation of atoms. Sometimes the law is expressed: 'In a chemical change the weight of the reacting substances is equal to the weight of the substances produced'.

Chapter summary

In this chapter we have discussed some of the ways in which scientists work. A chemist is a scientist who extracts and purifies substances, or who makes new substances by building up and breaking down existing substances. Chemists doing their job use processes such as distillation, filtration, sublimation, and centrifuging. Chemists believe that all matter is in particles. Sometimes the particles are atoms (e.g., neon), but usually the atoms are joined together into groups called molecules (e.g., in water H_2O and carbon dioxide CO_2). A compound always has elements in the same proportion by weight, and when compounds are formed, the weight of the reacting substances is equal to the weight of the substances produced.

Questions

1. Which would you expect to be purer, filtered water or distilled water? Explain your answer.

2. Solutions of copper sulphate are (*a*) filtered, (*b*) evaporated to dryness. In each case sketch the apparatus you would use, and describe what you would see during the experiment.

3. Distinguish between (*a*) distillation and fractional distillation, (*b*) an atom and a molecule, (*c*) a symbol and a formula.

4. Describe briefly, without giving details of apparatus, two experiments which help to show that matter consists of many minute particles.

5. State what is meant by each term and name a substance to which each could be applied; (*a*) radioactive, (*b*) sublimation, (*c*) centrifuging, (*d*) an element.

6. Explain why you would not consider the mixture of sand and salt put on roads in winter to be a compound. When the mixture has done its job only the sand is left on the road; where has the salt gone to?

2

Water

Water is a wonderful and precious substance. We are lucky that in Great Britain in the 'seventies it is plentiful and cheap. We take our supply of good, pure, disease-free water for granted, and grumble if it is turned off for repairs, or if it is discoloured, or if we are asked to economize on our water use. Our rainy weather is useful—we would think very differently of water if we had to carry all our supply in buckets for several miles, as some people in hot, dry countries do. In this chapter we are going to look at some of the properties of water to see why it is so useful, and why we miss it so badly when there is none.

One of the most obvious facts about the Earth is that it is largely covered by water. About four-fifths of our planet's surface is covered by water or the frozen water of the polar caps. Where did all this water come from? Scientists think that water, which is a very stable compound, was formed early in the history of the Earth, several thousand million years ago. It has been here ever since, helping to shape the surface of the land—making river valleys, washing soil into the sea, and so on. As well as this water which has been here for a long time, more water is being made all the time. All fires give off smoke, which is composed of small pieces of ash plus steam. Car exhausts give off steam (as well as noxious fumes). A gas flame makes steam, and many other examples could be given. In fact, the burning of any natural material (for example, wood, coal, natural gas, cotton, wool, and rubber) and of many manufactured materials (for example, candlewax, paper, plastics, and petrol) gives off water in the form of steam.

Physical properties of water

When heated, pure water **boils** at 100°C under normal atmospheric pressure. Water at or about this temperature is used for heating foods, washing white articles, and sterilizing. If the pressure on the water is increased, the boiling point is raised. A domestic pressure cooker usually uses what a housewife describes as 'fifteen pounds pressure'. She means that there is a pressure inside the cooker of normal atmospheric pressure plus fifteen pounds per square inch. The total pressure inside the cooker is then about twice normal atmospheric pressure (thirty pounds per square inch or $2 \cdot 1$ kg cm^{-2}), which raises the boiling point of water to 120°C. This rise in temperature causes food to cook about four times faster than it would at 100°C.

Cold water direct from a tap may be boiled without heating it if a good vacuum pump is available. This water really is boiling (bubbling and turning

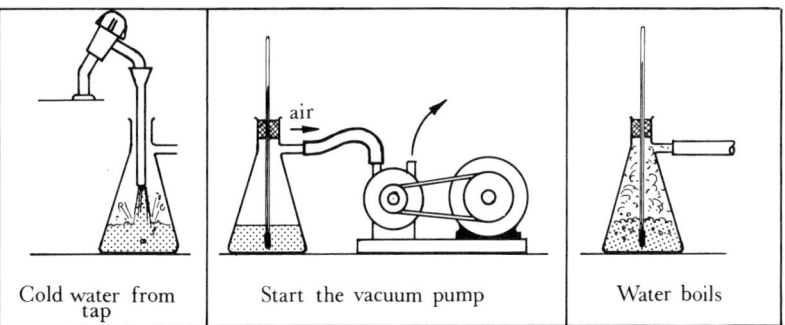

Figure 2.1   Water boiling under reduced pressure

freely into vapour inside the liquid), although it is not hot, and it would not make tea or cook an egg. We tend to use the expression 'boiling water' as if it specified the temperature of 100°C: it does not do this unless the normal atmospheric pressure is mentioned.

The method of reducing the pressure to lower a liquid's boiling point is much used in industry; salt solutions from salt mines are evaporated under reduced pressure to decrease heating costs.

Experiment 2.1   *Boiling impure water*

(*a*) Put solid ammonium chloride into a boiling tube to a depth of one centimetre, then add cold water until the water surface is three centimetres from the bottom of the tube. Boil the mixture and put a thermometer into the boiling liquid. Note the reading of the thermometer.

(*b*) Repeat the experiment using twice as much ammonium chloride, i.e., two centimetres depth of solid, in the same depth of water. Note the reading as before.

Experiment 2.1 shows that water made impure by dissolving ammonium chloride in it has a higher boiling point than pure water, and that the more impurity there is the higher the boiling point becomes. This is true for all dissolved solid impurities, and the result is often summarized by saying that a solution of a solid in water has a higher boiling point than pure water.

Pure water **freezes** at 0°C. Increasing or decreasing the pressure has only a very small effect on the freezing point, but adding something like sodium chloride to the water lowers the freezing point. A solution has a lower freezing point than pure water, and the more dissolved solid there is the lower the freezing point becomes. This lowering of the freezing point explains the use of antifreeze in car radiators (enough antifreeze is added to bring the freezing point of the mixture in the car radiator below the lowest temperature expected), and the fact that the sea freezes at about −3°C.

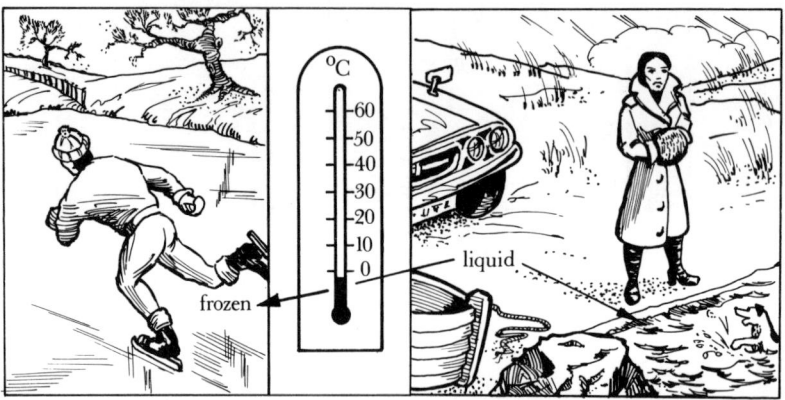

Figure 2.2 A fresh-water pond is frozen at −2°C, but the sea and the water plus antifreeze in the car radiator are both still liquid

Water spilled on a laboratory bench, and rain on clothes or roads, **evaporate**, forming water vapour. Evaporation is the turning of a liquid to a vapour, and it takes place at all temperatures. Evaporation is much quicker at high temperatures than it is at low ones. If a solution of a solid in water evaporates, the solid is left and the water becomes water vapour in the air. Examples of this process are the drying of ink on paper, leaving the colouring materials of the ink on and under the surface of the paper, and the evaporation of sea-water from skin after bathing in the sea, leaving on the skin salts which have a sticky feel.

There is a limit to the amount of water vapour that air can accept; when this limit is reached the air is said to be **saturated** with water vapour. We put a cap on a felt-tipped pen because the small volume of air inside the cap soon becomes saturated, and then no further loss of water takes place. If the cap were left off, all the water from the pen would soon be evaporated. Evaporation of water produces a cooling effect on the remaining water. This effect cools us when we perspire, and is responsible for the working of non-mechanical refrigerators such as those used in some caravans. These rely on

WATER

the evaporation of water producing a cooling effect on the contents. Milk coolers work similarly.

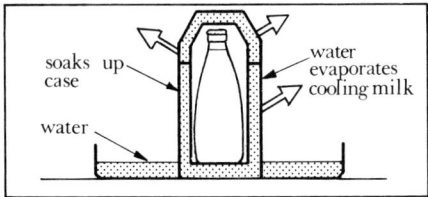

Figure 2.3 An evaporative milk-cooler

Many **drying** procedures depend on evaporation. These include the evaporation of the final film of water on crockery left to drain, water from washing on a line, or a damp towel or bathing costume. Heating the object to be dried or using moving air quickens evaporation, and this is done by, for example, hot air hand driers, tumble driers in launderettes, and hair driers. Other drying processes depend on chemical reaction. Some compounds, notably silica gel, concentrated sulphuric acid, and tetraphosphorus decoxide (sometimes called phosphorus pentoxide), absorb water by combining with it. Silica gel is especially useful because it releases the water if it is heated strongly, and it can then be used again. Small amounts of silica gel are often put in expensive scientific instruments which might be harmed by water vapour. It is also possible to buy biscuit tins containing silica gel. Any water vapour is absorbed by the silica gel, so the biscuits stay crisp instead of becoming damp and soggy.

Water has a **density** of one gram per cubic centimetre (1 g cm^{-3}). Although when you carry a bucket of water it feels very heavy, water is not among the densest substances known, nor is it among the least dense. Table 2.1 shows

Table 2.1 Approximate weights of 1000 cm^3 (1 litre) of various substances

hydrogen	0·1 g		conc. sulphuric acid	1800 g
air	1·2 g		granite	2500 g
carbon dioxide	2·0 g		lead	11 000 g
expanded polystyrene	22 g	water 1000 g	mercury	14 000 g
balsa wood	310 g		uranium	19 000 g
petrol	800 g		osmium	23 000 g

that hydrogen, the least dense element, is 10 000 times less dense than water, and osmium, the densest element, is 23 times denser than water.

Any of the substances named in the left-hand column would float in water. The gases would bubble to the top and escape. Some substances which are too dense to float can nevertheless be carried along by a swift stream of water. Examples include mud hosed off cars and lorries, solids in sewage, silt and gravel carried by rivers, and dirt cleaned from our streets by rain. A considerable volume of water is used for these purposes.

Solutions and solubility

It is easy to distinguish a laboratory used mainly for chemistry rather than for physics or biology; a chemistry laboratory contains rows and rows of bottles of liquids. These liquids, many of which are coloured, are called **reagents** because they take part in reactions. They are nearly all solutions of chemicals in water. Reactions take place much more readily when the reacting substances are dissolved in water, because liquids mix more readily than solids. Examples of this are common in cookery: compare the quick, easy mixing of milk and water with the long, vigorous beating needed to mix flour, sugar, and cooking fat.

Experiment 2.2   *Solubility*

Put small equal volumes (e.g., heaps on the end of a wooden splint) of potassium nitrate, manganese dioxide, sodium chloride, potassium permanganate, and sulphur in five test tubes, and add water to each tube to a depth of about four centimetres. Shake each tube vigorously for about two minutes, then stand all the tubes in a rack or beaker. Examine each tube in turn.

Caution: avoid splashing potassium permanganate on your clothes. It might stain your fingers brown but this is temporary and not harmful.

Has the solid dissolved? How do you know? Has it dissolved fully or partly?

Experiment 2.2 divides substances into those which are **soluble** in water and those which are **insoluble**. The potassium nitrate and the sodium chloride dissolve completely, and are said to be soluble in water. The manganese dioxide and the sulphur can still be seen as solids, and the water does not become coloured. They do not dissolve and are described as being insoluble in water. The potassium permanganate must dissolve because it turns the water purple, but it does not dissolve completely. It is soluble, but not as soluble as the potassium nitrate or the sodium chloride.

Experiment 2.3   *Solutions in other liquids*

Take several dry test tubes and use a glass rod or wooden splint to put a small smear of grease—petroleum jelly (Vaseline) is suitable—in the bottom of each tube. Pour water, alcohol (ethanol, methylated spirits, or industrial spirit), carbon tetrachloride, benzene, acetone (as available), one into each tube to a depth of about two centimetres. Shake the tubes and then look at them to see which of the liquids dissolve the petroleum jelly.

Caution: it is not safe to use some of these liquids if there are naked flames in the laboratory.

Substances which, like grease, are insoluble in water (see experiment 2.3), are sometimes soluble in other liquids. A liquid which will dissolve something is called a **solvent**; e.g., benzene is a solvent for grease. The substance which dissolves is called the **solute**. Solvents other than water are often used to remove stains caused by tar, oil, grease, or wet paint from clothes. The so-called 'dry cleaning' uses a liquid cleaner in which the clothes are agitated. The cleaner is a solvent for grease and dirt. The process is described as dry because the liquid is not water. The clothes are put in a large spin drier after cleaning, and then pressed.

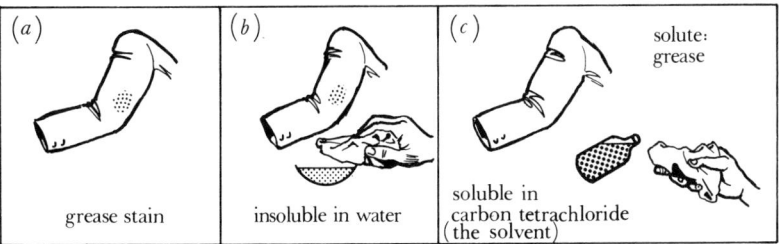

Figure 2.4 Stain removal

So far we have considered cases where the solute is a solid (e.g., sodium chloride, potassium nitrate, and grease) but gases may also be solutes. The gas carbon dioxide dissolves readily in water, if pressure is applied, forming soda-water. If the soda-water has colouring and flavouring added to it it becomes fizzy pop. When a bottle of soda-water or fizzy pop is opened, the pressure is released, and some of the dissolved carbon dioxide escapes. If the bottle is left opened for several hours all the carbon dioxide escapes and the drink becomes flat.

Liquids can also be solutes, if they dissolve in other liquids. There are many examples in everyday life, for example:

oil is dissolved in the petrol used in two-stroke engines which power some lawn-mowers, scooters, and mo-peds;

alcohol is dissolved in water in beer, wines, and spirits;

perfumes and toilet waters consist of perfume essences dissolved in an alcohol base.

CHEMISTRY

Experiments 2.4 to 2.9   *Work with solutions*

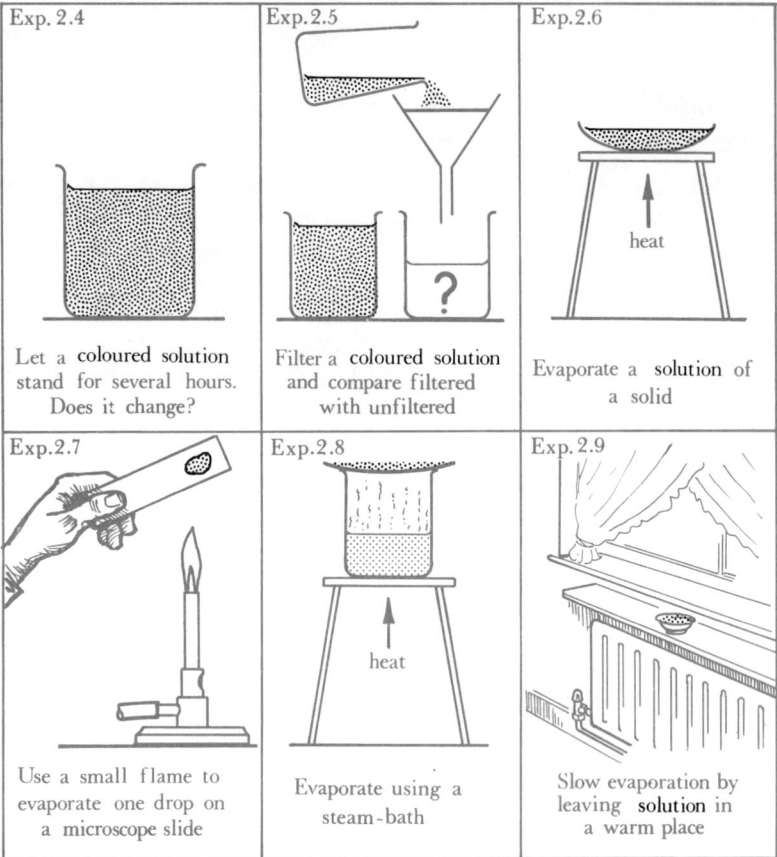

Figure 2.5   **Experiments with solutions**

Suitable solutions include copper sulphate, methyl orange, potassium permanganate and potassium dichromate.

A solution, once made, stays a solution (in which solute and solvent particles are thoroughly jumbled up) and need not be stirred to keep the solute dissolved. A solution can be filtered without change, because the solute particles are so small that they go through the holes in the filter paper, as do the solvent particles. These two properties of a solution help to distinguish it from a suspension, which settles if left and is separated by filtration. If a solution is evaporated the solvent escapes into the air and the solute is left. Dried milk is made by evaporating the water present in liquid milk; adding water to the dried milk powder produces a liquid similar to fresh milk.

WATER

Solubility and temperature

Experiment 2.10 *The solubility of ammonium chloride*

Take a boiling tube and put in it ammonium chloride to a depth of about two centimetres. Now add cold water until its depth is three centimetres (measured from the bottom of the tube). Shake the mixture hard for two minutes.

| Does any of the ammonium chloride dissolve? Does it all dissolve?

Now warm the tube and shake the mixture again.

| Does any more ammonium chloride dissolve?

Next, boil the mixture, and see what happens to the ammonium chloride. Finally, allow the solution to cool, giving the tube a single shake occasionally.

| What do you see as the hot solution cools?

Experiment 2.10 shows that the solubility of ammonium chloride in water increases when the water is heated. The cold water, which has a temperature of, say, 20°C, dissolved some of the ammonium chloride, but could not dis-

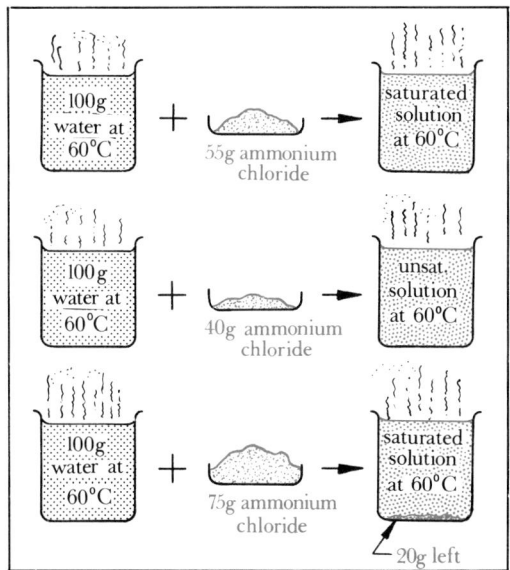

Figure 2.6 Saturated and unsaturated solutions

25

solve it all. The water which had dissolved as much ammonium chloride as it could was then **saturated** with the solid at 20°C. After warming, more ammonium chloride had dissolved, but there was still some of the solid left. The solution was saturated at the higher temperature. The warm saturated solution contained more dissolved solid than the cold saturated solution. A **saturated solution** is one which, at the temperature stated, contains the maximum possible weight of the solute.

A saturated solution of ammonium chloride at 60°C contains 55 g of ammonium chloride to every 100 g of water. Three different mixtures of ammonium chloride and water would produce the results shown in Fig. 2.6.

It is usual to quote solubilities by referring to the weight of the solute which will dissolve in 100 g of water, and the information is often displayed as a graph.

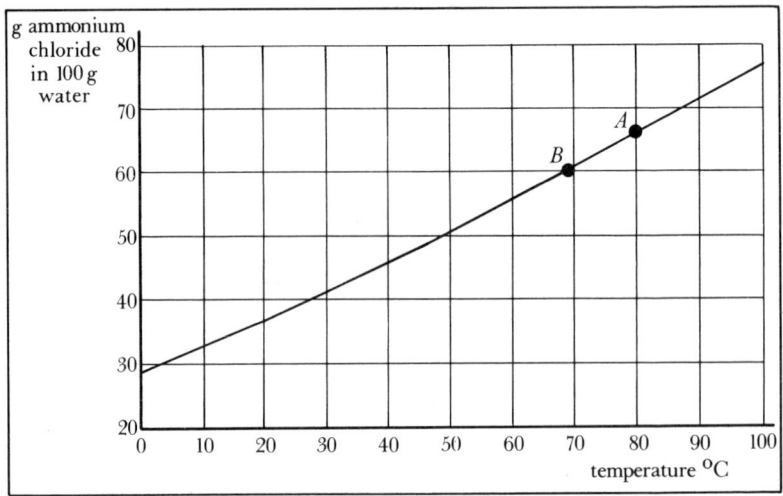

Figure 2.7 Solubility of ammonium chloride

> Use the graph to answer these questions; then check your answers by looking at the end of the chapter.
> What weight of ammonium chloride will dissolve in 100 g of water at 46°C?
> At what temperature can 100 g of water just dissolve 40 g of ammonium chloride?
> What does the graph tell us at point A?
> What does the graph tell us at point B?
> What weight of ammonium chloride will dissolve in 1000 g of water at 20°C?

Crystallization

If a hot solution saturated with a solid is cooled, the solvent is then unable to hold all the solute, and some of the solid reappears, as you saw in experiment 2.10. The process is called crystallization, and the small particles of solid are called crystals.

Experiment 2.11 *Crystal shapes*

Examine some crystals, preferably with a hand-lens or a low-powered microscope. Sodium chloride and granulated sugar are convenient substances to use, but you should also look at other substances if any are available. Notice particularly the shapes of the crystals.

Experiment 2.11 shows that crystals have flat sides, straight edges, and sharp corners, and that all the undamaged crystals of any one substance look alike. This similarity of shape is not always easy to see because some crystals do not grow perfectly, and others get damaged after growth.

Many shapes of crystal are possible, but sodium chloride crystals, for example, are cubes. Sometimes corners get knocked off, or faces or edges are damaged, but a perfect crystal of salt would have flat sides, straight

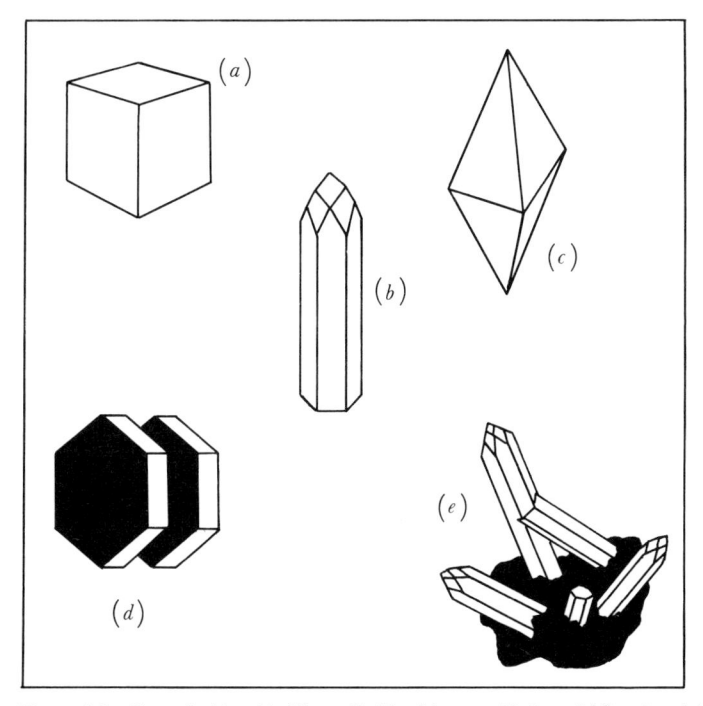

Figure 2.8 Crystals (*a*) **cubic** (*b*) **needle-like** (*c*) **pyramid-shaped** (*d*) **twinned** (*e*) **natural**

CHEMISTRY

edges and sharp corners, and all the angles between the faces would be 90°.

You discovered in experiment 2.10 that when a hot saturated solution of a solid is cooled, some of the solid is deposited in the form of crystals. There are two other methods by which crystals are often made. When certain melted substances cool and solidify they form crystals. Many natural crystals which are found in the Earth's crust have been made this way, the best known example being diamonds. Another method is to take a small crystal and hang

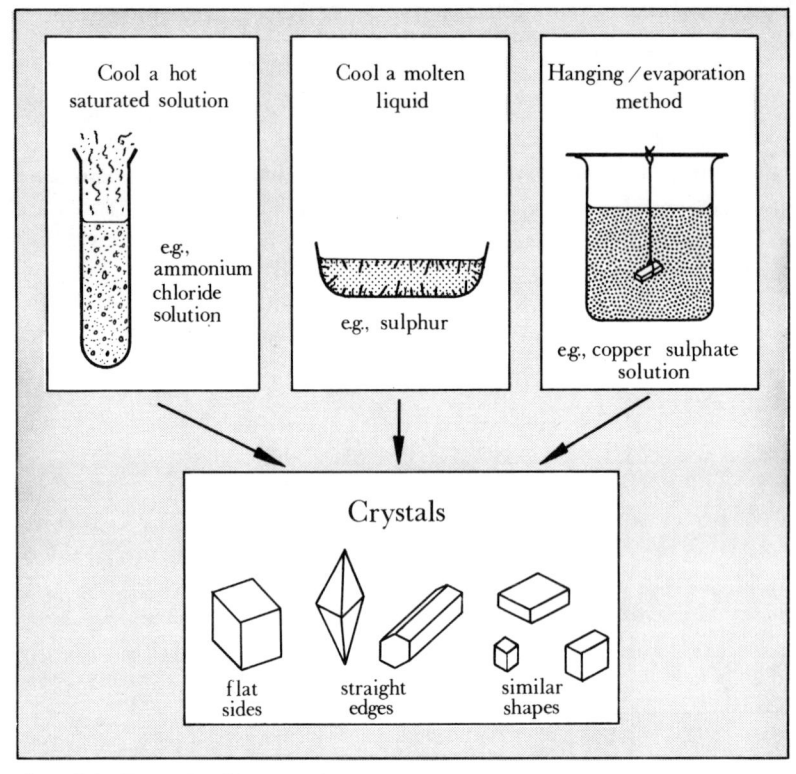

Figure 2.9 Ways of making crystals

- Cool a hot saturated solution — e.g., ammonium chloride solution
- Cool a molten liquid — e.g., sulphur
- Hanging / evaporation method — e.g., copper sulphate solution

Crystals: flat sides, straight edges, similar shapes

it in a cold saturated solution of the same substance, for example, a copper sulphate crystal is hung in copper sulphate solution. The water from the solution evaporates slowly, and because the solution was saturated the solid from this water must deposit somewhere in the inside of the beaker. Some of the solid deposits on the thread holding the crystal, and some on the sides and bottom of the beaker, but some attaches itself to the suspended crystal, which grows larger. The crystals which grow on the thread and on the surface of the beaker should be removed daily. If this method is to succeed the temperature of the solution must be kept constant. If the room temperature

WATER

rises, the solution warms up and the water in the beaker is able to dissolve more solid (i.e., it becomes unsaturated). It therefore dissolves the only supply available, the hanging crystal, and instead of a fine, large crystal, all there is in the beaker when you look at it next is a piece of thread. Common alum (potassium aluminium sulphate) and copper sulphate are crystals which may be grown this way.

Growing crystals by this method reveals one of the reasons why crystals are often imperfect: a crystal which grows while resting on the bottom of the beaker cannot grow downwards, so it always has one side undeveloped.

Water of crystallization

Many crystals contain water of crystallization. This is water which is locked up inside the crystals. The crystals are not wet in the sense that, for example, a used bath towel is wet, because the water is chemically combined with the material of the crystals, and forms part of them. These crystals are said to be **hydrated**: the normal blue copper sulphate is called hydrated copper sulphate. If the water is removed from hydrated crystals by moderate heating, the crystals break down into a powder, whose properties are not the same as those of the original crystals. Hydrated copper sulphate always contains the same proportion of water, 36 per cent by weight. This applies to other hydrated substances (the actual percentages being different, of course), and it is an example of the working of the Law of Constant Composition (see page 15). In this case, the composition of copper sulphate crystals always contains the item '36 per cent water'. Other hydrated compounds frequently seen in the school laboratory include hydrated iron sulphate and hydrated sodium carbonate.

Chemical properties of water

Experiment 2.12 *Action of water on calcium*

Put a piece of freshly cut calcium into a small beaker half-full of water.

What happens to the calcium?
Describe two other things which happen.

Experiment 2.13 *Action of water on sodium*

Put water into a tall beaker to a depth of about 2 cm. Test the water by dipping in either some universal indicator paper or both red and blue litmus papers. Drop into the beaker a lump of freshly cut sodium about one-quarter the size of a pea, put a wire gauze over the top of the beaker, and watch the experiment from a distance of 2 m or more. When the action has finished test again with the type of indicator used previously.

29

CHEMISTRY

Caution: the substances in this experiment are harmful to skin and clothes; use dry tongs to handle the sodium.

What do you hear as the action takes place?
What happens to the sodium?
What do the litmus paper tests tell you?

In experiment 2.12 the calcium decreases in size and finally vanishes, while white flakes form in the liquid, and bubbles of a colourless gas are given off. The white solid (which is calcium hydroxide) and the gas (which is hydrogen) were not there before the experiment: they were made during the experiment as some of the atoms present changed partners. What happened can be represented as a word equation:

$$\text{calcium} + \text{water} \longrightarrow \text{calcium hydroxide} + \text{hydrogen}$$

In experiment 2.13 the sodium, which obviously got hot (it melted to a silver coloured ball, and made a fizzing sound in the water), became smaller and smaller in size until it vanished. The red litmus did not turn blue when it was put into the water before the experiment, but it did turn blue afterwards, showing that there was something else present after the reaction. A further happening, not easy to see, was that a colourless gas was given off during the reaction. What happened can be represented as a word equation:

$$\text{sodium} + \text{water} \longrightarrow \text{sodium hydroxide} + \text{hydrogen}$$

Heat was produced in the reaction, and it would be correct to add ' + heat' to the end of this equation. The sodium hydroxide was in solution dissolved in the water and this turned the litmus blue. The hydrogen was the colourless gas given off. What happened was not a simple dissolving of sodium in the water, but a reaction of sodium with water. If the solution left in the beaker were evaporated it would leave solid sodium hydroxide, not sodium.

In both experiments a **chemical change** (or chemical reaction) has taken place. Some of the substances present at the beginning have been used up, and new substances have been made. Experiment 2.12 is summarized in Fig. 2.10. Some of the water was used up in the chemical change, and the atoms of the water molecules were separated. Part of the hydrogen in the H_2O came off as a gas, and the rest of the hydrogen and all the oxygen combined with the calcium to form the calcium hydroxide. It is difficult to reverse the change and get back the calcium and the water.

This process can be compared with a physical change such as the dissolving of ammonium chloride in water. Here, nothing new is made, the original substances are present in the solution, and the change can be reversed by evaporation, which is a simple process. The atoms in the water and ammo-

WATER

nium chloride are still joined in the same way (i.e., built-up into the same molecules or ions) after the physical change has taken place.

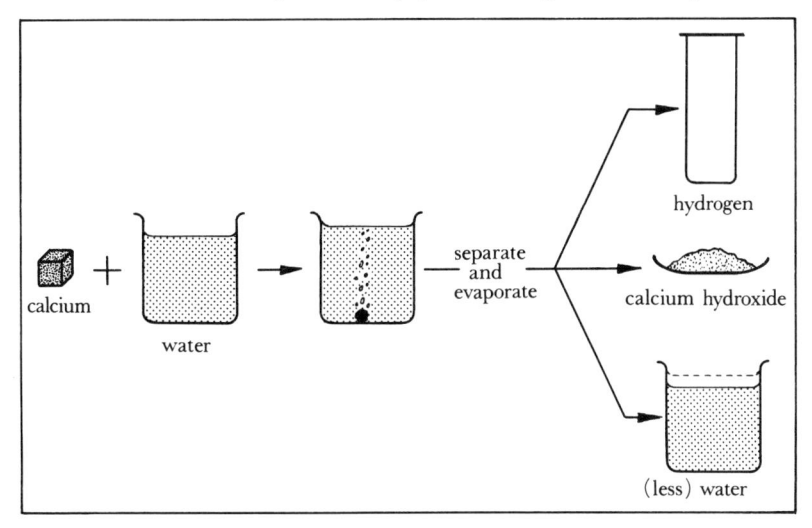

Figure 2.10 A chemical reaction between calcium and water

Summary of physical change and chemical change

After a physical change no new substance is made. The original substances are still present, and their atoms are still joined in the same way. A physical change is often easy to reverse.

After a chemical change one or more new substances have been made. The original substances have been used up, because their atoms have rejoined in new ways. Chemical change is often difficult to reverse.

Test for water

Figure 2.11 Is it water?

How could you tell if this colourless odourless liquid was water? The obvious answer 'Drink it!' won't do, because the liquid could be sulphuric acid or any one of many other poisonous substances if the colour and lack of smell were all the evidence used. Scientists need reliable tests to identify various substances with certainty. The best tests for a liquid suspected of being water are to measure the boiling point, freezing point, and density. These should be 100°C at normal pressure, 0°C and 1 g cm^{-3}. These tests take quite a long time. There is an alternative test, which is quicker but not as positive.

Experiment 2.14   *To detect the presence of water in a liquid*

Add about 1 cm^3 of the liquid to a little white anhydrous copper sulphate in a test tube. If the white solid turns blue there is water present in the liquid.

Note that experiment 2.14 shows only that the liquid has water in it, not that the liquid is pure water. Salt solution, or lime water, which both contain water, would turn the solid blue if they were tested. White anhydrous copper sulphate is not usually kept in the laboratory, but made when it is needed. It is made by gentle heating of blue hydrated copper sulphate crystals in a crucible or test tube. Steam is given off and the blue solid becomes paler and then turns white.

After a test with water the white powder becomes blue again. The chemical reaction which takes place when the water is removed by heating can be reversed, and the water put back into the solid again. This reaction is one of the special class of reactions called **reversible reactions**; in these reactions a change of conditions can reform the original substances from the products. An equation for a reversible reaction is written with double arrows. For example,

blue hydrated copper sulphate
$\rightleftharpoons$ white anhydrous copper sulphate + water

A useful word which describes the forward reaction, the removal of water, is **dehydration**. Any reaction in which water is removed from a compound is a dehydration reaction.

Water supply

Most of the water we use comes from reservoirs in the hills, or from great rivers such as the Severn, Scottish Dee, or Thames, although some is still drawn from wells.

In the purification process that it undergoes before it is fit to drink, the water is first pumped from the river or reservoir, and allowed to stand in a settling tank, where most of the suspended solid matter falls to the bottom in a sedimentation process. Smaller suspended particles, which are very slow to form sediment, are then removed by filtration. In slow sand filtration

WATER

water trickles through a bed of sand and gravel in a large tank. A slimy deposit forms on the sand, and although this sounds nasty and unhealthy it is in fact very beneficial, because the slime removes about 90 per cent of the bacteria present in the water. The filtered water is then treated with chemicals, usually chlorine and sodium fluoride. Chlorination kills the rest of the bacteria, and the addition of the sodium fluoride helps to prevent the decay of children's teeth. Some people objected to the addition of chlorine to water when this was first done about eighty years ago, but now everyone realizes that chlorination is sensible, because it checks the spread of diseases. The

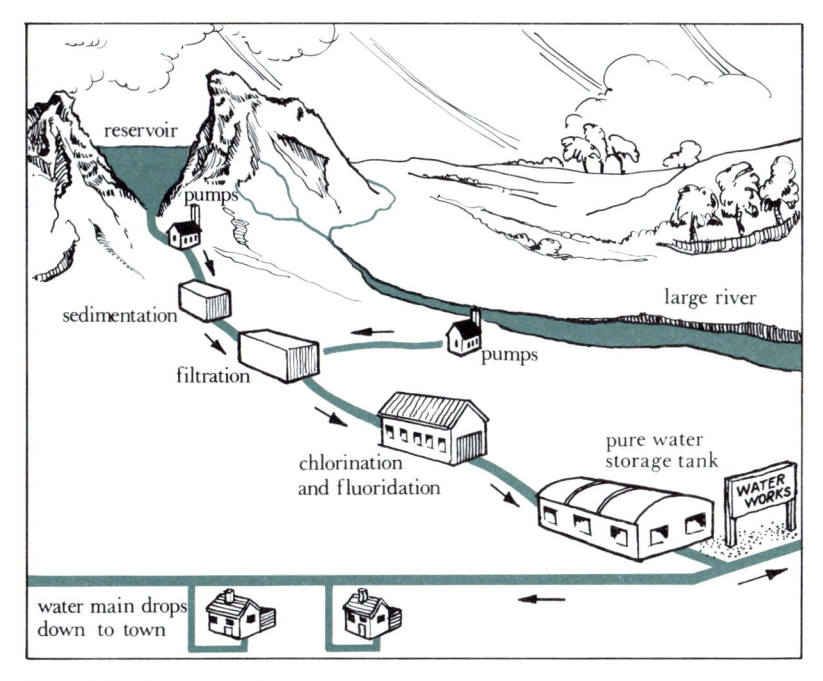

Figure 2.12 A water supply system

opposition to the fluoridation of water is similarly being overcome. The water, which is fit to drink although it still contains some dissolved solids, is then pumped into a large tank until it is ready for use. If possible this tank is built on a hill, so that the water flows downwards from it to the houses and factories, and does not need more pumping. In a flat area the tank is sometimes built into a high tower to give it the necessary height.

The water cycle

The collection, purification, and distribution of water are parts of the water cycle round which the water we use travels continuously. The most obvious changes in the cycle are evaporation and condensation, but other important

CHEMISTRY

processes are burning, and transpiration and plant growth. Transpiration and plant growth both involve water absorbed by the roots of plants.

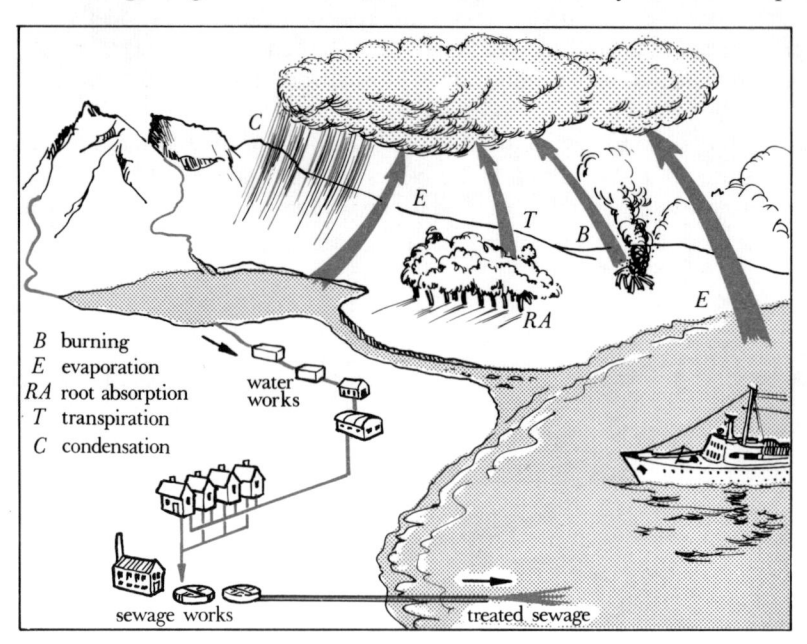

B burning
E evaporation
RA root absorption
T transpiration
C condensation

Figure 2.13 The water cycle

Kinetic theory

Experiments described in chapter 1 show that all matter consists of particles. In all the three states of water (solid, liquid, and vapour) the particles are molecules of water. Each of these molecules has the formula H_2O, because it consists of two atoms of hydrogen joined to one of oxygen, and the atoms stay joined when the water is frozen, evaporated, boiled, condensed, or melted. No new substances are made so these processes are physical changes.

In solid ice each molecule has its own position in the crystal, but the molecule does not stand still in that position—it vibrates all the time, and the position of the molecule in the crystal can be thought of as an average position. If the ice is heated the molecule vibrates more and more vigorously until, at 0°C, it has enough energy to break away from its position in the crystal and move more freely. We call this breaking away **melting**, and when the molecule is part of some liquid water, it can move anywhere in the water. As it moves about in the water it bounces off other water molecules, and off the walls and bottom of the container. The bouncing off the walls pushes on the walls, creating water pressure. If the molecule is moving fast enough and it approaches the surface of the water, it will break through the surface of

WATER

the water and escape, becoming part of the water vapour which always exists above a water surface. The process of escaping from the surface of the water is called **evaporation**. In water vapour the molecule will move about freely, bouncing off other molecules and off the surface of the container.

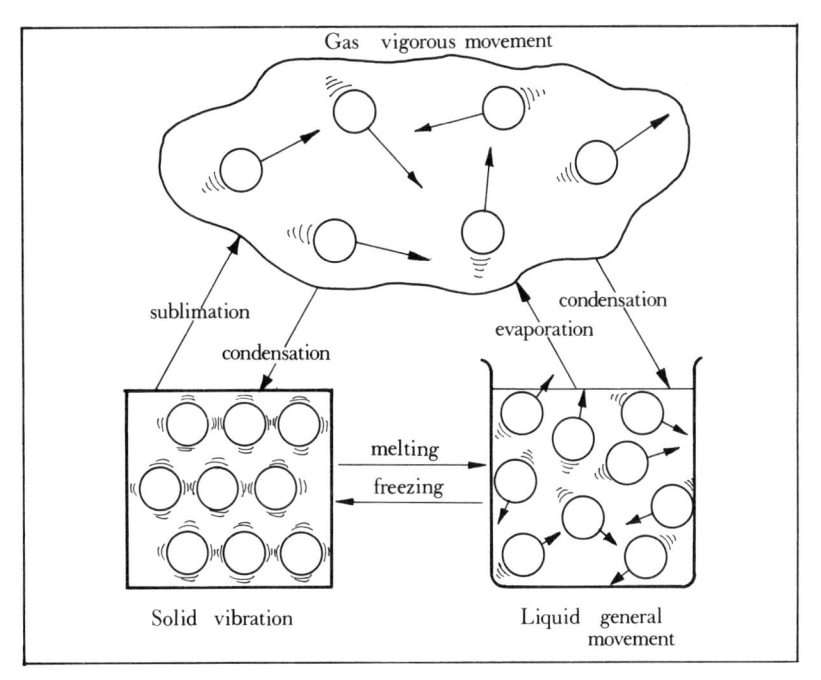

Figure 2.14 The particles of solids, liquids and gases move constantly

The molecules in the vapour state are on average much farther apart than those in the solid or liquid states. On cooling these changes are reversed, and the molecule becomes part of the liquid water again, and then ice.

The kinetic theory (the idea that the particles of substances are always moving) applies to all substances, not solely to water, and it provides an explanation for many things. Here are some simple examples:

evaporation is slow at low temperatures because the molecules are moving slowly and find it hard to escape;

evaporation produces cooling because the faster (hotter) molecules escape, leaving slower (cooler) ones behind;

gases are less dense than solids and liquids because their particles are farther apart;

a rubber balloon full of a gas expands when the gas is heated because the gas molecules move faster, hit the balloon walls harder and push them back;

35

solutions once made stay solutions and do not need shaking or stirring because the molecules in them move all the time and mix up the solute and solvent. Similarly gas mixtures such as air stay mixed;

the movement of the particles goes on and on, because it is frictionless, so there is no braking force available to slow down the particles; this is why Brownian Movement (experiment 1.8) carries on without external energy being supplied.

Chapter summary

Water, which covers most of the Earth, boils at 100°C under normal pressure, but at much lower temperatures if the pressure is reduced. Substances like potassium nitrate, sugar, and salt which dissolve in water are described as soluble, water being the solvent and the sugar or other substance the solute. A solution leaves its solid behind if the solvent is evaporated. Most solutes increase in solubility as the temperature rises, and decrease again as the temperature falls, which allows crystallization to take place. As well as these physical properties, in which the water molecules remain unchanged, water undergoes some chemical changes, e.g., with calcium and sodium and white anhydrous copper sulphate. Molecules in ice vibrate, those in liquid water and water vapour move about at random.

Answers to questions on the solubility graph

48 g
27°C
At 80°C, 66 g of ammonium chloride dissolve in 100 g water
At 69°C, 60 g of ammonium chloride dissolve in 100 g water
370 g (because 37 g dissolve in 100 g water at this temperature)

Questions

1. What is the essential difference between a physical and a chemical property? Classify as physical or chemical properties: (a) the boiling point of water, (b) the solubility of fat in benzene, (c) the evaporation of alcohol, (d) the crystallization of copper sulphate solution, (e) the action of calcium on water.

2. Mention two methods by which the boiling point of water may be raised above 100°C, and describe briefly a practical use of one of these.

3. Given a supply of sand, potassium nitrate, water, and acetone, and any apparatus you require, describe briefly how you would do experiments to illustrate the meaning of (a) solute, (b) insoluble, (c) evaporation. (It is not necessary to use all the chemicals in each experiment.)

4. Three beakers are known to contain distilled water, sodium hydroxide solution, and salt solution. Describe tests (excluding tasting) which you could do to distinguish the beakers.

5. Name an example of (*a*) a reversible reaction, (*b*) a substance used to kill bacteria in tap water, (*c*) a liquid which evaporates readily, (*d*) a chemical reaction of water, (*e*) a colourless gas, (*f*) a hydrated solid, (*g*) a substance eleven times as dense as water, (*h*) a solvent for grease.

6. Describe the changes in movement of a water molecule as the temperature of the water decreases from 130°C at normal pressure to −10°C.

7. Use the figures given to draw a solubility graph for potassium chlorate. From the graph determine (*a*) the solubility at 25°C, (*b*) the temperature at which the solubility is 12 g per 100 g, (*c*) whether a solution containing 130 g potassium chlorate in 1000 g water at 40°C is saturated or not.

Temp (°C)	0	10	20	30	40	50
Sol (g per 100 g water)	3·0	4·5	7·0	10	14	19

3

Oxygen and burning

A visitor from another galaxy might start his description of our Earth by saying, 'It is covered by an ocean many kilometres deep, consisting of a mixture of gases'. We all live at the bottom of this ocean of air, which has hot and cold currents, and tides, just like the seas. If we move out of our ocean, as when men and women explore the sea-bed, or go into space, we must take some of it with us to breathe. The oxygen in the air is our most

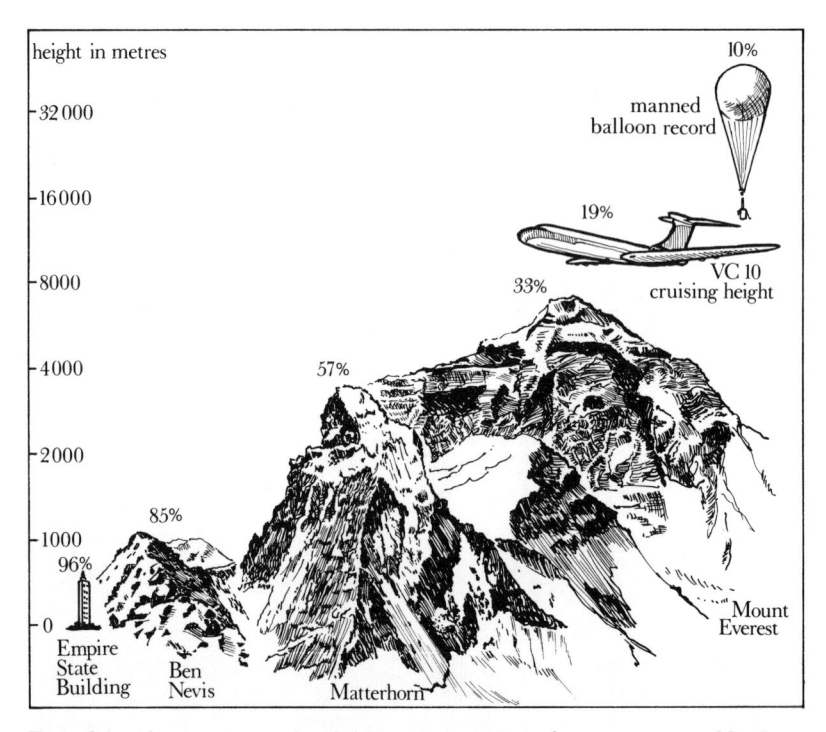

Figure 3.1 Air pressure at various heights as a percentage of pressure at ground level

OXYGEN AND BURNING

vital need; we can live several weeks without food, days without water, but only minutes without air. In this chapter we shall discuss the atmosphere, the gases in it, and the properties and reactions of the gas most important to us, oxygen.

The atmosphere

The visitor from space would not be able to report how deep or, as we on Earth would put it, how high our atmosphere was. Unlike the seas, which start at the sea-bed and finish at the water surface, the air has no upper boundary. The air just gets thinner and thinner at greater and greater heights.

The Earth has an atmosphere because its gravitational attraction is large enough to prevent the molecules in the air escaping into space. An atmosphere has probably always surrounded the Earth, although its composition has changed and is still changing. If air were a chemical compound, it would have fixed unvarying proportions because the Law of Constant Composition would apply. Since air is not a compound but a mixture, its composition can vary; the air in a city street, crowded with vehicles and people, has more carbon dioxide and carbon monoxide in it than country air has.

Experiment 3.1 *Measuring the percentage of oxygen in the air*

(a) Using steel wool to remove the oxygen

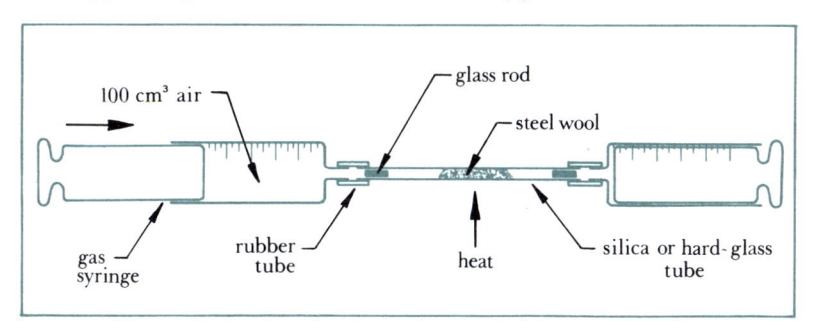

Figure 3.2 Removing oxygen by hot steel wool

Set up the apparatus as shown in the diagram, with 100 cm^3 air in the left-hand syringe. Heat the tube containing the steel wool, and when the wool glows red hot remove the flame and push the left-hand syringe slowly in so that the wool continues to glow and burn. If the burning steel wool goes out before all the air has passed through, reheat it. Push all the air out of the left-hand syringe, allow the apparatus to cool, and measure the volume of gas in the right-hand syringe.

(b) Using alkaline pyrogallol to remove the oxygen

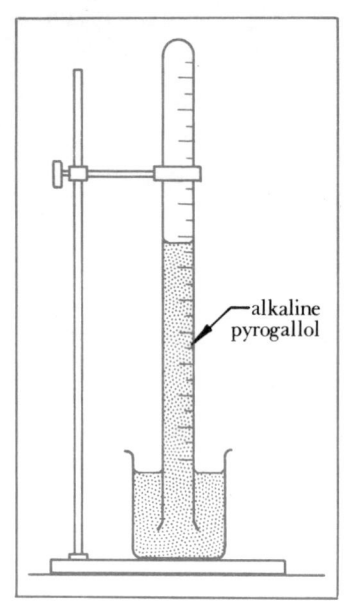

Figure 3.3 Removing oxygen by alkaline pyrogallol

Dissolve about one gram of pyrogallol in 30 cm^3 of water. Pour some of this solution into a graduated gas tube and put in two pellets of solid sodium hydroxide. Put a rubber stopper in the tube and read the volume of air it contains. Shake the tube gently until the solid sodium hydroxide has dissolved. Invert the tube, take out the bung under the surface of water in a beaker, clamp the tube, and leave it until all the oxygen has been absorbed.

What colour does the alkaline pyrogallol go? How do you know when all the oxygen has been absorbed?

In both these experiments, and in that shown in Fig. 7.9, oxygen is absorbed from the air. In experiment 3.1(a) the steel wool removes the oxygen while burning, forming a solid oxide of iron, and the remaining gases pass to the right-hand syringe. In experiment 3.1(b) the alkaline pyrogallol combines with the oxygen forming a rather complicated brown compound. The level of the solution rises until all the oxygen has been absorbed. It is important to handle the tube as little as possible when taking the final measurement, or the gas left will be warmed and expanded, making the answer inaccurate. The gas left in the tube after the experiment is mostly nitrogen. The result is

OXYGEN AND BURNING

calculated by:

$$\% \text{ oxygen} = \frac{(\text{first vol. of air}) - (\text{vol. of gas left at end})}{(\text{first vol. of air})} \times 100$$

The gases in the air

Experiments like experiment 3.1, and others done with more accurate and expensive apparatus, tell us the amounts of all the gases in the air.

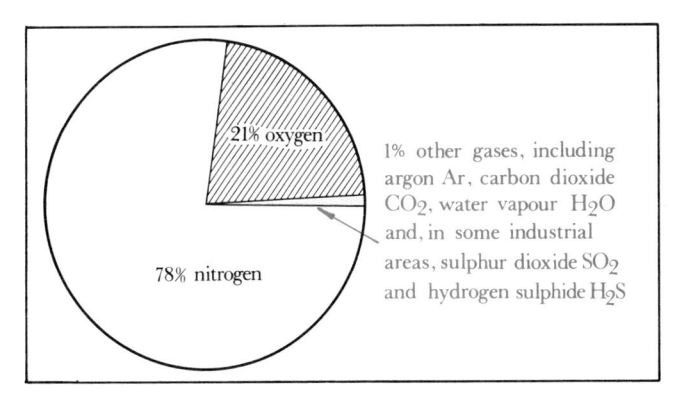

21% oxygen

78% nitrogen

1% other gases, including argon Ar, carbon dioxide CO_2, water vapour H_2O and, in some industrial areas, sulphur dioxide SO_2 and hydrogen sulphide H_2S

Figure 3.4 The gases in the air

Argon is one of a group of elements called the **inert gases** (rare or noble gases). Other members of this group include helium, neon, krypton, and xenon. Helium is used to fill airships, because it is a gas of very low density and is non-flammable. Neon glows red when electricity passes through it, and is used in neon lamps and signs. Argon is used to fill gas-filled electric lamps; the filaments would burn and break if air were put in, but they do not burn in argon. All these uses depend on the unreactive nature of these gases. They have so few chemical reactions that for many years it was thought they had none, but a few reactions have recently been discovered. Another consequence of the fact that these inert gases have few reactions is that their atoms go about singly (e.g., helium He, neon Ne), and do not combine to form molecules as do the atoms of most non-metallic elements (e.g., in oxygen O_2, two atoms have reacted to form a molecule).

Air contains oxygen, water vapour, and carbon dioxide. These three substances, acting together, are **corrosive** to iron and steel, and cause them to rust. Corrosive is a general word for eating away by chemical reaction, but the word rusting is used only for the corrosion of iron and steel. The addition of sulphur dioxide, SO_2, makes damp air even more corrosive. Sulphur dioxide is made whenever sulphur-containing fuels such as oil and coal are burned, and the air which contains it attacks curtain fabrics, which fall to

CHEMISTRY

pieces when washed, metal railings, and certain types of stone, which crumble to powder when touched.

Figure 3.5 Corrosion of an iron gate and a gravestone

Solids in the air

Air also contains small particles of solid material which we call dust. Even in country air there are small particles of soil, but in industrial areas the air contains much larger amounts of solid, mostly from incompletely burned fuels. When, by such things as the replacement of steam locomotives by diesel or electric traction, and the replacement of coal fires and furnaces by coke, oil, gas, or electrical heating, smoke is reduced, not only does the air become cleaner, but the annual hours of sunshine in a city can be increased by as much as 30 per cent when the smoke pall lifts (see also chapter 5). Air also contains fine asbestos fibres from worn brake shoes.

Air in water

Have you ever noticed what happens to a glass of cold water which stands in a warm room? If not, try the experiment now, using a glass or beaker. You can hurry it by putting the glass in a warm place. The bubbles of gas which appear are usually described as air, but their composition is not quite the same as ordinary air.

OXYGEN AND BURNING

Figure 3.6 What are the bubbles?

Experiment 3.2 *To find the proportion of dissolved gases in tap water*

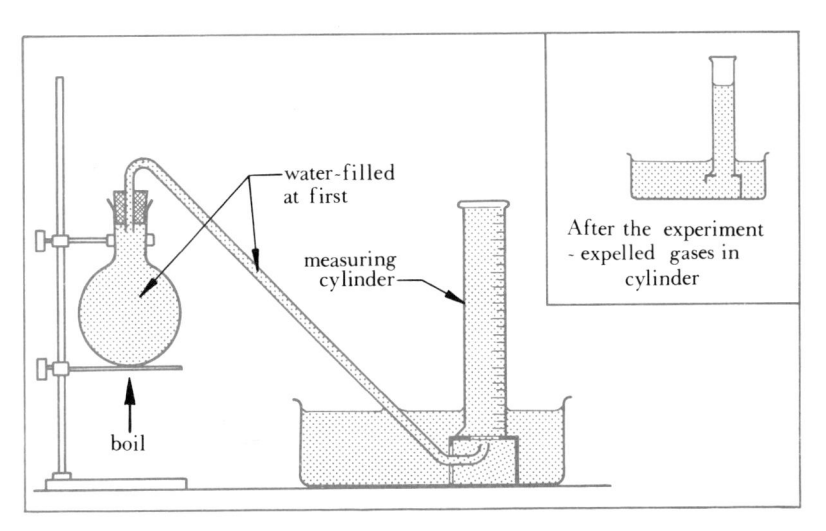

Figure 3.7 Boiling gases out of water

Set up the apparatus as shown in Fig. 3.7 and heat the water in the flask until it boils. Keep the water boiling until no more bubbles collect in the measuring cylinder. Take away the bunsen burner, and when the water in the trough has cooled, note the volume of gas in the measuring cylinder.

When water is boiled for several minutes all the gases are swept out of solution and can be collected and measured. A typical result from this experiment would be the collection of about 30 cm^3 of gas from 1000 cm^3 of water.

CHEMISTRY

Analysing this gas by the method of experiment 3.1 would show that it contained one-third oxygen, but we usually call this gas mixture 'air' for simplicity. The oxygen content is high because oxygen is more soluble in water than nitrogen is.

Fish breathe the oxygen dissolved in water, and if the water becomes warm there is sometimes not enough oxygen for them, and the fish suffocate (or drown, if you like to use the term!).

When a solid dissolves in water this is a physical change, not a chemical reaction. Similarly, the dissolving of air in water is a physical change. Unlike the dissolving of a solid in water, air is **less** soluble at higher temperatures. It is the absence of dissolved air that makes previously boiled water taste peculiar. This taste is often described as 'metallic', but it has nothing to do with any metal vessel in which the water has been boiled.

Experiment 3.3   *Obtaining gas jars of oxygen*

Method (*a*)

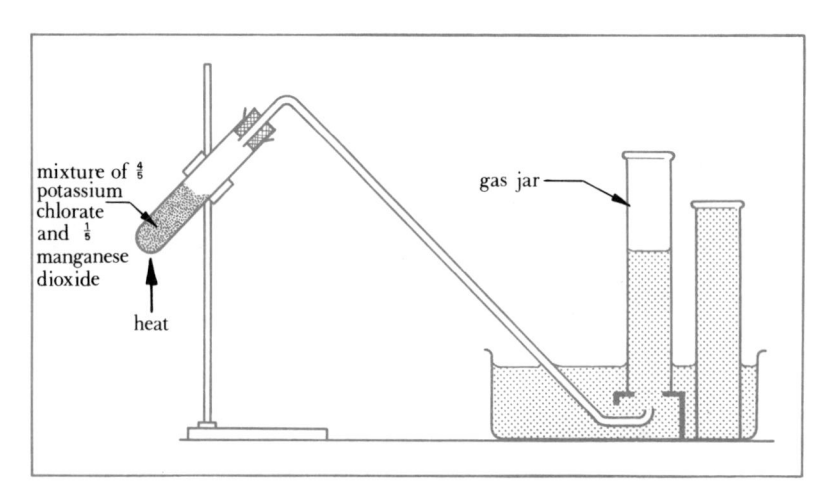

Figure 3.8   Preparation of oxygen from $KClO_3$

Set up the apparatus as shown in Fig. 3.8. Heat the test-tube gently but allow the first few bubbles to escape before starting to collect oxygen in the gas jar. Replace each full jar on the beehive shelf by a jar of water. If the stream of bubbles becomes very fast, stop heating until the reaction slows. Remove the delivery tube from the water when you have finished collecting oxygen.

Why are the first bubbles allowed to escape? What colour does the oxygen in the gas jars appear to be? What colour is the residue in the test-tube?

OXYGEN AND BURNING

Method (*b*)

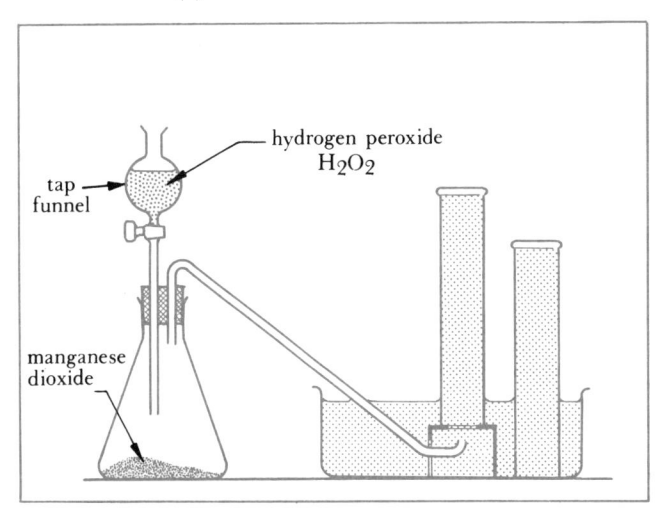

Figure 3.9 **Preparation of oxygen from hydrogen peroxide H$_2$O$_2$**

Set up the apparatus as shown in Fig. 3.9 and then allow some of the hydrogen peroxide to drop into the flask. Allow the first few bubbles to escape, and then collect the gas jars of oxygen as described above in method (*a*).

What do you see happening in the flask? What appears to be left in the flask when the reaction has finished?

Method (*c*)

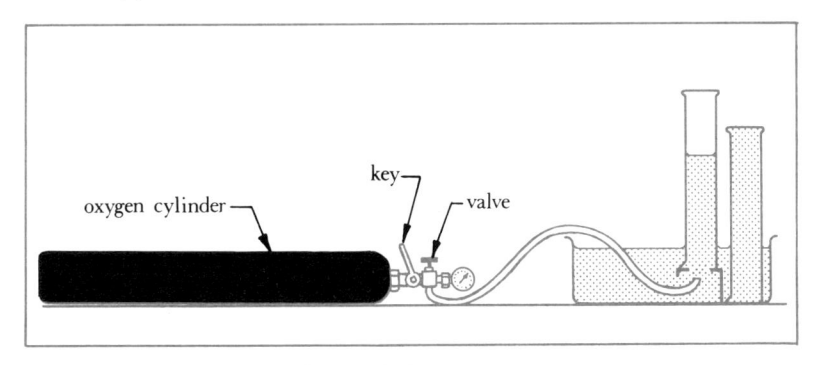

Figure 3.10 **Obtaining oxygen from a cylinder**

First use the key to open one of the valves of the oxygen cylinder, then open carefully the other valve. Oxygen comes from the outlet tube and may be led into a gas jar as shown in Fig. 3.10.

45

Oxygen may be obtained in the laboratory in several ways.

(a) The decomposition (splitting up) of potassium chlorate yields oxygen. A mixture of approximately one-fifth manganese dioxide and four-fifths potassium chlorate is heated in a hard glass test-tube, and the oxygen is collected over water as shown in Fig. 3.8. The first bubbles are allowed to escape because they consist of the air which is in the test-tube and delivery tube. The oxygen, which is collected over water often appears to be grey in colour. This is because as it leaves the test-tube it is very hot, and steam is formed as the hot gas passes through the water. The oxygen comes from the potassium chlorate in the mixture.

$$\text{potassium chlorate} \longrightarrow \text{potassium chloride} + \text{oxygen}$$

The residue in the test-tube is a mixture of potassium chloride and manganese dioxide.

(b) Oxygen may be made by decomposing hydrogen peroxide with manganese dioxide. The manganese dioxide is put in a flask as in experiment 3.3(b) and hydrogen peroxide is dropped on to the solid from a tap funnel. Vigorous frothing is seen and oxygen is produced. The first bubbles in the pneumatic trough are allowed to escape because they contain air from the flask and delivery tube, and then the oxygen is collected over water. Water and manganese dioxide are left in the flask after the experiment.

$$\text{hydrogen peroxide} \longrightarrow \text{water} + \text{oxygen}$$

(c) Oxygen may also be obtained from an oxygen cylinder, which is a strong steel container holding highly compressed oxygen. You should note that this is not a preparation of oxygen, merely the transfer of oxygen from a storage cylinder to your gas jar.

Catalysis

In experiments 3.3(a) and 3.3(b) you probably noticed that the manganese dioxide you put in seemed to be there still at the end of the experiment. You could have weighed the manganese dioxide at the start of the experiment, then washed it, filtered, dried, and reweighed it after the experiment; you would have found the same weight of manganese dioxide after the experiment as you started with. Does the manganese dioxide do anything at all?

If you are not sure of the answer to this put a little hydrogen peroxide solution (about 1 cm in depth) into each of two test-tubes. Add a small quantity of manganese dioxide to one of the tubes and watch what happens. In the tube containing hydrogen peroxide only, you will see a few bubbles. A very slow reaction will go on for several hours. In the other test-tube very rapid bubbling will take place.

OXYGEN AND BURNING

The manganese dioxide speeds up the slow reaction which takes place in the other test-tube. The manganese dioxide is not used up when it speeds up the reaction and it is called a **catalyst**. A reaction in which a catalyst is involved is called a catalysed reaction. Similarly, in the reaction with potassium chlorate, the manganese dioxide acts as a catalyst. It becomes spread out in the test-tube as the reaction takes place, but is not consumed, and there is the same weight of manganese dioxide present at the end of the experiment as was put into the test-tube at the beginning.

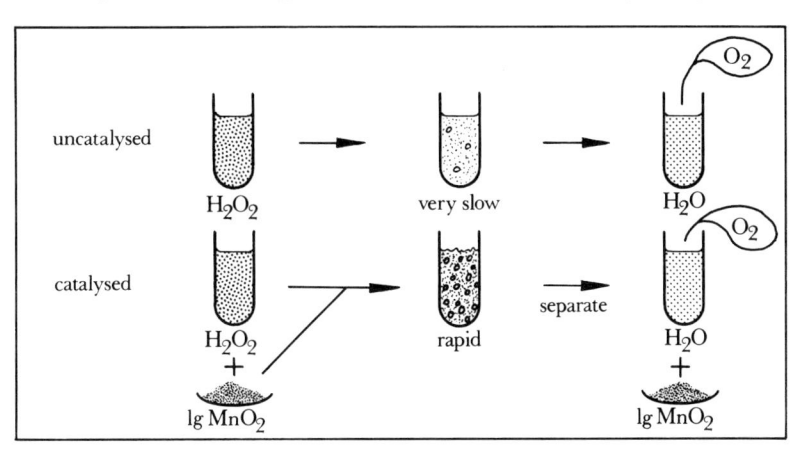

Figure 3.11 A typical catalyst in action

Equations

We saw in chapters 1 and 2 that it is often convenient to summarize chemical reactions in words, e.g.,

$$\text{iron} + \text{sulphur} \longrightarrow \text{iron sulphide}$$

A method even shorter than using these word equations is the use of chemical symbols and formulae. We call these equations **symbol equations**, or more usually chemical equations.

Word equation: iron + sulphur $\longrightarrow$ iron sulphide
Symbol equation: Fe + S $\longrightarrow$ FeS

Both word equations and symbol equations represent the overall changes taking place in a chemical reaction, i.e., atoms separating and joining, the original molecules breaking up and new ones being made. No atoms vanish and none appear so there is the same number of each type of atom on either side of the arrow. In the example above there is one atom of iron and one of sulphur on each side of the arrow. The word **equation** is related to the **equal** numbers of each sort of atom on either side of the arrow.

47

CHEMISTRY

Consider the decomposition of hydrogen peroxide using a manganese dioxide catalyst. The catalyst is not consumed in the reaction so it is not usually put in the equation

$$\text{hydrogen peroxide} \longrightarrow \text{water} + \text{oxygen}$$

Various ways of representing water

$H_2O \qquad H\text{-}O\text{-}H \qquad H\overset{O}{}H \qquad$ (diagrams)

Two representations of a chemical reaction

(diagrams)

$H_2O_2 \ + \ H_2O_2 \ \longrightarrow \ H_2O \ + \ H_2O \ + \ O_2$

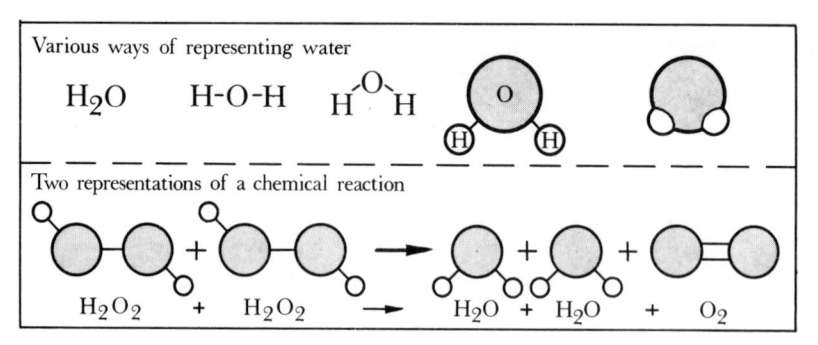

Figure 3.12 The decomposition of hydrogen peroxide

The equation shown in Fig. 3.12 is usually written

$$2H_2O_2 \longrightarrow 2H_2O + O_2$$

On the left-hand side of this balanced chemical equation the large 2 multiplies the whole of the formula H_2O_2, and on the right-hand side the large 2 multiplies the whole of the formula H_2O, but not the O_2. To check that the equation is balanced add up the number of atoms of each type.

For example, starting with hydrogen: on the left-hand side H_2O_2 contains two hydrogen atoms, so $2H_2O_2$ contains four hydrogen atoms. Therefore there are four hydrogen atoms on the left-hand side. On the right-hand side H_2O contains two hydrogen atoms, so $2H_2O$ contains four hydrogen atoms. Thus there are four hydrogen atoms on the right-hand side. This balances the four hydrogen atoms on the left-hand side. The only other type of atom in this equation is the oxygen atom:

H_2O_2 contains two oxygen atoms, so $2H_2O_2$ contains four oxygen atoms.

On the right-hand side there are two oxygen atoms in $2H_2O$ and two more in the O_2, so there are four oxygen atoms on the right-hand side. Therefore the symbol equation as written is balanced.

As a second example we can consider the production of oxygen from potassium chlorate. Again manganese dioxide acts as a catalyst, so is not consumed in the reaction, and need not be shown in the equation.

$$\text{potassium chlorate} \longrightarrow \text{potassium chloride} + \text{oxygen}$$
$$2KClO_3 \longrightarrow 2KCl + 3O_2$$

OXYGEN AND BURNING

The large two in front of the $KClO_3$ multiplies the whole of this formula. This means that on the left-hand side of the equation there are two potassium atoms, two chlorine atoms and $2 \times 3 = 6$ oxygen atoms. Checking the right-hand side reveals two potassium atoms and two chlorine atoms in $2KCl$, and six oxygen atoms in $3O_2$. Again, the number of atoms of each sort on either side of the equation is the same so the equation is balanced.

Summary of equations

The word equation is a convenient way of representing a chemical reaction, and shows the substances which react (the reactants), and the substances which are made (the products). A symbol equation shows what atoms and molecules react and are made. Since atoms don't appear or vanish in a chemical reaction, all atoms present at the start of the reaction must be accounted for; i.e., all the atoms on the left-hand side of the equation must appear on the right-hand side so that the equation is balanced.

Properties of oxygen

Oxygen is a gas at room temperature but it condenses to a liquid if it is made cold enough. The temperature needed is $-183°C$ (90 K). Everyday observation of the oxygen present in the air tells us that oxygen is colourless and has no smell. Oxygen is slightly denser than air, and slightly soluble in water, as 30 cm³ oxygen dissolve in 1000 cm³ water at 20°C.

Experiment 3.4 *Do things burn in oxygen?*

Using the methods shown in the diagram, try to burn various substances in gas jars of oxygen. Note the colour and fierceness of the flame if any, and the colour and type of 'ash' left after burning. Suitable substances are wood, paper, a candle or wax taper, a piece of coal, benzene, a town gas flame, sulphur, phosphorus, magnesium ribbon, iron wire, a jet of hydrogen, magnesium oxide, and zinc oxide. Keep the burning substances away from the walls of the gas jar.

Caution: some of these substances burn violently, throwing off sparks and molten material.

Your teacher will probably demonstrate the burning of phosphorus, as it can be dangerous.

CHEMISTRY

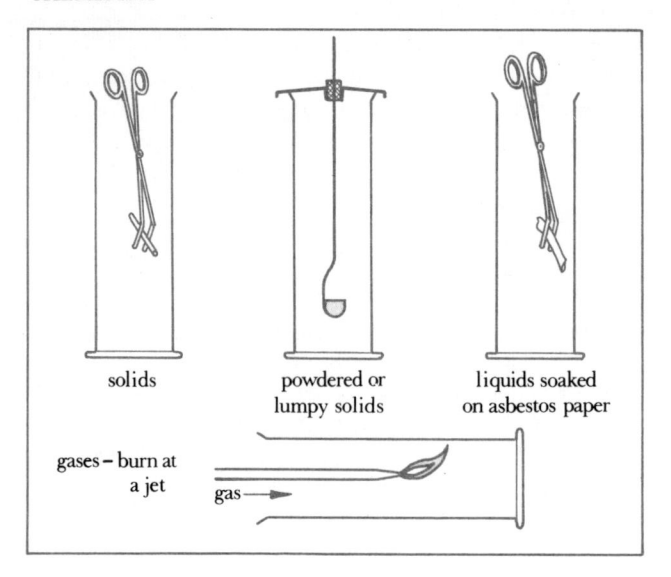

solids

powdered or lumpy solids

liquids soaked on asbestos paper

gases – burn at a jet

gas →

Figure 3.13 Burning substances in oxygen

All the substances in experiment 3.4 burn vigorously except for magnesium oxide and zinc oxide which have no reaction. A summary of the results is shown in Table 3.1.

Look at the table and decide in what ways these reactions are similar to each other.

The reactions in which burning occur are all similar because in each case an oxide is produced. Sometimes two, or even more oxides are produced. When an element or compound combines with oxygen it is said to be oxidized, and the reaction is called an **oxidation**. All the reactions in the table above are therefore oxidation reactions. The reactions are also similar in that in each one heat is produced, and a flame is seen. The reactions are also therefore examples of combustion. A **combustion** is an oxidation reaction which goes on so vigorously that heat and light are produced. Oxygen is a vigorous supporter of combustion, and anything which burns in air, burns faster, more brightly and with a hotter flame in oxygen. The nitrogen and other gases present in the air dilute the oxygen and make combustion less fierce.

Test for oxygen

The presence of oxygen is usually detected by putting a glowing wooden splint into the gas being tested. Oxygen relights a glowing splint.

OXYGEN AND BURNING

Table 3.1 Burning things in oxygen

Substance	Formula	Flame	Product(s)	Symbol equation
wood or paper	*	yellow, bright	charcoal, steam and carbon dioxide—gas and solid	*
candle wax	*	yellow, bright	carbon, steam, and carbon dioxide—gas and solid	*
coal	*	yellow, bright	carbon, steam, and carbon dioxide—gas and solid	*
benzene	C_6H_6	yellow, bright	carbon, steam, and carbon dioxide—gas and solid	$2C_6H_6 + 3O_2 \rightarrow 12C + 6H_2O$
sulphur	S	blue	sulphur dioxide—gas	$S + O_2 \rightarrow SO_2$
phosphorus	P_4	yellow, bright	tetraphosphorus decoxide smoke—solid	$P_4 + 5O_2 \rightarrow P_4O_{10}$
magnesium	Mg	white, bright	magnesium oxide powder—solid	$2Mg + O_2 \rightarrow 2MgO$
iron	Fe	white sparks bright	iron oxide powder—solid	$3Fe + 2O_2 \rightarrow Fe_3O_4$
hydrogen	H_2	blue	steam—gas	$2H_2 + O_2 \rightarrow 2H_2O$

Notes: Substances marked * are not simple compounds. They have variable composition—i.e., they are mixtures—and so have no fixed formula and no simple equation for burning. They all contain carbon and hydrogen, and would form carbon dioxide and steam if completely burned, but might make carbon if incompletely burned.

The two substances which did not burn, magnesium oxide and zinc oxide, are substances which have been burned already. The zinc oxide turns yellow when it is heated, and goes white again as it cools.

Extraction and uses of oxygen

Very large amounts of oxygen are used in industry. This oxygen is extracted from air by a process in which air is condensed to a liquid by cooling, then distilled to separate the oxygen from the nitrogen.

The first part of this process is the liquefaction (i.e., making liquid) of air. When you pump up a bicycle tyre, the air compressed in the pump gets hot and heats the end of the pump. When the compressed air is let out of the tyre it is very cold as it rushes out. These processes—compression and expansion—are used in the liquefaction of air. Pure dry air is compressed, which heats it, and then cooled. The cooled compressed air is allowed to expand, which cools it still further, and it liquefies, producing a mixture of liquid nitrogen

CHEMISTRY

and liquid oxygen. Liquid nitrogen boils at 77 K (i.e., 77° Absolute or −196°C) and liquid oxygen boils at 90 K (90°A or −183°C). The nitrogen at 77 K has a lower boiling point than the oxygen at 90 K so when the mixture is warmed the nitrogen distils off as a gas. Although we say the nitrogen boils off it is still very cold, and it is used to pre-cool the air and help it to liquefy in the first stage of the process. When the nitrogen has boiled away liquid oxygen remains; this is allowed to warm slightly, when it turns into a gas which is compressed and put into cylinders. Some industries such as steel-making use so much oxygen that they have their own oxygen-making plant, and pump the oxygen in pipes directly to the place where it is needed. Occasionally liquid oxygen is transported in rail or road tanker wagons.

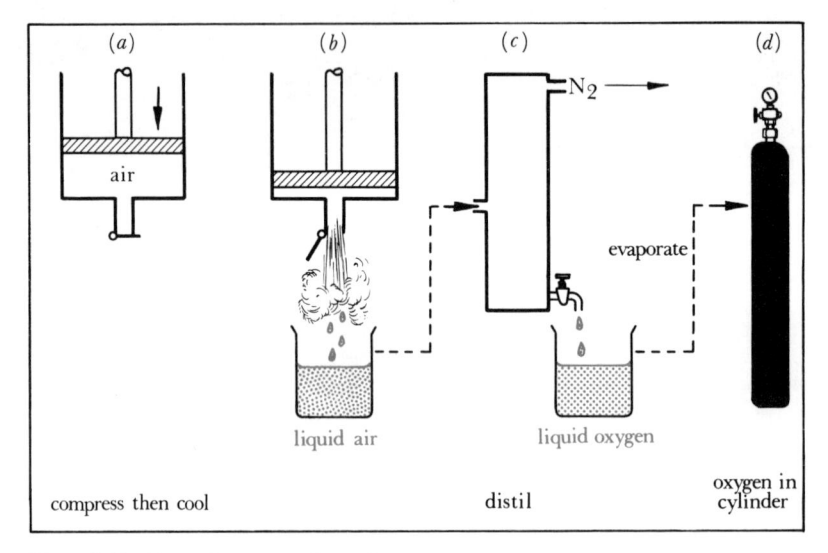

Figure 3.14 Extracting oxygen from air

Many of the uses of oxygen are connected with breathing. If someone is very ill it is a waste of energy for him to breathe air, four-fifths of which is no use to him. Patients are often given oxygen to breathe, either through a mask or by putting them into a plastic tent which is kept filled with oxygen. Men and women going to places where there is no air must carry their own supply and they usually take oxygen rather than air because a smaller volume is needed. Mountaineers at high altitudes, astronauts, firemen wearing breathing apparatus in smoky atmospheres, pilots of high-flying aircraft which are not pressurized, and skin divers all commonly carry oxygen supplies with them in cylinders.

Other uses of oxygen include the oxy-acetylene and oxy-hydrogen flames.

OXYGEN AND BURNING

In these, the gases acetylene or hydrogen are mixed with oxygen and burned.

$$\text{oxygen} + \text{acetylene} \longrightarrow \text{carbon dioxide} + \text{steam} + \text{heat}$$
$$5O_2 + 2C_2H_2 \longrightarrow 4CO_2 + 2H_2O + \text{heat}$$

$$\text{hydrogen} + \text{oxygen} \longrightarrow \text{steam} + \text{heat}$$
$$2H_2 + O_2 \longrightarrow 2H_2O + \text{heat}$$

These hot flames are used to raise metals to high temperatures so that they may be welded or cut. This is done by raising the metal to a high temperature and then turning off the acetylene or hydrogen, leaving an oxygen jet which simply burns away the metal (see Fig. 7.7).

Photographic flash bulbs contain aluminium wire or foil and oxygen. The aluminium burns brilliantly when an electric current is passed through it.

Liquid oxygen is also used in large rockets. Any fuel needs oxygen to burn so tanks of liquid oxygen are taken in the rocket. The liquid oxygen turns to gas and is used to burn the fuel which is often paraffin. An advantage of the use of liquid oxygen is that it is very cold and helps to cool the combustion chamber.

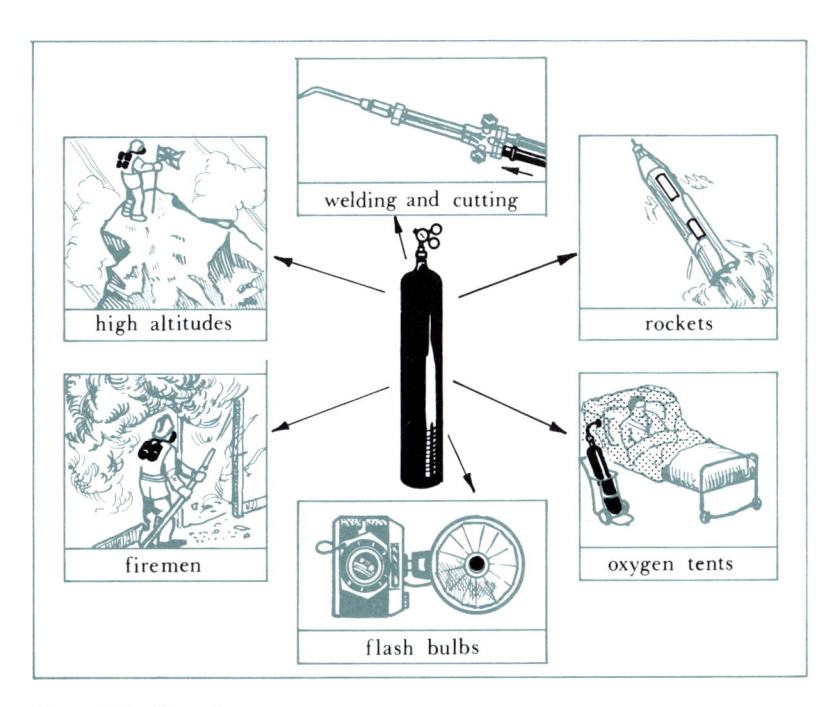

Figure 3.15 Uses of oxygen

CHEMISTRY

Chapter summary

Air consists of about one-fifth oxygen by volume, almost four-fifths nitrogen, and one-hundredth other gases, mainly argon, water vapour, and carbon dioxide. Oxygen can be made in the laboratory by heating potassium chlorate with a catalyst of manganese dioxide, or by decomposing hydrogen peroxide solution using a manganese dioxide catalyst. A catalyst is a substance which speeds up a reaction but is not consumed and therefore may be recovered after the reaction. Chemical reactions may be represented by equations, which must be balanced—i.e., the same number of atoms of each type must appear on either side of the equation.

Oxygen supports the combustion (burning giving heat and light) of many elements and compounds, which become oxidized to form oxides, e.g., Mg gives MgO and S gives SO_2. Industrially, oxygen is extracted by liquefying air by cooling and then allowing the nitrogen to boil away. Oxygen is used for breathing, and burning substances at high temperatures.

Questions

1. Name and give the chemical symbols and uses of three of the inert gases.

2. Explain the meaning of each term and give an example of its use: (*a*) corrosive, (*b*) catalyst, (*c*) combustion.

3. A manufacturer claims that each cubic centimetre of his hydrogen peroxide can give off fifty cubic centimetres of oxygen. Describe how you would check his claim.

4. Quote in words and formulae the equation for:
    (*a*) the decomposition of potassium chlorate,
    (*b*) any reaction which makes water or steam,
    (*c*) a reaction which makes sulphur dioxide,
    (*d*) a reaction of oxygen with a metal.

5. What are two essential points about a catalyst? Explain why oxygen is not a catalyst in the burning of magnesium.

6. Explain briefly how you would determine the percentage of oxygen in air breathed out by a pupil who has just run in a race.

4

The simplest atom—hydrogen—and others

Experiment 4.1 *Making and collecting jars of hydrogen*

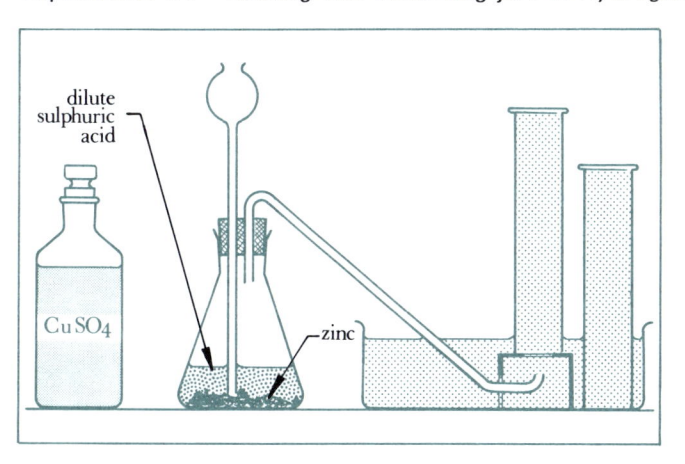

Figure 4.1 Hydrogen is made using zinc, dilute sulphuric acid and a catalyst

Set up the apparatus as shown in the diagram, and add a little copper sulphate solution to form a catalyst. Allow a few bubbles to escape from the end of the delivery tube, and then collect some gas in a test tube and attempt to burn it. When the gas in the test tube burns with a very faint pop and you see a blue flame travel down the test tube, start to collect the hydrogen.

What do you see happening in the flask while the experiment is going on? What do you see left in the flask after the experiment has finished?

Hydrogen may be made by the action of zinc on dilute sulphuric acid. If the reaction is very slow some copper sulphate solution is added to the mix-

CHEMISTRY

ture; this forms finely divided copper which acts as a catalyst, and the bubbling seen in the flask immediately becomes more vigorous. A colourless solution of zinc sulphate is formed as well as hydrogen.

$$\text{zinc} + \text{sulphuric acid} \longrightarrow \text{zinc sulphate} + \text{hydrogen}$$
$$Zn + H_2SO_4 \longrightarrow ZnSO_4 + H_2$$

To check that all the air from the apparatus has been swept out by hydrogen collect a test-tube full of the gas coming out of the delivery tube, and bring a flame to the mouth of the test-tube. If there is a squeak or a loud pop there is still air mixed with the hydrogen. If the gas in the tube lights with a very

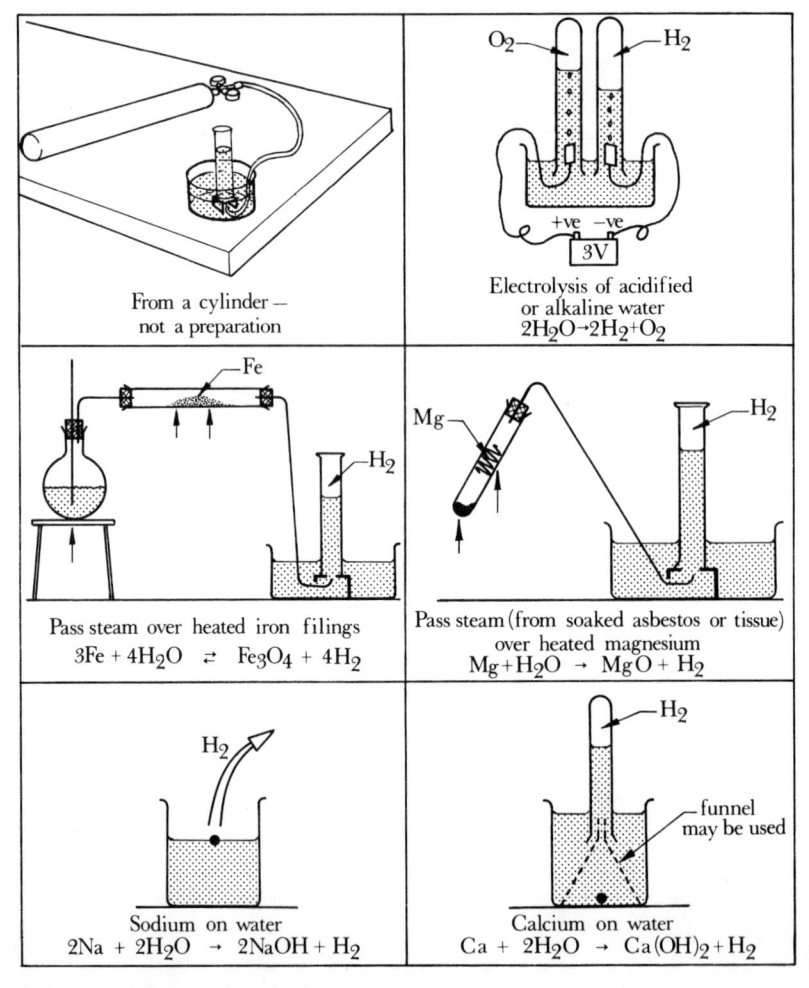

From a cylinder — not a preparation	Electrolysis of acidified or alkaline water $2H_2O \rightarrow 2H_2 + O_2$
Pass steam over heated iron filings $3Fe + 4H_2O \rightleftharpoons Fe_3O_4 + 4H_2$	Pass steam (from soaked asbestos or tissue) over heated magnesium $Mg + H_2O \rightarrow MgO + H_2$
Sodium on water $2Na + 2H_2O \rightarrow 2NaOH + H_2$	Calcium on water $Ca + 2H_2O \rightarrow Ca(OH)_2 + H_2$ funnel may be used

Figure 4.2 Other methods of obtaining hydrogen

THE SIMPLEST ATOM—HYDROGEN—AND OTHERS

quiet pop and a blue flame burns down the test tube, the gas is all hydrogen. It is important to do this test before collecting any hydrogen, because lighting even a moderate volume of a mixture of air and hydrogen can cause an unpleasant explosion. If the supply of hydrogen stops while there is still zinc left in the flask, this is because all the dilute sulphuric acid has been used, so a little concentrated sulphuric acid is cautiously poured down the thistle funnel.

Properties of hydrogen

As can be seen from the preparation, hydrogen is colourless. It has no smell and is only slightly soluble in water—if it were more than slightly soluble it could not be collected over water as was done in experiment 4.1.

Experiment 4.2   *The density of hydrogen*

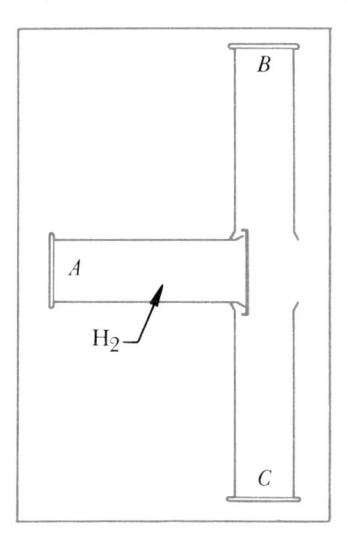

Figure 4.3   Does the hydrogen escape into *B* or *C*?

With your partner hold three gas jars as shown in Fig. 4.3. *A* is at first full of hydrogen, and *B* and *C* contain air. Take the cover off *A*, hold it off for about twenty seconds, and then cover *B* and *C*. Put a lighted taper to each of *B* and *C*.

Which jar makes a pop when the taper is held to its mouth? When the hydrogen escaped from *A* did it go upwards or downwards? What does this tell you about the density of hydrogen?

Hydrogen is less dense than air. This is shown in experiment 4.2 in which the top is taken off a jar full of hydrogen, and jars *B* and *C* are then tested to see whether the hydrogen has gone upwards or downwards. A flame put to *B* gives a pop, showing that hydrogen is present, but there is no reaction with gas jar *C*. The experiment shows that the hydrogen has floated upwards and is therefore less dense than air.

Hydrogen is not only less dense than air but is less dense than any other known substance. (For a table of densities see page 21.)

Figure 4.4 Methods of showing hydrogen is less dense than air

Demonstration experiment 4.3 *The diffusion of hydrogen*

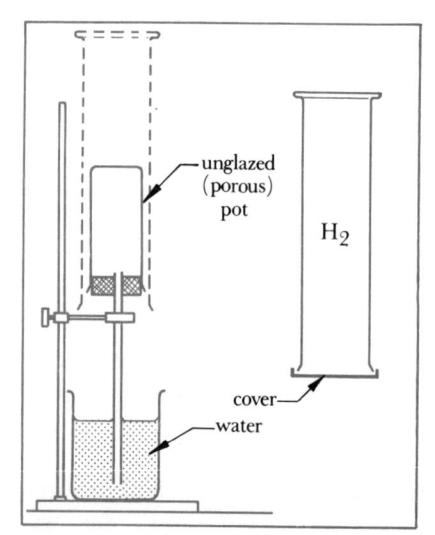

Figure 4.5 The diffusion of hydrogen and air

THE SIMPLEST ATOM—HYDROGEN—AND OTHERS

(*a*) Remove the cover from the gas jar, keeping the jar mouth downwards, and place the gas jar in the position shown by the dotted outline on Fig. 4.5. Hold the jar here for twenty seconds.

> What do you see happening in the beaker? Is gas going into or out of the porous pot?

(*b*) Now remove the gas jar.

> What do you see happening to the apparatus? Is gas going into or out of the porous pot?

Experiment 4.3 shows the **diffusion** of hydrogen, that is, the passing of hydrogen through the fine holes in the walls of an unglazed (porous) pot. When the jar of hydrogen is put round the porous pot in (*a*), hydrogen diffuses in quickly, and air is pushed down the glass tube and bubbles out through the water in the beaker. (At the same time some air diffuses out through the porous pot into the hydrogen in the gas jar, but this only happens very slowly.)

When the gas jar is removed in (*b*), the hydrogen in the pot diffuses out quickly, so water rises up the glass tube to take the place of this hydrogen. (Some air diffuses inwards, but as before this only takes place slowly.)

Hydrogen diffuses quickly because it has a low density—that is, because the molecules of hydrogen are small and light, they easily get through the holes in the porous pot. The fact that these small molecules are moving quickly makes for quick diffusion. The denser a gas is, the slower it diffuses, so hydrogen diffuses faster than air, which in turn diffuses faster than carbon dioxide.

The burning of hydrogen

Demonstration experiment 4.4   *Burning dry hydrogen in air*

> Set up the apparatus as shown in Fig. 4.6, and after testing the hydrogen to show that it does not contain any air, light the jet of hydrogen coming from the glass tube. Let the hydrogen flame touch the side of a flask full of cold water. When this flame has been burning for a few minutes, put a little white anhydrous copper sulphate into the drops of liquid which appear on the side of the cooled flask.

> What happens to the white anhydrous copper sulphate? What does this show?

If hydrogen is made and is then dried by passing it through a tube containing either anhydrous calcium chloride or silica gel, it can be proved that water is made when hydrogen burns. The hydrogen is allowed to burn with the flame touching a cold, dry flask, and the small drops of liquid which collect on the side of the flask are tested by putting a little white anhydrous copper sulphate on to them. The white anhydrous copper sulphate turns to blue hydrated copper sulphate which shows that the drops contain water.

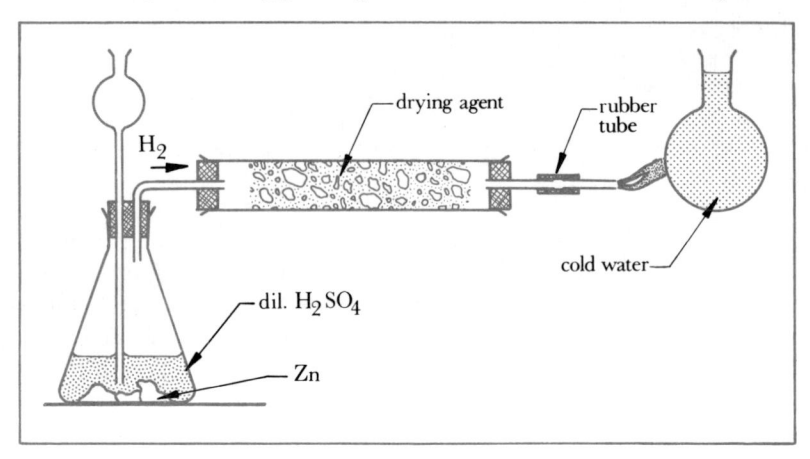

Figure 4.6 Burning dry hydrogen

Since the hydrogen has been dried, the water must have been made when the hydrogen was burned. Because the flame is hot, the water is actually made in the form of steam, which condenses on the surface of the cold flask. This experiment can be regarded as the building up of a compound (water) from its elements (oxygen and hydrogen), and it is sometimes called the synthesis of water. **Synthesis** means the building up of a compound from simpler substances.

$$\text{hydrogen} + \text{oxygen} \longrightarrow \text{water} + \text{heat}$$
$$2H_2 + O_2 \longrightarrow 2H_2O + \text{heat}$$

$$\text{anhydrous copper sulphate} + \text{water} \longrightarrow \text{hydrated copper sulphate}$$
$$CuSO_4 + 5H_2O \longrightarrow CuSO_4 \cdot 5H_2O$$

Demonstration experiment 4.5   *Lighting a mixture of two volumes of hydrogen and one volume of oxygen*

Collect over water in a large plastic measuring cylinder a mixture of two volumes of hydrogen to one volume of oxygen (e.g., 400 cm³ and 200 cm³, or 150 cm³ and 75 cm³). Pour this mixture into a plastic detergent bottle and put in a cork. Bury the charged bottle in a box of straw or woodwool so that only the neck is exposed. Remove the cork and put a lighted taper to the open neck.

THE SIMPLEST ATOM—HYDROGEN—AND OTHERS

A mixture of two volumes of hydrogen to one volume of oxygen (i.e., two-thirds and one-third) explodes violently when lit, giving a flame and a large amount of energy. Steam is produced at the same time.

We have met in this chapter three ways of burning hydrogen:

a jet of pure hydrogen burns quietly with a blue flame;
a mixture of air and hydrogen burns with a squeak or pop, or sometimes a squeaky pop;
a 2:1 mixture of hydrogen and oxygen burns with a loud explosion.

The chemical change which takes place is the same in all three cases, so all the equations are the same, and one gram of hydrogen burned by each of the three methods produces the same amount of heat energy. In the explosion this energy is produced very quickly but in the other less violent methods the energy is produced over a longer time.

Reducing properties of hydrogen

Experiment 4.6 *The action of hydrogen on copper oxide—reduction*

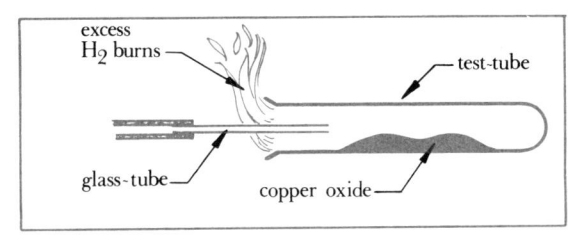

Figure 4.7 **The reduction of copper oxide by hydrogen**

Put some copper oxide in a test-tube and pass hydrogen over the copper oxide. After the stream of hydrogen has been passing for about thirty seconds (to make sure that there is no air mixed with the hydrogen), light the stream of hydrogen coming from the mouth. Heat the copper oxide with a bunsen flame, starting at the end farther from the mouth, and moving the bunsen flame slowly along so that all the copper oxide is heated. Remove the bunsen flame, and let the test-tube cool with hydrogen still passing through it. When the tube is cool stop the supply of hydrogen, tip out the solid, and examine it.

What colour changes take place in this experiment? What do you think is left in the tube after the experiment? What has been removed from the copper oxide and where do you think it has gone?

Copper oxide can be changed to copper by heating it in an atmosphere of hydrogen. The apparatus of experiment 4.6 is suitable, and as the change takes place the black copper oxide becomes very hot and turns to reddish-brown copper powder. The oxygen from the copper oxide is removed by the hydrogen; the oxygen combines with the hydrogen forming steam, which passes out of the test-tube with the excess hydrogen. This removal of oxygen from the copper oxide is called the **reduction** of copper oxide by hydrogen.

$$\text{copper oxide} + \text{hydrogen} \longrightarrow \text{copper} + \text{steam}$$
$$CuO + H_2 \longrightarrow Cu + H_2O$$

In a similar way hydrogen can reduce other oxides to their metals, e.g., iron oxide (Fe_2O_3), to iron (Fe).

$$Fe_2O_3 + 3H_2 \longrightarrow 2Fe + 3H_2O$$

Hydrogen acting in this way is said to be a **reducing agent**.

Action of hydrogen on chlorine

If equal volumes of hydrogen and chlorine are mixed and a light is applied the two gases combine with a violent explosion, forming hydrogen chloride gas.

$$\text{hydrogen} + \text{chlorine} \longrightarrow \text{hydrogen chloride} + \text{energy}$$
$$H_2 + Cl_2 \longrightarrow 2HCl$$

However, if chlorine and hydrogen are mixed and passed over a charcoal catalyst, they combine smoothly and quietly forming hydrogen chloride, and giving out the heat more gradually.

Test for hydrogen

Hydrogen burns with a blue flame forming steam. If the hydrogen is in a cool, dry container such as a test-tube or gas jar, the steam condenses on the walls as a faint mist.

Uses of hydrogen

Large volumes of hydrogen are used for making ammonia by the Haber Process. A mixture of nitrogen and hydrogen at 500°C and 250 atmospheres is pumped over a finely divided catalyst of iron. The reaction is reversible so not all the nitrogen and hydrogen combine and the mixture has to be pumped round again.

$$\text{nitrogen} + \text{hydrogen} \rightleftharpoons \text{ammonia}$$
$$N_2 + 3H_2 \rightleftharpoons 2NH_3$$

Hydrogen is also used for making margarine from vegetable oils. Oil is squeezed out of ground-nuts (peanuts), soya beans, or other seeds and mixed with a catalyst containing nickel. The hydrogen combines with the oil to produce fats which are solid. These fats are then blended into margarine.

THE SIMPLEST ATOM—HYDROGEN—AND OTHERS

This process of making hydrogen combine with oils in the presence of a catalyst is called **catalytic hydrogenation**.

Because it has a very low density, hydrogen is used for filling balloons and airships. The balloons are sometimes sold as toys but scientists use hydrogen-filled balloons in meteorology. Small hydrogen-filled balloons are released, and as they rise they indicate wind speed and direction, and larger balloons are used to carry instruments such as barometers and thermometers to high altitudes.

Small quantities of hydrogen are used for burning, and for reduction of certain precious metal oxides to metals.

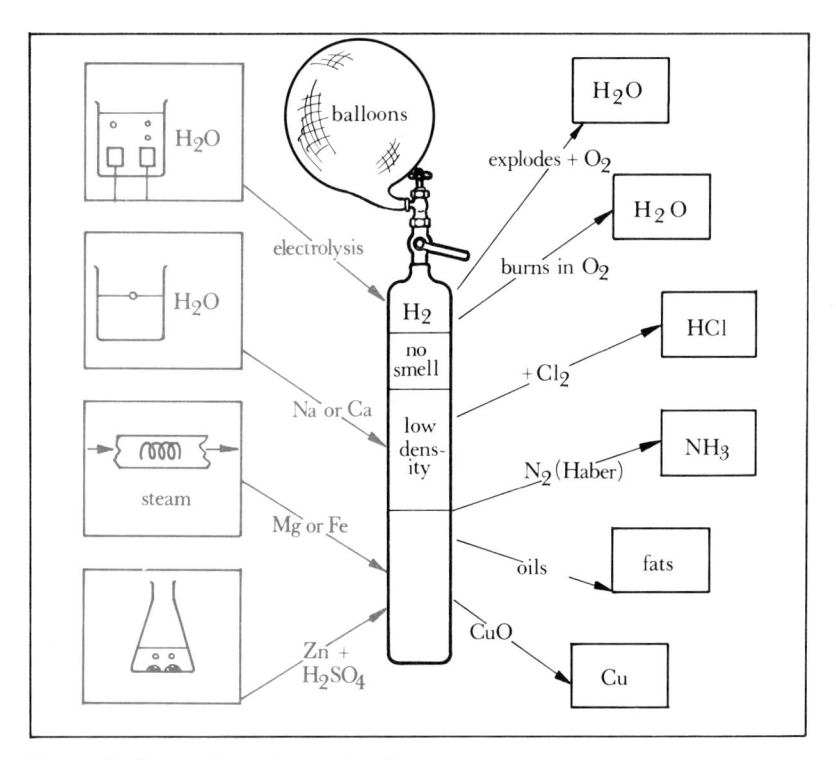

Figure 4.8 Preparation and properties of hydrogen

Oxidation and reduction

When hydrogen reacts with copper oxide to form copper and steam

$$CuO + H_2 \longrightarrow Cu + H_2O$$

the copper oxide is converted to copper by removal of oxygen. Copper oxide is said to be reduced to copper by the loss of oxygen. The hydrogen in the reaction is converted to steam by the addition of oxygen, and is said to be oxidized. We can summarize this by writing

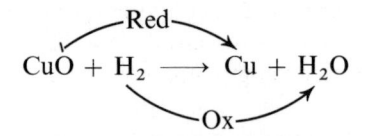

$$\underset{\underset{Ox}{\longleftarrow}}{\overset{\overset{Red}{\longrightarrow}}{CuO + H_2 \longrightarrow Cu + H_2O}}$$

The oxygen which is removed when something is reduced does not simply vanish; this would be impossible as atoms are not created or destroyed in a chemical reaction, they merely change partners. The oxygen always combines with one of the reactants, which becomes oxidized. Therefore oxidation and reduction happen together in this experiment, and in others.

The hydrogen reacting with the copper oxide is acting as a reducing agent. Hydrogen is not the only reducing agent in chemistry; carbon for example can reduce lead oxide to lead (see experiment 1.2). At the same time the carbon is oxidized to carbon monoxide.

$$\underset{\underset{Ox}{\longleftarrow}}{\overset{\overset{Red}{\longrightarrow}}{C + PbO \longrightarrow CO + Pb}}$$

Reduction, as well as meaning the removal of oxygen, can also mean addition of hydrogen. For example, in the reaction

hydrogen + chlorine $\longrightarrow$ hydrogen chloride
H_2 + Cl_2 $\longrightarrow$ 2HCl

the chlorine is reduced by the addition of hydrogen.

Similarly oxidation usually means the adding of oxygen. For example, in the reaction

sulphur + oxygen $\longrightarrow$ sulphur dioxide
S + O_2 $\longrightarrow$ SO_2

the sulphur is oxidized to sulphur dioxide and the oxygen is acting as an oxidizing agent. Oxidation can also mean the removal of hydrogen.

Experiment 4.7 **The action of manganese dioxide on concentrated hydrochloric acid**

Put concentrated hydrochloric acid into a test-tube to a depth of about 2 cm. Warm, but be careful not to boil, the hydrochloric acid and then drop in a little manganese dioxide. Hold the test-tube against a background of white paper, and look to see if any coloured substance is visible. Hold a piece of damp blue litmus in the gas at the top of the test-tube and observe any colour changes in the litmus.

Warm concentrated hydrochloric acid reacts with manganese dioxide to form chlorine.

$$\text{manganese dioxide} + \text{hydrochloric acid} \longrightarrow \text{manganese chloride} + \text{chlorine} + \text{water}$$
$$MnO_2 + 4HCl \longrightarrow MnCl_2 + Cl_2 + 2H_2O$$

In this action the hydrochloric acid is oxidized to chlorine by the removal of hydrogen. The chlorine can be recognized by its green colour and the fact that it turns damp blue litmus red, and then bleaches it white.

Summary of oxidation and reduction

Oxidation is usually the addition of oxygen. Reduction is usually the removal of oxygen. Oxidation can also mean removal of hydrogen, and reduction can also mean addition of hydrogen.

Atomic structure

We read in chapter 1 that all substances are made of atoms, and that the atoms are usually joined forming groups which are either molecules or ions. We are now going on to consider what atoms are made of. This is a difficult topic, but we shall start with the simplest atom, the atom of hydrogen.

No one has ever seen an atom, because atoms are too small to be seen, even with a powerful microscope. As with the existence of matter in particles, there is no single conclusive experiment which can show us the structure of atoms. Over the years, many pieces of evidence have been used to build up a reasoned guess about the nature of atoms. We call this reasoned guess a **model** of an atom. The first model (guess) was that atoms were hard, solid, and spherical, like tiny billiard balls. Then there was, about eighty years ago, an indication that this was wrong. Experiments showed that tiny bits of negative electricity (now called electrons) could be torn off atoms, so the billiard ball model was modified. Many more experiments of different types have since been done, and scientists are still not sure of all the details of atomic structure, but the current model supposes that atoms all have a hard heavy nucleus, with electrons surrounding it, moving about in large volumes of space.

Hydrogen

The hydrogen atom is the simplest and smallest atom. One model of it consists of a nucleus containing one particle only, a proton, and one electron moving about in association with the proton. We can represent this in a diagram.

CHEMISTRY

A model proposed about fifty years ago by the Danish physicist Niels Bohr supposed that the electron went round the nucleus like a planet round a sun. This planetary or Bohr model of atomic structure is still useful because it can be used to represent the three most vital facts about an atom—the composition of its nucleus and the numbers and energies of its electrons. Other models

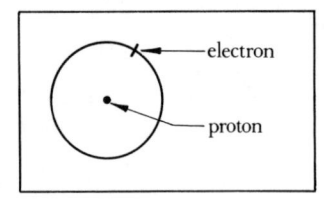

Figure 4.9   A representation of a hydrogen atom

of atoms exist, and although they are superior to the Bohr model in some ways, they are more difficult to understand, so in the rest of this chapter the Bohr model will be used. It is helpful to think of the diagrams as a convenient way of counting electrons into groups which we call shells. We shall use a stroke to represent an electron.

Helium

A helium atom is more complex than a hydrogen atom. Its nucleus contains two protons and two neutrons, and there are two electrons associated with the atom. The protons each have a positive electric charge and the electrons

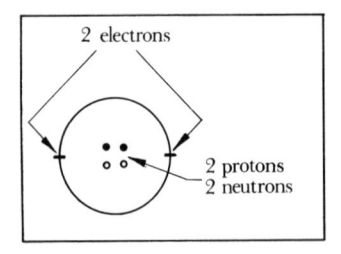

Figure 4.10   A helium atom

have a negative charge, so, because it contains two positive and two negative charges, the atom as a whole is neutral. The atom conforms to the general picture of a small, heavy nucleus with electrons outside the nucleus. The electrons are very light compared to the protons and neutrons. We have now met the three particles in our model of the atom and can summarize them in this table:

THE SIMPLEST ATOM—HYDROGEN—AND OTHERS

Table 4.1 Summary of particles in atoms

Name	Where found	Charge	Weight
proton	nucleus	+ve	1
neutron	nucleus	none	1
electron	outside nucleus	−ve	about 0·0005

Lithium

The next simplest atom is that of lithium, which is a grey metal of such low density that it floats on water (Fig. 4.11). The nucleus contains four neutrons

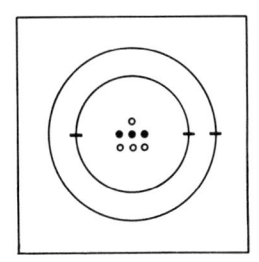

Figure 4.11 A lithium atom

and three protons. The three electrons are in two groups or shells, two in the first and one in the second. The two electrons in the inner shell have energies different from that in the outer shell. Electrons can be removed from atoms if a large enough voltage is applied and the single electron in the second shell is easier to remove than either of the electrons in the inner shell. You should remember that the diagram is not a picture of a lithium atom, and it is certainly not drawn to scale.

Other atoms

Figs. 4.12 to 4.16 show some atoms which are larger, heavier, and more complicated still. We do not always need to know the exact composition of the

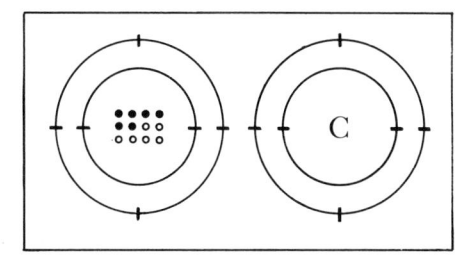

Figure 4.12 Two ways of representing a carbon atom

67

nucleus and sometimes we write the symbol for the atom instead of a representation of the nucleus. A further simplification is to show the numbers of electrons in the various shells instead of drawing a diagram to give this information. For example, we can write C 2.4 to show a carbon atom with two electrons in the first shell and four in the second.

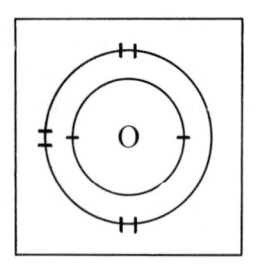

Figure 4.13 An oxygen atom, O 2.6

In the nucleus of oxygen there are eight protons and eight neutrons and, as Fig. 4.13 shows, there are eight electrons. It is not significant that all these three numbers are the same, but the number of protons in an uncombined atom is always equal to the number of electrons.

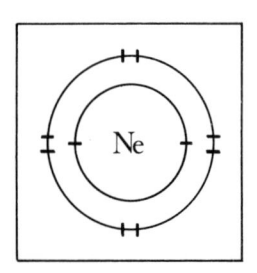

Figure 4.14 A neon atom, Ne 2.8

Neon is one of the family of inert gases. The second shell of electrons is now full (Fig. 4.14). In various atoms from lithium to neon, the second shell can hold one to eight electrons, but it never holds more than eight. Neon may also be represented as Ne 2.8 and its nucleus holds ten protons and ten neutrons.

THE SIMPLEST ATOM—HYDROGEN—AND OTHERS

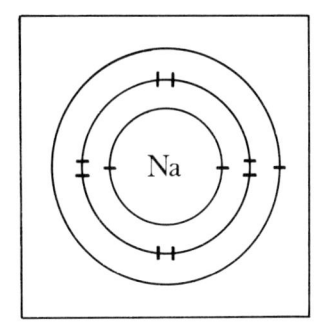

Figure 4.15 A sodium atom Na 2.8.1

Sodium may be written Na 2.8.1. A new shell has been started as the second one is now full.

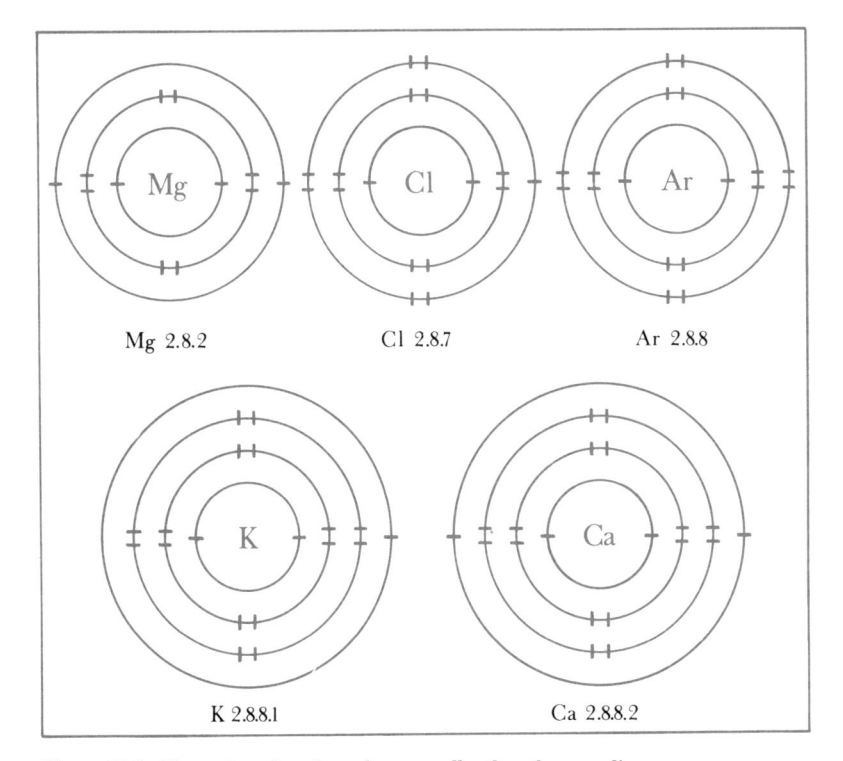

Mg 2.8.2   Cl 2.8.7   Ar 2.8.8

K 2.8.8.1   Ca 2.8.8.2

Figure 4.16 These atoms have been drawn smaller than the preceding ones

The most complicated natural atom known, that of uranium, has a total of 330 particles—92 protons and 146 neutrons in the nucleus, and 92 electrons arranged in 7 shells, some of which hold up to 32 electrons.

CHEMISTRY

The weight of an atom expressed in everyday units is very small, for example, the weight of a hydrogen atom is 0·00000000000000000000000000017 kg. This number and others like it are so inconvenient to use that a special scale of relative **atomic weights** has been devised. The numbers on this scale are nearly equal to the number of protons plus the number of neutrons in an atom. The weight of an electron is so small that it can be ignored compared to the weights of the protons and neutrons. For instance, the atomic weight of oxygen is 15·9994, which is very nearly equal to the number of protons plus the number of neutrons in its nucleus, $8 + 8 = 16$.

The **atomic number** of an atom is the number of protons in its nucleus: neon with ten protons in its nucleus has the atomic number 10.

Summary of atomic structure

Atoms are made of protons (+ve), neutrons (no charge), and electrons (−ve). In a normal uncombined atom of an element the number of protons is equal to the number of electrons, so the atom as a whole is neutral. The electrons are in groups called shells, the first three having maximum capacities of two, eight, and eight. The atomic number of an element is equal to the number of protons in its nucleus.

Molecular structure

Part 1   Electrovalent (ionic) bond formation

The eleven electrons of the sodium atom can be shown by experiments to be arranged 2.8.1 and not 2.9. Similarly, magnesium is 2.8.2 and not 2.10 or 2.9.1. These examples and others show that the second shell can hold eight but no more than eight electrons. The fact that the inert gas neon, which has no known chemical reactions, has the structure 2.8 confirms the stability of eight electrons in the second shell. Eight electrons in the second shell seems to be a specially favoured number.

Two different atoms, given suitable circumstances, will rearrange their electrons to obtain eight in their second shells. One way in which this happens is by electron robbery, when one atom takes an electron from another during a chemical reaction (Fig. 4.17). An isolated sodium atom has been robbed of

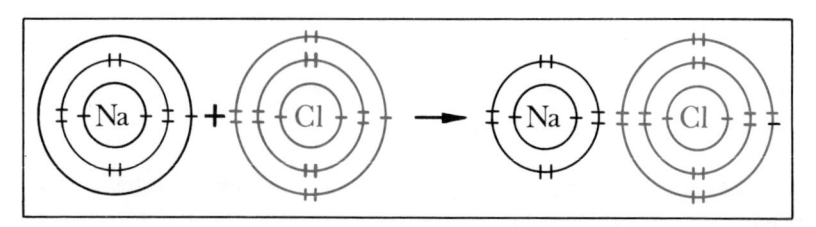

Figure 4.17   Na 2.8.1 + Cl 2.8.7 ⟶ Na^+ 2.8 + Cl^- 2.8.8

THE SIMPLEST ATOM—HYDROGEN—AND OTHERS

an electron by an isolated chlorine atom, resulting in two charged atoms or ions which make up sodium chloride. Both the sodium ion and the chloride ion formed have eight electrons in their outer shell and this is a favoured number for both the second and third shells.

Why have we written Cl and called it chlorine on the left-hand side, but Cl^- and called it chloride on the right-hand side? Originally chlorine had seventeen electrons $(2 + 8 + 7)$ and seventeen protons in the nucleus and so was electrically neutral. After the reaction the chlorine atom, having gained an electron, now has eighteen (arranged 2.8.8) but still has only seventeen protons. Overall therefore, the chlorine has a negative charge and is now called an **ion**. To distinguish the atom from the ion we change its name to chloride. A chloride ion is an example of an **anion** (remember **n**egative charge—a**n**ion). In a similar way the sodium atom originally had eleven electrons and eleven protons and was therefore neutral. After combination, it has lost an electron reducing the number to ten, but still has eleven protons in its nucleus and is therefore a positive sodium ion Na^+, which is a **cation**.

This method of combination is called **electrovalency** or **ionic bonding** and always results in the formation of ions; that is, atoms or groups of atoms which are not neutral but carry electric charges. The attraction between the positive and negative electric charges holds the ions firmly together in a regular pattern, so ionic substances at normal temperatures are solids. A typical example of one of these patterns is shown in Fig. 4.22, labelled 'strong bonding in all directions'. When an ionic substance is melted, or dissolved in water, the melt or solution conducts electricity as the ions move, and electrolysis takes place.

Sometimes the robber atom takes more than one electron from the other atom. In the example in Fig. 4.18 the oxygen atom takes two electrons from

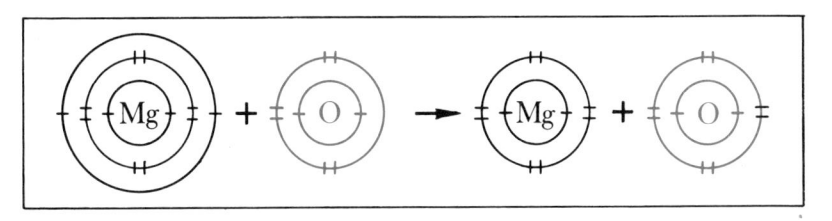

Figure 4.18 $Mg\ 2.8.2 + O\ 2.6 \longrightarrow Mg^{++}\ 2.8 + O^{--}\ 2.8$

the magnesium, becoming a doubly charged oxide ion, and the magnesium becomes a doubly charged positive ion.

An aluminium atom becomes triply charged Al^{+++} in some compounds, and an iron atom becomes Fe^{+++} in some iron(III) or ferric compounds, but there are no common compounds in which an atom is more than triply charged. Metals always become positive ions (cations) when they form electrovalent compounds.

CHEMISTRY

As a final example of electrovalency, let us consider the formation of an electrovalent bond between calcium and chlorine atoms. Calcium is 2.8.8.2 and chlorine is 2.8.7. If a chlorine atom takes one electron from a calcium atom the chlorine atom becomes a chloride ion with structure 2.8.8, so it has reached a stable state. The calcium atom, however, has become Ca^+, structure 2.8.8.1 which is not a stable state because it has one electron in its outer shell. If a second chlorine atom removes the one lone electron the calcium becomes Ca^{++}, structure 2.8.8, and has reached a stable state. Looking at the whole process we have

$$Ca\ 2.8.8.2 + \begin{matrix}Cl\ 2.8.7 \\ Cl\ 2.8.7\end{matrix} \longrightarrow Ca^{++}\ 2.8.8 + \begin{matrix}Cl^-\ 2.8.8 \\ Cl^-\ 2.8.8\end{matrix}$$

Summary of electrovalency (ionic bonding)

When atoms form electrovalent (ionic) bonds one atom takes an electron or electrons from the other, leaving a complete electron shell and completing its own outer shell. Two ions are made by this process, the robber atom becoming a negative ion or anion, the other atom becoming a positive ion or cation. The ions are arranged in a regular pattern and an ionic substance is a solid at room temperature. In a complicated example, three or more ions may be formed by the electron transfers.

Part 2   Covalent bond formation

In the hydrogen molecule H_2 the bond holding the two atoms together cannot be electrovalent. If an electrovalent bond were formed one hydrogen atom would have to pull an electron from another hydrogen atom, and two hydrogen atoms competing for an electron would be equivalent to two exactly equal tug-of-war teams—there could be no winner. Similarly, one hydrogen atom could not take an electron from another to form an electrovalent bond. The two hydrogen atoms share their electrons and the shared electrons can count as being in the outer shell of both atoms. Two shared electrons make up one covalent bond. For example, hydrogen:

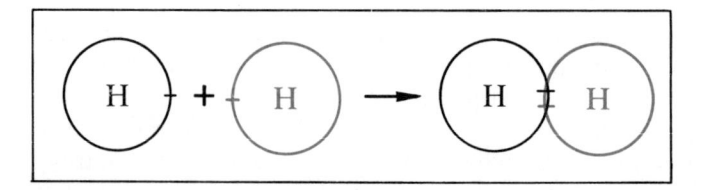

Figure 4.19   Formation of a covalent bond between two hydrogen atoms

THE SIMPLEST ATOM—HYDROGEN—AND OTHERS

An alternative and simpler way of representing a covalent bond is to write it as a dash so we could write

$$H + H \longrightarrow H-H$$

instead of showing the electrons in shells as we did in the first example.

Two isolated chlorine atoms combine in a similar way, but each of them uses only one of the seven electrons in its outer shell to share with the other chlorine atom. The electrons in the full inner shells do not take any part in bond formation.

$$Cl + Cl \longrightarrow Cl-Cl$$

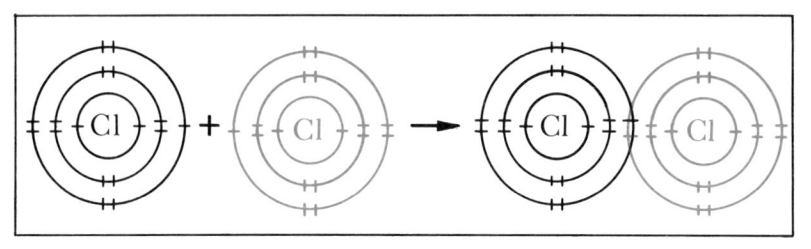

Figure 4.20 Formation of a covalent bond between two chlorine atoms

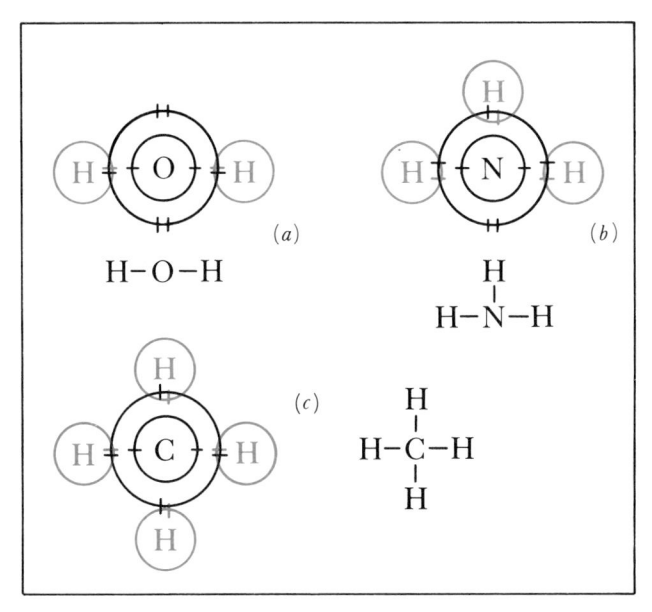

Figure 4.21 Covalent bonds in (a) water (b) ammonia and (c) methane

CHEMISTRY

In both the examples of covalent bond formation the shared electrons, which can be regarded as being in the outer shells of both atoms, bring the number of electrons in the outer shells up to their maximum values. When the bond has been formed each hydrogen atom has two electrons in its outer shell, and each chlorine has eight. The diagrams are printed in two colours merely for the sake of clarity; you should not think that there are two sorts of electrons, blue and black.

Other examples of covalent bonding include the compounds water, ammonia, and methane.

When electrons are shared and covalent bonds are made, molecules, usually containing small numbers of atoms, are formed. No ions are made. The bonds within the molecule, e.g., the bonds between hydrogen and oxygen in the water molecule or the bond between the two chlorine atoms in a chlorine molecule, are very strong. The force which attracts one molecule to another molecule is weak, so covalent substances are often gases or liquids at room temperature. (Compare ionic substances—solids at room temperature.)

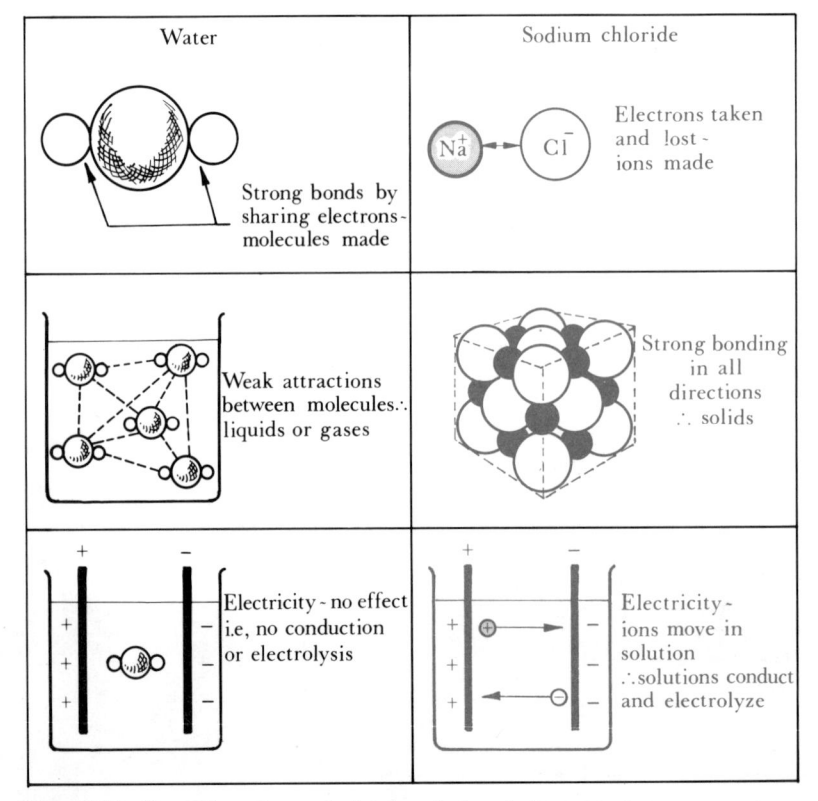

Water	Sodium chloride
Strong bonds by sharing electrons - molecules made	Electrons taken and lost - ions made
Weak attractions between molecules ∴ liquids or gases	Strong bonding in all directions ∴ solids
Electricity - no effect i.e, no conduction or electrolysis	Electricity - ions move in solution ∴ solutions conduct and electrolyze

Figure 4.22 Comparison of a covalent and an electrovalent compound

THE SIMPLEST ATOM—HYDROGEN—AND OTHERS

Since no ions are present covalent substances do not conduct electricity, e.g., pure water is a good insulator.

Summary of covalency (covalent bonding)

When atoms form covalent bonds electrons are shared by two atoms. Two shared electrons make up one covalent bond. Molecules are produced, not ions, and when the number of atoms in the molecule is small a covalent substance is a gas or liquid at room temperature.

Valency

The valency of a metal atom is a number which depends on the combining power of the atom. The valency of sodium is one, and this is often expressed by writing sodium as Na^+. Similarly, calcium has a valency of two and calcium can be written Ca^{++} or Ca^{2+}. Non-metals also have valencies and these are shown as negative charges, e.g., chloride is written Cl^- and oxide O^{--} or O^{2-}. When a metal combines with a non-metal, they do this so as to equalize the positive and negative charges. One sodium Na^+ goes with one chloride Cl^-, giving Na^+Cl^-. It is often convenient to omit the charges when writing the formula of a compound, so sodium chloride is often written NaCl.

One calcium Ca^{++} goes with two chlorides Cl^- and Cl^-; this forms calcium chloride which may be written $CaCl_2$.

One calcium Ca^{++} goes with one oxide O^{--} to form calcium oxide CaO, but two sodiums Na^+ are required to go with one oxide O^{--} in the formation of sodium oxide Na_2O.

Table 4.2 Valencies

		Cations			
silver	Ag^+	calcium	Ca^{++}	aluminium	Al^{+++}
sodium	Na^+	copper	Cu^{++}	iron(III) or ferric	Fe^{+++}
potassium	K^+	iron(II) or ferrous	Fe^{++}		
hydrogen	H^+	magnesium	Mg^{++}		
ammonium	(NH_4^+)	zinc	Zn^{++}		
		Anions			
hydrogen carbonate or bicarbonate		(HCO_3^-)		carbonate	(CO_3^{--})
chloride		Cl^-		oxide	O^{--}
hydroxide		(OH^-)		sulphate	(SO_4^{--})
nitrate		(NO_3^-)		sulphide	S^{--}

This method, by which the formula of a compound can be deduced from the valencies of its component parts, can be extended to include groups of atoms called **radicals** as well as single atoms. In the table above, brackets have been drawn round all the radicals, i.e., groups containing two or more atoms. It is useful to learn the valencies in the table, which are those frequently used in this book. An atom with its charge is called an ion, and a group of atoms with its charge is also called an ion. To distinguish positive from negative ions, atoms and groups of atoms having positive charges are called cations, atoms and groups of atoms having negative charges are called anions. (Remember anions—**n**egative.)

To construct a formula write the cation and anion with their positive and negative charges. If the numbers of positive and negative charges are not equal add extra ions of one type until the charges balance.

For example, sodium nitrate Na^+ (NO_3^-): the charges balance so no extra ions are needed. The formula may then be rewritten without the charges and becomes $NaNO_3$. The brackets are omitted unless there are two or more of the ions in brackets.

For example, sodium carbonate Na^+ (CO_3^{--}) becomes Na^+ Na^+ (CO_3^{--}) when the charges are balanced. This may be rewritten Na_2CO_3.

In ammonium sulphate, however, NH_4^+ (SO_4^{--}) becomes NH_4^+ NH_4^+ (SO_4^{--}) which may be rewritten $(NH_4)_2SO_4$. The small two multiplies both the N and the H_4 of the ammonium ion. The brackets must also be retained in aluminium hydroxide, which is $Al(OH)_3$.

When aluminium and iron(III) (or ferric) compounds are formulated it is sometimes necessary to increase the numbers of both ions to balance the charges.

For example, aluminium oxide from Al^{+++} and O^{--} becomes Al^{+++} Al^{+++} O^{--} O^{--} O^{--} which may be rewritten Al_2O_3, and similarly iron(III) sulphate or ferric sulphate is $Fe_2(SO_4)_3$. The (III) in iron(III) sulphate shows that the valency of iron in this compound is three.

Valency and electrons

Some of you might have seen already the simple connection between valency and ionic structure: the valencies in the table are the charges on the ions forming an ionic (electrovalent) bond. Sodium Na, valency one, is written in the table as Na^+, and sodium actually forms this ion (which has the electronic structure 2.8) when it reacts with chlorine. Chlorine Cl, valency one, is written in the table as Cl^- and Cl^- is the actual formula of the chloride ion. When one electron is transferred from a sodium atom to a chlorine atom a sodium ion Na^+ with one positive charge is formed, and a chloride ion Cl^-

THE SIMPLEST ATOM—HYDROGEN—AND OTHERS

with one negative charge is formed. The number of positive and negative charges must always be equal.

The result, Na^+Cl^-, represents the actual state of sodium chloride which has an ordered pattern containing alternate sodium and chloride ions. The fact that we usually write it as NaCl means that we are not always interested in stating the charges on the atoms. Writing NaCl does not mean that a molecule of sodium chloride exists; it merely means that in any crystal of sodium chloride there is one chloride ion for each sodium ion. The formula for sodium chloride (and for all other ionic substances) tells us the ratio in which the ions are found.

Chapter summary

Hydrogen, the least dense substance known, is made by the electrolysis of acidified water, the action of zinc on dilute sulphuric acid, and by the action of certain active metals on water or steam. Hydrogen burns forming steam, and acts as a reducing agent when it removes oxygen from oxides such as copper oxide. Hydrogen has the simplest atom, containing only one proton and one electron, but all other atoms have a nucleus containing protons and neutrons, and also contain electrons which are outside the nucleus. The electrons, which are light and have a negative charge, are found in groups according to the energy they have, and the first three groups can hold a maximum of two, eight, and eight electrons. In the Bohr model of the atom the electrons are in shells round the nucleus. In a normal neutral atom the number of electrons is equal to the number of protons which is equal to the atomic number, but atoms sometimes combine by electrovalency giving charged ions, a positive ion which has lost one or more electrons and a negative ion which has gained one or more electrons. Atoms also combine by sharing electrons (covalency), producing neutral molecules. Atoms combining by either method do so to bring the number of electrons in the outermost group to a stable number such as two or eight. The combining power of an atom is called its valency.

Questions

1. Write word and chemical equations for:
    (*a*) a reaction in which zinc sulphate is made,
    (*b*) the reduction of copper oxide,
    (*c*) a synthesis of water,
    (*d*) an oxidation of carbon,
    (*e*) a preparation of chlorine.

2. Describe briefly three different ways in which hydrogen may be burned, and give chemical equations for three different preparations of hydrogen.

CHEMISTRY

3. A 'Wonder Dry-cleaning Fluid' is stated to contain no water. Describe how you would check such a claim.

4. Name these particles, atoms, or molecules, and draw diagrams of the structures of (a) and (d):
(a) an atom containing two protons, (b) a particle with a single positive charge, (c) an atom with eight protons, (d) a molecule containing two chlorine atoms.

5. Describe as fully as you can the structure of a magnesium atom (it has twelve neutrons), and explain how it forms ionic bonds in magnesium chloride.

6. Write the formulae (omitting any charges), of (a) calcium hydroxide, (b) magnesium sulphate, (c) ammonium carbonate, (d) ammonia, (e) a silver ion, (f) potassium nitrate, (g) methane, (h) potassium hydrogen carbonate, (i) zinc sulphate, (j) aluminium sulphate.

5

Carbon, fuels, flames, and energy

Nearly all the fuels we burn contain carbon. The molecules of these fuels are covalent, most of the bonds being between a carbon and a hydrogen atom, or one carbon and another carbon atom. There are also some important substances consisting of carbon atoms only and this chapter deals with these first.

The allotropes of carbon

The element carbon exists in several different forms which are called the allotropes of carbon. Elements which can exist in different forms in the same physical state are said to exhibit allotropy.

Diamond

Diamond is a pure crystalline form of carbon, and at high temperatures it burns forming carbon dioxide—a very expensive experiment! Natural diamonds are found in a bluish or yellowish clay, or in sandy gravel. Diamonds are found in many parts of the world, notably in the Congo, South Africa, and Tanzania. These diamonds have been made by the crystallization of hot carbon under enormous pressure exerted by the Earth's crust. Many attempts to produce artificial diamonds have been made, and recently these have been successful although the diamonds tend to be small and discoloured.

Diamond is one of the hardest substances known. It has a very high melting point and does not conduct electricity. These properties arise from the structure of a diamond crystal which is shown in the Fig. 5.1. The covalent bonds hold the carbon atoms firmly in position. It is therefore difficult to separate the atoms and the melting point is high. This also explains why a diamond is hard. A single crystal of diamond is in fact one giant covalent molecule; there are therefore no ions in it and diamond does not conduct electricity.

A diamond as found in the earth looks like a small pebble. Skilled cutters split it in certain directions so that the split travels between the planes of atoms (see Fig. 5.1), or saw the crystal using a thin bronze wheel impregnated with diamond dust, to wear away a cut. The splitting or sawing process, followed by polishing with diamond dust, produces the shaped diamonds with many small faces, or facets, which we see in jewellery. Ninety per cent of the diamonds discovered are small or discoloured and are used as cutting tools (e.g., in rock drills or glass cutters) or as bearings in watches or other accurate instruments. The 10 per cent of diamonds used as gemstones are mostly colourless or slightly pink. (Other gemstones which are also hard and crystalline include sapphires and rubies, which are mainly aluminium oxide, and emeralds, which are a complex silicate of aluminium and beryllium. Pearls, which are much softer, are a form of calcium carbonate.)

Graphite

Graphite, which is another crystalline allotrope of carbon, is a very soft black solid which conducts electricity. This sharp contrast with the properties of diamond can be explained by the molecular structures of the two allotropes.

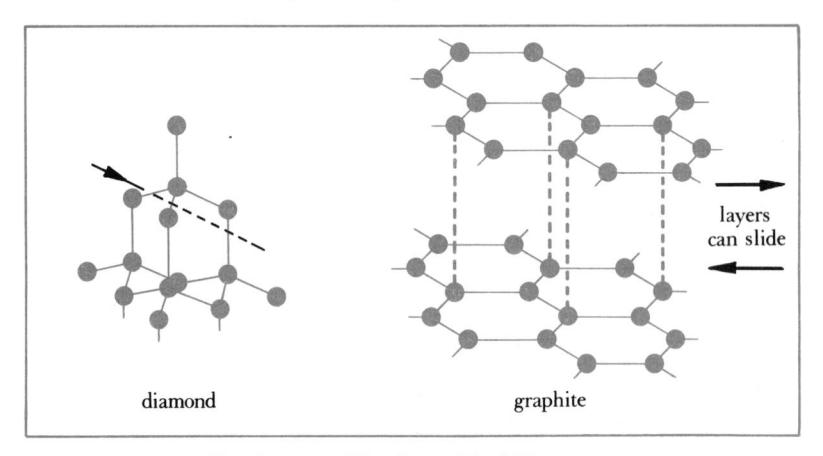

Figure 5.1 The graphite planes can slide; diamond is rigid

Graphite is used to make pencil 'leads'. The graphite is mixed with clay and the mixture extruded through a nozzle rather as toothpaste is squeezed out of a tube. The mixture is then baked. A hard, or grade H, pencil is made by adding more clay than in a black or grade B pencil. As the pencil is pulled across the piece of paper layers of graphite slide off on to the paper. Graphite is also used as a lubricant, e.g., for locks, and wooden surfaces such as drawer slides.

Although natural deposits of graphite are found in many parts of the world, much graphite is made artificially by heating coke to a very high temperature in an electric furnace. Graphite mines in the Lake District are not now worked, but brand names for pencils such as Cumberland, Lakeland,

CARBON, FUELS, FLAMES, AND ENERGY

and Borrowdale still exist. Coloured pencil leads are made from wax, clay, and a finely ground pigment.

Wood charcoal

Experiment 5.1 *Making wood charcoal*

Wood charcoal is made by heating wood in a limited supply of air. Break a wooden splint into pieces about 3 cm long, put the pieces in a test tube, cover them with sand, and heat the tube.

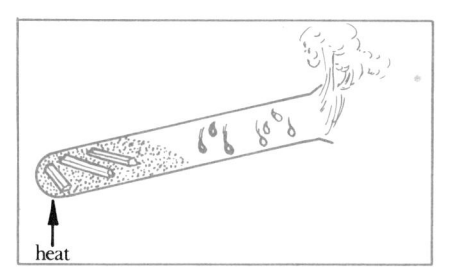

Figure 5.2 Heating wood without air

Look for a smoky gas coming off. Does it burn? How many different liquids can you see on the sides of the tube? Has the pale liquid any action on indicator paper? Can you write with the charcoal after it has cooled?

Wood charcoal is a soft black solid form of carbon made by heating wood in a limited supply of air. (The charcoal burners of old used to cover a pile of logs with turf, light the logs and let only a little air into the pile. Some logs burnt, others were converted to charcoal, as in experiment 5.1.) As the charcoal is made, smoky flammable wood gas comes off, a watery liquid containing acetic acid is made, and a brown or yellowish wood tar also appears. In the earlier charcoal burners' method these by-products were lost, but modern manufacture consists of passing logs in trucks through a long oven, and the by-products are caught and used.

Charcoal removes oxygen from certain oxides, and is therefore a reducing agent, e.g., lead(II) oxide PbO is reduced to lead if it is heated on a charcoal block, or mixed with powdered charcoal and heated. The lead is seen as silvery beads which are soft enough to make a scratchy grey mark on paper.

$$\text{lead(II) oxide} + \text{carbon} \longrightarrow \text{lead} + \text{carbon monoxide}$$
$$\text{PbO} + \text{C} \longrightarrow \text{Pb} + \text{CO}$$

For full details see experiment 1.2.

CHEMISTRY

Experiment 5.2   *The action of charcoal on colouring materials*

Take a 250 cm^3 beaker full of water and add ten drops of methyl orange solution. Set aside half of the coloured solution, into the other half put about half a teaspoonful of powdered charcoal and boil the mixture briskly for five minutes. Filter the hot solution and compare the filtrate with the untreated solution.

Charcoal removes certain colouring materials from solutions. It will, for example, remove the dye methyl orange from its solution. Charcoal is very porous and therefore has a large surface area. The molecules of methyl orange become trapped on the surface of the charcoal. Charcoal will also remove the molecules of some poisonous gases, and it was one of the absorbing agents used in the gas masks issued during the Second World War.

Mixed with sulphur and potassium nitrate charcoal forms gunpowder, the first explosive used by man. Gunpowder is not now used in guns, but it is put in fireworks, and is sometimes used for blasting, when it is called black powder.

Carbon black (lamp black)

Demonstration experiment 5.3   *Making carbon black*

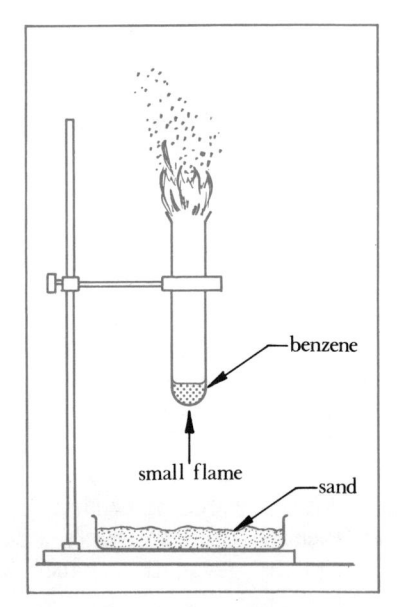

Figure 5.3   **Burning a small volume of benzene C_6H_6**

In a retort stand clamp a hard glass boiling tube containing 0·5 cm^3 benzene. As a safety precaution put a tin lid or small tray containing sand below the

CARBON, FUELS, FLAMES, AND ENERGY

tube. Heat the tube with a small flame, and light the benzene vapour when it reaches the mouth of the tube.

What colour is the flame? What do you see in the air above and around the flame?

Carbon black or lamp black is a form of carbon, usually seen as soft black specks above the flame made when benzene or various gas or oil fuels

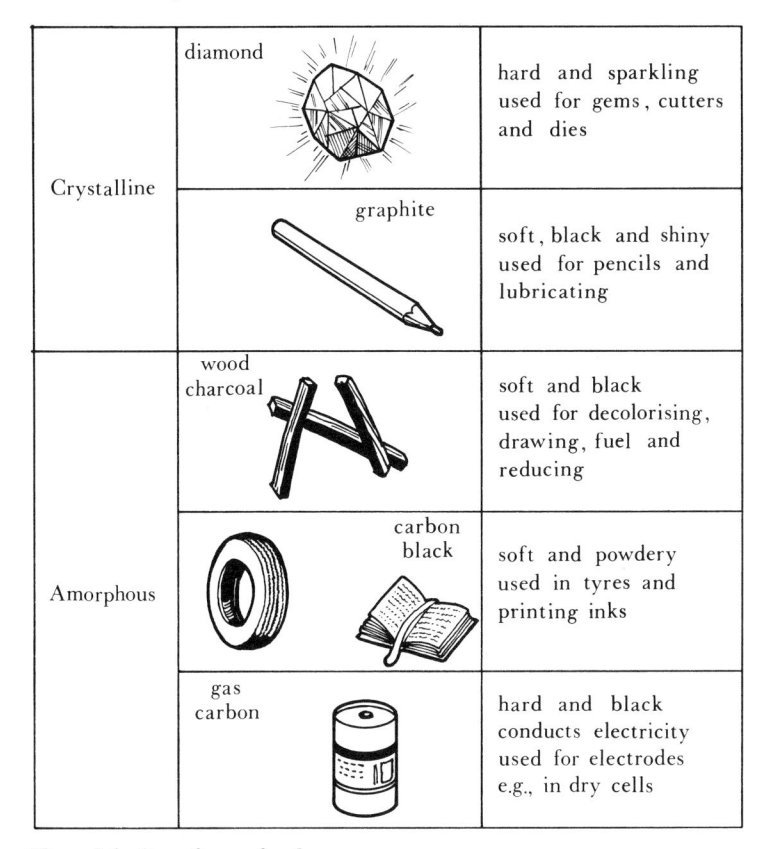

Crystalline	diamond	hard and sparkling used for gems, cutters and dies
	graphite	soft, black and shiny used for pencils and lubricating
Amorphous	wood charcoal	soft and black used for decolorising, drawing, fuel and reducing
	carbon black	soft and powdery used in tyres and printing inks
	gas carbon	hard and black conducts electricity used for electrodes e.g., in dry cells

Figure 5.4 **Some forms of carbon**

burn with a limited supply of air. Carbon black is used as a pigment in Indian ink, printer's ink and black shoe polish. It is also put in rubber tyres to make them more resilient, and is used as a filler and pigment in plastics.

Gas carbon

Gas carbon is a hard black form of carbon which is made on the sides of coke ovens in which coal is being heated to make coke and coal gas. The gas carbon is chipped off and is then ready for use. As gas carbon conducts electricity it is used to make electrodes; the carbon rod in the middle of a dry battery is made of gas carbon.

Carbon monoxide

Carbon, for example charcoal in a barbecue, burns to carbon monoxide if there is a lot of carbon and only a little oxygen, as in the middle of a bed of red hot charcoal.

$$\text{carbon} + \text{oxygen} \longrightarrow \text{carbon monoxide}$$
$$2C + O_2 \longrightarrow 2CO$$

Carbon monoxide rises to the surface where it meets more oxygen and burns with a blue flickering flame forming carbon dioxide.

$$\text{carbon monoxide} + \text{oxygen} \longrightarrow \text{carbon dioxide}$$
$$2CO + O_2 \longrightarrow 2CO_2$$

Figure 5.5 Formation of CO and CO_2 in a barbecue

Carbon monoxide is poisonous because it combines with the haemoglobin in the red cells of the blood, rendering them unable to carry oxygen. Sometimes carbon monoxide escapes from burning stoves and boilers without being oxidized to carbon dioxide, so care should be taken when coke is burned in a confined space. Similar reactions happen when other fuels containing carbon are burned. For example petrol is rarely fully burned in a car engine, so the exhaust fumes contain carbon monoxide and are therefore poisonous.

Since carbon monoxide can combine with oxygen it can act as a reducing agent and remove oxygen from other compounds. In a blast furnace one of the reactions which reduce the iron oxide to iron is

$$\text{carbon monoxide} + \text{iron(III) oxide} \longrightarrow \text{carbon dioxide} + \text{iron}$$
$$3CO + Fe_2O_3 \longrightarrow 3CO_2 + 2Fe$$

CARBON, FUELS, FLAMES, AND ENERGY

Carbon dioxide

Experiment 5.4 *Preparing and investigating carbon dioxide*

(a) Cover the bottom of the flask with lumps of calcium carbonate then add moderately concentrated hydrochloric acid. After about one minute lift the paper cover of the gas jar and hold a lighted splint at the place marked X on the diagram. If the splint goes out the jar is full of carbon dioxide; fill four jars and then three wide test tubes or boiling tubes.

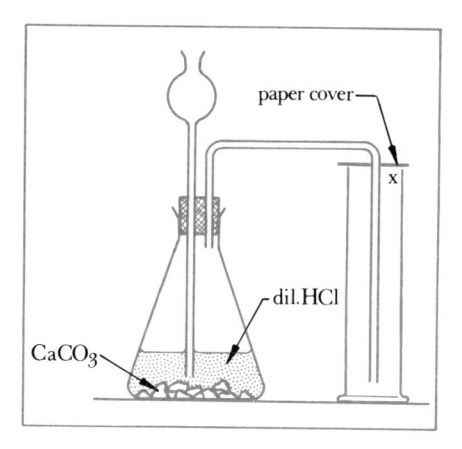

Figure 5.6 Preparation of carbon dioxide

| What do you see happening in the flask? What is left in the flask when the experiment is over? What colour is carbon dioxide?

(b) Smell some of the gas coming from the delivery tube.

(c) Into one of the test tubes of carbon dioxide pour a little lime-water. Cork the tube and shake it.

| What do you see?

(d) With your partner hold three gas jars as shown in the Fig. 5.7. Take the top off gas jar A, hold the jars in place for 30 seconds, then test jars B and C by pouring in lime-water.

| Into which jar has the carbon dioxide gone and what does this show about the density of carbon dioxide?

(e) Into one of the test-tubes of carbon dioxide pour about 3 cm depth of water, then stopper the tube tightly and shake it for about three minutes. Put the tube mouth down in a beaker of water and remove the stopper under water. Test the solution in the test-tube with universal indicator.

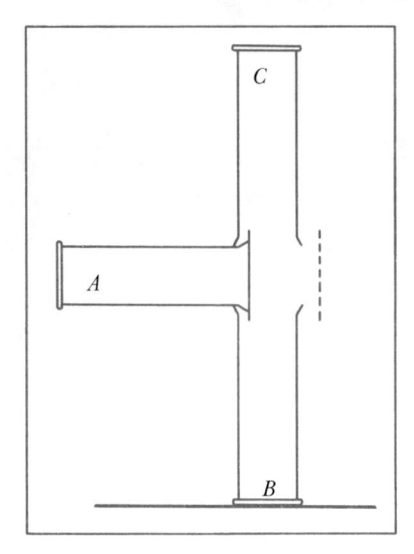

Figure 5.7 The three gas jars experiment on the density of CO_2

| What do you see happening and what does this show?

(f) Repeat experiment (e) but use dilute sodium hydroxide solution in the tube. (Use water in the beaker.)

| What do you see happening and what does this show?

(g) Hold a piece of magnesium ribbon about 10 cm long in crucible tongs. Light the ribbon in a bunsen flame and plunge it into a gas jar of carbon dioxide, being careful not to touch the walls of the jar with the burning ribbon. Try to find two different solids in the jar after the experiment.

| What colour are they and what might they be?

Carbon dioxide is usually made by the action of moderately concentrated hydrochloric acid on calcium carbonate. (Marble chips are suitable.) Fizzing is seen in the flask and a colourless solution of calcium chloride is left.

$$\text{calcium carbonate} + \text{hydrochloric acid} \longrightarrow \text{calcium chloride} + \text{water} + \text{carbon dioxide}$$

$$CaCO_3 + 2HCl \longrightarrow CaCl_2 + H_2O + CO_2$$

CARBON, FUELS, FLAMES, AND ENERGY

Carbon dioxide is collected by downward delivery, which means that it falls to the bottom of the gas jar while the air that was originally in the jar floats upwards on top of the carbon dioxide. This shows that carbon dioxide is denser than air.

Carbon dioxide is colourless and has no smell. Carbon dioxide reacts with lime-water producing small white particles in the lime-water which make it look cloudy or milky or turbid. Lime-water is a solution of calcium hydroxide and the white particles produced are small pieces of calcium carbonate.

calcium hydroxide + carbon dioxide ⟶ calcium carbonate + water
$Ca(OH)_2$ + CO_2 ⟶ $CaCO_3$ + H_2O

This reaction is used as a test for carbon dioxide. The white flakes of calcium carbonate are called a **precipitate** of calcium carbonate. (A precipitate is a solid produced in a reaction.) If a very large volume of carbon dioxide is passed through turbid lime-water the mixture clears because the precipitate reacts with the excess carbon dioxide forming calcium hydrogen carbonate (calcium bicarbonate) which dissolves in water (see page 178).

Carbon dioxide reacts slowly with water forming carbonic acid solution, which changes the colour of indicator papers.

water + carbon dioxide ⟶ carbonic acid
H_2O + CO_2 ⟶ H_2CO_3

Carbonic acid is only a weak acid and a solution of it known as soda-water may be drunk. The acidity explains the sharp taste of soda-water.

Carbon dioxide reacts with sodium hydroxide solution forming sodium hydrogen carbonate (sodium bicarbonate).

sodium hydroxide + carbon dioxide ⟶ sodium hydrogen carbonate
$NaOH$ + CO_2 ⟶ $NaHCO_3$

This reaction is an example of an acidic oxide reacting with a base forming a salt.

Burning magnesium continues to burn in carbon dioxide because it is hot enough to split the carbon dioxide, reducing it to carbon and using the oxygen to form magnesium oxide.

magnesium + carbon dioxide ⟶ carbon + magnesium oxide
$2Mg$ + CO_2 ⟶ C + $2MgO$

Uses of carbon dioxide

(a) Carbon dioxide is used in fire extinguishers. The carbon dioxide extinguisher consists of a cylinder of carbon dioxide at high pressure, a tap, and a large nozzle. When the nozzle is aimed at the fire and the tap turned, a noisy blast of very cold carbon dioxide rushes out, cooling the fire and blanketing it, thus excluding the air. Carbon dioxide extinguishers make less mess than water or foam extinguishers and may be used safely on electrical equipment.

(b) Solid carbon dioxide sublimes (i.e., turns from solid to a gas without melting) at $-78°C$. It is a white waxy-looking solid which appears to smoke in moist air because the extreme cold turns the water vapour in the air to tiny crystals of ice. It is used to make artificial smoke on stage and in films. It is also used for cooling ice cream and frozen foods during transit in insulated vans, and for production of low temperatures in scientific experiments. Its advantages over ice are that it is much colder, and when it has sublimed no residue is left, whereas when ice is used for cooling, the water formed must be drained away.

(c) Soda-water is a solution containing carbonic acid, H_2CO_3, which is made by dissolving carbon dioxide in water under pressure. When the pressure is released the carbon dioxide comes out of solution so bubbles are seen and the soda-water eventually becomes flat. Bottled fizzy drinks are made of soda-water together with colouring and flavouring materials.

(d) In a gas-cooled nuclear reactor carbon dioxide is blown through the reactor core and comes out very hot. It then passes through tubes surrounded by water. The water turns to steam which is used to drive turbo-alternators for the production of electricity.

(e) Baking powder contains tartaric acid and sodium hydrogen carbonate (sodium bicarbonate). When the baking powder is mixed with water and heated in the mixture which is being cooked, carbon dioxide is made, forming bubbles in the mixture, which therefore swells or rises. (See also health salts, page 230.)

(f) The carbon dioxide in the air is used by plants in the process of photosynthesis. It also helps in the setting of mortar. The mortar starts to set by the drying out of water but the dry mortar continues to harden because it contains calcium hydroxide which is alkaline and reacts with the carbon dioxide in the air.

$$Ca(OH)_2 + CO_2 \longrightarrow CaCO_3 + H_2O$$

The calcium carbonate formed binds the mortar into a hard solid mass. (See also page 225.)

Other reactions in which carbon dioxide is made

(a) Nitric, sulphuric, hydrochloric, and acetic acids all react with any carbonate or bicarbonate (hydrogen carbonate) giving off carbon dioxide. For example:

$$\text{copper carbonate} + \text{sulphuric acid} \longrightarrow \text{copper sulphate} + \text{water} + \text{carbon dioxide}$$

$$\underset{\text{(green solid)}}{CuCO_3} + H_2SO_4 \longrightarrow \underset{\text{(blue solution)}}{CuSO_4} + H_2O + \underset{\text{(fizzing)}}{CO_2}$$

Mixing a compound with an acid to see if carbon dioxide is formed is a test to discover whether or not the compound is a carbonate or bicarbonate. (See Fig. 6.2.)

(b) When sodium hydrogen carbonate is heated sodium carbonate is made and steam and carbon dioxide are given off.

$$2NaHCO_3 \longrightarrow Na_2CO_3 + H_2O + CO_2$$

Potassium hydrogen carbonate reacts similarly.

(c) When calcium carbonate is heated carbon dioxide and calcium oxide are made. (See experiment 7.11.)

$$\begin{aligned} \text{calcium carbonate} &\longrightarrow \text{calcium oxide} + \text{carbon dioxide} \\ \text{limestone} &\longrightarrow \text{quick lime} + \text{carbon dioxide} \\ CaCO_3 &\longrightarrow CaO + CO_2 \end{aligned}$$

Copper carbonate, zinc carbonate, and lead carbonate react similarly.

$$\begin{aligned} CuCO_3 &\longrightarrow CuO + CO_2 \\ ZnCO_3 &\longrightarrow ZnO + CO_2 \\ PbCO_3 &\longrightarrow PbO + CO_2 \end{aligned}$$

(d) The complete burning of carbon, carbon monoxide, or any other carbon-containing material such as oil, petrol, paraffin, natural gas, wood or other plant tissues, coal or coke, produces carbon dioxide.

(e) The breathing of plants and animals (including human beings) is a process in which oxygen is removed from the air and an equal volume of carbon dioxide put back into the air.

The carbon cycle—the natural circulation of carbon

The atmosphere contains 0·04 per cent carbon dioxide. You might think that the amount of carbon dioxide in the air should be increasing rapidly because all burning and breathing processes are putting more carbon dioxide into the air at the expense of oxygen. Fortunately photosynthesis is reversing this change. Using energy trapped from sunlight by chlorophyll, plants build up starches from water and carbon dioxide, and give out oxygen.

$$\text{carbon dioxide} + \text{water} + \text{energy} \xrightarrow{\text{chlorophyll}} \text{starches} + \text{oxygen}$$

Recently, however, there has been a detectable increase in the amount of carbon dioxide present in the air; this is one of the ways in which industrial development is polluting the Earth.

Another process which is helping to remove carbon dioxide from the air is the dissolving of the gas in water.

CHEMISTRY

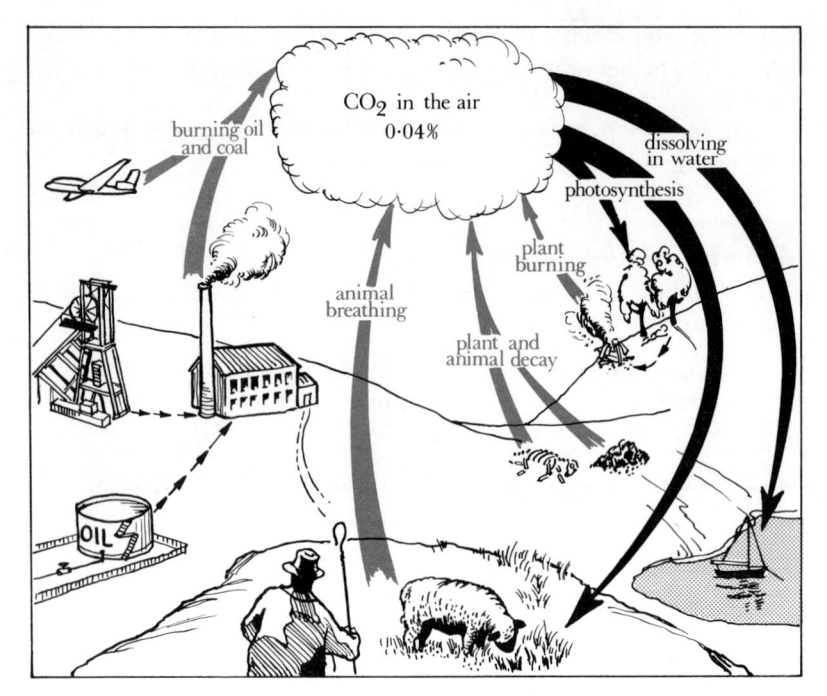

Figure 5.8 Some important processes in carbon circulation—the carbon cycle

Coal and coke

Now that pits are closing and coal is losing its place as the most prominent source of energy, it is hard to appreciate the immense importance that coal had in making the United Kingdom a prosperous industrial nation. The coal, which has for thousands of years been dug out of the ground and burned, started life as vegetation—large fern-like plants some of which were as big as present day trees. As these died they fell to the forest floor and became covered with further layers of plant remains, and later, as the Earth's crust crumpled and heaved, sand and rock layers were laid down on top of them. Decaying under conditions of high pressure for millions of years, these vegetable remains eventually formed coal. Ordinary household coal is only one of several types.

Among the elements present in coal are carbon, hydrogen, oxygen, sulphur, nitrogen, magnesium, and silicon. These elements combine forming a large variety of compounds, and the types and proportions of these compounds govern the sort of coal formed. The older, harder coals contain less water and more combined carbon, so have a greater calorific value (heating power per kilogram or per ton). If coal burns in an adequate supply of oxygen, the main chemical products are steam and carbon dioxide. If there is not

CARBON, FUELS, FLAMES, AND ENERGY

enough oxygen for full burning, black specks of carbon are made and appear as soot or in smoke. Ash is magnesium silicate; small particles of it are carried up chimneys by convection currents and eventually return to earth. In London before smoke control orders were made, 240 tons of dirt, largely ash and carbon, fell yearly on each square mile (almost 0·1 kg per square metre per year). As well as solids, steam, and carbon dioxide, burning coal produces sulphur dioxide pollution in the atmosphere.

Table 5.1 **Properties of coal-like fuels**

Name	Appearance	Properties	Use	Ease of burning
peat	brown, fibrous	▇ increasing age, hardness, calorific value ▇ decreasing ash and volatile matter ⬇	mainly horticultural	burns with fumes when dry
brown coal	soft, brown solid		burned in some power stations (Australia, Eire)	made into briquettes which burn when dried
household bituminous coal	shiny, black, shatters if hit		on open fires	burns freely with smoke and flame
anthracite	very hard, black and shiny		in boilers	forced draught needed— e.g., in closed stove

Experiment 5.5 *Destructive distillation of coal*

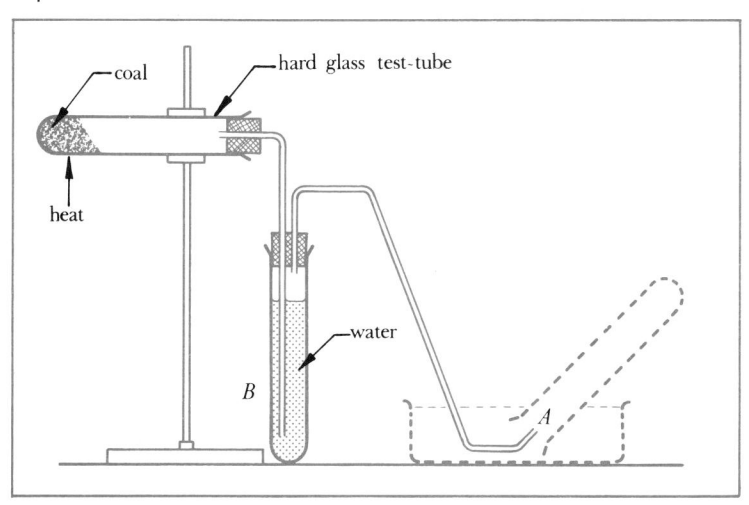

Figure 5.9 **A small-scale coke oven**

CHEMISTRY

Crush coal to lumps approximately the size of peas and heat these in the apparatus shown. The gas coming from *A* is initially air but is later an impure form of coal gas. Try to light the gas, then collect some over water in a boiling tube. When the tube is full examine the gas and then burn it.

What is the appearance of the substances in tube *B* after the experiment? What is left in the hard glass test tube?

Coal heated in a very limited supply of air decomposes forming coal gas, coal tar, ammoniacal liquor, and coke. In experiment 5.5 the tar, which is dark brown, and the ammoniacal liquor (ammonia solution) collect in tube *B*. Although the domestic use of coal gas is declining as the burning of natural gas increases, the destructive distillation of coal is still carried on because coke, coal tar, and the other products are valuable materials. A steel works may have its own coke ovens (which are a type of gas works) primarily because of the need for coke in a blast furnace.

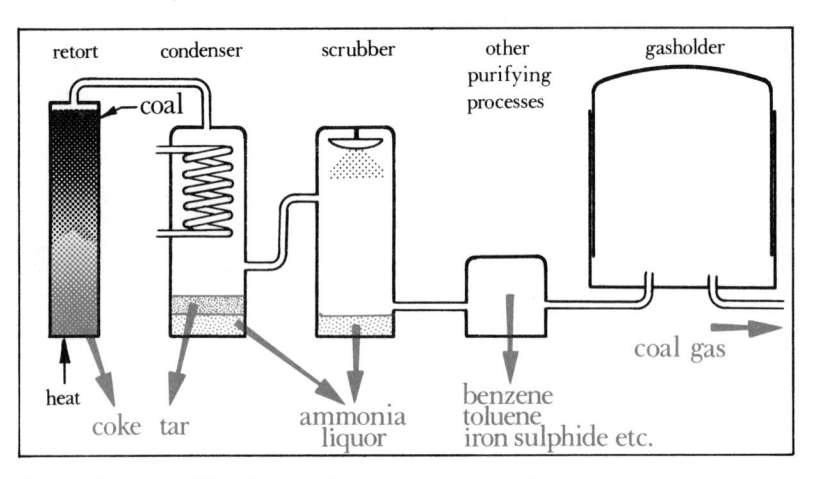

Figure 5.10 A simplified diagram of a coal-gas plant or coke-oven

In a gas works or coke oven coal is heated for many hours at a temperature higher than 500°C. Gas flames heat metal retorts lined with fire bricks until the coal is converted to coke and gas carbon which remain in the retort, and volatile materials which pass on. Coal tar condenses when the gases are cooled in condensers, and ammonia is removed when a water spray passes through the gas in the scrubber. Other processes remove various oil-like products, dust, and hydrogen sulphide before the gas is metered and stored ready for sale. Coal tar contains hundreds of different chemical compounds, and from these many things including drugs, dyes, insecticides, plastics, and explosives are made. Ammonium sulphate, a fertilizer, is made from the

CARBON, FUELS, FLAMES, AND ENERGY

ammonia liquor, and the sulphur in the hydrogen sulphide is made into sulphuric acid.

The **coke** left is largely carbon. It is used as a fuel in furnaces and central heating boilers, and as a fuel and reducing agent in the smelting of iron ore into iron. If the supply of oxygen is adequate the overall reaction in the burning of coke is

$$C + O_2 \longrightarrow CO_2 + \text{heat}$$

Coke is also used for making water gas and producer gas.

Most **smokeless fuels** are substances intermediate in properties between coal and coke. They burn more easily than coke but less smokily than coal.

Fuel gases

Coal gas

Coal gas has been used for over a hundred years in many parts of the world. In common with all gaseous fuels it is clean, smokeless, and exactly controllable, but there is always a danger of explosion if a fuel gas accumulates

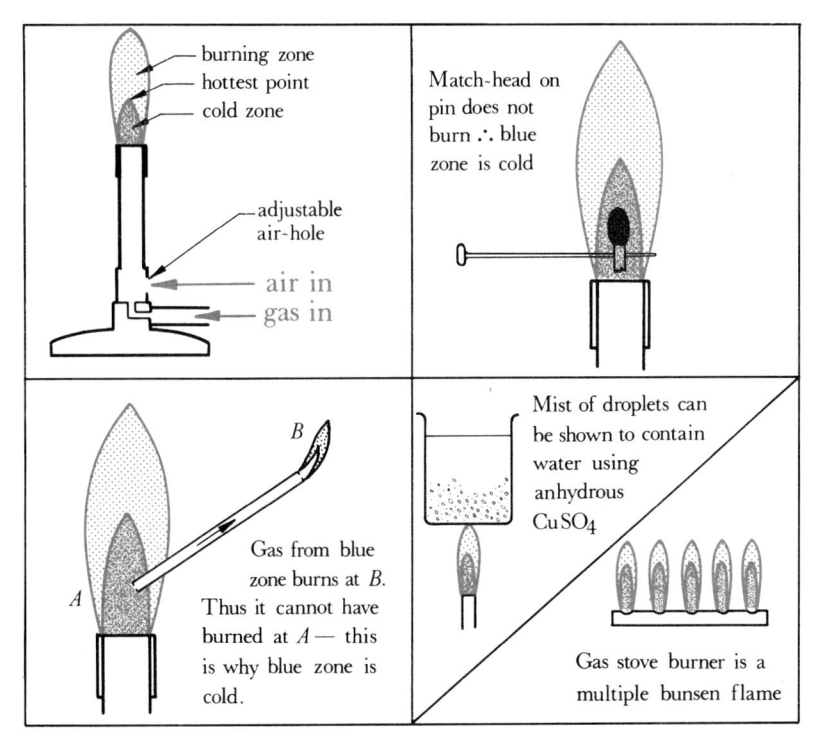

Figure 5.11 The bunsen burner

in a confined space. Coal gas has a further disadvantage in that it is poisonous. The exact composition of coal gas varies according to the type of coal in the retort and the temperature to which it is heated, but a typical analysis would be

$$50\% \text{ hydrogen } H_2$$
$$30\% \text{ methane } CH_4$$
$$10\% \text{ carbon monoxide } CO$$
$$10\% \text{ other gases}$$

The burning of coal gas produces carbon dioxide and steam according to the following equations:

$$2H_2 + O_2 \longrightarrow 2H_2O + \text{heat}$$
$$CH_4 + 2O_2 \longrightarrow CO_2 + 2H_2O + \text{heat}$$
$$2CO + O_2 \longrightarrow 2CO_2 + \text{heat}$$

Water gas and producer gas

When steam is blown through white-hot coke the coke reduces the steam, forming a mixture containing equal volumes of carbon monoxide and hydrogen.

$$H_2O + C + \text{heat} \xrightarrow{\text{Ox} \atop \text{Red}} CO + H_2$$

The mixture of carbon monoxide and hydrogen is called water gas. This reaction is **endothermic**, which means that heat is absorbed as the reaction takes place. The coke therefore cools and the rate of production of water gas slows. To heat the coke again a blast of air is blown through it. The oxygen in the air combines with the coke making carbon monoxide but the nitrogen passes through unchanged.

$$\text{air} + \text{coke} \longrightarrow \text{carbon monoxide} + \text{nitrogen} + \text{heat}$$
$$4N_2 + O_2 + 2C \longrightarrow 2CO + 4N_2 + \text{heat}$$

Because this reaction produces heat it is called an **exothermic reaction**. The mixture of carbon monoxide and nitrogen is called producer gas.

Water gas and producer gas are both used as fuels in industry.

Natural gas

Natural gas consists almost entirely of methane CH_4. It is found underground in the North Sea, Algeria, USA, and Nigeria and in many other parts of the world. The gas is pumped at high pressure to the point of use, where it passes through a pressure-reducing valve before being burned.

$$CH_4 + 2O_2 \longrightarrow CO_2 + 2H_2O + \text{heat}$$

CARBON, FUELS, FLAMES, AND ENERGY

Natural gas can be obtained by the Gas Boards at about one-fifth of the price it costs to make coal gas and is also non-poisonous. The jets at which natural gas burns must be smaller than those for coal gas so expensive conversion of all appliances is needed before natural gas can be used. The flame

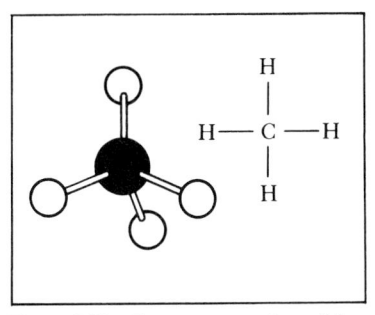

Figure 5.12 Two representations of the methane molecule

of natural gas burns more slowly than that of coal gas so the flame easily becomes detached from the jet and small flames blow out readily. Natural gas is harder to light than coal gas, and the flame is more difficult to adjust, but the cheapness of the fuel is thought to outweigh these disadvantages to the consumer, and all piped gas supplies in the United Kingdom will soon be converted to natural gas.

Oil

Experiment 5.6 *Fractional distillation of crude oil*

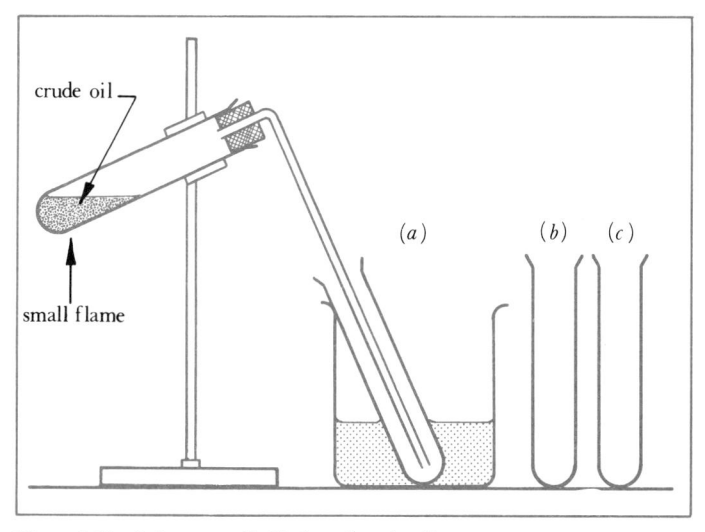

Figure 5.13 Laboratory distillation of crude oil

CHEMISTRY

Put crude oil in the test-tube to a depth of approximately 3 cm and heat cautiously, (Fig. 5.13). Into three separate test tubes, (*a*), (*b*) and (*c*), distil three portions (fractions) each about 1 cm depth, and then allow the undistilled residue to cool.

Shake the three tubes containing the fractions and compare their viscosity with each other and with that of the undistilled portion.

Smell each of the fractions, then dip a piece of rolled-up paper into each one and hold it to a flame. Finally put one drop of each fraction on a microscope slide and observe the order in which they evaporate to dryness.

What do you observe about the smells, boiling points, and order of evaporation of the fractions?

Experiment 5.6 shows the separation of crude oil into four fractions. Three of these distil as colourless or faintly yellow liquids and the fourth is left as a dark brown liquid in the distilling tube. The first fraction smells of petrol, the second of diesel fuel, and the third is an oil similar to light lubricating oil. The first fraction is very volatile (i.e., evaporates quickly), smells strongly, and splashes about a great deal in the tube. The second fraction is

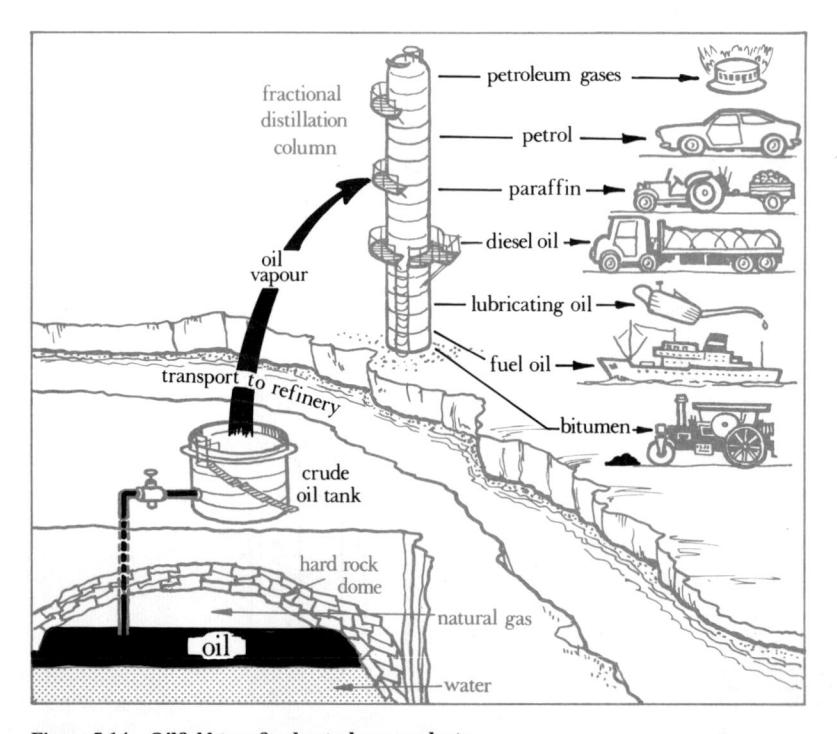

Figure 5.14 Oilfield to refined petroleum products

CARBON, FUELS, FLAMES, AND ENERGY

less volatile, evaporates more slowly, and is less mobile than the first. The third and fourth fractions are less volatile still and also less mobile. All the fractions burn, the first more readily than the second and so on, the flames becoming more smoky and yellower from the first to the fourth fraction.

Crude oil is a thick brown liquid which has probably been formed by the decay of small sea organisms under conditions of high pressure. Natural gas is formed at the same time and the two fuels are often found in the same place. Crude oil is separated into many fractions by fractional distillation in a petroleum refinery.

Crude oil is a mixture which consists largely of **hydrocarbons** (that is, compounds of hydrogen and carbon) called alkanes. The refinery products formed by distillation are also mixtures and consist of those few of the hydrocarbons in crude oil which have boiling points close together. Petroleum gases are used as fuels; e.g., Propagas is liquid propane C_3H_8, and Calor gas is a mixture of liquid butane C_4H_{10} with a little propane.

propane C_3H_8　　　　butane C_4H_{10}

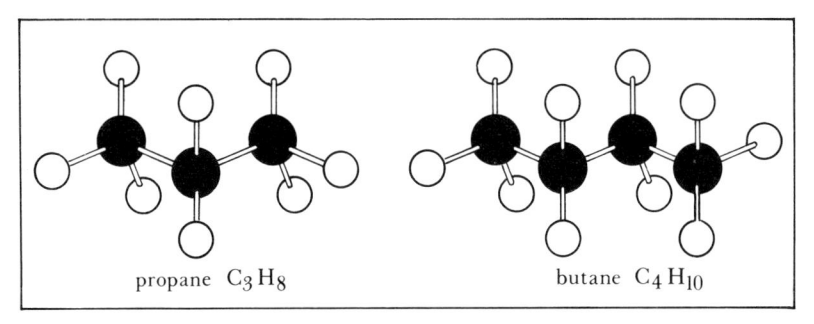

Figure 5.15 Hydrocarbon molecules present in Calor gas

Petrol contains compounds such as hexane C_6H_{14}, heptane C_7H_{16}, and octane C_8H_{18} which come from the crude oil, but various other substances known as additives are put in by the refining companies. These include lead compounds to reduce pinking, bromine and chlorine compounds to remove the lead when it has done its job, and various substances designed to keep the engine clean and reduce wear. Lead used in this way escapes with the engine exhaust gases and pollutes the atmosphere.

When the refinery products are listed in order from petroleum gases to bitumen the materials become less volatile, less readily flammable, and more viscous, because the molecules of the substances lower down the list are larger and heavier. Experiment 5.6 illustrates this, and so does the fact that fuel oil, which contains molecules such as $C_{14}H_{30}$ and $C_{16}H_{34}$, is thicker, harder to light, and less volatile than petrol. The world demand for petrol is so great that large molecules such as those found in oil are split into parts to provide more of the small molecules needed for petrol. This process is called **cracking** the molecules and it is carried out using a catalyst in a giant tower known in the trade as a cat-cracker. A typical example of cracking would be the splitting of $C_{16}H_{34}$ to yield C_8H_{18} and other molecules.

Most of the refined oil-products listed above are burned, producing heat and adding carbon dioxide to the atmosphere. For example:

$$\text{propane} + \text{oxygen} \longrightarrow \text{carbon dioxide} + \text{steam} + \text{heat}$$
$$C_3H_8 + 5O_2 \longrightarrow 3CO_2 + 4H_2O + \text{heat}$$

Many of the refinery products, however, are extremely valuable starting materials for the manufacture of plastics, detergents, and other useful substances. If we go on burning refinery products as we are doing now, alternative raw materials will be needed for the manufactured items, and their prices will probably rise steeply.

Ethyl alcohol (ethanol)

The compound ethyl alcohol C_2H_5OH is in general usage called alcohol without any qualification; its proper chemical name is ethanol. Methylated spirit is largely ethyl alcohol together with some methyl alcohol (methanol), water, and small amounts of other substances intended to make it unpleasant to drink.

Experiment 5.7   *To make ethyl alcohol (ethanol) by fermentation*

Dissolve about 100 g of sugar (sucrose) in about 500 cm³ of warm water in a litre flask. Add a few grams of yeast which has been mixed to a cream with a little water, and put a tuft of cotton wool in the neck of the flask. Leave the flask in a warm place (about 25°C) for several days until the reaction dies down. Use the method shown in Fig. 6.2 to test the gas above the liquid in the flask for carbon dioxide.

Filter the liquid in the flask through a fine filter paper, then try to separate some of the ethyl alcohol produced from the water by fractional distillation as in experiment 1.4.

| What substances are made by fermentation of sugar solution?

A solution of sugar (sucrose) ferments when yeast is added yielding ethyl alcohol (ethanol) and carbon dioxide, which causes the mixture to froth.

$$\text{sugar} + \text{water} \longrightarrow \text{ethyl alcohol} + \text{carbon dioxide}$$
$$C_{12}H_{22}O_{11} + H_2O \longrightarrow 4C_2H_5OH + 4CO_2$$

The yeast contains **enzymes** (naturally-occurring catalysts) which catalyse this change. This process has been used since prehistoric times to make alcoholic liquors. The yeasts necessary for this process are present on the

CARBON, FUELS, FLAMES, AND ENERGY

skins of grapes, so if the grapes are crushed the sugary juice contains yeast and it ferments without further treatment.

Wines are largely water but also contain ethyl alcohol, colouring and flavouring materials. When wines are distilled the alcohol, colouring, and flavouring materials distil over before the water, so a more concentrated liquor known as a spirit is made. Distillation of spirits produces thick syrupy liquids known as liqueurs. Home winemaking is legal in the United Kingdom but the domestic production of spirits by distillation is definitely not.

Ethyl alcohol (ethanol) is also an important industrial chemical. It is used as a fuel, as a starting material for making other compounds and as a solvent—phenolphthalein, for example, is dissolved in ethyl alcohol for use as an indicator. The ethyl alcohol used for industrial purposes is not now made by fermentation, but from petroleum chemicals.

Organic chemistry

Ethyl alcohol C_2H_5OH, methane CH_4, propane C_3H_8, butane C_4H_{10}, octane C_8H_{18}, and many other compounds mentioned in this chapter are organic compounds, and the study of them is called organic chemistry. All organic compounds contain carbon and they often contain fairly large complex molecules; compare, for example, chlorophyll (organic) $C_{55}H_{72}O_5N_4Mg$ with hydrogen chloride HCl and ammonia NH_3, which are inorganic compounds. Organic compounds include both natural products such as cellulose, starch, sugars, and rubber, and synthetic substances such as DDT, polythene, nylon, and polystyrene. All plastics, detergents and antibiotics are organic compounds.

Flames and explosions

Experiment 5.8 *Brightness and colours of flames*

(*a*) Take two wooden splints or small rolls of paper, dip one into benzene and the other into ethyl alcohol. Apply a light to each.

What do you observe about the brightness of the flames produced, and any products of burning appearing from the flames?

(*b*) Use the method described in experiment 3.4 to burn phosphorus and carbon in two separate gas jars of oxygen.

What do you observe about the brightness of the flames, and any products of burning appearing in the flames?

(c) Take a piece of nichrome wire or pencil lead, dip it into some concentrated hydrochloric acid on a watch-glass, and then into a little potassium chloride on a second watch-glass. Put the wire, together with some of the potassium chloride stuck to it, into the hot part of a bunsen flame and observe any colour produced. When the colour dies away repeat the experiment using calcium chloride, then copper chloride, then sodium chloride.

| What is the colour of the flame in each case?

A **flame** is a region in which burning is going on so vigorously that heat and light are produced. If the substance burning produces a solid oxide the flame is very bright. The flame of burning phosphorus is bright because the white solid oxide phosphorus(V) oxide (tetraphosphorus decoxide) is produced, and benzene burns with a bright flame because it produces solid specks of carbon. Substances which produce only gaseous oxides burn with flames producing little light. Carbon burnt in oxygen forms carbon dioxide, and ethyl alcohol burns to carbon dioxide and steam, so neither of these substances gives a bright flame. The very bright sparks produced when iron filings are flicked into a bunsen flame arise because a solid oxide of iron is made; the sparks made by certain fireworks and by the grinding of steel tools on a sharpening wheel arise from the same reaction.

Certain metallic compounds give rise to colours when they are introduced into a flame. The colour produced by the compounds of any metal is always the same and can be used to identify the metal. This type of experiment is called a flame test (see Appendix 2). Sodium compounds colour a flame yellow, potassium compounds lilac, copper compounds greenish blue, and calcium compounds red. The flames of fireworks, signal flares, and distress rockets often contain small amounts of metallic compounds to produce colours.

Demonstration experiment 5.9 *Gas explosions*

(a) Drill a hole approximately 5 mm diameter into the base of a tin of about 500 cm^3 capacity, and a slightly smaller hole in the lid. Fill the tin with coal gas or natural gas, balance it on a tripod with the lid downwards and put a lighted splint to the upper hole. Stand back.

(b) Put a mixture containing approximately one-third oxygen and two-thirds hydrogen in a polythene bottle volume 350 cm^3 or less. Clamp the bottle in a retort stand and apply a light to the mouth of the bottle.

Pure natural gas or coal gas burns quietly in air, but a mixture of gas with an appropriate proportion of oxygen explodes when lit. In experiment 5.9(a) air enters the tin by the bottom hole as gas burns at the top hole. The percentage of oxygen in the mixture in the tin increases until a certain limit is reached. At this limit the gas mixture explodes.

CARBON, FUELS, FLAMES, AND ENERGY

In experiment 5.9(b) the oxygen and hydrogen mixture is in the proportions required for complete combustion, and the mixture explodes when lit. In both these experiments the explosive mixture contains a fuel (gas or hydrogen) and an oxidizing agent (oxygen).

A chemical explosion is simply a very rapid combustion reaction. The heat produced expands the gases made in the reaction and a blast wave results. High explosives such as nitroglycerine and dynamite (which is a mixture of nitroglycerine with a special sort of earth) burn very much more quickly than low explosives such as gun powder. The high explosives shatter objects near by, but low explosives produce a slower push and may be used as propellants in guns and solid fuel rockets. Both low and high explosives contain a fuel and an oxidizing agent.

Most people connect explosives with guns, bombs, and war, but explosives have many other uses such as quarrying, mining, tunnelling, road making, and other civil engineering works, while rockets can be used for signalling and carrying lifelines and space capsules, as well as nuclear warheads. The energy stored in explosives can be used for peaceful as well as warlike purposes.

Energy for the world

Apart from the new materials produced by chemists, the main difference between an industrial country now and the same country a hundred years ago is that machines rather than muscles are moving people and goods from place to place, cutting and shaping wood, stone and metal, quarrying and digging, doing household washing and cleaning, and harvesting and processing food. Machines often use coal, oil, or natural gas as a primary source of energy. When one of these fossil fuels is used, either to do mechanical work, to produce electricity directly in a fuel cell, or simply to produce heat, the long carbon chains of the fuel form carbon dioxide, which escapes into the atmosphere along with steam. It is difficult to estimate the reserves of these fuels, but it seems probable that if in future their consumption goes on increasing as it is doing now, all the world's oil, for example, will be used in under fifty years. This must not be allowed to take place. These fuels are needed also as raw materials for the chemical industry, and although alternative sources of energy will probably be used increasingly in the future, other sources of raw materials will be hard to find. Our present burning of oil and coal is a wasteful use of resources, comparable to the wasteful methods of farming which produced dust-bowls in the USA. Possibilities for energy supply include hydro-electric power, tide, wind, and sun power, burning alcohol produced from starches made by quick-growing plants, heat from the interior of the earth, and nuclear energy.

All animals, human beings included, need energy for moving and communicating, and warm-blooded animals need extra energy to maintain their body temperature. (A normal person has a body temperature some 15° or 20° above a comfortable room temperature.) The process of food oxidation is similar to, although more complex than, combustion.

$$\text{food} + \text{oxygen} \longrightarrow \text{carbon dioxide} + \text{water} + \text{energy}$$

The supply of food to an animal is similar to the supply of fuel to a machine; both animal and machine need oxygen to oxidize the fuel and produce energy, and if the supply of food is inadequate an animal works inefficiently.

Chapter summary

Carbon atoms join in various ways to produce several forms of carbon. Some forms are crystalline (diamond, graphite) and some are amorphous or non-crystalline (wood charcoal, carbon black, and gas carbon).

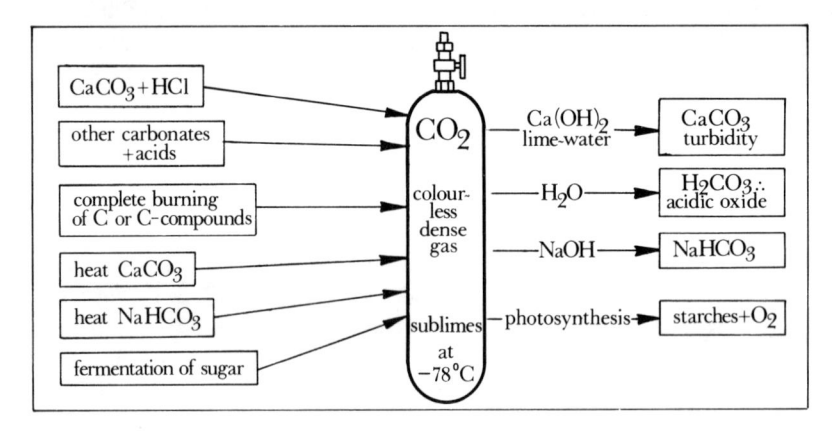

[Diagram: Reactions producing and consuming CO_2 (colourless dense gas, sublimes at $-78°C$).
Inputs to CO_2: $CaCO_3 + HCl$; other carbonates + acids; complete burning of C or C-compounds; heat $CaCO_3$; heat $NaHCO_3$; fermentation of sugar.
Outputs from CO_2: $Ca(OH)_2$ lime-water → $CaCO_3$ turbidity; H_2O → H_2CO_3 ∴ acidic oxide; $NaOH$ → $NaHCO_3$; photosynthesis → starches + O_2.]

All important fuels contain carbon, e.g., coal, natural gas (CH_4, methane), and oil products. Oil, on fractional distillation, splits into various mixtures including petroleum gases, petrol, paraffin, diesel oil, lubricating oil, fuel oil, and bitumen. Oil products are valuable as chemicals as well as fuel. All oil products are hydrocarbons—compounds of hydrogen and carbon.

Ethyl alcohol (ethanol C_2H_5OH) is made by fermentation of sugar solution using catalysts called enzymes from yeast. Ethyl alcohol is an organic compound.

Questions

1. Name in each case a form of carbon which (*a*) is amorphous, (*b*) conducts electricity, (*c*) is used to make an explosive, (*d*) is a reducing agent, (*e*) is used as a pigment, (*f*) is used as a lubricant.

CARBON, FUELS, FLAMES, AND ENERGY

2. Construct a table comparing the heating without air of wood and coal. Include in your table the headings: solid product, liquid products, and gas made. In the table name and describe each product.

3. A solid A, when put into a flame, turns the flame red. A bubbles freely when put into dilute hydrochloric acid and a gas B is evolved. B reacts with limewater producing a white solid C. Identify A, B and C.

4. Describe how carbon dioxide affects (a) blue litmus solution, (b) sodium hydroxide solution, (c) a small fire (e.g., an overheated electrical flex).

5. Describe briefly two processes which tend to increase the amount of carbon dioxide in the air, and two which tend to decrease it.

6. Explain what is meant by, and give an example of, (a) an endothermic reaction, (b) a precipitate, (c) allotropy, (d) a hydrocarbon, (e) fermentation.

7. What differences in physical properties and chemical formulae would you find by comparing petrol and lubricating oil? In what ways are petrol and oil similar?

8. Devise an experiment to compare the densities of coal gas and natural gas.

9. Fuel oil, coke, coal, and natural gas are all used as fuels. Construct a table showing their origin, appearance, formula (where known), and main products of burning.

6

Acids, bases, and salts

Acidic, basic, and neutral oxides

Demonstration experiment 6.1 *The action of water on oxides*

Into a gas jar containing a little sulphur dioxide put a strip of damp red and a strip of damp blue litmus paper. Into a gas jar containing some phosphorus(V) oxide (tetraphosphorus decoxide) smoke put a strip of damp red and a strip of damp blue litmus paper. On to damp red and damp blue litmus paper rub a little magnesium oxide.

Use a spatula to rub a little calcium oxide powder on to a strip of damp red and a strip of damp blue litmus paper. In each case record the action on the litmus paper and state what this shows.

In experiment 6.1 four oxides react with water on the damp litmus paper and the acidic or alkaline nature of the product is checked. The sulphur dioxide reacts with water to produce a compound which turns litmus paper red. The compound produced is an acid—sulphurous acid H_2SO_3.

$$\text{water} + \text{sulphur dioxide} \longrightarrow \text{sulphurous acid}$$
$$H_2O + SO_2 \longrightarrow H_2SO_3$$

The oxide of phosphorus reacts with water to produce an acid—orthophosphoric acid H_3PO_4

$$6H_2O + P_4O_{10} \longrightarrow 4H_3PO_4$$

The magnesium oxide reacts with water to produce a compound which turns litmus paper blue. This compound is an alkali—magnesium hydroxide.

$$\text{magnesium oxide} + \text{water} \longrightarrow \text{magnesium hydroxide}$$
$$MgO + H_2O \longrightarrow Mg(OH)_2$$

ACIDS, BASES, AND SALTS

The calcium oxide also reacts with the water producing a compound which turns litmus paper blue. This compound is the alkali calcium hydroxide.

$$\text{calcium oxide} + \text{water} \longrightarrow \text{calcium hydroxide}$$
$$\text{CaO} + \text{H}_2\text{O} \longrightarrow \text{Ca(OH)}_2$$

The results of experiment 6.1 are typical of the oxides of many metals and non-metals. Most non-metallic elements burn, as do sulphur and phosphorus, producing an **acidic oxide**, i.e., an oxide which reacts with water to produce an acid. Most metals burn to produce **basic oxides**, which are the chemical opposites of acidic oxides. Some basic oxides react with water to produce hydroxides as do the oxides of magnesium and calcium. These basic oxides form a special class called **alkaline oxides**. Other basic oxides do not react with water, an example of this type being copper oxide. To summarize, most metallic oxides are basic, and some of these basic oxides are alkaline oxides.

Summary of classification of oxides

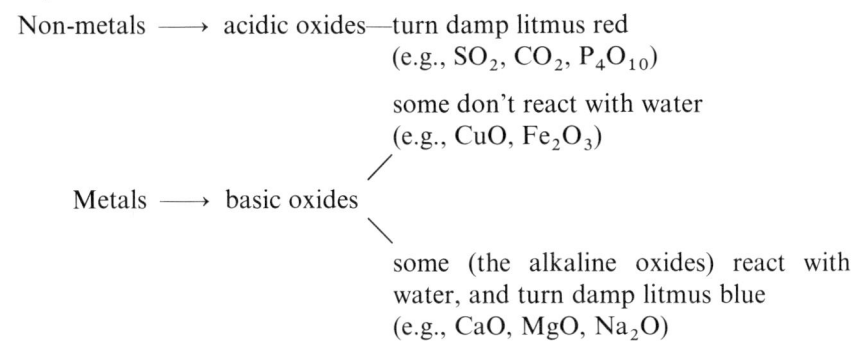

Non-metals ⟶ acidic oxides—turn damp litmus red
(e.g., SO_2, CO_2, P_4O_{10})

Metals ⟶ basic oxides
- some don't react with water (e.g., CuO, Fe_2O_3)
- some (the alkaline oxides) react with water, and turn damp litmus blue (e.g., CaO, MgO, Na_2O)

A few non-metallic oxides are neutral oxides, e.g., H_2O, CO, and show no reaction with damp litmus.

Indicators

The litmus used in experiment 6.1 showed which of the compounds made were acidic and which were alkaline. Litmus, which is an example of an indicator, is a plant product. Solutions of litmus sometimes go mouldy, and the colour changes from red through purple to blue in a gradual way so that the change is often hard to see. Dozens of synthetic (man-made) indicators have been developed to overcome these difficulties, and three of the most useful are:

methyl orange—red in acidic, yellow in alkaline solutions;
phenolphthalein—colourless in acidic, pink in alkaline solutions;
universal indicator—see experiment 6.14 for colours.

Acids

The average person, and most writers of comics, have a fixed idea of an acid: it is a highly dangerous, flesh-consuming, fuming liquid which bubbles and froths of its own accord. Although there is no acid of this exact nature many acids are dangerous and all must be treated with great care. The best immediate treatment for acid on flesh or clothes is to dilute the acid with a large volume of water, but all spills on yourself or your clothes, or the floors or bench should be reported to the teacher in charge as soon as possible, as further treatment may be necessary. The three acids most used in the laboratory are sulphuric, nitric, and hydrochloric.

Sulphuric acid H_2SO_4

The manufacture of sulphuric acid

Four million tons of sulphuric acid are made every year in the United Kingdom. In the Contact Process sulphur is first burned forming sulphur dioxide.

$$S + O_2 \longrightarrow SO_2$$

The hot (450°) purified sulphur dioxide and air are passed over a catalyst (usually an oxide of vanadium) spread out on shelves in large boxes. On contact with the catalyst, the sulphur dioxide is oxidized to sulphur trioxide.

$$2SO_2 + O_2 \longrightarrow 2SO_3$$

The sulphur trioxide is then dissolved in concentrated sulphuric acid, and water is added as well. The effective reaction is

$$H_2O + SO_3 \longrightarrow H_2SO_4$$

The Contact Process may be summarized:

$$S \xrightarrow{O_2} SO_2 \xrightarrow[\text{cat}]{O_2} SO_3 \xrightarrow{H_2O} H_2SO_4$$

The acid produced by this process is pure and concentrated.

The properties of sulphuric acid

The concentrated sulphuric acid usually supplied to laboratories contains 98 per cent acid and 2 per cent water. It is a colourless odourless oily liquid which does not fume and is almost twice as dense as water, so that a bottle containing concentrated sulphuric acid is noticeably heavier than a similar bottle containing most other liquids. This concentrated acid is particularly corrosive and must always be handled with care. Concentrated sulphuric acid has a very high boiling point, 335°C.

ACIDS, BASES, AND SALTS

Experiment 6.2 *Concentrated sulphuric acid and water*

(*a*) Into about 1 cm depth of concentrated sulphuric acid in a test-tube put a blue crystal of copper sulphate pentahydrate $CuSO_4.5H_2O$.

(*b*) Into a similar volume of sulphuric acid dip a wooden splint.

(*c*) Put sugar $C_{12}H_{22}O_{11}$ into a test-tube to a depth of 1 cm, hold the tube in a test-tube holder and pour in an equal depth of concentrated sulphuric acid.

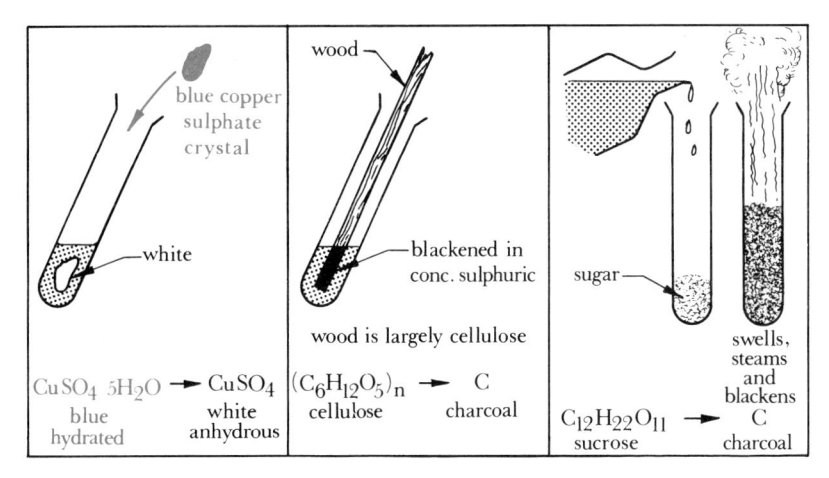

Figure 6.1 **Water removal (dehydration) by concentrated sulphuric acid**

$CuSO_4.5H_2O \rightarrow CuSO_4$
blue hydrated — white anhydrous

$(C_6H_{10}O_5)_n \rightarrow C$
cellulose — charcoal

$C_{12}H_{22}O_{11} \rightarrow C$
sucrose — charcoal

Note that only concentrated sulphuric acid acts as a water absorber. The concentrated acid if left unstoppered will absorb water vapour from the air, and very gradually become diluted as it does so. Any substance which absorbs water vapour from the air is said to be **hygroscopic**, so concentrated sulphuric acid is a hygroscopic substance.

Demonstration experiment 6.3 *Adding concentrated sulphuric acid to water*

Put 50 cm^3 of cold water in a 250 cm^3 beaker and take the temperature using a 200°C thermometer. Stir the water round, and in a steady stream pour in 50 cm^3 of cold concentrated sulphuric acid. Listen, observe any vapour evolved, and take the final temperature.

When concentrated sulphuric acid is mixed with water as in experiment 6.3 much heat is produced. A solution of equal volumes of cold water and cold concentrated sulphuric acid frequently attains a temperature of 120°C, steam is produced, and fizzing is heard as the acid is poured in. Although the mixture reaches 120°C it does not boil because it is not water, but 50 per cent sulphuric acid solution, which has a much higher boiling point than water.

Dilution should always be done this way because if water is added to concentrated sulphuric acid the first small quantity of water to touch the acid may boil and throw the mixture out of the beaker. Remember, 'Make the mixture as you oughta, add the acid to the water'.

Concentrated sulphuric acid, especially when hot, acts as an oxidizing agent. It will, for example, oxidize carbon to carbon dioxide.

$$\overset{\overset{\text{O}}{\overbrace{}}}{\underset{\underset{\text{R}}{\underbrace{}}}{C + 2H_2SO_4 \longrightarrow CO_2 + 2H_2O + 2SO_2}}$$

In any reaction in which sulphuric acid acts as an oxidizing agent, the acid is itself reduced to sulphur dioxide.

Because sulphuric acid is a strong acid with a high boiling point it can turn other acids out of their salts, and so can be used to make nitric acid from sodium nitrate, and hydrochloric acid from sodium chloride.

$$\begin{array}{c}\text{sulphuric} \\ \text{acid}\end{array} + \begin{array}{c}\text{sodium} \\ \text{nitrate}\end{array} \longrightarrow \begin{array}{c}\text{sodium hydrogen} \\ \text{sulphate}\end{array} + \begin{array}{c}\text{nitric} \\ \text{acid}\end{array}$$
$$H_2SO_4 + NaNO_3 \longrightarrow NaHSO_4 + HNO_3$$

$$\begin{array}{c}\text{sulphuric} \\ \text{acid}\end{array} + \begin{array}{c}\text{sodium} \\ \text{chloride}\end{array} \longrightarrow \begin{array}{c}\text{sodium hydrogen} \\ \text{sulphate}\end{array} + \begin{array}{c}\text{hydrogen} \\ \text{chloride}\end{array}$$
$$H_2SO_4 + NaCl \longrightarrow NaHSO_4 + HCl$$

For details see experiments 6.8 and 6.11. Other acidic properties are usually demonstrated using dilute sulphuric acid.

Experiment 6.4 The action of dilute sulphuric acid on sodium hydroxide solution–neutralization

Put approximately 25 cm^3 of dilute sulphuric acid in a 100 cm^3 beaker and add about 20 cm^3 of dilute sodium hydroxide solution (caustic soda). Remove a drop of the mixture on the end of a clean glass rod and test with litmus. If you are using litmus paper put the drop on to the paper but if you are using litmus solution put a drop of the solution on a white tile or microscope slide and add to this the drop on the end of the glass rod. If the solution is still acidic add sodium hydroxide solution a little at a time, testing after each addition until the indicator shows neither the acidic nor the alkaline colour, i.e., the solution is **neutral**. It is often advisable to use a dropper to add small volumes of the alkali. If you overshoot the neutral point and make the solution alkaline, use a fresh dropper to add some acid. When the solution is neutral boil away water from it until you have a hot saturated solution. To test when the hot solution is ready to crystallize dip in a cold dry glass rod. If the solution crystallizes on the rod when it is removed from the liquid set the beaker aside to cool.

ACIDS, BASES, AND SALTS

When the solution has crystallized filter it and examine some of the crystals, using a hand lens if they are small.

Sulphuric acid reacts with alkalis to form sulphates. If the alkali used is sodium hydroxide, sodium sulphate is formed.

$$H_2SO_4 + 2NaOH \longrightarrow Na_2SO_4 + 2H_2O$$

This is an example of an important type of reaction:

$$acid + base \longrightarrow salt + water$$

When the acid used is sulphuric acid the salt is a sulphate or bisulphate.

Experiment 6.5 *The action of dilute sulphuric acid on copper oxide*

Into a boiling tube or wide test-tube pour dilute sulphuric acid to a depth of about 3 cm. Boil the acid gently, remove the tube from the flame, and put in a little copper oxide powder. When the bubbling stops, boil the mixture again and add a little more copper oxide. Repeat this until the copper oxide does not all react but remains as a grey or black cloudiness in the solution. At this stage, all the original sulphuric acid is used. Add two more drops of acid and boil again to remove the last traces of copper oxide, then pour the hot solution into a cold watch-glass or evaporating dish. Crystals will probably form as the solution cools. If not, pour the liquid back into the test-tube and boil away some water to concentrate the solution. Then try again to obtain the copper sulphate crystals. Filter and examine the crystals made, using a hand lens if they are small.

Hot dilute sulphuric acid reacts with black copper oxide forming a blue solution of copper sulphate and water. This is another example of the general reaction:

$$acid + base \longrightarrow salt + water$$
$$H_2SO_4 + CuO \longrightarrow CuSO_4 + H_2O$$

If the copper sulphate is crystallized, copper sulphate pentahydrate crystals are formed ($CuSO_4 \cdot 5H_2O$).

Similar reactions would occur using other oxides which act as bases, e.g.,

$$ZnO + H_2SO_4 \longrightarrow ZnSO_4 + H_2O$$

Experiment 6.6 *The action of dilute sulphuric acid on carbonates*

Put dilute sulphuric acid to a depth of about 2 cm into four test-tubes and add small powdered samples of copper carbonate, zinc carbonate, sodium carbonate, and potassium carbonate. If fizzing (effervescence) takes place, collect some of the gas evolved as shown in Fig. 6.2.

(a) squeeze bulb

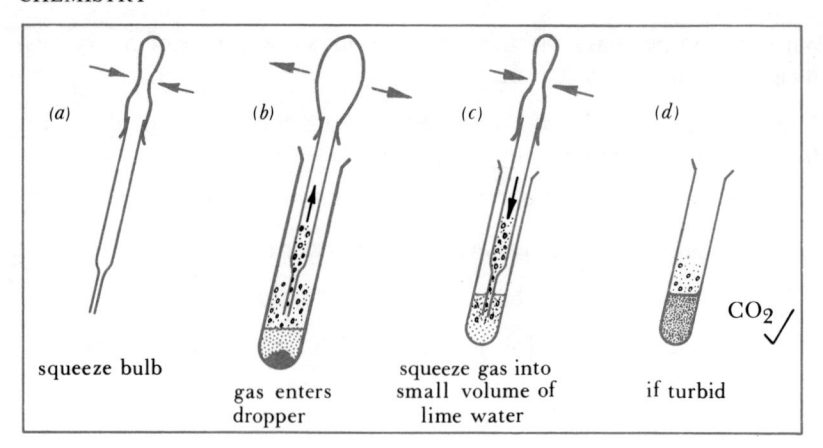

(b) gas enters dropper

(c) squeeze gas into small volume of lime water

(d) if turbid CO_2 ✓

Figure 6.2 Testing for carbon dioxide

Note which carbonates produce carbon dioxide, and the colours of the solutions left.

Dilute sulphuric acid reacts with all carbonates, producing carbon dioxide which causes fizzing or effervescence. A solution of a sulphate, and water are made at the same time, e.g.,

sulphuric acid + copper carbonate ⟶ copper sulphate + water + carbon dioxide

$$H_2SO_4 + CuCO_3 \longrightarrow CuSO_4 + H_2O + CO_2$$

Sodium hydrogen carbonate and potassium hydrogen carbonate react similarly.

$$H_2SO_4 + 2NaHCO_3 \longrightarrow Na_2SO_4 + 2H_2O + 2CO_2$$

Experiment 6.7 *The action of dilute sulphuric acid on metals*

Fill a test-tube to a depth of about $\frac{1}{2}$ cm with small pieces (chips or powder if possible) of metal, and add dilute sulphuric acid to a depth of about 2 cm. If there is a reaction and a gas is given off put your thumb on the end of the tube while gas collects for about a minute, then hold the mouth of the tube close to a flame and take your thumb off the end of the tube. A small pop indicates the presence of hydrogen made by the reaction between the metal and the sulphuric acid. In separate tubes try the reaction with magnesium, iron, lead, zinc, copper, and aluminium. If there is no reaction or if the reaction is very slow, heat the tube gently but do not boil the acid.

Dilute sulphuric acid reacts with certain metals forming hydrogen and a solution of a sulphate. The metals which do this are those which are above hydrogen in the electrochemical series (see page 168). Of these reactions, that

ACIDS, BASES, AND SALTS

between zinc and dilute sulphuric acid is used for a laboratory preparation of hydrogen; the reaction with aluminium is very slow.

SUMMARY OF SULPHURIC ACID

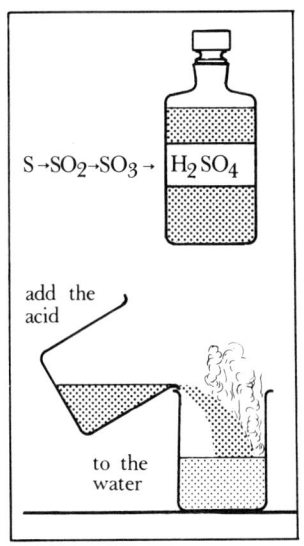

$S \rightarrow SO_2 \rightarrow SO_3 \rightarrow H_2SO_4$

Concentrated

Dense, oily, corrosive dangerous liquid; high boiling point;

dehydrates copper sulphate crystals, wood, sugar, flesh;

oxidizes when hot (e.g., $C \rightarrow CO_2$);

acts as an acid e.g., on NaCl forming HCl gas and on $NaNO_3$ forming HNO_3.

Dilute

Acts only as an acid;
  with alkalis gives salt + water,
  with bases gives salt + water,
  with carbonates gives salt + water + carbon dioxide,
  with Al, Mg, Zn, and Fe gives hydrogen and a salt.

add the acid to the water

Uses of sulphuric acid

Sulphuric acid has very many uses in a large number of different industries. Probably every manufacturing industry uses the acid or a product made from it at some stage of its processes.

Sulphuric acid is used concentrated in the soda-acid type of fire extinguisher (see Fig. 6.3). The reaction between the concentrated sulphuric acid and

concentrated sulphuric acid

sodium hydrogen carbonate solution

CO_2

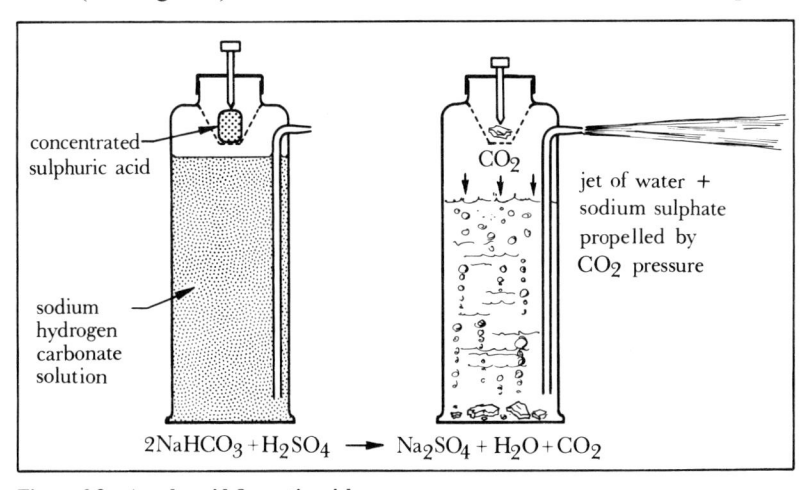

jet of water + sodium sulphate propelled by CO_2 pressure

$2NaHCO_3 + H_2SO_4 \longrightarrow Na_2SO_4 + H_2O + CO_2$

Figure 6.3 A soda-acid fire extinguisher

sodium hydrogen carbonate solution produces carbon dioxide under pressure which drives a jet of water on to the fire.

Dilute sulphuric acid containing about 19 per cent of the acid is used in lead acid accumulators for car, motor cycle, and submarine batteries. This battery acid is three times more concentrated than the usual dilute acid used in laboratories.

Sulphuric acid is used to make fertilizers such as ammonium sulphate and calcium superphosphate. Some synthetic detergents are made from crude oil fractions and concentrated sulphuric acid.

Sheet steel must be very clean before it can be plated with tin or zinc to make tin plate or galvanized steel. One method of cleaning steel is to dip sheets of it into dilute sulphuric acid, which reacts with the surface layer of iron oxide, dissolving it by an acid + base gives salt + water reaction, leaving a clean new steel surface.

Sulphuric acid is also used in petrol refining, for making other acids, and for making the white pigment titanium dioxide (which is used in most white paints) by reaction with an ore containing iron and titanium.

Hydrochloric acid HCl

Hydrochloric acid differs from the other two common acids in that it is a solution of a gas (hydrogen chloride) in water. It is possible for the gas to become freed from the solution, so concentrated hydrochloric acid fumes in air. When the solution of hydrochloric acid in water reaches the proportion of one-third hydrochloric acid to two-thirds water, the solution is saturated and no more hydrochloric acid can be dissolved in it. Therefore the most concentrated hydrochloric acid it is possible to make contains two-thirds water. This is still a strong acid, and although it is not as corrosive as concentrated sulphuric acid it should be treated with care.

Experiment 6.8   *Laboratory preparation of hydrochloric acid*

In the apparatus shown (Fig. 6.4) drop concentrated sulphuric acid slowly on to sodium chloride. Lead the hydrogen chloride gas into a beaker of water containing a piece of blue litmus paper. The funnel gives a large area of contact between the gas and the water and prevents the sucking back of water into the flask.

$$NaCl + H_2SO_4 \longrightarrow NaHSO_4 + HCl$$

When concentrated sulphuric acid is dropped on to sodium chloride the mixture bubbles and the colourless gas hydrogen chloride is given off. This gas dissolves readily in water making hydrochloric acid, and a piece of blue litmus paper in the water changes to red. The acid produced in this experi-

ACIDS, BASES, AND SALTS

ment could be made concentrated if enough gas were passed into the water. After the experiment sodium hydrogen sulphate is left in the flask.

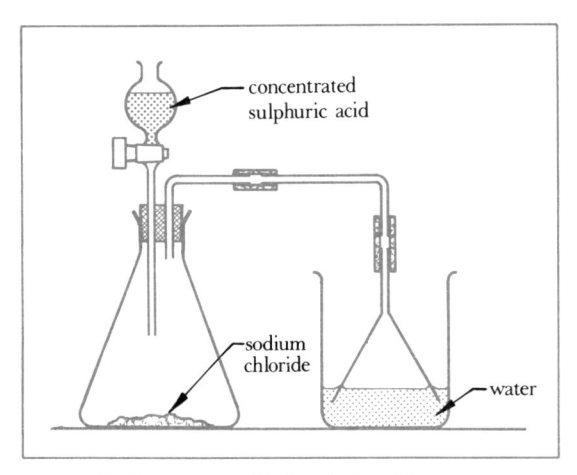

Figure 6.4 Preparation of hydrochloric acid

Hydrochloric acid is made industrially by burning hydrogen in an atmosphere of chlorine, or by allowing the gases to mix in the presence of a catalyst of activated charcoal. This produces hydrogen chloride gas, which is then dissolved in water.

$$H_2 + Cl_2 \longrightarrow 2HCl$$

Properties of hydrochloric acid

Concentrated hydrochloric acid is a colourless liquid which fumes slightly in air and has a choking smell. Damp blue litmus paper held in the fumes immediately turns red. If a glass rod dipped in concentrated ammonia solution is held near the mouth of the bottle, dense white fumes of ammonium chloride are produced. The ammonia solution gives off ammonia and this reacts with the hydrochloric acid in the fumes.

$$NH_3 + HCl \longrightarrow NH_4Cl$$

Experiment 6.9   *The reactions of dilute hydrochloric acid*

(*a*) Test the action of dilute hydrochloric acid on indicators such as blue litmus, pink phenolphthalein, and yellow methyl orange.

(*b*) Action on an alkali: take about 3 cm depth of dilute sodium hydroxide solution in a test-tube. Test this with an indicator and gradually add dilute hydrochloric acid until the acid and alkali have neutralized each other. Use

113

the method described in experiment 6.4. The sodium chloride made may be extracted by boiling the solution almost to dryness (**care: beware of spurting**), and the crystals examined.

(c) Action on a base: warm about 3 cm depth of dilute hydrochloric acid in a wide test-tube, and drop in zinc oxide a little at a time until some remains undissolved. Add a little more dilute hydrochloric acid to react with this zinc oxide.

(d) Action on a carbonate: put powdered sodium carbonate or crystals of sodium carbonate decahydrate in a test-tube to a depth of about $\frac{1}{2}$ cm, and then pour in dilute hydrochloric acid to a depth of about 2 cm. Test any gas evolved with lime-water, and observe the solution left in the test-tube after the sodium carbonate has reacted.

(e) Action on metals: put small pieces of a metal (chips or powder if possible) in a test-tube to a depth of about $\frac{1}{2}$ cm, and add dilute hydrochloric acid to a depth of about 2 cm. If any gas is evolved test it for hydrogen as described in experiment 6.7, and observe the colours of the solutions left in the test tube. Use magnesium, iron, lead, zinc, copper and aluminium for this experiment.

(f) Action on iron(II) sulphide (ferrous sulphide): take a small piece of iron(II) sulphide and if possible powder it. Drop the solid into an ignition tube containing about 1 cm depth of dilute hydrochloric acid. When some bubbles appear smell the product which is a gas, and then hold in the mouth of the ignition tube a strip of filter paper damped with lead nitrate solution. As soon as you have finished this experiment put the ignition tube into a fume cupboard.

Dilute hydrochloric acid shows all the typical reactions of an acid.

(a) Dilute hydrochloric acid turns litmus red, phenolphthalein colourless and methyl orange red.

(b) Dilute hydrochloric acid reacts with sodium hydroxide solution forming sodium chloride solution and water. This is a reaction of the type

$$\text{acid} + \text{base} \longrightarrow \text{salt} + \text{water}$$
$$HCl + NaOH \longrightarrow NaCl + H_2O$$

The point at which all the sodium hydroxide has been converted to sodium chloride can be determined using an indicator. In this example the base used is the alkali sodium hydroxide, but other alkalis would also produce chlorides by this reaction, which can be described as the **neutralization** of the acid by a base.

(c) Dilute hydrochloric acid reacts with zinc oxide forming zinc chloride solution and water.

$$2HCl + ZnO \longrightarrow ZnCl_2 + H_2O$$

ACIDS, BASES, AND SALTS

This is another example of an acid reacting with a base to give salt and water, but here the base is an oxide of a metal.

(d) Dilute hydrochloric acid reacts with carbonates forming carbon dioxide, a salt which is always a chloride, and water. Fizzing is seen and heard as the carbon dioxide escapes.

$$\text{acid} + \text{a carbonate} \longrightarrow \text{salt} + \text{water} + \text{carbon dioxide}$$
$$2HCl + Na_2CO_3 \longrightarrow 2NaCl + H_2O + CO_2$$

The usual laboratory preparation of carbon dioxide uses the reaction of hydrochloric acid on calcium carbonate (experiment 5.4), which is an example of this type of reaction.

(e) Dilute hydrochloric acid reacts with magnesium, aluminium (slowly), zinc, and iron giving off hydrogen, which can be seen and heard fizzing, and forming a colourless solution of the chloride of each metal.

$$Mg + 2HCl \longrightarrow MgCl_2 + H_2$$
$$Zn + 2HCl \longrightarrow ZnCl_2 + H_2$$
$$Fe + 2HCl \longrightarrow FeCl_2 + H_2$$
$$2Al + 6HCl \longrightarrow 2AlCl_3 + 3H_2$$

(f) Dilute hydrochloric acid reacts with iron(II) sulphide (ferrous sulphide) forming hydrogen sulphide and iron(II) chloride solution.

$$FeS + 2HCl \longrightarrow FeCl_2 + H_2S$$

Hydrogen sulphide can be detected by its obnoxious smell. Although hydrogen sulphide is poisonous its smell is so objectionable that even a small amount of it is readily detected, and poisoning by it is quite uncommon. A chemical test for hydrogen sulphide is its action on lead nitrate solution, which forms a black precipitate of lead sulphide, PbS.

$$Pb(NO_3)_2 + H_2S \longrightarrow PbS + 2HNO_3$$

Concentrated hydrochloric acid also acts as an acid. With indicators, alkalis, bases, carbonates, metals, and iron(II) sulphide (ferrous sulphide) it reacts similarly to dilute hydrochloric acid but more vigorously.

Concentrated hydrochloric acid also can be oxidized. Oxidation can consist of adding oxygen or removing hydrogen; when concentrated hydrochloric acid has hydrogen removed it forms chlorine.

Experiment 6.10 *Oxidation of concentrated hydrochloric acid by potassium permanganate*

Put a small pile of potassium permanganate in the bottom of a gas jar and pour in concentrated hydrochloric acid to a depth of about $\frac{1}{2}$ cm. Put a cover on the jar, observe the reaction, and hold in the jar some damp blue litmus paper.

Potassium permanganate oxidizes cold concentrated hydrochloric acid to chlorine by the removal of hydrogen. The green gas chlorine is seen in the gas jar and the damp blue litmus is first turned red, and then bleached by the chlorine.

Manganese(IV) oxide (manganese dioxide) MnO_2 will also oxidize concentrated hydrochloric acid to chlorine, but the hydrochloric acid must be warm for this reaction (see experiment 4.7).

SUMMARY OF HYDROCHLORIC ACID

Industry
$H_2 + Cl_2 \longrightarrow 2HCl(gas)$
Laboratory
$NaCl + H_2SO_4 \longrightarrow NaHSO_4 + HCl(gas)$
$\longrightarrow H_2O \longrightarrow$

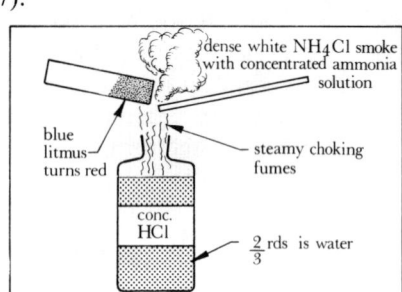

(diagram: conc. HCl bottle — dense white NH_4Cl smoke with concentrated ammonia solution; blue litmus turns red; steamy choking fumes; $\frac{2}{3}$rds is water)

Dilute hydrochloric acid reacts with:
an alkali, giving a chloride (acid + base → salt + water);
a base, giving a chloride (acid + base → salt + water);
a carbonate, giving a chloride + carbon dioxide;
Mg,Al,Zn, or Fe giving a chloride + hydrogen;
iron(II) sulphide (ferrous sulphide), giving H_2S (smell!).

Concentrated hydrochloric acid reacts with:
alkalis, bases, carbonates, metals and iron(II);
sulphide similarly to dilute;
MnO_2 or $KMnO_4$ forming chlorine by oxidation.

Uses of hydrochloric acid

Hydrochloric acid is used to make ammonium chloride (for dry cells) by reaction with ammonia solution.

It is used like sulphuric acid for cleaning metals before coating with tin or zinc.

It is used in industry for the manufacture of many drugs, dyes, and plastics.

Nitric acid HNO_3

Demonstration experiment 6.11   *Making concentrated nitric acid*

Into the distilling flask put about 20 g of sodium nitrate and cover it with concentrated sulphuric acid. Heat gently and collect the distillate of very

ACIDS, BASES, AND SALTS

concentrated nitric acid in the water-cooled boiling tube. Note that there is no bare cork or rubber in the apparatus. Polythene is used as this has a better resistance to attack by nitric acid.

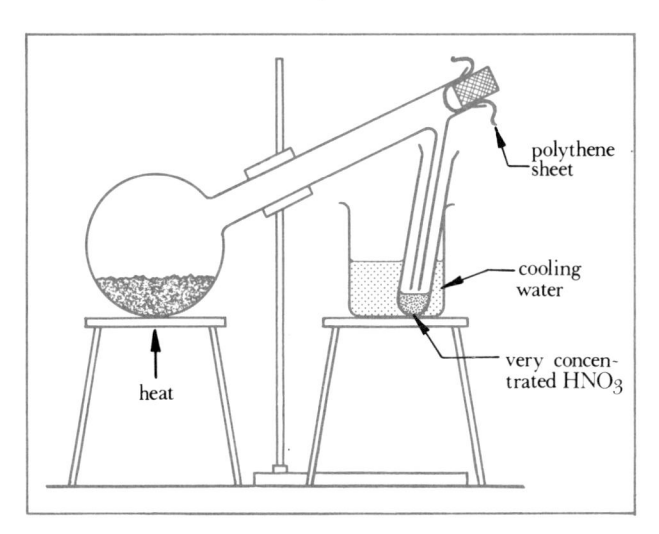

Figure 6.5 Making concentrated nitric acid HNO_3

Nitric acid is made in the laboratory by boiling concentrated sulphuric acid with sodium nitrate.

$$\text{sulphuric acid} + \text{sodium nitrate} \longrightarrow \text{sodium hydrogen sulphate} + \text{nitric acid}$$
$$H_2SO_4 + NaNO_3 \longrightarrow NaHSO_4 + HNO_3$$

Very concentrated nitric acid distils from this mixture and may be condensed. This acid is very corrosive and is often brown because it contains dissolved nitrogen dioxide which is a brown gas. The reaction is an example of the action of sulphuric acid, which has a very high boiling point, turning the more volatile nitric acid out of its salt, sodium nitrate.

Nitric acid is made industrially by a process involving the **catalytic oxidation** of ammonia. Ammonia, NH_3, is oxidized by mixing it with air and passing the mixture over a catalyst of hot platinum gauze.

$$\text{ammonia} + \text{oxygen} \longrightarrow \text{nitrogen monoxide} + \text{steam}$$
$$4NH_3 + 5O_2 \longrightarrow 4NO + 6H_2O$$

In this example of oxidation the ammonia has both lost hydrogen and gained oxygen. When cooled, the nitrogen monoxide (nitric oxide) reacts with more oxygen forming nitrogen dioxide, NO_2.

$$2NO + O_2 \longrightarrow 2NO_2$$

CHEMISTRY

The nitrogen dioxide then reacts with water and oxygen forming nitric acid. This takes place in a series of reactions which may be summarized

$$4NO_2 + O_2 + 2H_2O \longrightarrow 4HNO_3$$

The concentrated nitric acid produced by this process contains some water.

Properties of nitric acid

The concentrated nitric acid usually supplied to laboratories is a colourless liquid containing about two-thirds nitric acid and one-third water. The acid fumes slightly and has a characteristic smell. It must be treated with care because it is very harmful to clothes, flesh, benches, and floors. Apply quickly a large volume of water to any spillage.

Demonstration experiment 6.12   *The actions of warm concentrated nitric acid on carbon and on iron*

(a) Put concentrated nitric acid to a depth of about 2 cm in a boiling tube. Warm the acid, remove it from the flame, and, being careful not to point the mouth of the tube at anybody, drop in a piece of charcoal about the size of a pea. Observe any gas evolved.

(b) Put a small quantity of iron filings in a test tube and add concentrated nitric acid to a depth of about 2 cm. Observe any reaction.

Concentrated nitric acid is an oxidizing agent, especially when hot. In experiment 6.12(a) the nitric acid oxidizes the carbon to carbon dioxide, and is itself reduced to nitrogen dioxide which is given off as brown fumes.

$$C + 4HNO_3 \longrightarrow 2H_2O + 4NO_2 + CO_2$$

In experiment 6.12(b) the concentrated nitric acid attacks the iron, oxidizing it to iron oxide. The nitric acid itself is reduced to nitrogen dioxide and some bubbling is seen. On the surface of the iron filings a thin film of iron oxide forms and this film protects the iron from further attack so the reaction stops. Iron coated in this way is said to have been made **passive**.

Dilute nitric acid also acts as an oxidizing agent but not so vigorously as the concentrated acid.

Experiment 6.13   *The action of concentrated nitric acid on copper*

To a few copper turnings in a test-tube add concentrated nitric acid to a depth of about 2 cm. Observe the reaction but do not breathe in the gas made.

Concentrated nitric acid reacts vigorously with copper. The mixture froths, and a large volume of the brown gas nitrogen dioxide is made. A blue solution of copper nitrate is left.

$$Cu + 4HNO_3 \longrightarrow Cu(NO_3)_2 + 2H_2O + 2NO_2$$

ACIDS, BASES, AND SALTS

Experiment 6.14 *The reactions of dilute nitric acid*

The reactions of dilute nitric acid with indicators, alkalis, bases, and carbonates may be investigated using the methods from experiment 6.9, parts (*a*), (*b*), (*c*), and (*d*). (*e*) Action on metals: put dilute nitric acid to a depth of 2 cm into two test-tubes. Into one put water until the depth of liquid is 4 cm, and also a piece of magnesium; put into the other a piece of zinc. Observe the reactions and test for hydrogen any gases made.

Dilute nitric acid has the reactions of a typical acid: it changes the colours of indicators, forms salts (nitrates) with alkalis and bases, and gives carbon dioxide with carbonates. For example,

$$HNO_3 + NaOH \longrightarrow NaNO_3 + H_2O$$
$$2HNO_3 + CuO \longrightarrow Cu(NO_3)_2 + H_2O$$
$$2HNO_3 + Na_2CO_3 \longrightarrow 2NaNO_3 + CO_2 + H_2O$$

Dilute nitric acid has complicated reactions with metals, forming nitrates and various oxides of nitrogen. The brown gas nitrogen dioxide is usually one of the products. Magnesium is the only metal which makes hydrogen with dilute nitric acid, which should be more dilute than the usual bench acid.

$$Mg + 2HNO_3 \longrightarrow Mg(NO_3)_2 + H_2$$

SUMMARY OF NITRIC ACID

Industry

$$N_2 \xrightarrow[\text{Haber}]{H_2} NH_3 \xrightarrow[\text{oxn.}]{\text{cat.}} NO \xrightarrow{O_2} NO_2 \xrightarrow{H_2O} HNO_3$$

Laboratory

$$NaNO_3 + H_2SO_4 \longrightarrow NaHSO_4 + HNO_3$$

Concentrated nitric acid *oxidizes*:

carbon to CO_2
iron to iron oxide (film, passive)
copper to copper nitrate

In all these cases NO_2 is given off.

Dilute nitric acid *acts as an acid*:
with indicators
with alkali (e.g., NaOH) gives a nitrate (acid + base → salt + water)
with a base (e.g., CuO) gives a nitrate (acid + base → salt + water)
with a carbonate (e.g., Na_2CO_3) gives salt + water + carbon dioxide
with magnesium gives hydrogen

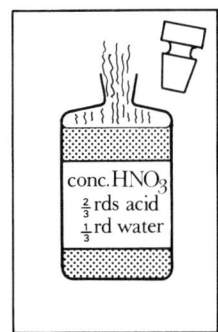

CHEMISTRY

Uses of nitric acid

Nitric acid is used to make nitrates which are used as fertilizers because they provide a supply of fixed nitrogen (see Fig. 10.5). Examples include ammonium nitrate and nitro-chalk (a mixture of equal weights of ammonium nitrate and calcium carbonate). Nitric acid is used extensively to make explosives. Many high explosives (e.g., nitro-glycerine and TNT) are related to nitric acid. The nitro parts of their molecules contain the groups $-NO_3$ or $-NO_2$, and the oxygen in these groups is used in the burning of the rest of the molecule.

Carbonic acid H_2CO_3

Carbonic acid is made by dissolving carbon dioxide in water.

$$H_2O + CO_2 \rightleftharpoons H_2CO_3$$

This is a reversible reaction so if the acid is heated, or even left in an open beaker, it splits up and carbon dioxide is given off, leaving water in the beaker. Carbon dioxide is not very soluble in water so high pressure is often used to increase the amount dissolving. Even when high pressure is used the carbonic acid made is so weakly acidic that it can be drunk, when it is known as soda-water (see Fig. 6.6). The acidity of soda-water is responsible for its sharp taste.

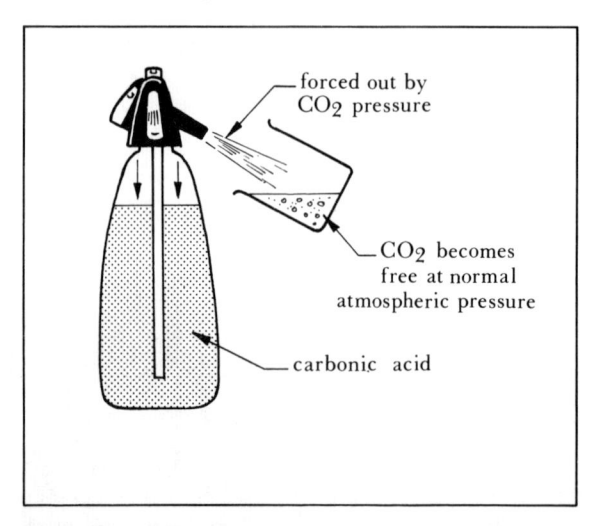

Figure 6.6 A soda-syphon

The reaction of carbonic acid with calcium carbonate to form a solution of calcium hydrogen carbonate (calcium bicarbonate) is involved in the formations of caverns in limestone areas, the production of temporarily hard

ACIDS, BASES, AND SALTS

water, and the clearing of cloudy limewater when a large excess of carbon dioxide is passed through it (see Fig. 8.9).

$$CaCO_3 + H_2CO_3 \longrightarrow Ca(HCO_3)_2$$

Acetic acid CH_3COOH

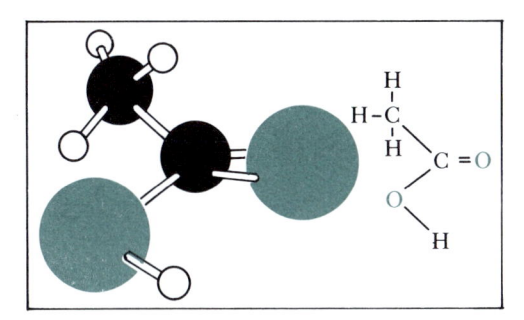

Figure 6.7 An acetic acid molecule

Fig. 6.7 shows a model of the molecule of acetic acid, in which the black spheres represent carbon atoms, the white spheres hydrogen atoms, and the blue spheres oxygen atoms. The formula of acetic acid, which is an organic compound, is sometimes written $C_2H_4O_2$, but CH_3COOH is usually preferred because this tells us more about the arrangement of the atoms within the molecule. Although acetic acid is not as strong an acid as sulphuric, hydrochloric, or nitric acid it should be handled with care because concentrated acetic acid burns skin, i.e., it is **caustic**.

Experiment 6.15 *The properties of acetic acid*

(*a*) Pour a little concentrated acetic acid into a test tube. Smell the liquid cautiously then tip the tube from side to side and observe whether the acid is a viscous or a mobile liquid.

(*b*) Use the methods described in experiment 6.9 to investigate the action of dilute acetic acid on indicators, sodium carbonate, and magnesium.

Concentrated acetic acid is a colourless, viscous (thick) liquid with a characteristic sharp smell. Although it is a weak acid, even dilute acetic acid can change the colour of indicators, react with carbonates giving off carbon dioxide, and react with magnesium giving off hydrogen. It will also neutralize bases forming salts which are called acetates.

As the smell suggests, there is acetic acid in vinegar, which is a solution usually containing 4 to 5 per cent of the acid. Vinegar may be made from wine which has gone sour, but much vinegar is now made synthetically. A non-brewed vinegar contains acetic acid (made from crude oil), water, and charred sugar (caramel) as a colouring material.

A very large amount of acetic acid is used to produce cellulose acetate. This is made into acetate rayon which is sometimes called artificial silk.

How acidic is an acid—pH

So far we have described substances as acidic (e.g., H_2SO_4), alkaline (e.g., NaOH solution), or neutral (e.g., H_2O or CO). There are, however, gradations of acidity and alkalinity and these are measured on a scale of numbers called the pH scale. The part of the pH scale most used runs from pH 0 to pH 14.

← pH 2 and lower	← pH 5	← pH 7 →	pH 9 →	pH 12 and higher →
acidic, e.g., very dilute HCl	slightly acidic, e.g., cabbage juice	neutral, e.g., pure water	slightly alkaline, e.g., milk of magnesia	alkaline, e.g., very dilute NaOH solution

Demonstration experiment 6.16   *Colour changes and pH using Universal Indicator*

Fill a large beaker almost to the top with tap water and add enough universal indicator to give a distinctly coloured solution. Observe the colour then add ten to twenty drops of sodium hydroxide solution from a dropper. Stir thoroughly and note the colour of the mixture. Wash the dropper and add two or three drops of dilute hydrochloric acid. Stir and notice the colour. Repeat the addition of hydrochloric acid until no further colour change takes place. Refer to the colour chart provided with the indicator and determine the pH at each stage of the experiment.

A universal indicator is a mixture of indicators which can show as many as six colours in solutions of different pH value. For example, BTL universal indicator is:

purple	above	pH 12
blue	at	pH 10
green	at	pH 8
yellow	at	pH 6
orange	at	pH 4
pink	at	pH 2
red	at	pH 1 or below

ACIDS, BASES, AND SALTS

Intermediate pH readings may be made by matching colours. There are, for example, various shades of orange about pH 4 for BTL universal indicator.

Many types of universal indicator are available for the determination of pH. Gardeners use them to check the acidity or alkalinity of soil before planting certain types of plants, e.g., rhododendrons need a much more acidic soil than do peas or beans. Gardeners call an acidic soil a sour soil and an alkaline soil a lime soil. If necessary they neutralize excess acidity with slaked lime (calcium hydroxide) which is an alkali, and they put peat on a soil which is too alkaline.

Experiment 6.17 *The pH of various substances*

Use universal indicator to determine the pH of indigestion powder or tablets, lemon juice, household bleach, toothpaste, acid drops, juice from a potato, rhubarb juice, soda-water, and sodium bicarbonate.

If the substance is a liquid, dip in indicator paper, or add two drops of liquid indicator to $\frac{1}{2}$ cm depth of the substance in a test-tube. If the substance is a solid, crush it in a mortar with a little water then dip in indicator paper, or add two drops of liquid indicator.

Many substances we eat or drink are mildly acidic or alkaline. Substances with a sharp taste, such as lemon juice, acid drops, or soda water, are usually acidic. The digestive juices in the stomach contain hydrochloric acid and are therefore acidic, but they become too strongly acidic in people suffering from certain types of indigestion. When this takes place alkalis are taken to reduce the acidity, so that indigestion powders usually contain substances such as magnesium hydroxide, magnesium carbonate, or calcium carbonate which react with acids.

Summary of acids, bases, and salts

An acid is a compound containing hydrogen which turns litmus red, reacts with a base to give a salt plus water, and reacts with a carbonate to give a salt plus water plus carbon dioxide.

A base is the oxide of a metal, e.g., copper oxide. Some bases react with water to give hydroxides. These hydroxides are called alkalis. For example, Na_2O forms $NaOH$. Bases and alkalis react with acids to form salts plus water.

A salt is made by the reaction of an acid with a base, an acid with an alkali, an acid with a carbonate, or an acid with a metal.

Various gradations of acidity and alkalinity may be measured using the pH scale. Low numbers such as 1 and 2 indicate acidic solutions, pH 7 is neutral, and pH 13 and 14 are alkaline.

CHEMISTRY

The weights of atoms and molecules

In experiment 6.4 you made sodium sulphate by adding sodium hydroxide solution gradually to dilute sulphuric acid, then testing the solution many times to see when the correct amount of sodium hydroxide had been added. This rather tedious method would not have been necessary if you had known the correct weights of sodium hydroxide and sulphuric acid to use. The weights can be calculated by a method you are going to learn. One molecule of sulphuric acid reacts with two molecules of sodium hydroxide, i.e., the two atoms of hydrogen, one atom of sulphur, and four atoms of oxygen in sulphuric acid react with the two atoms of sodium, two atoms of oxygen, and two atoms of hydrogen in the sodium hydroxide. To calculate the weights of the two compounds we need to know the weights of the various atoms.

Atomic weights

The weight of an atom of sodium is

approximately 0·00000000000000000000004 g.

This is not a convenient number to remember and use, so instead of weighing atoms in grammes we use another scale in which the weights of atoms are assigned numbers based on calling carbon 12. To understand how the weights are determined, consider the imaginary experiment shown in Fig. 6.8.

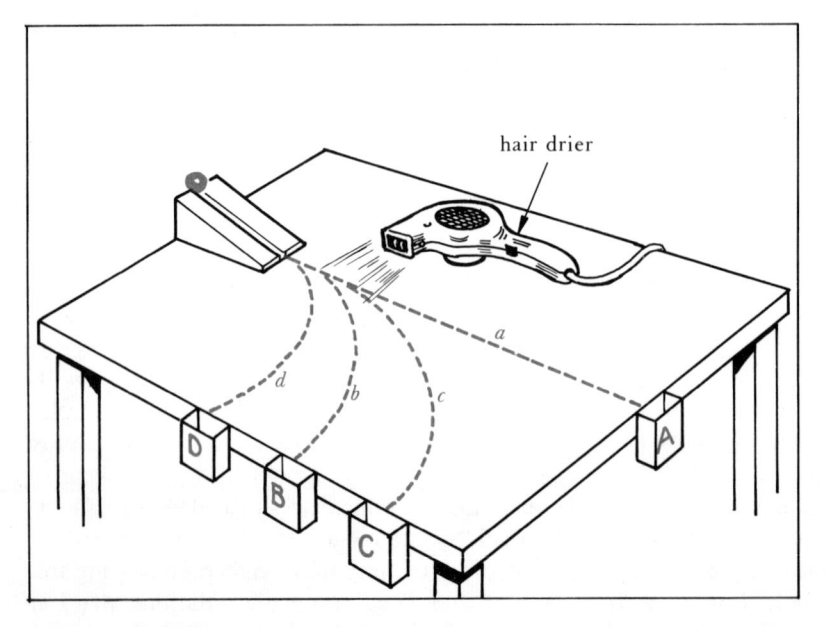

Figure 6.8 Rolling balls across a table

ACIDS, BASES, AND SALTS

If a golf ball is rolled down the channel in the block of wood it will roll across the table along track *a* into box *A*. If the hair dryer is switched on the air blast will deflect the ball so that it follows track *b* into box *B*. Any number of golf balls rolled down the slot will follow the same track if they all start from the same place on the block. Suppose now a table tennis ball rolls down the block: is it more likely to follow track *c* or *d*? Which of these two tracks would a heavy steel ball-bearing be likely to follow?

This experiment is a method which could be used to sort a mixture of table tennis balls, golf balls, and ball-bearings. The lightest (table tennis) balls would be deflected most by the air blast and fall into box *D*, and the heaviest (ball-bearings) would be deflected least and fall into box *C*. If a ball of unknown weight were rolled down the slope we could compare its weight with that of a table tennis ball, a golf ball, and a ball-bearing by seeing what track it followed.

A similar experiment can be done with atoms (see Fig. 6.9). The atoms are converted into charged atoms (ions) and shot out of an ion gun in a fine

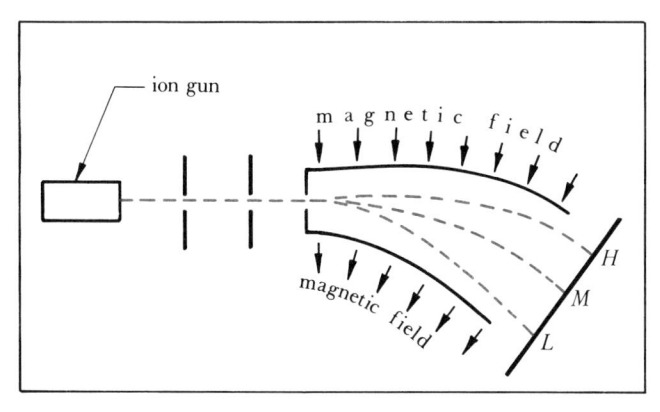

Figure 6.9 Sorting out atoms by weight

beam. They are deflected by a magnetic field and fall on a photographic plate. Light atoms are deflected most, medium-weight atoms next most, and the most massive atoms least of all. Dots are made where the ions fall on the photographic plate, and when this is developed, the relative weights of the atoms can be worked out, giving results such as H = 1·008, O = 15·999, and Na = 22·990. To simplify arithmetic in elementary work it is usual to express these to the nearest whole number, e.g., H = 1, O = 16, Na = 23. A table of approximate atomic weights appears in Appendix 5.

Formula weights

As was pointed out in chapter 1, atoms do not usually stay single, but join together to form molecules, so we need to be able to calculate the total

CHEMISTRY

weights of the atoms in each formula—the formula weight. The weight of a formula is determined by adding together the weights of all its atoms. For example, the formula weight of oxygen O_2 is $2 \times 16 = 32$. The formula weight of sulphur dioxide SO_2 is $32 + 2 \times 16 = 64$. The formula weight of sulphuric acid H_2SO_4 is $2 \times 1 + 32 + 4 \times 16 = 98$. The formula weight of calcium hydroxide $Ca(OH)_2$ is $40 + 2(16 + 1) = 74$. (The 2 outside the bracket in $Ca(OH)_2$ multiplies both the oxygen and the hydrogen.) The formula weight of copper sulphate pentahydrate $CuSO_4.5H_2O$ is $64 + 32 + 4 \times 16 + 5(2 \times 1 + 16) = 250$. The 5 multiplies all the H_2O.

Now try to work out the formula weights of:
(a) magnesium oxide (b) sodium oxide (c) copper chloride
(d) sulphur trioxide SO_3 (e) magnesium hydroxide (f) ammonium chloride
(g) ammonium carbonate (h) calcium hydrogen carbonate (calcium bicarbonate)

The formulae and the answers are given at the end of the chapter.

Percentage composition

The compound calcium oxide CaO has a formula weight of $40 + 16 = 56$. Forty of these fifty-six parts are calcium so

$$\% \text{ Ca} = \frac{40}{56} \times \frac{100}{1} = 71\%$$

In a similar way we can calculate the percentage of sodium in sodium oxide. The formula weight of sodium oxide Na_2O is $2 \times 23 + 16 = 62$.

$$\% \text{ Na} = \frac{2 \times 23}{62} \times \frac{100}{1} = 74\%$$

Now try to work out the percentages of:

(i) sulphur in sulphur trioxide
(j) copper in anhydrous copper sulphate
(k) water in copper sulphate pentahydrate

Reacting weights

Using formula weights and equations, the weights of reacting substances can be calculated. For the burning of sulphur the equation is $S + O_2 \rightarrow SO_2$.
 The atomic weight of sulphur is 32
 The formula weight of sulphur dioxide is $32 + 2 \times 16 = 64$
Thus from 32 units of sulphur 64 units of sulphur dioxide are made. The units

ACIDS, BASES, AND SALTS

may be grammes, kilogrammes, pounds, tons, or any other unit. For example:

32 g of sulphur produce 64 g of sulphur dioxide
32 tonnes of sulphur produce 64 tonnes of sulphur dioxide

Let us look at another example: what weight of magnesium oxide is made by burning 4·8 g of magnesium? The equation is $2Mg + O_2 \rightarrow 2MgO$.

The atomic weight of magnesium is 24
The formula weight of magnesium oxide is $24 + 16 = 40$

It is useful to underline substances whose weight is known or asked about, and to put their atomic or formula weights under the equation, multiplying each by the figure in front of its formula. The equation becomes

$$\underline{\frac{2Mg}{2 \times 24}} + O_2 \longrightarrow \underline{\frac{2MgO}{2 \times 40}}$$

Translating to grammes we have

48 g magnesium produce 80 g magnesium oxide

This is not the answer required, which must be worked out by proportion thus

1 g magnesium produces $\frac{80}{48}$ g magnesium oxide

4·8 g magnesium produce $\frac{80 \times 4·8}{48}$ g magnesium oxide

i.e., 4·8 g magnesium produce 8·0 g magnesium oxide.

Note that in calculations of this type it is not necessary to work out all the atomic or formula weights in the equation.

Summary of reacting weight calculations

(i) Write and balance the equation for the reaction.

(ii) Underline in the equation the substances whose weights are given or asked about.

(iii) Work out the atomic or formula weights of the substances underlined.

(iv) Write these under the equation multiplying each by any figure in front of its formula.

(v) Translate to grammes, kilogrammes or other units.

(vi) Work out the answer by proportion.

Now try to do these examples:

(*l*) What weight of sodium chloride can be made from 4·0 grammes of sodium hydroxide by reaction with hydrochloric acid?

127

CHEMISTRY

(m) What weight of zinc is needed to react with acid containing 3·65 grammes of hydrogen chloride?

(n) What weight of sulphur trioxide is made when 8·0 kilogrammes of sulphur dioxide is oxidized?

(o) What weight of iron(III) oxide (ferric oxide) reacts with concentrated hydrochloric acid to produce 65 grammes of iron(III) chloride (ferric chloride)?

(p) What weight of nitric acid could be made by heating 17 grammes of sodium nitrate with concentrated sulphuric acid?

Answers to numerical problems in this chapter

(a) MgO 40
(b) Na_2O 62
(c) $CuCl_2$ 135
(d) SO_3 80
(e) $Mg(OH)_2$ 58
(f) NH_4Cl 53·5
(g) $(NH_4)_2CO_3$ 96
(h) $Ca(HCO_3)_2$ 162
(i) SO_3 40%
(j) $CuSO_4$ 40%
(k) $CuSO_4 \cdot 5H_2O$ 36%
(l) 5·85 g
(m) 3·25 g
(n) 10 kg
(o) 32 g
(p) 12·6 g

Questions

1. If you knew that four unlabelled bottles contained distilled water, dilute nitric acid, dilute sulphuric acid, and lime-water, describe how you would do a series of tests to find out which was which.

2. Name an example of (a) an acidic oxide, (b) an indicator, (c) an acid which is always a solution in water, (d) a neutral oxide, (e) a dehydrating agent, (f) a brown gas, (g) a viscous liquid, (h) a substance whose pH is 7.

3. Give an example of sulphuric acid acting as (a) an acid, (b) an oxidizing agent, (c) a dehydrating agent. In each case describe what you would see as the reaction went on, and give a chemical equation.

4. How, and under what conditions of temperature and concentration does nitric acid react with (a) iron, (b) copper, (c) sodium carbonate, (d) magnesium?

5. Draw a flow-chart for hydrochloric acid, showing two preparations, and its reactions with MnO_2, NaOH, CuO, $CaCO_3$, Fe, Zn, FeS, and NH_3 (from ammonia solution).

6. Make a table comparing the preparation, physical properties, action on magnesium, action on sodium hydroxide, and uses of sulphuric, nitric, hydrochloric, and acetic acids.

7. An advertisement claims that a certain indigestion remedy is 'more effective at neutralizing acids' than others on the market. Describe how you would check this claim by a laboratory experiment.

ACIDS, BASES, AND SALTS

8. Determine the formula weights of (a) methane CH_4, (b) nitric acid, (c) chlorine, (d) sodium hydrogen carbonate, (e) ammonium sulphate, (f) potassium sulphate, (g) acetic acid.

9. What are the percentages by weight of (a) hydrogen in methane CH_4, (b) carbon in acetic acid, (c) magnesium in magnesium oxide, (d) carbon in ammonium carbonate?

10. What weight of:
   (a) potassium hydroxide will react with a solution containing 49 g of sulphuric acid?
   (b) calcium oxide is made by heating strongly 10 g calcium carbonate?
   (c) iron is needed to produce 7·6 g of iron(II) sulphate (ferrous sulphate) by reaction with dilute sulphuric acid?
   (d) sodium nitrate is needed to produce 30 g of sodium hydrogen sulphate by reaction with concentrated sulphuric acid?

7

Metals old and new

Early man used to dig using a spade made from the bone of an animal, and his wife would pound grain using two stones. The metals from which modern spades, mincers, and food mixers are made are among the most important of the new materials which make our life easier and more comfortable today. If a metal is to be used extensively it must be present in the Earth's crust in masses large enough to be worth digging out, the extraction from the ore must not be too difficult, and the properties of the metal itself must be appropriate to the use—shininess for jewellery, corrosion resistance for chemical plant, high melting point for lamp filaments, low density for aircraft parts, and so on.

Metals and non-metals

Most people would agree that gold and copper were metals and, if asked, would say that a metal was a hard, shiny, heavy solid which was cold to the touch. There are, however, metals which are soft (e.g., potassium), dull (e.g., lead), low in density (sodium floats on water), and liquid at room temperature (mercury). Also, the hardest substance known, and one of the shiniest when polished, is diamond, which is certainly not a metal. These points show that it is hard to make up an exact definition of a metal using physical properties such as hardness, shine, density, malleability (the ability to be beaten into thin sheets), and ductility (the ability to be drawn into a wire). Even the fact that metals, without exception, conduct electricity is not much use, because graphite and gas carbon conduct electricity. There are usually exceptions to the physical properties in the table below, and a metal or non-metal will have most but not all of the properties listed. Investigation of the physical properties mentioned so far involves only physical changes such as polishing the metal, or making a dent to assess its hardness. The investigation of chemical properties involves chemical changes such as turning the metal into another substance, for example, a metal oxide. When the oxides are classified, using experiments similar to experiment 6.1, it is found that all metals have at least one basic oxide (that is, an oxide which reacts with acid forming salt and water). Another distinguishing chemical property is that when a metal forms a simple ion it is always a cation (positive ion) such as Na^+ or Mg^{++}, while a non-metal forming a simple ion always gives an anion (negative ion) such as the chloride ion Cl^- or the oxide ion O^{--}

Table 7.1 **Properties of metals and non-metals**

METAL	NON-METAL
Usual physical properties	
solid at room temperature	may be solid, liquid or gas at room temperature
shiny	dull
high density	low density
good conduction of heat and electricity	poor conduction of heat and electricity
malleable and ductile	not malleable or ductile
Chemical properties	
always has at least one basic oxide	never has a basic oxide oxide usually acidic
forms positive ions—cations	forms negative ions—anions

Although gold, silver, copper, and sodium are clearly metals, and oxygen, sulphur, and chlorine clearly non-metals there is no exact borderline between the two classes. Some elements have properties intermediate between a metal and a non-metal and are called **metalloids**. Silicon and germanium are typical metalloids. Since they are neither very good nor very poor conductors of electricity, silicon and germanium are called semiconductors and are used to make semiconducting devices such as diodes and transistors. These metalloids undergo some of the most thorough purification processes performed in any industry before they are suitable to be raw materials for making semiconducting devices. The finished transistors and diodes are small, light, robust, cheap to make and run, and have made possible not only transistor radios but large computers.

Grouping things together

This exercise on grouping similar things together shows that we make groups, that is, classify things, in the way most useful for our immediate purpose. The metal/metalloid/non-metal classification is only one of many possible ways in which we can arrange the chemical elements. We could do it according to their oxidizing powers, the colours of their oxides, their use-

CHEMISTRY

fulness as catalysts, or the number of electrons in their outer shell. Grouping the elements in all these different ways produces a similar arrangement which is often written in a form known as the Periodic Table of the elements.

Figure 7.1 In how many ways can you separate these things into two groups?

A copy of the table appears at the back of the book. Elements with similar chemical and physical properties such as sodium and potassium; silicon and germanium; helium, neon, and argon; and chlorine, bromine, and iodine all occur close together in the table. This method includes the metal/non-metal classification because all the non-metals appear towards the top right-hand corner of the table.

Having discussed what metals are, and some of the ways in which they differ from non-metals, we shall now consider the properties of some well-known metals.

Silver and gold Ag and Au

Silver and gold have been known and used since prehistoric times. Because they are expensive, and have fairly good resistance to corrosion (eating away by chemical attack), they are called precious or noble metals. Both silver and gold can be found **native**, which means uncombined with other elements,

METALS OLD AND NEW

and so they need only be separated from rock particles and then melted before use. This simple process explains why they were used in the early history of man, before complicated extractions were possible. Gold is still found native, but most of the silver is now extracted from silver sulphide by chemical processes, as supplies of native silver are very small.

Silver has good resistance to attack by air and water, but compounds containing sulphur tarnish the surface by forming black silver sulphide Ag_2S. This is seen to happen when silver is exposed to an industrial atmosphere polluted by hydrogen sulphide, and when an egg containing sulphur compounds is eaten with a silver-plated spoon. The fact that gold rings and other ornamental articles are always shiny indicates that gold is resistant to attack by air and water. Pure gold is malleable and can be beaten into sheets so thin that a gold coin as big as a fivepenny piece would cover a football pitch if beaten out. This gold leaf is used for gilding, on expensive books for example. Gold used for jewellery and ornaments is usually hardened by the addition of silver or an alloy of silver and copper. (Any mixture of metals is known as an **alloy**.) The amounts of silver, or silver/copper alloy, added are described by carat measure. One carat is 1/24th part so 22 carat gold is 22/24ths gold, and 9 carat gold is only 9/24ths gold. The largest and smallest

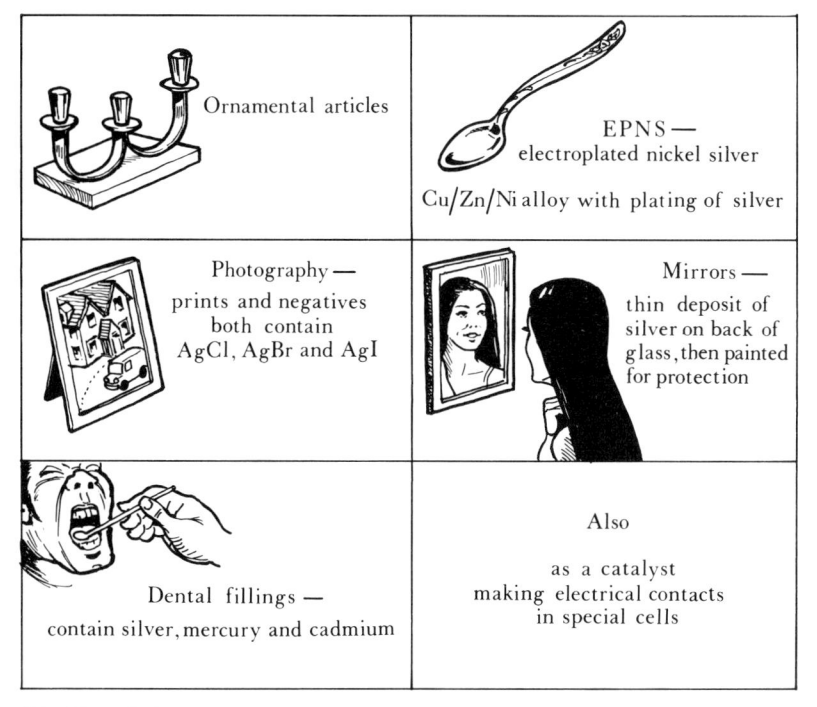

Ornamental articles	EPNS — electroplated nickel silver $Cu/Zn/Ni$ alloy with plating of silver
Photography — prints and negatives both contain AgCl, AgBr and AgI	Mirrors — thin deposit of silver on back of glass, then painted for protection
Dental fillings — contain silver, mercury and cadmium	Also as a catalyst making electrical contacts in special cells

Figure 7.2 Uses of silver

CHEMISTRY

carat measures in common use are 22 and 9. Rolled gold consists of a very thin coating of 9 carat gold on a brass or steel base.

Silver and gold are both very good conductors of heat and electricity. Silver is sometimes used to coat the contacts of electrical switch gear.

Experiment 7.1 *Making and decomposing silver chloride*

To a test-tube half full of dilute silver nitrate solution add a solution of any chloride—dilute hydrochloric acid is suitable. Shake the mixture formed, then pour half of it into a second test-tube. Put one test-tube into a dark cupboard, then leave the other in a bright light such as direct sunlight. After several hours compare the contents of the two tubes.

When silver nitrate solution is mixed with a solution containing a chloride silver chloride appears as a white precipitate.

$$AgNO_3 + HCl \longrightarrow AgCl + HNO_3$$

When the silver chloride is exposed to light the white precipitate turns purplish grey and finally darkens to black because the light turns the silver chloride to silver, which looks black when it is in a very finely divided state. Silver chloride left in the dark remains white. The blackening of silver chloride, silver bromide, or silver iodide when exposed to light is the basis of photography. When light falls on a film the film blackens, so a negative is produced. A print is formed by passing light through the stabilized negative and treating the positive so made to make it permanent.

The formation of a white precipitate of silver chloride when a substance is mixed with silver nitrate solution is used as an indication that the substance is a chloride. When the reaction is used as a test, dilute nitric acid is added to the silver nitrate to prevent certain other reactions from interfering (see Appendix 2).

Copper Cu

The main source of copper is copper sulphide. This is found mixed with rock and clay, and is separated by crushing the ore, then churning it with water and a foam-making substance. The rock and clay particles fall to the bottom but the valuable ore collects in the froth and is skimmed off. The ore is roasted in air, and then heated very strongly until the heat energy supplied to the copper sulphide converts it all to copper and sulphur dioxide. The copper is then purified, often by an electrolytic process.

Experiment 7.2 *Purification of copper by electrolysis*

(*a*) Heat a piece of copper foil in a bunsen flame for about 2 minutes. Let the copper cool and look to see whether heating has changed its appearance.

METALS OLD AND NEW

(b) Take the heated piece of copper foil, put it into a beaker of copper sulphate solution, and connect it to the positive (red) terminal of a four volt DC supply. Connect an untreated copper sheet to the negative terminal, switch on the current, and let it pass for about 15 minutes. Examine the copper sulphate solution and both sheets of copper to see if any changes have taken place.

When copper is heated in the presence of air, as in experiment 7.2(a), a film of black copper oxide appears on the surface.

$$2Cu + O_2 \longrightarrow 2CuO$$

The copper has been oxidized to copper oxide by the addition of oxygen. As the copper is heated the flame turns a greenish-blue colour, showing there is a small amount of copper present in the flame.

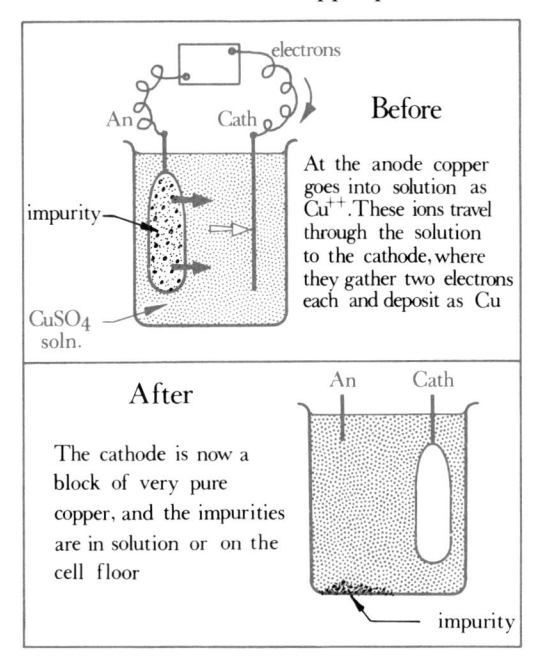

Before

At the anode copper goes into solution as Cu^{++}. These ions travel through the solution to the cathode, where they gather two electrons each and deposit as Cu

After

The cathode is now a block of very pure copper, and the impurities are in solution or on the cell floor

Figure 7.3 **Purification of copper by electrolysis**

If impure copper, such as a sheet of copper with a copper oxide film on the surface, is made the anode of an electrolytic cell, a sheet of pure copper made the cathode, and a current passed through the cell, copper is removed from the anode, passes through the solution, and deposits on the cathode. Impurities such as copper oxide fall to the bottom of the cell, and other impurities go into solution. Copper, and no other metal, deposits on the cathode, which grows. This method is used industrially to purify copper.

135

Copper, a reddish brown metal, may be rolled into sheets or drawn through a thin hole in a hard material such as diamond (a die) which converts rods into wire.

Copper forms copper oxide when heated in air (see experiment 7.2(*a*)), but if left exposed to air copper slowly reacts with oxygen, water, carbon dioxide, and sulphur dioxide if present, giving a green deposit, which is seen not only on copper pipes, wires, and roofing sheets but also on alloys of copper such as brass and bronze. It forms slowly so copper has good resistance to corrosion and may be used for water pipes, lightning conductors, roofing sheets, and similar articles exposed to weather.

Copper is a very good conductor of heat and is therefore used for boilers, steam condensers, and the bits of soldering irons which must give up heat quickly to the article being soldered. It is also a very good conductor of electricity; a very pure form of copper is used for wiring and parts of switches.

Alloys of copper include brasses, which are about two-thirds copper and one-third zinc, and bronzes, which are usually about four-fifths copper and one-fifth tin, although bronzes may include other metals as well. 'Silver' coins such as 5, 10, and 50p pieces are made of cupro-nickel which is four-fifths copper and one-fifth nickel. 'Copper' coins are 97 per cent copper, $2\frac{1}{2}$ per cent zinc, and $\frac{1}{2}$ per cent tin.

Experiment 7.3   *The action of concentrated nitric acid on copper*

Add concentrated nitric acid to a depth of about 2 cm to some copper turnings in a test-tube. Observe the colour changes and try to pour downwards the gas evolved. Do not breathe in large quantities of this gas.

Concentrated nitric acid reacts vigorously with copper forming a greenish blue solution of copper nitrate.

$$Cu + 4HNO_3 \longrightarrow Cu(NO_3)_2 + 2NO_2 + 2H_2O$$

This action involves the dissolving of the surface layer of copper, and it can therefore be used to clean copper or copper alloys such as brass. Old blackened coins can be cleaned by this method, but this decreases their value as collectors' items.

Copper oxide CuO

Copper oxide is a black powder which can be made by heating copper in air. This is not a good preparation because only the surface reacts, unchanged copper being left underneath, so copper oxide is usually made by heating copper carbonate $CuCO_3$.

$$CuCO_3 \longrightarrow CuO + CO_2$$

METALS OLD AND NEW

As the copper carbonate, a green powder, is split up (decomposed) by heating (thermally) the reaction is called a **thermal decomposition**.

If copper oxide is heated in an atmosphere of hydrogen, the oxygen is removed and the black powder is reduced to reddish brown copper (see experiment 4.6).

$$CuO + H_2 \longrightarrow Cu + H_2O$$

Copper oxide is a basic oxide and therefore reacts with acids forming a copper salt plus water (see experiment 6.5). For example,

$$CuO + 2HNO_3 \longrightarrow Cu(NO_3)_2 + H_2O$$

Copper sulphate $CuSO_4$

Copper sulphate solution is made by the action of dilute sulphuric acid on copper oxide or copper carbonate (see experiments 6.5 and 6.6).

$$H_2SO_4 + CuO \longrightarrow CuSO_4 + H_2O$$
$$H_2SO_4 + CuCO_3 \longrightarrow CuSO_4 + H_2O + CO_2$$

Copper sulphate crystals are blue, contain five molecules of water of crystallization, and are called copper sulphate pentahydrate. The action of water on white anhydrous copper sulphate gives blue hydrated copper sulphate again plus heat.

$$CuSO_4 + 5H_2O \longrightarrow CuSO_4.5H_2O + heat$$

This reaction can be used as a test for the presence of water (see experiment 2.14).

Experiment 7.4   *The action of iron and zinc on copper sulphate solution*

Take two test-tubes containing copper sulphate solution to a depth of 2 cm. Into one put pieces of granulated zinc and into the other put iron filings. After a few minutes observe any changes in the temperature and appearance of the chemicals in the tubes.

Zinc reacts with copper sulphate solution forming a colourless solution of zinc sulphate and reddish-brown flakes of copper. The mixture becomes warm as the reaction takes place.

$$Zn + CuSO_4 \longrightarrow ZnSO_4 + Cu + heat$$

This type of reaction is called the **displacement** or **replacement** of copper by zinc. Similarly, iron replaces the copper in copper sulphate forming a pale green solution of iron(II) sulphate (ferrous sulphate) and a precipitate of copper.

$$Fe + CuSO_4 \longrightarrow FeSO_4 + Cu + heat$$

CHEMISTRY

As a variation of this experiment it is possible to coat a steel knife blade with copper by dipping it into copper sulphate solution for a few seconds. The copper plating is of poor quality and flakes off very easily because it has been applied too quickly to an unprepared surface. Commercial plating processes are slow and the object being plated is carefully cleaned beforehand.

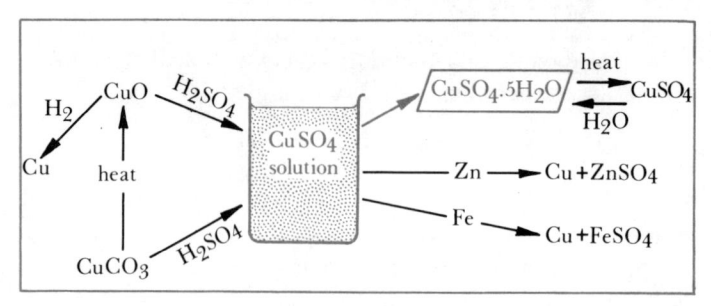

Figure 7.4 Summary of copper compounds

Tin Sn

Tin is a shiny metal with very good resistance to corrosion by air and water. Its main use is for coating steel plate, either by dipping clean steel plate into molten tin, or by a process of electrolysis in which tin is deposited on the plate. Although the coating of tin is often as thin as a thousandth of a millimetre it protects the iron unless the coating is scratched, when the underlying iron rusts quickly. (An opened tin, which can be regarded as scratched along the cut edge, rusts rapidly if left exposed to air and water.) Tins for the storage of food or drink are often varnished on the inside to preserve the flavour of the goods in them.

A pool of molten tin is used in the float glass process developed by Messrs Pilkington for making very flat glass. The surface of the molten tin is very flat, and molten glass allowed to solidify on this surface is so flat and smooth that it does not need grinding or polishing before it is ready for use.

Tin is used to make alloys such as bronze (Cu/Sn), type metal (Sn/Pb/antimony), and solder (Sn/Pb).

Experiment 7.5 *The melting point of an alloy*

Cut pieces of tin, lead, and solder, making them as equal as possible in size and shape. Put the three pieces at the corners of an equilateral triangle drawn on a sheet of metal, and arrange a small bunsen flame to strike the middle of the triangle so that the pieces are heated equally. Watch to see the order of melting.

METALS OLD AND NEW

The melting point of solder, which is an alloy of tin and lead, is lower than that of either tin or lead, as is revealed when the specimens melt in the order solder first, then tin, then lead. It is usual for the melting point of an alloy to be lower than the melting point of any of its constituents.

Iron Fe

This morning you got out of your bed which had steel springs, ate your breakfast with a stainless steel knife, fork, and spoon, and came to school probably by bus, train, car, or bicycle, all of which are largely steel. Even if you walked to school your heels are probably held on to your shoes by steel nails, and as you read this book you are likely to be sitting on a chair with a steel frame, or a wooden frame held together with steel screws. Iron and its close relative steel are vital to modern life and industry, so we are going to study iron and steel manufacture in detail.

Iron ore which contains iron(III) oxide, ferric oxide, is reduced to impure iron called pig iron in a blast furnace. Most of the pig iron produced is then converted to steel.

The blast furnace

A blast furnace, which is made of steel lined with fire-bricks, is charged with a mixture containing:

iron ore—impure iron(III) oxide Fe_2O_3
a fuel and reducing agent—coke C
an impurity-remover—calcium carbonate $CaCO_3$

The fuel is burned by a blast of hot air, sometimes containing added oxygen, entering through a ring of nozzles set near the bottom of the furnace. The burning not only makes carbon monoxide, which is the main reducing agent in the smelting process, but supplies heat energy necessary for the reducing reaction and the melting of the products.

$$2C + O_2 \longrightarrow 2CO + \text{heat}$$

The hot carbon monoxide rises up the furnace and reduces the iron(III) oxide in the ore to iron.

$$Fe_2O_3 + 3CO \longrightarrow 2Fe + 3CO_2$$

The iron melts and trickles to the bottom of the furnace. The high temperature in the blast furnace causes the calcium carbonate to split up (thermal decomposition). The calcium oxide formed then reacts with the main impurity in the ore, the silicon dioxide (silica) present in sand and clay, forming calcium silicate.

$$CaCO_3 \longrightarrow CaO + CO_2$$
$$\text{then } CaO + SiO_2 \longrightarrow CaSiO_3$$

The calcium silicate melts, runs down the furnace, and collects as **slag** on top of the molten iron.

The carbon dioxide produced from the calcium carbonate, together with that from the reduction reaction, passes up the furnace along with nitrogen from the air blast and dust from the charge. The hot gases are led away from the top of the furnace and used to heat towers containing bricks. There are several of these towers, and when one is hot the air is passed through it before being blasted into the furnace. This preheating avoids the cooling effect that cold air would produce on entering the furnace, and this saves fuel.

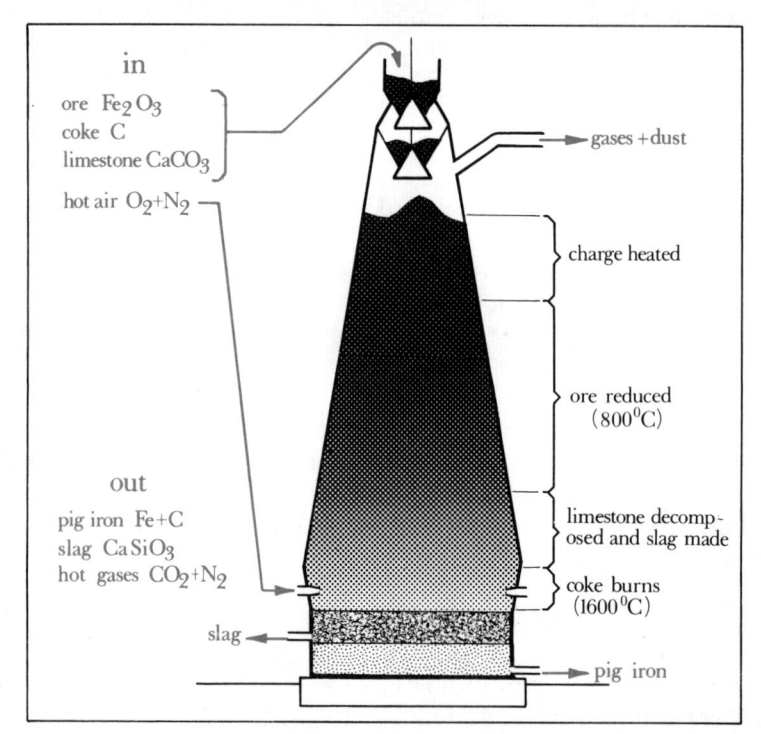

Figure 7.5 The blast furnace

A blast furnace is an impressively large structure which dwarfs the operating crew. Some furnaces stand as high as a fifteen-storey building and are surrounded by large heat-exchanging towers and dust-catching devices. The furnace, once lit, is never allowed to stop until it needs repair, and it might produce 1000 tonnes of pig iron each day. The furnace is tapped by breaking away a clay plug at the bottom, and molten iron, white-hot and sparking, runs down channels, usually into a large ladle for carrying to a steel-making process nearby. The slag is tapped and allowed to cool, then broken up for use as railway ballast, road-making or building material, or fertilizer.

The **pig iron** coming from a blast furnace contains 90 to 95 per cent iron together with about 5 per cent carbon and varying amounts of silicon, manganese, and phosphorus according to the impurities in the iron ore used. The elements carbon, silicon, manganese, and phosphorus make the pig iron hard but brittle, so it cannot be used to make things which have to bend (for example, springs) or suffer shocks (such as nails, car bumpers). Lamp posts, car cylinder blocks, turbine casings, and machine-tool beds are among the articles made from pig iron with little further treatment. They are cast by pouring molten iron into a mould and are said to be made of cast iron.

Conversion of iron to steel

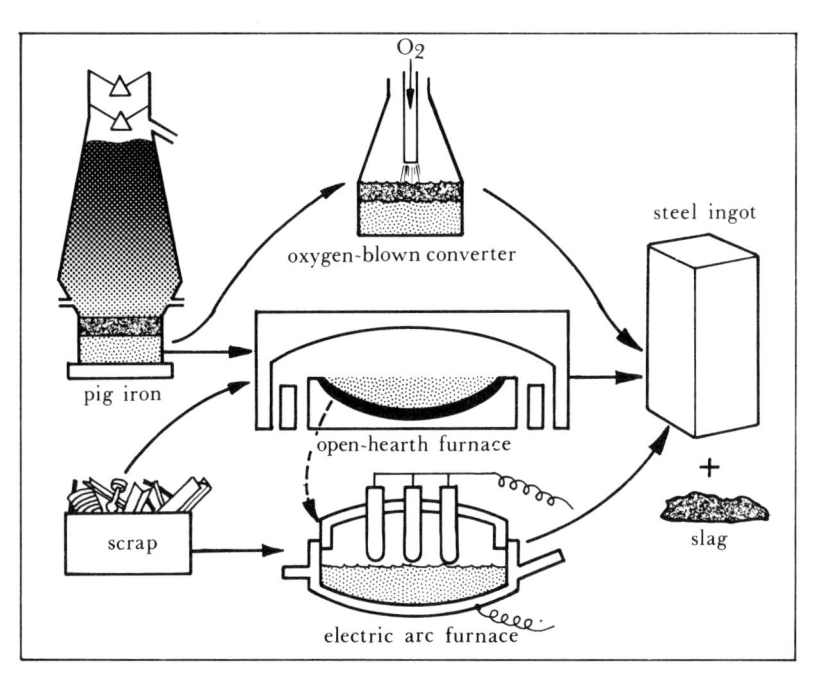

Figure 7.6   Iron into steel

The majority of the pig iron now produced is converted to steel, which has between 0·1 and 1·5 per cent carbon. For over 2000 years steel has been expensively and painstakingly made in small quantities for swords and armour, but the first cheap steel-making process was introduced in Sheffield

CHEMISTRY

Table 7.2 Turning iron into steel

Name	Produces	Source of energy	Reactions	Notes
Bessemer Converter	steel from pig iron	burning of excess carbon within pig iron by hot air blast	$2C + O_2 \rightarrow 2CO$ CO burns at mouth of converter	almost obsolete in UK
LD, Kaldo, and Rotor processes	steel from pig iron	burning of excess carbon within pig iron using supersonic oxygen jet	$2C + O_2 \rightarrow 2CO$	modern development of original Bessemer
Open hearth furnace	steel from pig iron plus scrap	gas or oil flames burning over pool of molten iron	excess C in pig iron reduces iron(III) oxide $3C + Fe_2O_3 \rightarrow 2Fe + 3CO$ (reaction similar to blast furnace)	oxygen blast helps to remove unwanted carbon, by burning it out
Electric arc furnace	high-grade steel from ordinary steel	large arc from carbon electrodes to the steel	excess carbon reduces iron(III) oxide $3C + Fe_2O_3 \rightarrow 2Fe + 3CO$	furnace can be closed off from atmosphere so high purity possible. Expensive to run

METALS OLD AND NEW

about 120 years ago by Sir Henry Bessemer. This process turned steel from a rare and expensive material to a common everyday substance used for bridges, machines, railway lines, locks and keys, ships, trains, cooking utensils, and thousands of other objects. The original Bessemer process is not now common but many variations of it have been developed. In all of them carbon is removed by oxidation, and other elements (e.g., phosphorus and silicon) are removed in the slag, which is used for fertilizers, or making roads and building blocks.

Uses of steel

Mild steel containing about 0·1 per cent carbon is used to make steel plate for car bodies, refrigerators, ovens and the like, tin plate, and many other steel articles. A high-carbon steel containing up to 1·5 per cent carbon is used for making axe heads, scissors, punches, drills and other tools.

Figure 7.7 An oxy-acetylene cutting torch being used to cut steel plate in a Scottish quarry. The short cylinder contains acetylene C_2H_2, the tall one oxygen.

In addition to these ordinary steels there are many different alloy steels used for special purposes. Stainless steels have very good resistance to rusting; one type known as 18/8 contains 18 per cent chromium and 8 per cent nickel. Manganese steel containing 14 per cent manganese is very hard, and is used for the jaws of rock crushers, railway points, and armour plate. Tungsten steel, which remains hard even at comparatively high temperatures,

CHEMISTRY

is used for cutting tools on lathes. Chromium vanadium steel is very tough and resists wear and rust, so it is used for spanners.

Chemistry of iron

Table 7.3 Some reactions of iron

Reaction	Equation	Notes
burn iron filings or steel wool (see experiment 3.1(a))	$3Fe + 2O_2 \rightarrow Fe_3O_4$ magnetic iron oxide made	sparks made as in 'sparklers' (fireworks), steel cutting and tool sharpening (see Fig. 7.7)
iron on dilute sulphuric acid	$Fe + H_2SO_4 \rightarrow FeSO_4 + H_2$ iron(II) sulphate (ferrous sulphate) made	pale green solution made, H_2 bubbles evolved
iron on dilute hydrochloric acid	$Fe + 2HCl \rightarrow FeCl_2 + H_2$ iron(II) chloride (ferrous chloride) made	pale green solution produced
iron on copper sulphate solution	$Fe + CuSO_4 \rightarrow FeSO_4 + Cu$ iron(II) sulphate made	pale green solution and red-brown precipitate produced by displacement
red-hot iron on steam	$3Fe + 4H_2O \rightleftharpoons Fe_3O_4 + 4H_2$ iron(II) iron(III) oxide, magnetic iron oxide made	used industrially to produce hydrogen. Reaction is reversible

Rusting

The word rusting is applied to the corrosion of iron and steel.

Experiment 7.6 *Conditions necessary for the rusting of iron*

Set up test-tubes as shown in Fig. 7.8, each containing a bright iron nail, and examine the nails after a day or two.

In (a) the nail is exposed to air and water, in (b) it is exposed to air but not water, and in (c) to water but not to air because air has been removed from the water by boiling, and the layer of oil or Vaseline prevents air from redissolving in the water.

Iron exposed to air and water rusts, but on exposure to air only or water only no rusting takes place. This shows that air and water are both needed to rust iron. (It is in fact the oxygen in the air which is used in rusting.) Rust is hydrated iron(III) oxide (ferric oxide), $Fe_2O_3 \cdot xH_2O$. x is variable according to the amount of water available when the rust is formed.

$$4Fe + 3O_2 + 2xH_2O \longrightarrow 2Fe_2O_3 \cdot xH_2O$$

METALS OLD AND NEW

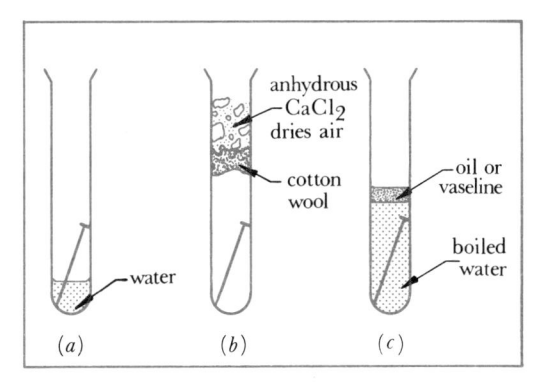

Figure 7.8 An experiment on rusting

Steel rusts under exactly the same conditions as iron so when the apparatus shown in Fig. 7.9 is set up, the water rises in the cylinder as the oxygen is removed.

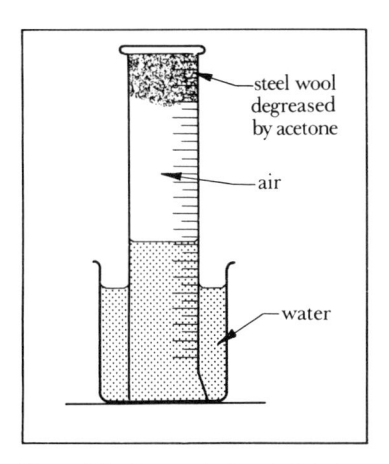

Figure 7.9 Oxygen is absorbed during rusting

When the water stops rising, nitrogen and water vapour are left in the cylinder.

Rusting car panels and exhaust pipes must be replaced, wire-wool pan scourers rust if left wet on the sink, steel screws rust and are hard to remove, and the Forth Rail Bridge is painted continuously to protect it, the painters restarting at one end as soon as they finish at the other (see also Fig. 3.5). These are just a few examples. It has been estimated that rusting and its prevention cost over a hundred million pounds a year in Great Britain. The rusting of iron and steel is prevented by keeping away air and water

by painting or greasing (cars, tools),
by plating with tin (tin plate for canned food),

by coating with aluminium (by rolling aluminium dust on to hot clean steel plate and then heating),
by plating with chromium (bicycle and car parts), and
by coating with plastics (dish draining racks).

The above processes protect the iron from rusting only when they form a complete covering which keeps out water and air. When the film is broken rusting starts. Zinc plating (**galvanizing**) acts in a different way and gives very long-lasting protection—a galvanized dustbin or corrugated iron sheet lasts many years before rusting. This is because zinc is attacked by air and water more readily than is iron, so the zinc starts to corrode first. This forms a coat of zinc oxide on the surface of the zinc which makes further attack on the zinc very slow. Since the iron is not attacked until all the neighbouring zinc has gone it is a long time before the iron starts to rust.

Stainless steel also resists rusting, but it would not be possible to make all steel into stainless steel by alloying it with chromium and nickel. This is not only because stainless steel is expensive but there is just not enough chromium and nickel available in the world to do this.

Rust may be removed from iron and steel by rubbing (e.g., using steel wool, a wire brush, or shot blasting), or by chemical means. Being a basic oxide rust reacts with acids, but the acids used must not affect the iron or steel. A solution of orthophosphoric acid H_3PO_4 is often used to react with rust.

Iron(II) sulphate heptahydrate (ferrous sulphate crystals) $FeSO_4.7H_2O$

When iron is allowed to react with dilute sulphuric acid, the solution filtered to remove carbon from the iron, and then crystallized, pale green crystals of iron(II) sulphate are formed. When heated, the crystals decompose, giving off steam, sulphur dioxide, and sulphur trioxide, and leaving a reddish brown residue of iron(III) oxide, ferric oxide.

$$2FeSO_4.7H_2O \longrightarrow Fe_2O_3 + SO_2 + SO_3 + 14H_2O$$

A green solution of iron(II) sulphate is converted to a brown solution of iron(III) sulphate, ferric sulphate, by mixing with dilute sulphuric acid and an oxidizing agent such as hydrogen peroxide or chlorine.

$$2FeSO_4 + H_2O_2 + H_2SO_4 \longrightarrow Fe_2(SO_4)_3 + 2H_2O$$
$$2FeSO_4 + Cl_2 + H_2SO_4 \longrightarrow Fe_2(SO_4)_3 + 2HCl$$

This conversion of iron valency two to iron valency three (ferrous to ferric) is regarded as a form of oxidation, and the reverse of this type of reaction, iron valency three to iron valency two, is correspondingly a form of reduction. If iron(II) sulphate solution is allowed to stand in contact with the oxygen in the air it is oxidized and turned brown as iron(III) compounds are formed.

METALS OLD AND NEW

Iron(III) oxide (ferric oxide) Fe_2O_3

Iron(III) oxide is reddish-brown powder made by heating iron(II) sulphate. It is a basic oxide and therefore reacts with acids to form iron(III) salts and water. For example,

$$Fe_2O_3 + 6HCl \longrightarrow 2FeCl_3 + 3H_2O$$

Demonstration experiment 7.7 *The thermit reaction*

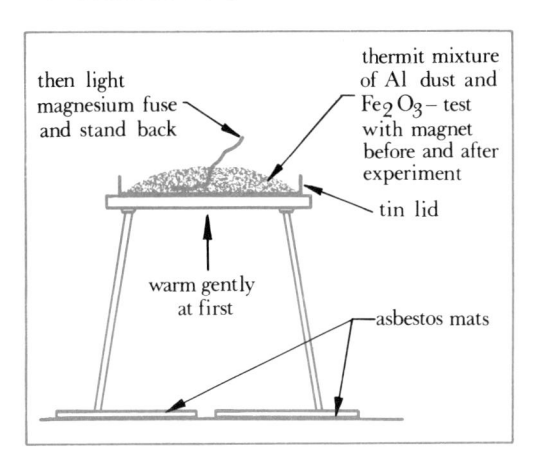

Figure 7.10 The thermit reaction

Iron(III) oxide can be reduced to iron by the removal of all the oxygen. Aluminium powder acts as the reducing agent and a very large amount of energy is released as the reaction occurs. If a mixture of iron(III) oxide and aluminium is warmed, and lit by a magnesium fuse, sparks fly off, the mass melts then becomes white-hot, giving off aluminium oxide as a white smoke.

$$Fe_2O_3 + 2Al \longrightarrow 2Fe + Al_2O_3$$

When the residue cools some of the globules left stick to a magnet, which indicates that they contain iron.

At high temperatures, iron(III) oxide may be reduced to iron by carbon monoxide as in a blast furnace.

$$Fe_2O_3 + 3CO \longrightarrow 2Fe + 3CO_2$$

Lead Pb

Experiment 7.8 *The action of charcoal on lead(II) oxide (lead monoxide)*

Scrape a hole 0·2 cm deep in a charcoal block and fill it with lead(II) oxide. Add one drop of water to hold the oxide in place, and press the powder down.

147

Shut the air hole of a bunsen burner and turn down the gas supply so that the flame is 5 cm high. Keeping the tip of the blow pipe out of the flame, blow gently to direct a small, hot flame on to the lead(II) oxide. Blow until you see the material in the hole melt. Allow the mixture to cool, examine the residue, and try to mark paper with one of the globules made.

Lead(II) oxide is reduced to lead by the action of carbon at high temperatures. The oxide becomes red hot and then silvery beads of lead form.

$$PbO + C \longrightarrow Pb + CO$$

These beads are soft enough to mark paper.

Lead was mined in Britain before the Romans arrived, and after the conquest England and Wales became the main sources of lead for the Roman Empire. The Romans called lead *plumbum*, a word which survives in our words plumber and plumb-line, and in the symbol Pb. The most useful ore of lead is galena, a sulphide of lead which is heated strongly in air to form lead(II) oxide. This oxide is then reduced to lead by heating with coke in a small furnace. This extraction is very similar to the reduction of lead(II) oxide to lead in experiments 1.2 and 7.8. As only a moderate amount of energy is needed to extract lead from its ores, lead was one of the earlier metals used by man. When the lead has been extracted it is often purified, especially if it is known to contain silver.

Lead is a dense grey metal, 1 cm^3 weighs 11·4 g, and we talk of things being 'as heavy as lead'. Lead is one of the softer metals; a sheet of it may be cut with a knife, it is easy to form into sheets, pipes, and tape, and it marks paper if rubbed on. The metal is not strong, a lead rod having a breaking strain about one twenty-fifth that of a mild steel rod of the same shape and size, so lead is not much used in engineering. It has, however, excellent resistance to corrosion, and is easily bent and joined, so for thousands of years it has been used for roofing, and for water containers and pipes. Roman pipes two thousand years old have been found in good condition at Pompeii and Bath. Lead is becoming very expensive so lead pipes in domestic water and central heating systems are not common now, copper being used instead.

Lead is resistant to attack by many chemical agents and is used to line the tanks which hold concentrated sulphuric acid. Its resistance to attack by sulphuric acid enables lead to be used in lead acid accumulators in car and submarine batteries.

Lead has a melting point of 327°C which is quite low for a metal. This makes lead and its alloys (whose melting points are even lower, see experiment 7.5) easy to cast into articles ranging from bullets, shot, and fishing weights to type metal. In soldering, a lead/tin alloy is melted between the surfaces to be joined. If both surfaces are clean, solder sticks to them when it solidifies and joins them.

Lead absorbs X-rays and gamma rays, so it is used as a shielding material.

Lead containers are used for storing and transporting radioactive substances, and protective clothing for operators of X-ray machines can be made from finely divided lead dispersed in polythene.

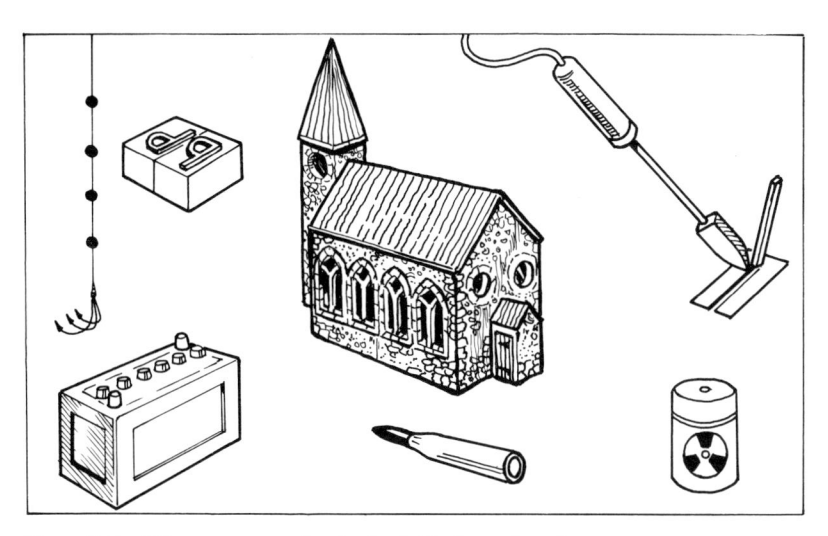

Figure 7.11 What property makes lead suitable for each use?

Compounds of lead

Among the oxides of lead are lead(II) oxide (lead monoxide), PbO, which is a yellowish-brown powder, and dilead(II) lead(IV) oxide (triplumbic tetroxide), Pb_3O_4, which is often called red lead. Both oxides may be reduced to lead by heating with carbon (experiments 1.2 and 7.8).

Lead(II) nitrate $Pb(NO_3)_2$ is a white crystalline solid made by the action of dilute nitric acid on lead(II) oxide, which acts as a base.

$$PbO + 2HNO_3 \longrightarrow Pb(NO_3)_2 + H_2O$$

Lead(II) nitrate decomposes when heated, giving off a mixture of oxygen and brown nitrogen dioxide, and leaving a yellowish-brown residue of lead(II) oxide.

$$2Pb(NO_3)_2 \longrightarrow 2PbO + 4NO_2 + O_2$$

The solid jumps about in the tube and crackles (decrepitates) as the heat splits the crystals.

Many lead compounds are poisonous and toys or furniture likely to be sucked or chewed by young children should be painted with lead-free paint. The use of lead compounds in petrol has also been criticized for this reason.

CHEMISTRY

Mercury Hg

Mercury is made very simply by heating mercury sulphide. Mercury vapour is given off and this condenses to form liquid mercury.

Mercury is shiny and silvery coloured, a good conductor of heat and electricity, and its oxide reacts with an acid to give a salt + water. These properties indicate that mercury is a metal. It is unusual in that it is the only metal which is liquid at room temperature. Mercury has a very high density, being 13·6 times as heavy as an equal volume of water: a bucketful of mercury would weigh 136 kg (i.e., as much as two men) and cost over £400. Its high density makes mercury suitable for use in a barometer, and the fact that it is easily visible and forms a column, which, owing to its high surface tension does not break easily, means that it is useful in thermometers. When an electric current is passed through mercury vapour at low pressure an intense blue-green light is given out. The mercury vapour lamps used for street lighting work on this principle. The alloys of mercury with other metals are called **amalgams** and may be solid or liquid according to the amount of mercury present. Solid amalgams containing mercury, silver, copper, and cadmium are used for filling teeth. Certain mercury compounds which are very poisonous are used to kill fungi.

Zinc Zn

Zinc is extracted from its ore (zinc sulphide) by roasting the ore to turn it to zinc oxide, then smelting the zinc oxide with carbon (powdered coal or coke). The zinc oxide is reduced to zinc, which vaporizes and is then condensed.

$$ZnO + C \longrightarrow Zn + CO$$

The zinc is then distilled again to purify it.

Zinc is a brittle silvery metal, but when exposed to moist air it gradually becomes covered with a grey film of zinc oxide and carbonate. This film sticks firmly to the zinc and prevents further corrosion, so zinc lasts well when exposed to air and water.

Experiment 7.9 *Reactions of zinc*

(a) Zinc, if heated strongly on an asbestos gauze until it melts, burns when it is stirred to expose fresh unoxidized surface. A bluish-green flame is seen and zinc oxide is made.

$$2Zn + O_2 \longrightarrow 2ZnO$$

Some of the zinc oxide escapes as a white smoke but some remains on the gauze. Zinc oxide is yellow when hot but as it cools it turns white.

METALS OLD AND NEW

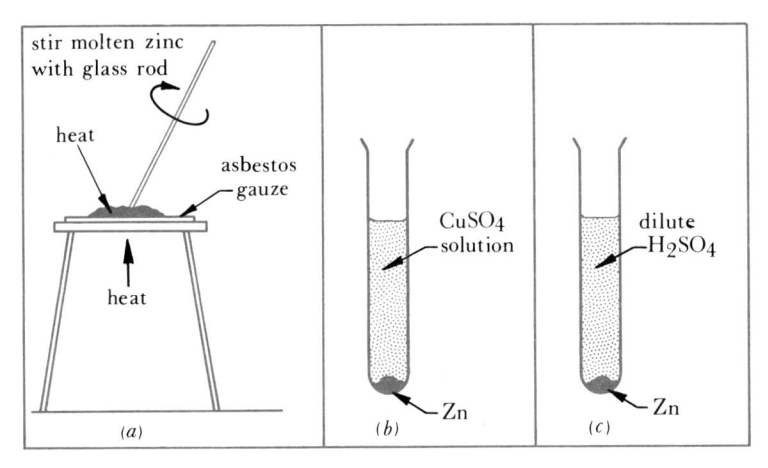

Figure 7.12 Some reactions of zinc

(b) Zinc displaces copper from copper sulphate solution. The blue solution turns colourless and a reddish-brown precipitate of copper appears.

$$Zn + CuSO_4 \longrightarrow ZnSO_4 + Cu$$

(c) Zinc reacts with dilute sulphuric acid forming zinc sulphate solution and hydrogen (experiment 4.1).

$$Zn + H_2SO_4 \longrightarrow ZnSO_4 + H_2$$

Experiment 7.10 *Zinc-plating of iron*

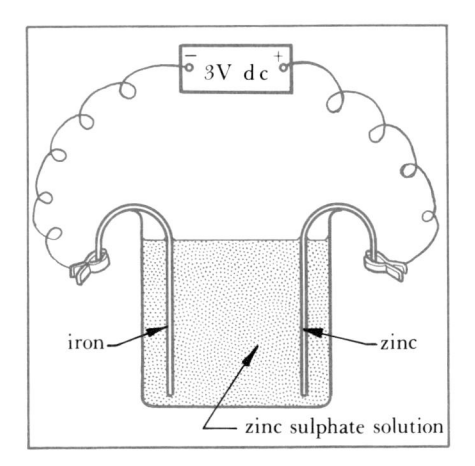

Figure 7.13 Plating zinc on to clean iron

CHEMISTRY

(a) Polish a piece of iron or sheet steel with emery cloth and bend over the end so that the piece will hang inside a small beaker containing zinc sulphate solution. After polishing do not touch the part that will be in the solution. Take a similar strip of zinc sheet and connect the apparatus to a source of three volts DC, fixing the iron strip to the negative (black) terminal of the power supply. Allow the current to flow until the iron is coated with a light-coloured layer of zinc, then examine the coating.
(b) Put the zinc-coated iron in a test-tube containing a little water and leave it, examining it from time to time for signs of rusting.

Zinc can be plated on to clean iron by the electrolytic method described in experiment 7.10. The zinc, as is usual with metals, deposits on the cathode or negative electrode. (This is because the positive ions Zn^{++} are attracted to the negative electrode.) Greasy fingers touching the iron after polishing prevent even plating. If the zinc-coated steel is exposed to air and water the exposed steel rusts but the zinc-coated part does not.

Sodium Na

The source of sodium is one of the most abundant of compounds—sodium chloride. Solid deposits of sodium chloride such as those of the salt mines of Cheshire and Droitwich are the remains of seas which dried up long ago as the land rose and fell. As with all extractions of metals from their compounds,

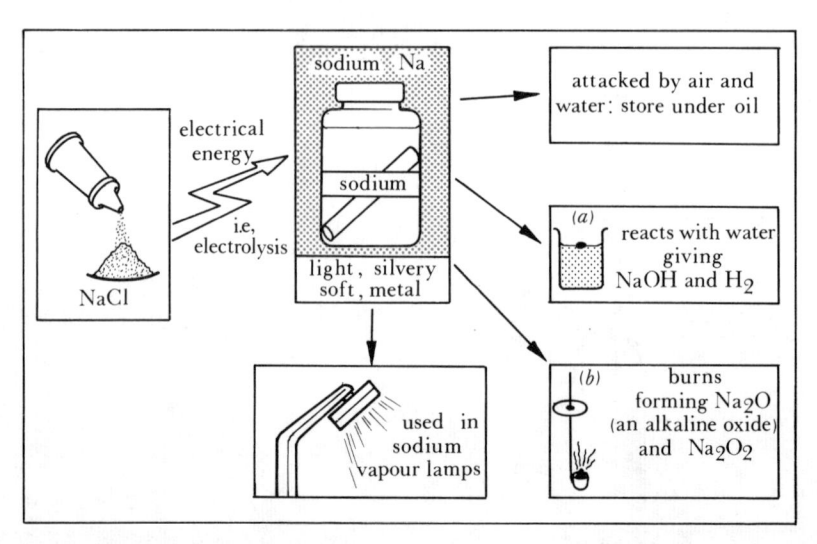

Figure 7.14 Properties of sodium Na
Equations (a) $2Na + 2H_2O \longrightarrow 2NaOH + H_2$ (Exp. 2.13)
(b) $4Na + O_2 \longrightarrow 2Na_2O$ (Exp. 3.4)

METALS OLD AND NEW

energy must be supplied to make the metal from its ore. Sodium is extracted from sodium chloride using electrical energy; when molten sodium chloride is electrolyzed, sodium is made at the cathode and chlorine is released at the anode of the cell (see Appendix 4).

$$2NaCl \longrightarrow 2Na + Cl_2$$

The fact that sodium oxide is an alkaline oxide (i.e., a basic oxide which reacts with water to give an alkali) is good evidence that sodium is a metal, as is the fact that sodium forms a positive ion Na^+.

Sodium is used in sodium vapour lamps. In these sodium is heated to vaporize it, and when an electric current is passed through the vapour a bright yellow light is made. Molten sodium is used in one type of nuclear power station as a heat transfer liquid. The sodium becomes heated in the hot part of the reactor and then travels round the system, giving out heat in boilers so that steam is generated.

Sodium hydroxide NaOH

Sodium hydroxide is a white solid made by the electrolysis of sodium chloride solution (for details see Appendix 4).

$$2NaCl + 2H_2O \longrightarrow 2NaOH + H_2 + Cl_2$$

A special cell is used to keep the chlorine from the sodium hydroxide, because if these two products mixed they would react and remake sodium chloride. The chlorine and hydrogen made are collected separately and sold as by-products.

Sodium hydroxide and its solution are often called caustic soda. Caustic, implying burning, is used because the substance attacks most animal and vegetable matter, including skin and natural fibres such as wool and cotton. Dilute sodium hydroxide solution is used to react with cotton thread, making it smoother and easier to dye, in the process of mercerizing. The solution slowly attacks even glass.

A pellet of solid sodium hydroxide put on a watch-glass in the laboratory is soon seen to be glistening with the water it absorbs from the air. Substances such as sodium hydroxide which absorb water from the air and become wet are said to be **deliquescent**.

Sodium hydroxide is an alkali, so it changes the colours of indicators (for example, turns litmus blue and phenolphthalein pink) and neutralizes acids, forming a salt plus water (experiments 6.4 and 6.9). For example,

$$HCl + NaOH \longrightarrow NaCl + H_2O$$

In a similar way sodium hydroxide reacts with acidic oxides, but in this case a salt only is made (experiment 5.4(f)). For example,

$$CO_2 + NaOH \longrightarrow NaHCO_3$$

If sodium hydroxide solution is boiled with an ammonium salt, e.g., ammonium chloride, ammonia gas is formed (see experiment 10.1).

$$NH_4Cl + NaOH \longrightarrow NaCl + H_2O + NH_3$$

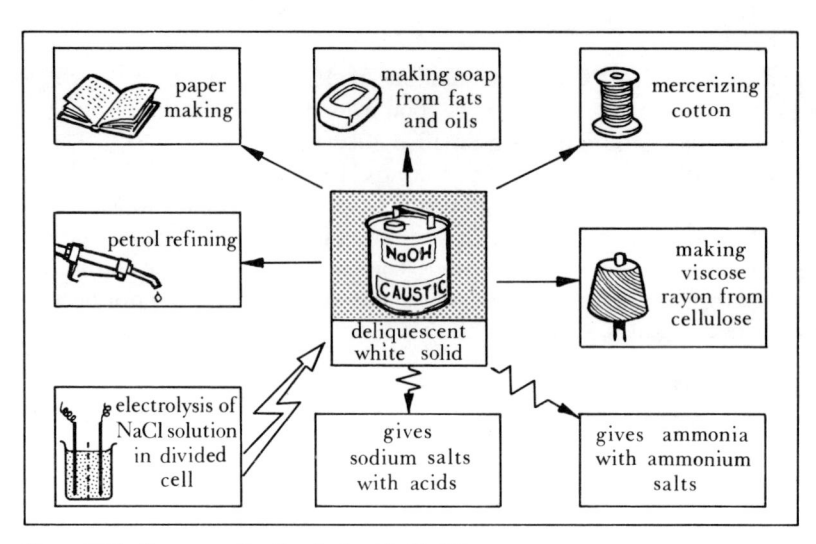

Figure 7.15 Summary of sodium hydroxide NaOH

Sodium nitrate $NaNO_3$

Large deposits of impure sodium nitrate occur naturally in rainless areas of Chile and it is known as Chile Saltpetre. Sodium nitrate can be made by the action of dilute nitric acid on sodium hydroxide or sodium carbonate, and the solid crystallized. It is a white solid which decomposes on heating, giving off oxygen and leaving sodium nitrite.

$$2NaNO_3 \longrightarrow 2NaNO_2 + O_2$$

If a small amount of sodium nitrate is heated in a test-tube with concentrated sulphuric acid, nitric acid is produced and sodium hydrogen sulphate is also made (see experiment 6.11).

$$NaNO_3 + H_2SO_4 \longrightarrow HNO_3 + NaHSO_4$$

The nitric acid, which is more volatile than sulphuric acid, has been turned out of its salt by the sulphuric acid.

Sodium nitrate is used as a fertilizer because it provides a supply of fixed (chemically combined) nitrogen.

Calcium Ca

Although calcium carbonate and calcium sulphate are the commonest naturally occurring compounds of calcium, calcium metal is usually extracted from calcium chloride. Heating does not convert calcium chloride to calcium; electrical energy must be used. The calcium chloride is melted and an electric current passed through it. Chlorine is evolved at the anode and calcium is released at the cathode.

Calcium is a fairly soft silver-grey metal which is hard to keep in the laboratory because it reacts readily with air, water, and carbon dioxide forming a powdery coating of calcium oxide, hydroxide, and carbonate. It burns with a red flame, forming calcium oxide.

$$2Ca + O_2 \longrightarrow 2CaO$$

Calcium reacts with water, giving off hydrogen and making a white precipitate of calcium hydroxide (experiment 2.12).

$$Ca + 2H_2O \longrightarrow Ca(OH)_2 + H_2$$

Calcium oxide (quicklime) CaO

Experiment 7.11 *Making and reacting calcium oxide*

(*a*) Put a large marble chip on the edge of a gauze, and for five minutes heat it strongly from above and below. Try to make the chip glow brightly. Use

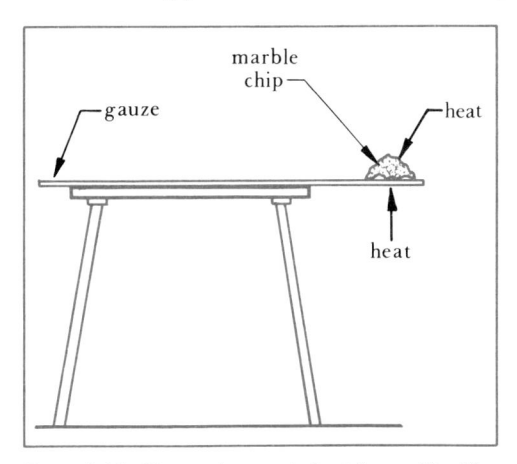

Figure 7.16 Use two bunsens to heat the marble chip

tongs to move the chip to a cool part of the gauze, let it cool, and compare its appearance with that of another chip which has not been heated.

(*b*) When you are sure that the chip is cool, start a tap dripping slowly, and watch what happens when you let one drop of water fall on the cold

CHEMISTRY

solid. Keep the chip on the gauze as you do this. Put more drops of water on the chip one at a time, continuing until you see no further changes in the chip. Use the wet solid for experiment 7.12.

When a shiny piece of marble (calcium carbonate) $CaCO_3$ is heated strongly it glows with a very bright light. This light, called limelight, was used in stage lighting before powerful electric spotlights were invented. The shiny surface of the chip becomes dull and powdery as the calcium carbonate loses carbon dioxide and becomes converted to calcium oxide, which is known as quicklime.

$$CaCO_3 \longrightarrow CaO + CO_2$$

The reaction is carried out on a very large scale in lime kilns, in which lumps of calcium carbonate (often in the form of chalk, which is cheaper than marble) are heated by gas flames. The carbon dioxide is allowed to escape.

If water is put on a piece of cold calcium oxide a vigorous reaction takes place. The lump of quicklime swells, crumbles to powder, and some of the water is turned to steam, showing that a considerable quantity of heat is produced by the reaction. Calcium hydroxide or slaked lime has been produced and the process is known as **lime slaking**.

$$CaO + H_2O \longrightarrow Ca(OH)_2 + heat$$

Calcium oxide is an alkaline oxide (a basic oxide which reacts with water forming a soluble hydroxide). It attacks flesh causing a burning feeling and should be treated with care.

Calcium hydroxide (slaked lime) $Ca(OH)_2$

Experiment 7.12 *Making lime-water*

Put calcium hydroxide (from experiment 7.11) to a depth of about $\frac{1}{2}$ cm in a test-tube and half fill the tube with water. Shake the mixture for about five minutes and then filter. Discard the undissolved solid, and use a glass tube to blow through the clear filtrate. Get someone else to blow through tap water for a similar length of time and compare the two tubes after blowing for about a minute.

Calcium hydroxide is a white powder which is slightly soluble in water. A solution of calcium hydroxide which has been separated from any undissolved solid is called lime-water. The solution reacts with carbon dioxide (e.g., in breathed-out air) forming a turbid or chalky suspension containing small particles of solid calcium carbonate. This is a reaction between an acidic oxide and an alkali forming a salt and water, and the reaction is used to test for carbon dioxide.

$$CO_2 + Ca(OH)_2 \longrightarrow CaCO_3 + H_2O$$

METALS OLD AND NEW

If turbid lime-water (i.e., a suspension of calcium carbonate) is shaken and divided into two parts, and then carbon dioxide is passed through one of these for a long time, comparison of the two tubes shows that this one is gradually clearing. This is because the calcium carbonate particles react with excess carbon dioxide and water, forming calcium hydrogen carbonate (calcium bicarbonate).

$$CaCO_3 + H_2O + CO_2 \longrightarrow Ca(HCO_3)_2$$

Calcium hydrogen carbonate is soluble in water, so eventually a clear solution forms. This reaction takes place in rivers running over rocks containing calcium carbonate, and results in the formation of water containing calcium hydrogen carbonate in solution—temporarily hard water (see Fig. 8.9).

Heating calcium hydroxide strongly dehydrates it, removing water and forming calcium oxide and steam. This is the reverse of slaking quicklime.

$$Ca(OH)_2 \longrightarrow CaO + H_2O$$

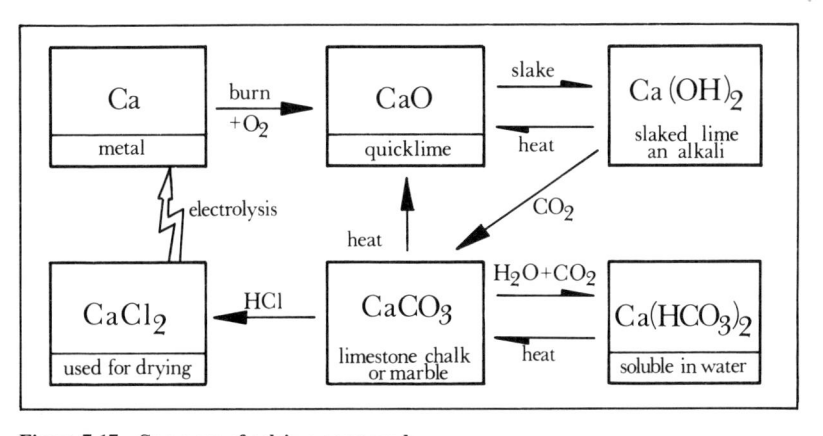

Figure 7.17 Summary of calcium compounds

Magnesium Mg

Magnesium, which is often used in the laboratory in the form of a ribbon, is extracted from molten magnesium chloride by electrolysis. The magnesium produced sticks to the cathode, and chlorine, which is produced at the same time, is led away to prevent it from reacting with the magnesium. There are magnesium compounds in sea water and these are used as raw materials to supplement magnesium compounds obtained by mining. There is a magnesium extraction plant near Amlwch in Anglesey.

Experiment 7.13 *Some properties of magnesium*

(*a*) Put a piece of magnesium ribbon in dilute hydrochloric acid and leave it until the surface is shiny, then take the ribbon out, wash it thoroughly, dry and leave it exposed to air. Look at it from time to time to see if its appearance changes.

(*b*) Hold a 5 cm length of magnesium ribbon in crucible tongs and light it in a bunsen flame. Do not look directly at the flame. Examine the residue and test it by rubbing a little on to moist red litmus paper.

(*c*) Fold a 10 cm length of magnesium ribbon several times and drop it into about 3 cm depth of dilute sulphuric acid in a test-tube. Close the top of the tube with your thumb for about 30 seconds, then bring the open mouth of the tube near to a flame.

| What happens, what does it show, and what is left in the test-tube when this reaction is finished?

Freshly cleaned magnesium is silvery coloured, but the metal usually looks grey because it is covered with a magnesium oxide layer formed by the attack of oxygen from the air.

Magnesium burns readily in air and brilliantly in oxygen giving a bright greenish-white light and leaving white magnesium oxide powder.

$$2Mg + O_2 \longrightarrow 2MgO$$

Magnesium oxide turns damp red litmus paper blue, showing that it is an alkaline oxide (experiment 6.1).

Magnesium reacts with dilute sulphuric and hydrochloric acids, and with very dilute nitric acid, giving off hydrogen which burns when lit, and leaving a colourless solution of a magnesium salt (experiments 6.7 and 6.9). For example,

$$Mg + H_2SO_4 \longrightarrow MgSO_4 + H_2$$

Magnesium is unusual in that it forms hydrogen with very dilute nitric acid (experiment 6.14).

Demonstration experiment 7.14 *Action of magnesium on steam*

Put water to a depth of 3 cm in a hard glass test-tube, then put in asbestos wool or paper tissues until all the water is soaked up. Put in a 15 cm length of magnesium ribbon folded as shown in Fig. 7.18, then set up the rest of the apparatus. Heat the magnesium ribbon strongly, occasionally flicking the flame down to the asbestos to ensure a constant supply of steam over the magnesium. When the reaction of the magnesium is over, take the end of the delivery tube from the water at once. Test the gas in the gas jar to see if it will burn.

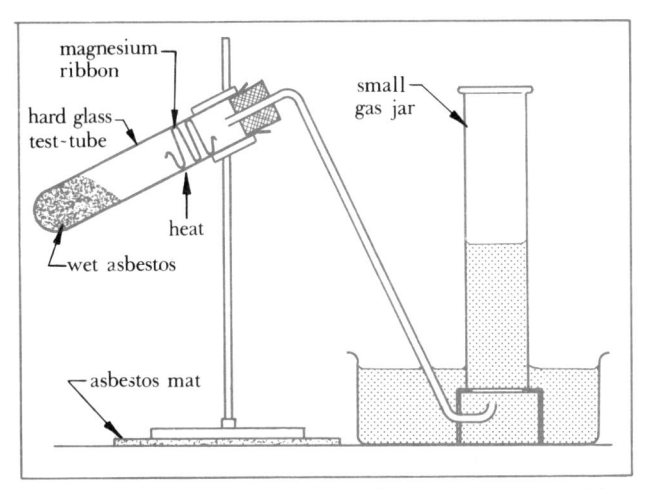

Figure 7.18 A wet-asbestos experiment: hot magnesium reacts with steam

Magnesium reacts with steam, burning in it to produce hydrogen, magnesium oxide, and a large quantity of heat.

$$Mg + H_2O \longrightarrow MgO + H_2 + heat$$

This is a reduction of the steam by removal of oxygen, the magnesium becoming oxidized at the same time.

Magnesium is used in flares, fireworks and incendiary bombs, and in the production of light, strong alloys with aluminium and zinc. The alloys are used principally in car and aircraft parts.

Magnesium oxide MgO

Magnesium oxide, which is a white powder sometimes called magnesia, is made by burning magnesium or by heating magnesium carbonate. It is an alkaline oxide and forms magnesium hydroxide, which is a mild alkali, by reaction with water. Milk of magnesia, a suspension containing magnesium hydroxide, is used to counteract excess acid in the stomach.

Magnesium oxide has a very high melting point indeed, and is used to make bricks for lining furnaces subject to high temperatures.

Aluminium Al

Remember that aluminium has a valency of three and forms an ion Al^{+++}. Try to make up the formula for the oxide, hydroxide, and sulphate of aluminium and iron(III) (ferric iron).

The ore of aluminium is bauxite, a form of hydrated aluminium oxide Al_2O_3. Aluminium oxide cannot be smelted with carbon as zinc and iron are; electrical energy has to be used to reduce it to aluminium. The ore is purified and dissolved in a suitable solvent, carbon electrodes are put into the mixture, and the passage of an electric current produces aluminium and oxygen (which slowly burns away the carbon electrodes). Because this extraction is difficult and expensive, and because aluminium, although the commonest metal in the Earth's crust, is thinly spread, it has only been used extensively for about a hundred years. This may be compared with the five thousand years for which copper has been used by man. Aluminium is extracted near Fort William and in other places where hydroelectric power provides a supply of cheap electricity.

Aluminium is a silvery coloured metal, and silver-coloured paint consists of aluminium dust suspended in a type of varnish. It is a malleable metal, easily rolled into thin sheets which are often used as 'silver' paper and cooking foil. Aluminium is a good conductor of heat, so is used to make kettles and pans, cylinder heads and pistons, and other car and motor cycle parts. It is also a good conductor of electricity, and the cables of the National Grid are thirty-seven or sixty-one strands of aluminium woven round a core of galvanized steel which provides extra strength. This steel-cored aluminium cable is cheaper, lighter, and stronger than a copper cable of equivalent current-carrying capacity.

When exposed to air and water, aluminium stays shiny for longer than most metals. There is attack of the surface of the metal, forming aluminium oxide, but this usually forms a thin layer which sticks firmly to the metal and prevents further reaction. This layer can be made thicker by an electrolytic process called **anodizing**. The aluminium article is put in a solution and made the anode of an electrolytic cell. By electrolysis, oxygen is made on the surface of the aluminium, and the oxygen thickens the aluminium oxide layer, making it hard and shiny in the process. If molecules of dye are put in the solution some of these are trapped in the layer of aluminium oxide. Thus highly coloured anodized articles (e.g., ashtrays, cycle mudguards, and pan lids) may be made as well as shiny silvery ones.

The density of aluminium is low; 1 cm^3 weighs 2·7 g, which is only about one-third the weight of the same volume of steel. The resistance to corrosion and light weight of aluminium make it suitable for outdoor uses, such as window frames, roofing sheets and aircraft, car, ship, and bicycle parts.

In many of the applications of aluminium an alloy containing usually less than 5 per cent of other elements, such as copper, zinc, manganese, or silicon, is used, because these alloys can be up to six times stronger than aluminium itself. Hundreds of aluminium alloys are available, many of them being sold under the group name Duralumin or Dural.

Aluminium reacts with dilute hydrochloric acid forming hydrogen and aluminium chloride solution.

$$2Al + 6HCl \longrightarrow 2AlCl_3 + 3H_2$$

Aluminium reacts with warm sodium hydroxide solution, giving hydrogen and a solution of sodium aluminate.

$$2Al + 2NaOH + 2H_2O \longrightarrow 2NaAlO_2 + 3H_2$$

For this reason aluminium kitchenware should not be cleaned with alkaline cleaners such as sodium bicarbonate, or it would be attacked.

It is very difficult to convert aluminium oxide to aluminium in the extraction of aluminium, so, conversely, aluminium itself is relatively easy to convert to aluminium oxide. Aluminium will, in fact, remove oxygen from other compounds, thus reducing them, as in the thermit reaction (experiment 7.7).

$$2Al + Fe_2O_3 \longrightarrow Al_2O_3 + 2Fe + heat$$

This reaction has been used for welding in situations where no electricity or oxygen/acetylene mixture is available. Thermit mixture consisting of aluminium dust and iron(III) oxide (ferric oxide) is packed round the parts to be joined and then lit by a fuse. The iron formed welds the joint together on solidification.

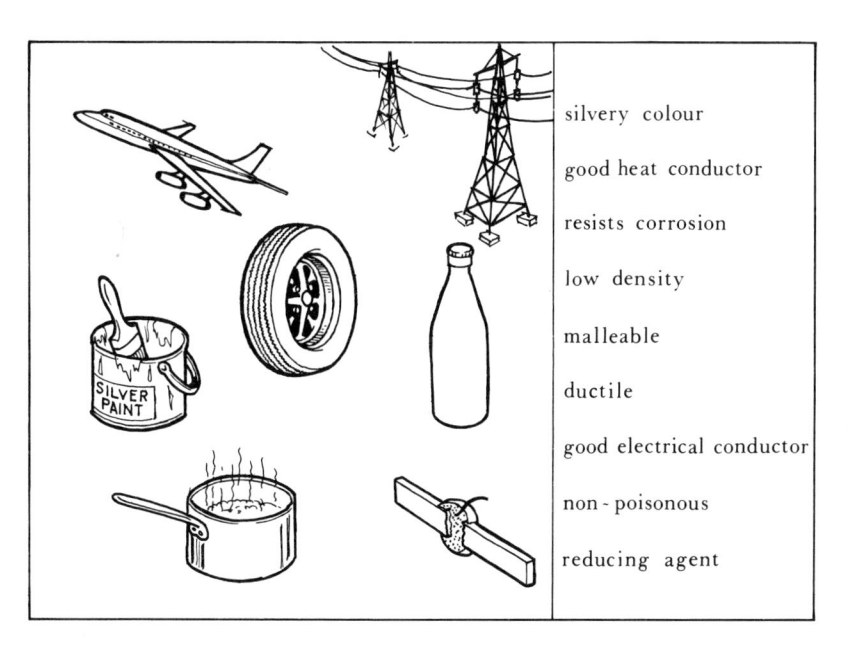

Figure 7.19 Which of the properties listed make aluminium suitable for each use?

CHEMISTRY

Aluminium sulphate $Al_2(SO_4)_3 \cdot 18H_2O$

Aluminium sulphate is a white powder which is soluble in water giving a solution which can be shown by the use of indicators to be acidic. Aluminium sulphate therefore releases carbon dioxide from sodium hydrogen carbonate solution. If sodium hydrogen carbonate solution plus detergent is mixed with aluminium sulphate solution, foam is produced by the carbon dioxide made. The reaction is used in foam fire extinguishers. The pressure of the carbon dioxide produced propels a jet of liquid containing bubbles of carbon dioxide on to the base of the fire, which is extinguished both by the carbon dioxide and the liquid.

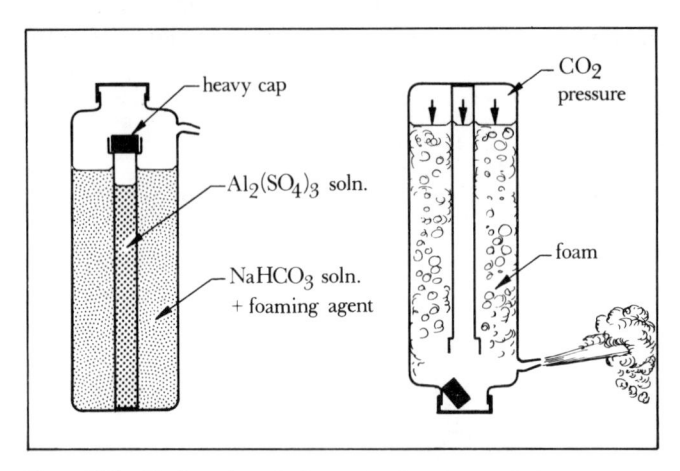

Figure 7.20 The foam from the fire extinguisher is propelled by the pressure of carbon dioxide made from sodium hydrogen carbonate and aluminium sulphate solution

You should compare this action with that of the soda-acid fire extinguisher shown in Fig. 6.3.

Aluminium sulphate is also used as an additive in paper-making to increase the strength and quality of the paper, and in sewage and water treatment.

Alums

There is a series of compounds known as alums, a typical example being potassium aluminium sulphate dodecahydrate (potash alum) $KAl(SO_4)_2 \cdot 12H_2O$. Other alums contain chromium or iron(III) instead of aluminium, or ammonium or sodium in place of potassium. Alums can be used (as can aluminium sulphate) as **mordants** in dyeing. A fugitive dye does not stick to the fabric well and is therefore washed off easily. Certain aluminium compounds stick to the fibres of fabrics, and the dye then sticks to the aluminium compound (mordant), which acts as a sort of glue between the fibres and the

METALS OLD AND NEW

dye molecules, forming a combination which will not wash off the fabric—a fast dye.

Uses of metals

Why is a cooker made of steel, a pan of aluminium, a coin of copper–nickel alloy, and the plating on a teaspoon of silver? The uses of a metal obviously depend on both its chemical properties (resistance to corrosion, and the readiness with which it may be plated) and its physical properties (strength, density, heat and electrical conductivity, appearance, and the ease with which it can be shaped, hardened, or softened). Another factor which always influences use is the price of the metal.

Table 7.4 Prices of metals

Metal	Percentage in Earth's crust	Price per kg £
aluminium	7·5	1·30
iron	4·7	0·45
calcium	3·4	7·55
sodium	2·6	1·50
potassium	2·4	10·15
magnesium	1·9	2·15
(hydrogen)	(0·9)	(3·20)
zinc	0·01	0·75
copper	0·007	1·85
tin	0·004	4·75
lead	0·002	1·00
mercury	0·00005	19·40
silver	0·00001	81·00
gold	0·0000005	1880·00

Note: the most abundant elements in the Earth's crust, the non-metal oxygen (49%) and the metalloid silicon (26%), have not been put in the table

Table 7.4 shows that although the price of a metal is connected with rarity (gold, for example, is very expensive), other factors are also at work. These include the ease of mining the ore, the concentration of metal within the ore, the difficulty of the extraction process, and the demand for the metal.

| Try to work out how each of these affects the price of the metal.

Although plastics are replacing metals to some extent, as in children's toys, food packing, rainwater guttering, and some car parts, the use of metals increases annually. Some of the metals used in a modern car are indicated in Fig. 7.21.

163

CHEMISTRY

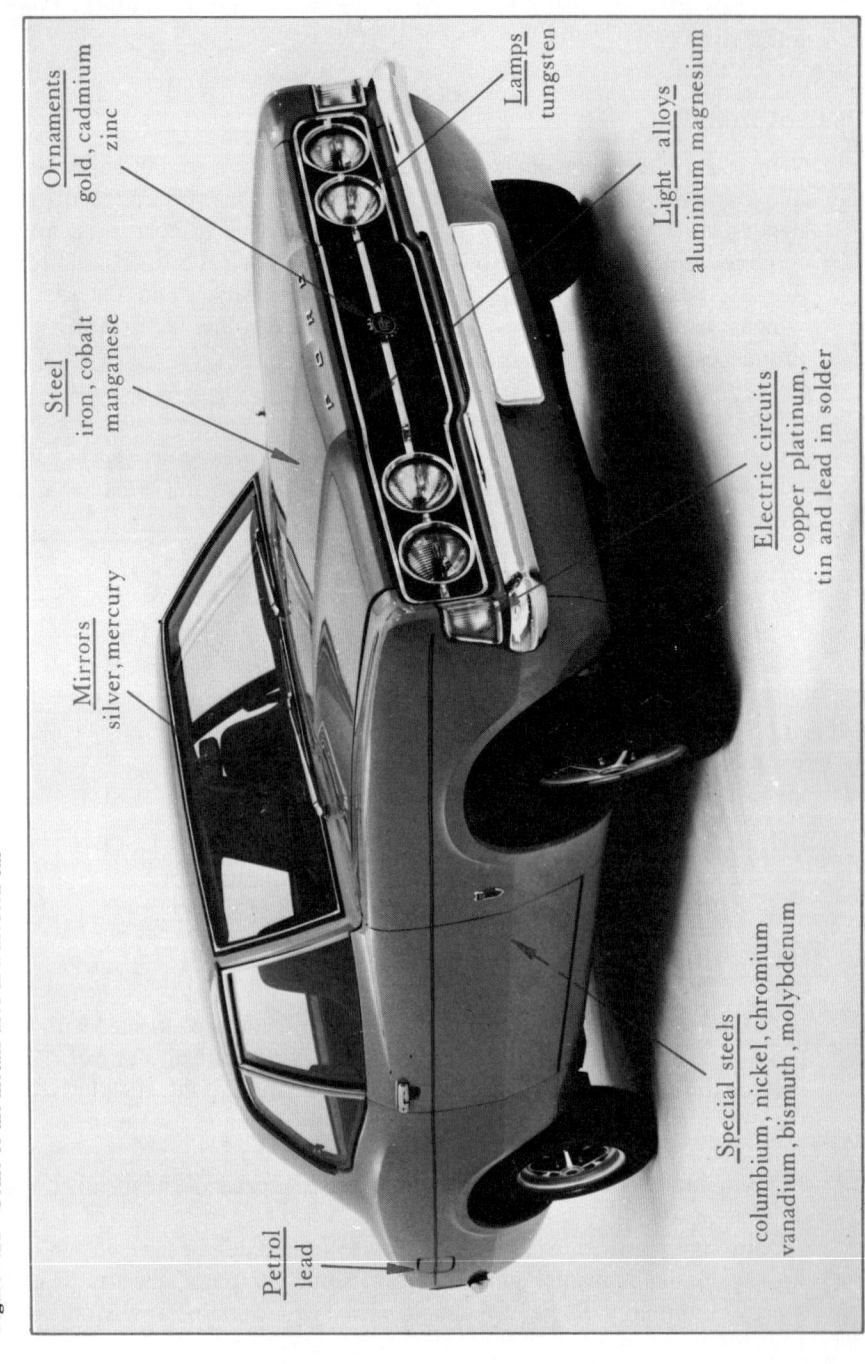

Figure 7.21 Some of the metals used in a modern car

- Ornaments: gold, cadmium, zinc
- Lamps: tungsten
- Light alloys: aluminium magnesium
- Steel: iron, cobalt, manganese
- Electric circuits: copper platinum, tin and lead in solder
- Mirrors: silver, mercury
- Special steels: columbium, nickel, chromium, vanadium, bismuth, molybdenum
- Petrol: lead

METALS OLD AND NEW

Physical properties of metals

Experimenting with metals and considering their physical properties show us that metals are usually dense, shiny, malleable solids which are good conductors of heat and electricity. The model or picture which scientists have of the structure of metals supposes that their atoms have one, two, or three electrons relatively loose. These electrons are easily detached from the atom forming a positive ion having the favoured structure with a full outer shell, plus one or more 'free' electrons.

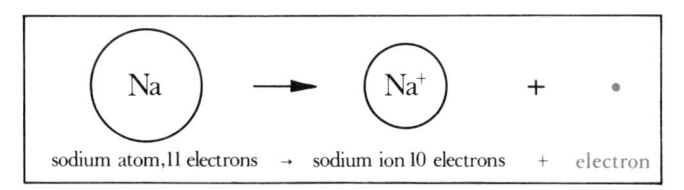

Na	→	Na⁺	+	•
sodium atom, 11 electrons	→	sodium ion 10 electrons	+	electron

Figure 7.22 A sodium atom becomes a sodium ion when an electron is removed

The easily removed electrons move about freely within an array of ions, making metals good conductors of heat and electricity. The loose electrons are sometimes described as an 'electron sea'. Because the electrons have negative charges they are attracted by the positive ions near them. These forces hold the ions together in a regular pattern, making metals solids. The layers of ions can slip over each other when enough force is applied and this explains the malleability of metals. Finally, the surfaces reflecting light efficiently make metals shiny.

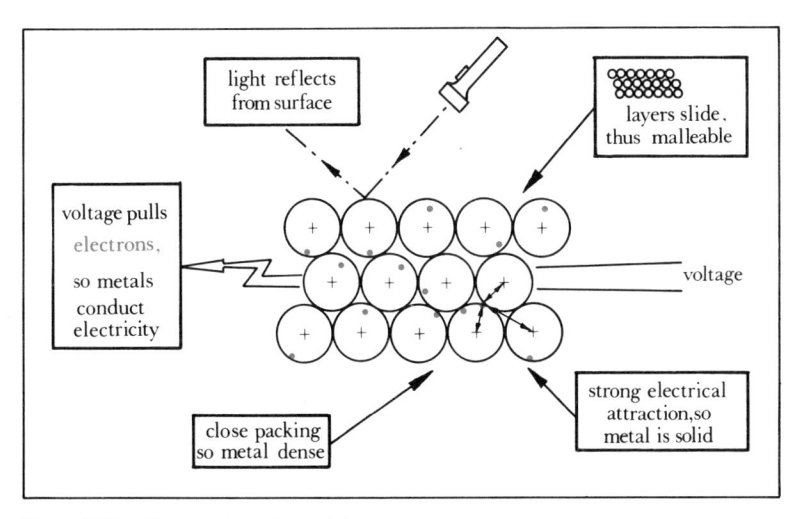

Figure 7.23 The structure of a metal

CHEMISTRY

Hardening and softening metals

Experiment 7.15 *Heat treatment of copper*

Use tongs to hold a piece of copper wire about 10 cm long and at least 1 mm in diameter, and heat it so that as much of the middle part as possible is red hot. Let the wire cool to room temperature, then use your fingers to bend it in the middle until it makes a right angle. Straighten the wire and repeat the bending twice.

Repeat the experiment but this time hammer the wire twenty times, holding it against a hard surface, before bending.

Is the wire always easy to bend?
What happened to the wire on repeated bending or hammering?

The perfectly regular pattern of ions in a piece of metal does not extend right through the metal. The piece is made of many small regions (crystals or grains). In each crystal the arrangement is similar to that shown in Fig. 7.23, but the crystals are not arranged regularly relative to each other. When the metal is bent the layers can slip only until they reach a crystal boundary.

When the copper is slowly cooled after being heated a small number of comparatively large crystals form, then the layers slip for long distances and the metal is soft. When the copper is bent or hammered a larger number of small crystals is formed, slipping is restricted, and the metal becomes hard. Metalworkers call this work-hardening.

Experiment 7.16 *Heat treatment of steel*

Take a steel knitting needle and try to bend it with pliers. Holding it in tongs, heat the needle until it is red hot, quickly plunge it into cold water, and stir it about until it is cool. Try to bend the needle at the blackened part. (**Warning:** it will probably snap, so be careful not to cut yourself on the sharp ends.)

Take the larger, brittle, broken part of the needle and polish it with emery cloth. Heat it cautiously until the blue colour which forms on the surface has spread for about 2 cm up the needle, then plunge it into the water again. Try to bend the needle at the part which is blue.

A steel knitting needle is hard but can be bent with pliers. If it is heated red hot (about 1000°C) and cooled rapidly it becomes very hard but brittle and can be snapped. Further heating to a moderate temperature (about 350°C, as indicated by the blue colour of the thin oxide film on the surface) followed by quenching in cold water tempers the steel. The tempered steel remains hard but is no longer brittle.

METALS OLD AND NEW

These changes in hardness and brittleness are caused by changes in the small crystals of which steel is composed. The changes are more complex than those in copper because there is carbon present in the steel in addition to the iron. The processes of hardening and tempering steel are of immense importance in toolmaking.

Chemical reactivities of various metals

Metals reacting with water

We have considered the action of water on various metals; some react vigorously with water, others only react with steam, and others do not react at all.

> Try to put these metals in order, the one which reacts most vigorously with water first, and the one that reacts least vigorously last: calcium, copper, iron, lead, magnesium, sodium.

The most spectacular and vigorous reaction is with sodium, followed by calcium (reacts with cold water), then magnesium and iron (react with steam), then lead and copper which do not react with water.

So, the order of reactivity to water is: Na, Ca, Mg and Fe, Pb and Cu.

Metals reacting with oxygen

If we consider burning, we can put the metals calcium, copper, iron, magnesium, sodium, and zinc in order of reactivity to oxygen.

> Try to do this for yourself.

The most ready reactions are with sodium, magnesium, and calcium which burn brilliantly in air or oxygen. Iron wire or filings burn giving off sparks if strongly heated, and granulated zinc burns if heated until it is molten and stirred vigorously. Copper does not burn, but a black surface film of copper oxide forms if copper is heated in air or oxygen.

The order of reactivity to oxygen is thus: Na and Ca and Mg, Zn and Fe, Cu.

Metals reacting with dilute hydrochloric acid

We can similarly arrange the metals copper, iron, magnesium and zinc in order of the vigour of their reaction with dilute hydrochloric acid.

> Try to do this for yourself.

167

The most ready reaction is magnesium, followed by zinc and iron, while copper does not react with dilute hydrochloric acid. The order of reactivity to dilute hydrochloric acid is thus: Mg, Zn and Fe, Cu.

Surveying all these results we see these orders:

to H_2O	Na		Ca		Mg	and		Fe, Pb Cu
to O_2	Na	and	Ca	and	Mg,	Zn	and Fe,	Cu
to HCl					Mg	Zn	and Fe,	Cu

The orders are essentially the same, and they represent a general order of chemical reactivity of the metals. This is the order of the ease with which a metal is willing to become part of a compound, i.e., to form an ion by electron robbery, such as happens when magnesium reacts with oxygen forming $Mg^{++}O^{--}$, magnesium oxide. Many other experiments could be done and these would give similar results. If the other metals were placed the order would become:

K Na Ca Mg Al Zn Fe Sn Pb Cu Hg Ag Au

This series is known as the **electrochemical series**.

If it is very easy for a metal to become a compound (e.g., sodium very readily becomes sodium oxide), it is very difficult to reverse this change and decompose the compound to get the metal back again. Thus the metals potassium, sodium, calcium, magnesium, and aluminium at the head of the electrochemical series, which are readily converted to oxides or to chlorides, cannot be smelted with carbon to prepare the metals. These metals are made by electrolysis, which means using electrical energy to release the metal.

The metals zinc, iron, tin, lead, and copper can be smelted using carbon. Mercury is extracted by heating the ore and silver and gold can be found uncombined. We can see that the electrochemical series is roughly the reverse of the order of ease of extraction of metals, and is therefore roughly the reverse of the order in time of their use by man, the metals easily extracted from their ores being those used first.

Experiment 7.17 *Replacement reactions of metals and salts*

(*a*) Into three test-tubes containing zinc sulphate, iron(II) sulphate (ferrous sulphate), and copper sulphate solutions to a depth of 3 cm, put small pieces of magnesium. Observe whether any reactions take place, and if so, what appears to be formed.

(*b*) Repeat the experiment using a small piece of zinc in magnesium sulphate, iron(II) sulphate, and copper sulphate solutions.

(*c*) Repeat the experiment using a piece of iron (wire or sheet steel is much better than filings) in magnesium sulphate, zinc sulphate, and copper sulphate solutions.

METALS OLD AND NEW

(*d*) Repeat the experiment using a piece of copper in magnesium sulphate, zinc sulphate, and iron(II) sulphate solutions.

If magnesium is put into copper sulphate solution a reddish-brown precipitate of copper is formed and the blue copper sulphate solution becomes paler and finally colourless, because magnesium sulphate solution is made.

$$Mg + CuSO_4 \longrightarrow Cu + MgSO_4$$

The magnesium is said to replace or displace the copper from the copper sulphate.

Magnesium similarly replaces zinc from zinc sulphate solution and iron from iron(II) sulphate solution, leaving magnesium sulphate solution in both cases.

The whole series of displacement experiments can be illustrated by a diagram where ✓ represents a displacement reaction and × represents no reaction.

Table 7.5 Results of displacement experiments

	$MgSO_4$	$ZnSO_4$	$FeSO_4$	$CuSO_4$
Mg		✓	✓	✓
Zn	×		✓	✓
Fe	×	×		✓
Cu	×	×	×	

Magnesium, which displaces three of the other metals, is obviously the most active of the three metals considered in these replacement reactions, followed by zinc, iron, and copper in this order. The order Mg, Zn, Fe, Cu is the same as the other activity orders. A metal will displace from its salt another metal which is lower in the electrochemical series. For this reason the electrochemical series is sometimes called the **activity series** or **displacement series**. This replacement order is as expected, because metals high in the electrochemical series more easily become parts of compounds (ions) than the lower metals.

Chapter summary

It is often convenient to divide elements into the classes metals and non-metals. There is no strict dividing line between metals and non-metals and elements such as silicon and germanium which do not fit properly into either class are put into a third category—metalloids.

CHEMISTRY

A metal always forms a simple positive ion (a cation) and always has at least one basic oxide. It is usually a dense, shiny, malleable solid which is a good conductor of heat and electricity. A metal has one, two, or three electrons detached from its atom and these electrons move quite freely within a closely packed array of positive ions.

Some metals are found uncombined, e.g., gold, others (e.g., silver) can be extracted merely by heating the ore. Most metals must be extracted by smelting, i.e., reducing with carbon in a furnace (e.g., zinc, iron, and lead), or by electrolysis (e.g., sodium, calcium, magnesium, and aluminium).

The electrochemical series is a list of elements in order of reactivity, and this order is in general the same for all simple reactions of metals, such as those with oxygen, water, and dilute hydrochloric acid, and their displacement reactions.

Questions

1. State three differences between metals and non-metals, and in two of the cases name a metal which is an exception to the general rule you have quoted.

2. A manufacturer decides to make an electric kettle with a stainless steel body and lid, and a plastic handle secured by brass nuts and bolts. Name and give the symbols for the five metals he is using, and explain why the two alloys are suitable for their purposes.

3. You find some old blackened coins when digging. How would you test one to see if it contained copper? Why could the Romans make coins of copper alloys, but not of aluminium alloys?

4. Of the metals magnesium, iron, zinc, and copper name the one which (*a*) is extracted electrolytically, (*b*) does not give hydrogen with a dilute acid, (*c*) reacts reversibly with steam, (*d*) is used to galvanize iron, (*e*) can be trivalent, (*f*) is lowest in the activity series (electrochemical series).

5. Explain what is meant by each term, and in each case give an example: (*a*) electrolysis, (*b*) amalgam, (*c*) deliquescent, (*d*) cation, (*e*) mordant, (*f*) alloy, (*g*) galvanizing.

6. Construct a flow-sheet illustrating the reactions of zinc with oxygen, sulphuric acid, hydrochloric acid, and copper sulphate solution.

7. Describe what you would see, name the products, and write the equation for the action of heat on (*a*) calcium carbonate, (*b*) sodium nitrate, (*c*) calcium hydroxide, (*d*) lead nitrate.

8. Iron(III) oxide (ferric oxide) may be reduced by carbon monoxide or by aluminium. Explain briefly how each reduction is done (no diagrams are needed), and mention a use of each reaction.

9. When dilute sulphuric acid is added to iron a gas A is evolved and a liquid B remains. If B is crystallized a pale green solid C is formed. On heating, the solid C leaves a brown residue D, and a mixture of gases E is evolved. Identify and give the formulae of A, B, C, D, and E.

8

Detergents

Queen Elizabeth I is said to have had a bath every month whether she needed it or not, whereas we now spend a lot of our time washing ourselves, our clothes, cars, cooking utensils, and other possessions. Chemists have made life easier for us by inventing detergents.

Detergents at work

A detergent is a general term for a cleaning agent used in solution in water. There are two main types of detergent—soap, and synthetic or soapless detergents. Using the word 'detergent' by itself to mean 'synthetic detergent' exclusively is misleading.

Both synthetic (soapless) and soapy detergents have similar molecular structures. Their molecules have long tails made of hydrogen and carbon,

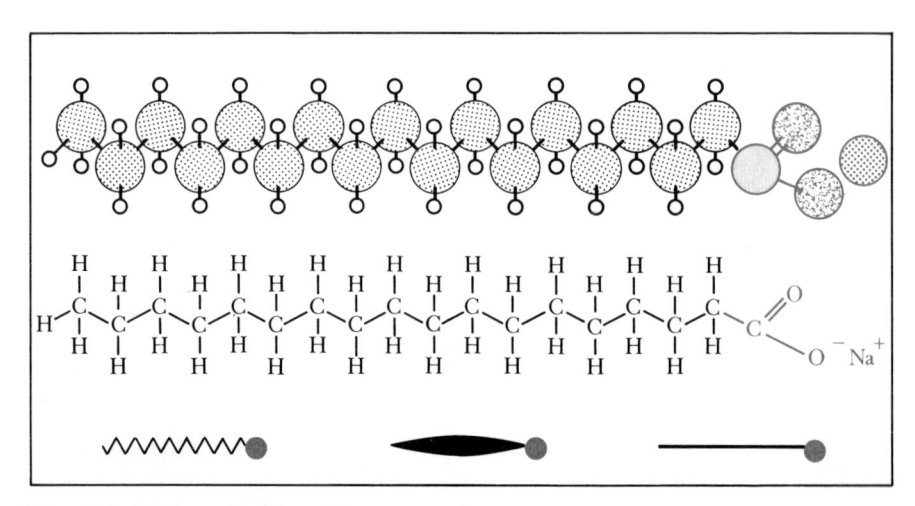

Figure 8.1 Five representations of the structure of soap

DETERGENTS

and short heads containing oxygen and other elements. The long tail is grease-loving and the head is water-loving. Fig. 8.1 above shows five ways in which a soap molecule may be represented; a model of one type of synthetic detergent molecule would be very similar, differing only in the type of atoms in the head.

Grease removal is the key to nearly all cleaning actions. Dirt is stuck on to collars and cuffs, a motor mechanic's hands, a used plate, grubby wallpaper near light switches, or hair which needs washing, by grease. (There are types of dirt such as ink, blood, grass, and dye stains which do not rely on the sticking power of grease, but most cleaning actions are directed to grease-held dirt.) The sequence of actions below shows how both soap and synthetic detergents remove grease from surfaces and fabrics (Fig. 8.2).

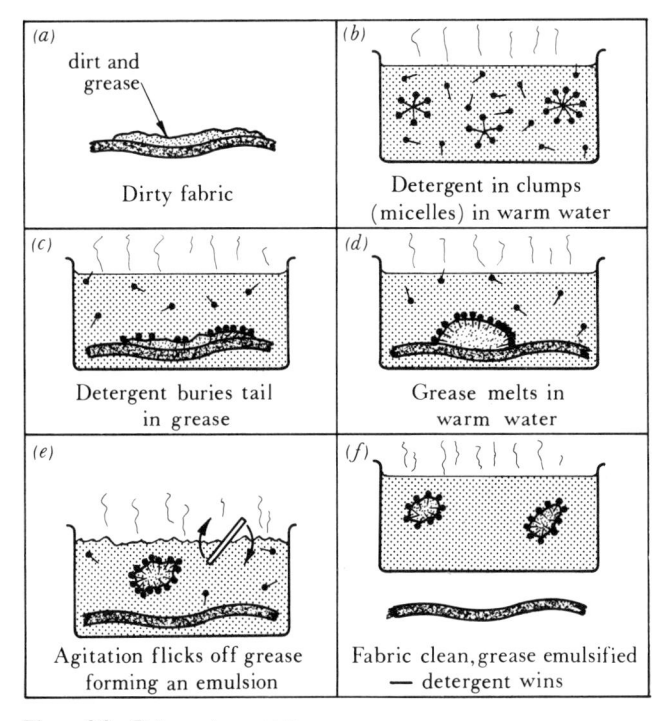

(a) Dirty fabric — dirt and grease	(b) Detergent in clumps (micelles) in warm water
(c) Detergent buries tail in grease	(d) Grease melts in warm water
(e) Agitation flicks off grease forming an emulsion	(f) Fabric clean, grease emulsified — detergent wins

Figure 8.2 Detergent *v.* grease

When put into water the detergent tries to keep its tail dry. Most of the molecules form little spherical clumps or **micelles** with their tails all together, leaving only a few free molecules. When a greasy fabric is put into warm water, the grease starts to melt and free detergent molecules bury their tails in it. As the free molecules are used up, micelles break open to provide a further supply of free molecules. Scrubbing or agitating the water then flicks the melted grease plus detergent molecules off the fabric, and it immediately forms a minute sphere surrounded and protected by detergent molecules. The formation of these protected spheres is an example of emulsification, and the grease plus detergent in the water is called an **emulsion**. The detergent coating on the surface repels other emulsified droplets, so the grease droplets cannot join together and redeposit on the fabric.

SOAP

Experiment 8.1 *Making soap*

Into a 100 cm^3 beaker put 5 cm^3 ethanol (industrial or methylated spirit is suitable), and 1 cm^3 olive oil. Then, carefully as it is caustic, add a very concentrated solution of sodium hydroxide. Stir the mixture and heat it to boiling. Keep it boiling for two minutes then add 25 cm^3 saturated salt solution. Reboil briefly, allow the mixture to cool, then filter.

Put a small quantity of the solid in a test-tube with some tap water and shake it to see if a lather is formed.

Soap has been made for hundreds of years by boiling fats or oils with alkalis. Animal fats, fish residues, and plant products such as palm oil and olive oil have been used, and the usual alkali is sodium hydroxide solution (caustic soda, which is known as lye in the soap industry). The mixture of fat and alkali is boiled to bring about a reaction called **saponification**. This reaction may be represented in several different ways:

$$\text{fat} + \text{alkali} \longrightarrow \text{glycerine} + \text{soap}$$

$$\text{glyceryl stearate} + \text{sodium hydroxide} \longrightarrow \text{glycerol} + \text{sodium stearate}$$

$$C_3H_5(C_{17}H_{35}COO)_3 + 3NaOH \longrightarrow C_3H_5(OH)_3 + 3C_{17}H_{35}COONa$$

The soap then has to be separated from the glycerine and the water which was added to the mixture as part of the sodium hydroxide solution. Sodium chloride solution is added to the mixture. Soap will not dissolve in salty water so the soap forms a curdled-looking mass which floats on top of the mixture. The wet mass of soap is skimmed off, squeezed to remove water, and prepared for sale. The glycerine (known chemically as glycerol) is extracted from the watery layer and sold as a by-product.

The conversion of fat to soap by boiling with alkali takes several days. A much quicker modern process has been invented, in which the fats or oils are boiled with steam at a very high pressure and temperature for about an hour. This converts the fats or oil to glycerine (glycerol) and an organic acid known as a **fatty acid**. The fatty acid is then neutralized with sodium hydroxide solution giving a salt (soap) plus water. This modern continuous **hydrolysis** (decomposition by water) process may be represented by:

DETERGENTS

First stage

$$\text{fat} + \text{water} \longrightarrow \text{glycerine} + \text{fatty acids}$$
$$\text{glyceryl stearate} + \text{water} \longrightarrow \text{glycerol} + \text{stearic acid}$$
$$C_3H_5(C_{17}H_{35}COO)_3 + 3H_2O \longrightarrow C_3H_5(OH)_3 + 3C_{17}H_{35}COOH$$

Second stage

$$\text{fatty acid} + \text{alkali} \longrightarrow \text{soap} + \text{water}$$
$$\text{stearic acid} + \text{sodium hydroxide} \longrightarrow \text{sodium stearate} + \text{water}$$
$$C_{17}H_{35}COOH + NaOH \longrightarrow C_{17}H_{35}COONa + H_2O$$

Whichever way it is made, soap is usually dried and mixed with colouring materials, preservatives, and perfume before it is sold. The soap and added substances are mixed together and either passed through large rollers to produce the thin sheets which break into soap flakes, or extruded. Extrusion is passing the soap through a nozzle so that it comes out as a long ribbon, which is then cut up, stamped into tablets and wrapped.

Synthetic detergents

Experiment 8.2 *Making a synthetic detergent*

Take about 0·5 cm depth of castor oil in a test-tube and carefully add concentrated sulphuric acid to a depth of approximately 1 cm. Stir and pour into a small beaker half full of water. Stir very gently to remove excess acid, pour away the water and repeat the washing process.

Shake a little of the product with tap water and see whether it lathers.

Types of synthetic detergent frequently used in the home are clothes washing powders, and the liquids used for dish washing and hair shampooing. The molecules of all types have a grease-soluble tail and a water-soluble head. The head is often the sodium salt of a sulphonate group —SO_3Na rather than the sodium salt of a fatty acid —$COONa$ present in soap. Synthetic detergents of this type are made by the action of concentrated sulphuric acid on substances extracted from crude oil. This produces a sulphonic acid head on a long grease-soluble chain, and the addition of sodium hydroxide solution neutralizes this acid, giving the sodium salt of the sulphonic acid, which is the synthetic detergent.

Synthetic detergents sold for dish washing are usually diluted with water before sale, often to the extent of containing 75 per cent water. Housewives prefer to put a large quantity of diluted synthetic detergent in their washing-up water, but hotels and hospitals use the concentrated synthetic detergent in smaller quantities. Selling synthetic detergents for clothes washing is a very complex and competitive business. Much money is spent on advertising and

CHEMISTRY

'free offers', and the synthetic detergent itself is mixed with many other substances before sale. Fig 8.3 gives an analysis of a typical washing powder.

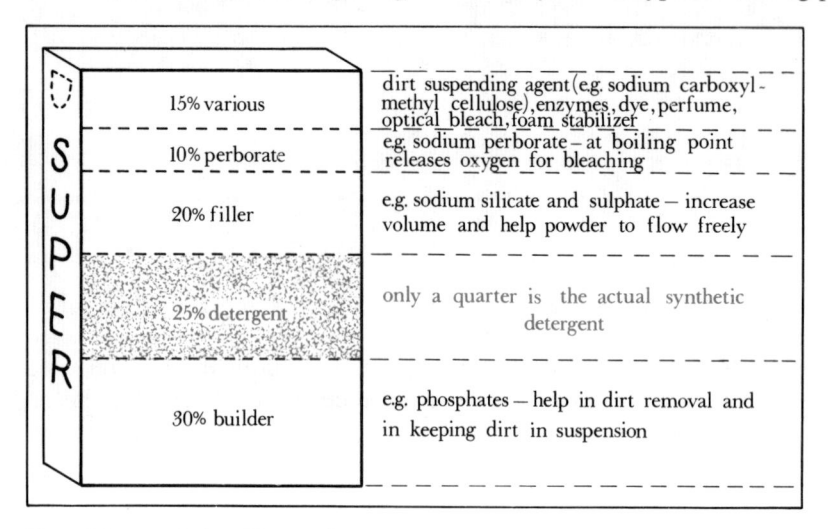

SUPER		
	15% various	dirt suspending agent (e.g. sodium carboxyl-methyl cellulose), enzymes, dye, perfume, optical bleach, foam stabilizer
	10% perborate	e.g. sodium perborate – at boiling point releases oxygen for bleaching
	20% filler	e.g. sodium silicate and sulphate — increase volume and help powder to flow freely
	25% detergent	only a quarter is the actual synthetic detergent
	30% builder	e.g. phosphates — help in dirt removal and in keeping dirt in suspension

Figure 8.3 A typical washing powder

The **enzymes** contained in enzyme detergents are catalysts extracted from living material, and their purpose in washing is to break down the proteins which help to hold stains like blood and gravy on to fabrics. Clothes are soaked overnight in the solution containing enzymes, and many people believe that it is the soaking rather than the enzymes which produces the results.

An **optical bleach** is a substance which absorbs ultra-violet light and re-transmits it as visible light. It is difficult to rinse out all the optical bleach from the fabric, so some dries on the surface. Figure 8.4 shows how extra light is reflected from a fabric containing optical bleach, making it appear whiter, lighter, and brighter, although it is no cleaner than a fabric with no optical bleach.

No optical bleach so UV (invisible to human eye) reflected	With optical bleach - extra visible light reflected so fabric looks bright

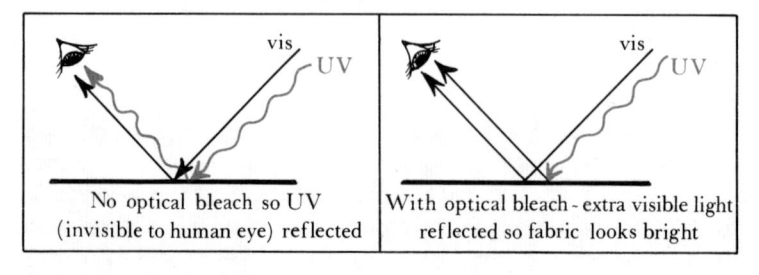

Figure 8.4 An optical bleach makes fabrics look whiter

Experiment 8.3 *Comparing soap and a liquid synthetic detergent*

(*a*) Fill a dropper with liquid synthetic detergent, watch closely, and squeeze out several drops to get an idea of the approximate size of one drop. Make a ball of soap about a quarter the volume of a drop—that is just over half the diameter of the drop—to allow for the water in the liquid synthetic detergent. Simultaneously add the ball of soap and a drop of the liquid synthetic detergent to two separate test tubes each half full of water. Which dissolves more readily?

(*b*) Add one soap flake to a test-tube containing distilled water, and add one drop of diluted synthetic detergent solution to another test-tube containing an equal volume of distilled water. Shake the two tubes vigorously and observe what happens.

(*c*) Repeat part (*b*) with salt water, hard water, and acidified water.

Experiment 8.3 shows that soap does not dissolve as readily as a liquid synthetic detergent, and that although soap lathers well in distilled water, the presence of hardness, dissolved sodium chloride, or acids decreases dramatically the efficiency of the soap. In practice, in areas where the water is very soft and pure, synthetic detergents have little advantage over soap other than their speed of dissolving, but over most of this country the water is hard and soap is inferior to synthetic detergents in convenience and washing power.

Causes of hard water

Experiment 8.4 *Evaporation of hard water*

Put one drop of hard water, specimen T, on a microscope slide. Hold the slide in your fingers about 25 cm above a small bunsen flame. When all the water has evaporated examine the residue, and then repeat the experiment with hard water, specimen P, and with distilled water on two more slides.

When hard water is evaporated an appreciable amount of solid is left, whereas distilled water leaves little or no residue. These solids were dissolved in the water originally, and were the cause of hardness in both types of hard water.

Experiment 8.5 *The two types of hardness*

Put about 3 cm depth of hard water (specimen T) in a boiling tube and boil it gently for about two minutes. Repeat the experiment with hard water, specimen P, and compare the results.

When one form of hard water is boiled a white precipitate is produced. This form is known as temporarily hard water (in our experiment we called it specimen T). The other form shows no change and so it is called permanently hard water. The precipitate looks similar to that produced when carbon dioxide reacts with lime-water. In fact both precipitates are calcium carbonate.

Temporary hardness is caused by a chemical reaction in water flowing over rocks such as limestone, chalk, and marble, which contain calcium carbonate. The water and the carbon dioxide dissolved in it react with the calcium carbonate to produce calcium hydrogen carbonate (calcium bicarbonate). The calcium hydrogen carbonate dissolves in the water and makes it temporarily hard. (Excess carbon dioxide clears turbid lime-water by this reaction.)

$$CaCO_3 + H_2O + CO_2 \longrightarrow Ca(HCO_3)_2$$

Because some of the carbon dioxide is combined with the water forming carbonic acid this equation is also written:

$$CaCO_3 + H_2CO_3 \longrightarrow Ca(HCO_3)_2$$

Permanent hardness is caused by water flowing over anhydrite, gypsum, or alabaster, which are rocks containing calcium sulphate. A little calcium sulphate dissolves in the water which therefore becomes permanently hard.

> Calcium hydrogen carbonate solution is temporarily hard water.
> Calcium sulphate solution is permanently hard water.

Properties of hard water

(*a*) Boiling hard water

Bringing permanently hard water to the boil has no chemical effect on it, but when, as in experiment 8.5, temporarily hard water is raised to boiling point the calcium hydrogen carbonate decomposes and a white precipitate of calcium carbonate appears.

$$Ca(HCO_3)_2 \longrightarrow CaCO_3 + H_2O + CO_2$$

Some of this precipitate sticks to the inside of kettles and boilers, coating them with a layer of stone, which decreases heating efficiency. This layer contributes to kettle fur and boiler scale.

(*b*) Evaporating hard water

The evaporation of either permanently or temporarily hard water leaves a residue (experiment 8.4). The residue is calcium sulphate if the water is permanently hard, but temporarily hard water leaves a residue of calcium carbonate. Calcium bicarbonate does not exist as a solid, so the reaction described in (*a*) above takes place on evaporation. That is, evaporation by boiling or at laboratory temperatures leaves a solid residue from both permanently and temporarily hard water. Thus both types of hard water can form boiler scale and kettle fur (Fig. 8.5).

Figure 8.5 The results of hard water—the pipe is almost blocked by boiler scale

(c) Action on soap

Both temporarily and permanently hard water react with soap to produce a scum floating on the surface of the water (experiment 8.3). This scum is also called lime scum, lime soap, and calcium soap, but it is, in fact, calcium stearate.

soap + temporary hardness $\longrightarrow$ scum + dissolved solid

sodium stearate + calcium hydrogen carbonate $\longrightarrow$ calcium stearate + sodium hydrogen carbonate

$$2C_{17}H_{35}COONa + Ca(HCO_3)_2 \longrightarrow Ca(C_{17}H_{35}COO)_2 + 2NaHCO_3$$

Similarly, for permanent hardness:

soap + permanent hardness $\longrightarrow$ scum + dissolved solid

sodium stearate + calcium sulphate $\longrightarrow$ calcium stearate + sodium sulphate

$$2C_{17}H_{35}COONa + CaSO_4 \longrightarrow Ca(C_{17}H_{35}COO)_2 + Na_2SO_4$$

These reactions use up soap which is thus wasted, and also form a sticky dirty scum or tide mark round the edge of a bowl or bath. The scum is particularly troublesome in hair washing, because it is hard to rinse off the hair and leaves it dull and greasy looking, so hair shampoos are made of synthetic detergent to avoid this scum. The entire detergent industry developed from the search for better hair shampoos during the 'thirties. Synthetic detergents have no reaction with hard water and are therefore as efficient in hard water as soft water areas. This and their speed of dissolving in water are the two main advantages synthetic detergents have over soaps (they also lather in sea water as when oil slicks are dispersed, and in water containing acids). Synthetic detergents have only slight advantages over soaps in areas where the water is very soft. The main disadvantage of synthetic detergents is that they sometimes make foams which last a long time, causing trouble at sewage works and on rivers into which sewage effluent is discharged.

Softening of hard water

Although hard water is acceptable for washing if synthetic detergents are used rather than soap, it is not suitable for certain other purposes such as dyeing, food preservation, bottle washing, photographic processing, or adding to car batteries. Also, many people dislike the taste of hard water and dislike washing in it as they use soap for personal washing. Many methods are available for softening water. The most obvious is distillation, which removes all the dissolved solids from hard water, but which is too expensive for everyday use.

Experiment 8.6 *Softening of hard water*

(a) Count the number of soap flakes necessary to produce a lather in a test-tube half full of hard water, any type, then repeat this, first putting in a small pinch of Calgon.

| Does Calgon soften hard water of the type you used?

(b) Repeat the experiment in part (a) but this time add a crystal of sodium carbonate decahydrate (washing soda) $Na_2CO_3.10H_2O$ instead of Calgon.

| Does washing soda soften hard water of the type you used?

(c) Set up the apparatus shown in Fig. 8.6 and pass hard water slowly through. Do not let the column run dry at any time during the experiment. Use the method described in part (a) to compare samples of water before and after passing through the ion exchange resin in the column.

| Does an ion exchange resin soften hard water of the type you used?

Experiments such as 8.6(a) show that both temporarily and permanently hard water can be softened chemically using Calgon, sodium hexametaphosphate. It is the calcium part of the calcium hydrogen carbonate or calcium sulphate in hard water which causes the reaction with soap. Calgon combines with this calcium (which is in the form of calcium ions Ca^{++}) making it unable to react with soap. Calgon dissolves readily if sprinkled into the temporarily or permanently hard water and the softened water is ready for use. Although the water still contains dissolved solids it is said to be softened because it does not react with soap.

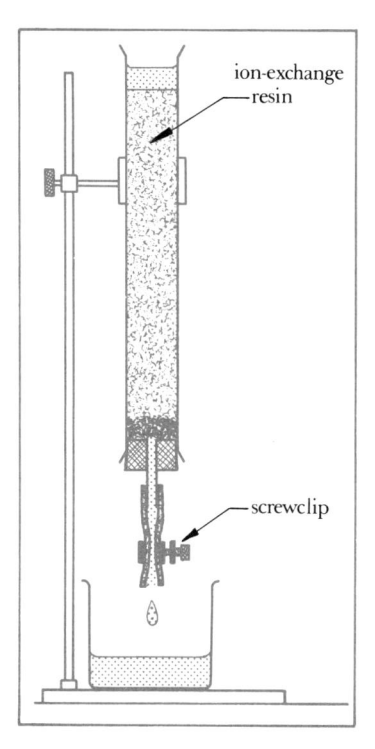

Figure 8.6 A model of a water-softener

Part (b) above shows that both temporarily and permanently hard water are softened by adding sodium carbonate decahydrate (washing soda crystals) $Na_2CO_3 \cdot 10H_2O$. When the crystals have dissolved they react with the calcium in the hard water to form a precipitate of calcium carbonate. The calcium in the calcium carbonate, although it is still in the form of calcium ions, is now in the solid state rather than dissolved in the water, and is unable to react with soap.

$$\text{thw} \quad Ca(HCO_3)_2 + Na_2CO_3 \longrightarrow CaCO_3 + 2NaHCO_3$$
$$\text{phw} \quad CaSO_4 + Na_2CO_3 \longrightarrow CaCO_3 + Na_2SO_4$$

Although the water still contains a dissolved solid (either sodium hydrogen carbonate or sodium sulphate) neither of these can react with soap so the water has been softened.

Bath salts and bath cubes are made from sodium sesquicarbonate crystals plus colouring and perfume. Their main effect is to soften the water so that soap lathers more easily.

As part (c) above shows, both temporarily and permanently hard water are softened by reaction with an ion exchange resin. Ion exchange resins are compounds containing long chains of carbon atoms with cross-links between

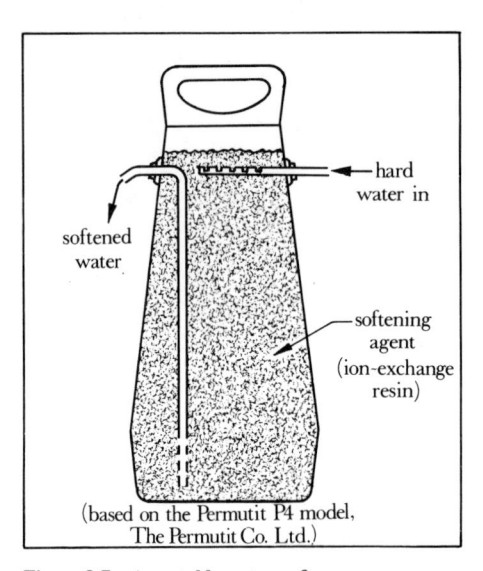

Figure 8.7 A portable water-softener

the chains. When water passes slowly through a water softener the reactions below take place. The resin is represented in the equation as $Na_2(res)$

$$\text{thw} \quad Ca(HCO_3)_2 + Na_2(res) \longrightarrow Ca(res) + 2NaHCO_3$$
$$\text{phw} \quad CaSO_4 + Na_2(res) \longrightarrow Ca(res) + Na_2SO_4$$

Both these equations may be represented by the ionic equation

$$Ca^{++}(\text{in water}) + 2Na^+(\text{in resin}) \longrightarrow Ca^{++}(\text{in resin}) + 2Na^+(\text{in water})$$

After the water has been softened it contains dissolved sodium hydrogen carbonate or sodium sulphate, but these do not react with soap. The resin is called an **ion exchange resin** because it exchanges calcium ions Ca^{++} in the hardness for the sodium ions Na^+, which are initially in the resin.

The used resin, i.e., calcium resin, stays in the water softener, which gradually becomes less efficient as the amount of sodium resin in it decreases. Fortunately it is not necessary to throw away used resin, as it may be turned back to sodium resin (regenerated) by leaving it overnight in contact with concentrated sodium chloride solution.

$$Ca(res) + 2NaCl \longrightarrow Na_2(res) + CaCl_2$$

This reaction may be represented by the ionic equation

$$Ca^{++}(\text{in resin}) + 2Na^+(\text{in water}) \longrightarrow Ca^{++}(\text{in water}) + 2Na^+(\text{in resin})$$

After the sodium chloride solution has stood in the water softener, water is flushed through to carry away excess salt and calcium chloride solution. The softener is then ready to work again.

	Cause	
T	$Ca(HCO_3)_2$ from calcium carbonate rocks $CaCO_3 + H_2O + CO_2 \rightarrow Ca(HCO_3)_2$	
P	$CaSO_4$ dissolved from rocks	

	Soap	Heat
T	forms calcium stearate scum	T $CaCO_3$ ptt. on boiling residue on evaporation
P	forms calcium stearate scum	$CaSO_4$ residue on evaporation only

Softening

Calgon — a polyphosphate — T✓ P✓

(distillation) T✓ P✓

washing soda $Na_2CO_3 \cdot 10 H_2O$ — T✓ P✓

ion-exchange resin — T✓ P✓

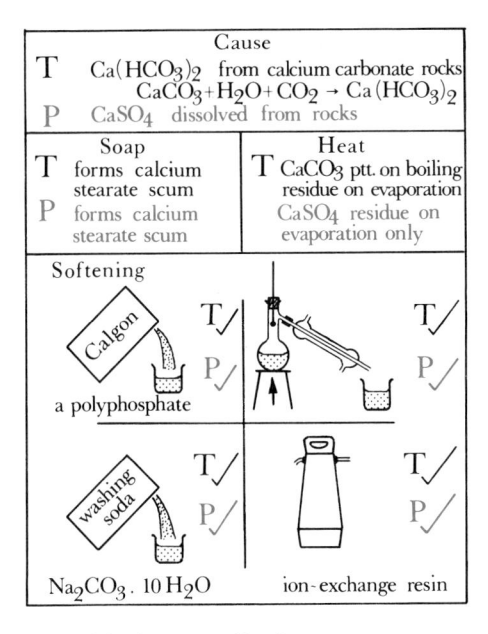

Figure 8.8 Summary of hard water

Advantages of hard water

Calcium is an essential item of diet. It is used in bone formation and is specially needed by young children and pregnant women. Hard water supplies a small amount of calcium.

Hard water is good for making beer, especially pale ale.

Very soft water dissolves small amounts of lead from water pipes. Lead is a cumulative poison so if your house has lead water pipes it is wiser not to drink water that has been standing in them for several days. This does not apply if the water is hard or if you have copper or plastic pipes.

Stalagmites and stalactites

Stalagmites, stalactites, and underground caves and passages in limestone areas are formed by the same reaction which makes water temporarily hard. Calcium carbonate in the limestone reacts with water containing carbon dioxide, which trickles down through cracks in the rocks. As the calcium carbonate reacts the cracks widen and caves eventually form. Stalactites (remember **c** in **c**eiling) are made when this reaction reverses and the calcium hydrogen carbonate (calcium bicarbonate) in the water drop on a cave ceiling decomposes and calcium carbonate is deposited. The reaction is reversible, dissolving of rock being one direction, and deposition of calcium carbonate the reverse.

$$CaCO_3 + H_2O + CO_2 \rightleftharpoons Ca(HCO_3)_2$$

The calcium carbonate slowly forms a stalactite, and the rest of the drop falling to the floor of the cave builds up a stalagmite from the ground.

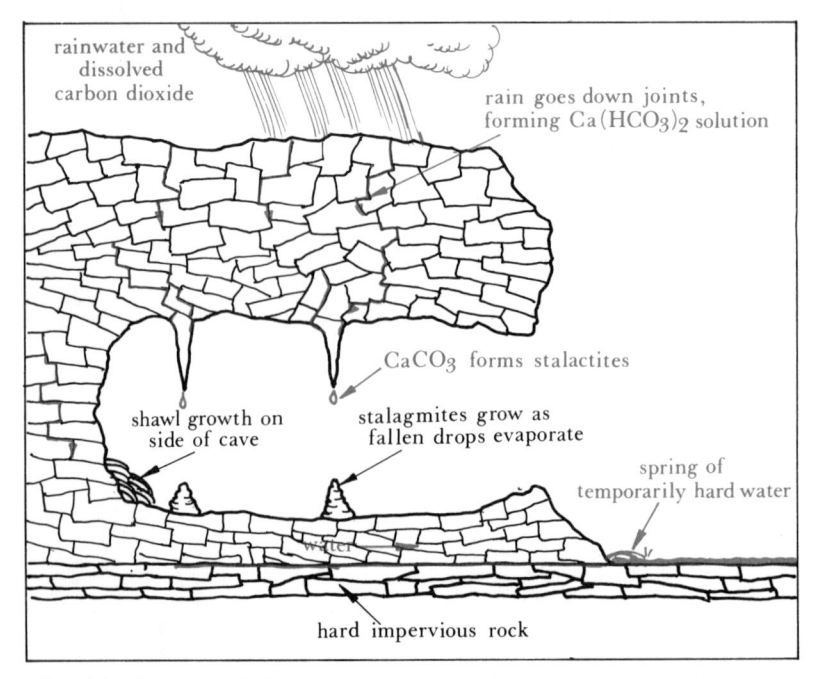

Figure 8.9 The reaction between calcium carbonate, water and carbon dioxide is involved in the formation of stalactites, stalagmites and temporarily hard water

Chapter summary

Synthetic detergents are made from oil and concentrated sulphuric acid, and soaps are made from fats and sodium hydroxide. Both synthetic detergents and soaps have molecules containing long grease-loving tails and water-soluble heads. They bury their tails in grease and emulsify it.

Temporarily hard water contains calcium hydrogen carbonate and permanently hard water contains calcium sulphate in solution. Soap reacts with these dissolved solids forming a scum, but synthetic detergents do not. Both types of hardness may be removed by Calgon, washing soda, ion exchange resins, or by distillation.

Questions

1. What is the meaning of (a) hydrolysis, (b) enzyme, (c) detergent, (d) micelle?

2. A new washing-up liquid is advertised as containing 'twice the lather' of its competitors. Explain how you would check (a) the manufacturer's claim, (b) whether the new product was better than other brands at washing crockery.

3. Describe an experiment to compare the hardness of water from your own home with the hardness of water from another town. How would you decide whether one of these specimens contained temporary or permanent hardness?

4. Describe, and give a word equation for a reaction in which calcium stearate is produced.

5. A piece of stalagmite is put into dilute hydrochloric acid. What would you see happening and why? (Give an equation.)

6. A friend argues with you that although soap X is twice as dear as soap Y, X lasts longer and washes cleaner, so is a better buy. Describe experiments to decide who is right. What other factors might influence your choice of soap?

9

Plastics

Most of you reading this book are wearing something made of a plastic material such as nylon or Terylene. Plastics now come into our lives so much that we take them for granted. They are used for one or more of these three reasons:

they can be **cheaper** than the traditional material, e.g., plastic hairbrush handles are cheaper than polished wood, plastic billiard balls are cheaper than ivory;

they can be **better** than the traditional material, e.g., plastic gutters are lighter than cast iron and do not rust, plastic washing-up bowls are quieter than metal and do not chip crockery;

they **differ** from natural materials and so are used when no natural material is suitable, e.g., ciné film and polythene bags.

Polythene

Compounds called hydrocarbons, which, as their name suggests, are made of hydrogen and carbon, occur in crude oil. These hydrocarbons are often

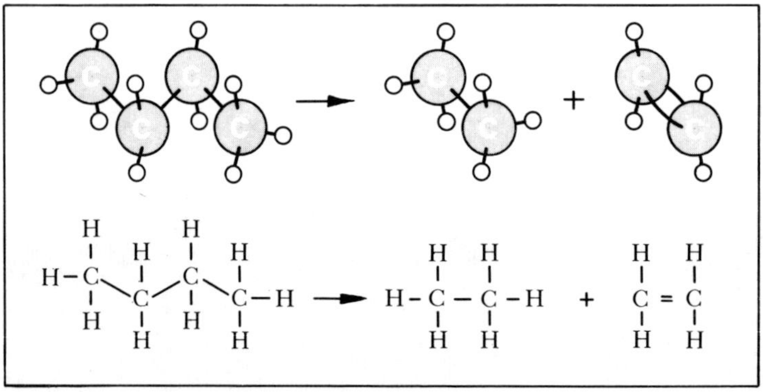

Figure 9.1   Cracking butane into smaller molecules

PLASTICS

cracked by using a catalyst to break them into smaller molecules which are needed for petrol and other purposes (chapter 5); e.g., if butane C_4H_{10} were cracked the results would be as shown in Fig. 9.1 on page 186.

The first of the molecules on the right-hand side of the equation is ethane C_2H_6, but the second is a type of compound different from ethane because it contains a double covalent bond between the carbon atoms, and has only four hydrogen atoms instead of the six which go with the two carbons in ethane. This compound is ethylene (ethene). Ethylene C_2H_4 is a colourless gas at room temperature, and is much used in the chemical industry because it is very reactive and can be made into many useful products. Road tanker lorries and rail tankers containing ethylene can often be seen.

Ethylene is the compound from which polyethylene is made. Using a substance called an initiator to start the reaction ethylene molecules can be made to join up in long chains in a process called **polymerization**. You should note that all ethylene molecules are the same, and they have been shown in two colours only to make Fig. 9.2 clear. The finished chain may consist of

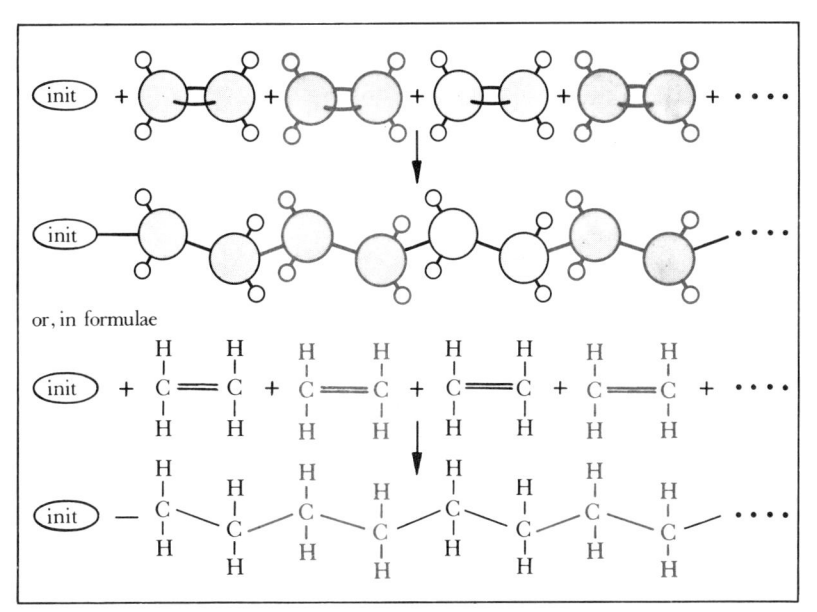

Figure 9.2 Polymerization of ethylene forming a chain

ten to twenty thousand individual ethylene units joined together. The chain stops growing when its growth point (i.e., the last ethylene molecule that is added on) meets and combines with another initiator particle. The initiator joins on the end and stops the chain from growing any more. The word 'poly' means many, as in 'polygon', and the long chain molecule is called a polyethylene, or polythene, molecule.

187

CHEMISTRY

Experiment 9.1 Properties of polythene

(a) Cut off the top and bottom of a polythene squeeze bottle and then weigh the cylinder you have made. Measure the volume of polythene in the walls by squashing the cylinder flat, rolling it up tightly, and pushing the roll fully into a measuring cylinder containing water. The rise in water level gives the volume of polythene. Work out the density of the polythene in g per cm^3.

A rough idea of the density of a specimen of polythene may be obtained by releasing it under water and seeing if it floats or sinks.

(b) From a polythene bag cut a strip of polythene about 1 cm × 15 cm. Draw a series of parallel lines a millimetre apart on a piece of paper, and make a mark on the polythene with a ballpoint pen. Arrange the mark on the polythene above the first line, hold the strip down firmly at the far end, and stretch the polythene gently until the mark is opposite the second line (see Fig. 9.3). Relax the pull and see if the polythene recovers its original length.

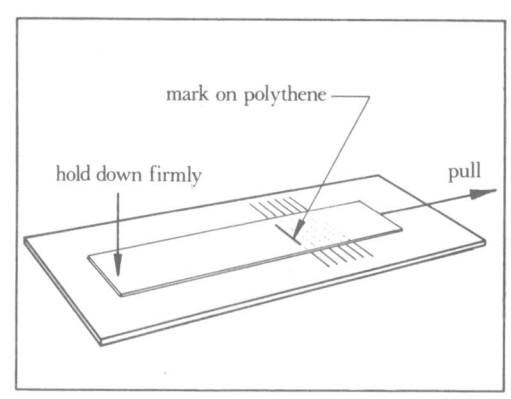

Figure 9.3 Is polythene elastic?

If it does, go on stretching a little farther each time and find out whether the polythene becomes permanently strained, i.e., does not recover its original length.

(c) Put a piece of polythene sheet over a piece of paper on which is written:

    conc. HNO$_3$ NaOH solution   acetone   alcohol(ethanol)   benzene

On to the polythene above its name put one drop of each of the compounds, being careful not to let the drops run together. Cover the drops with an upturned petri dish to slow evaporation. After ten minutes soak up each drop with a separate strip of filter paper, and examine the polythene to see if it has been attacked.

(d) Cut a strip 1 cm wide from a polythene bag and hold it in crucible tongs about $\frac{1}{2}$ metre above a small bunsen flame. Lower the polythene very

PLASTICS

slowly towards the flame so that it is heated gradually and observe what happens.
(*e*) Use a cell, wire, and lamp to test whether polythene conducts electricity.

Polyethylene, or polythene, is a waxy solid, transparent in thin sheets but translucent in thicker forms. It is less dense than water, but the densities of different specimens vary according to the manufacturing process used. It is completely waterproof, elastic, and has very good resistance to chemical attack. It is one of the best electrical insulators known. It is also cheap, easy to make into sheets, tubes, bottles, and solid articles, and can be coloured, made opaque or printed on. This list of its properties explains why it has so many uses. Its main disadvantage is that it softens at a fairly low temperature, and burns readily, forming carbon dioxide and steam if there is a sufficient supply of oxygen.

All these properties result from the structure of the molecules and their arrangement. It is a solid because the long-chain molecules are fairly strongly attracted to each other. The chains are twisted and become tangled, but they can slide past each other to a limited extent so under small forces polythene is elastic. When the polythene is heated, there is increased thermal motion of the molecules overcoming most of the attraction forces between the molecules, so the plastic softens and melts. When cooled the polythene resets in a new shape, so that it can be moulded into things such as bottles. Having a structure similar to that of mineral oils and paraffin wax (i.e., carbon and hydrogen atoms in long chains), polythene might be expected to repel water. This it does, so polythene is suitable for making squash bottles, film for wrapping food, for waterproofing paper and coating steel wire products such as dishdraining racks which must not rust. Finally, the fact that polythene contains no ions or free electrons (it is joined entirely by covalent bonds) makes it an electrical insulator.

Monomers and polymers, thermoplastics and thermosets

Experiment 9.2 *Types of plastic*

Collect small specimens of several types of plastic, drop them into a beaker of boiling water and boil for about two minutes. Take the plastics out of the water and sort them into two classes according to whether they have changed their shape or not.

There are two types of plastic material: **thermoplastics** such as polythene soften and melt easily when heated, but thermosetting plastics, often called **thermosets**, do not soften in boiling water. If heated strongly enough, thermosets decompose.

The formation of polythene by joining together of molecules of ethylene is an example of a simple type of reaction called **addition polymerization**.

189

Once the reaction has been started by an initiator, the double bond in ethylene opens out and provides a linking point for a further molecule to join to it. This continues until the chain ends—the molecules simply add on to each other. The starting material for polymerization reactions is called a **monomer** (mono – one) and the finished giant molecule containing thousands of monomers linked together is called a **polymer** (poly – many). All plastics, whether thermoplastics or thermosets, are polymers. Not all polymers are plastics, because some natural polymers such as rubber, starch, and cellulose are also known.

Thermoplastic — melts readily	Thermosetting — once made will not melt
e.g., cigarette melts hole into nylon sleeve	e.g., Bakelite ashtray unaffected by red-hot cigarette end
examples:- polythene polyvinyl chloride (PVC) polystyrene nylon Terylene	examples:- Bakelite, melamine–formaldehyde plastics urea – formaldehyde plastics

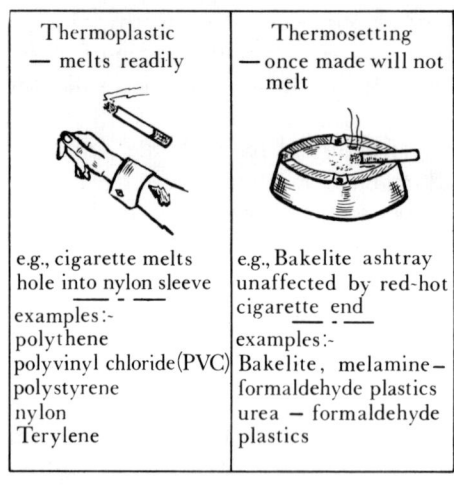

Figure 9.4 The two types of plastic

Now test yourself on some important words used in talking about plastics by seeing if you can understand this sentence and explain the technical terms in it to someone else.

Polymerization of monomers forms polymers, which may be of the thermosetting or thermoplastic type.

Close relatives of polythene

Ethylene (ethene), the monomer of polythene, has the formula C_2H_4.

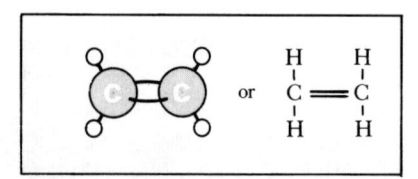

Figure 9.5 The structure of ethylene (ethene)

PLASTICS

A change in the structure of the monomer produces a similar change in the polymer. If a chlorine atom is substituted for one of the hydrogen atoms in ethylene, the monomer becomes vinyl chloride, and the polymer becomes polyvinylchloride PVC (Fig. 9.6).

$$\begin{array}{c} H \quad H \\ | \quad | \\ C=C \\ | \quad | \\ Cl \quad H \end{array} \text{ vinyl chloride}$$

or, in formulae

$$\cdots - \underset{Cl}{\overset{H}{\underset{|}{C}}}=\underset{H}{\overset{H}{\underset{|}{C}}} + \underset{Cl}{\overset{H}{\underset{|}{C}}}=\underset{H}{\overset{H}{\underset{|}{C}}} + \underset{Cl}{\overset{H}{\underset{|}{C}}}=\underset{H}{\overset{H}{\underset{|}{C}}} + \underset{Cl}{\overset{H}{\underset{|}{C}}}=\underset{H}{\overset{H}{\underset{|}{C}}} + \underset{Cl}{\overset{H}{\underset{|}{C}}}=\underset{H}{\overset{H}{\underset{|}{C}}} + \cdots$$

↓ polymerization

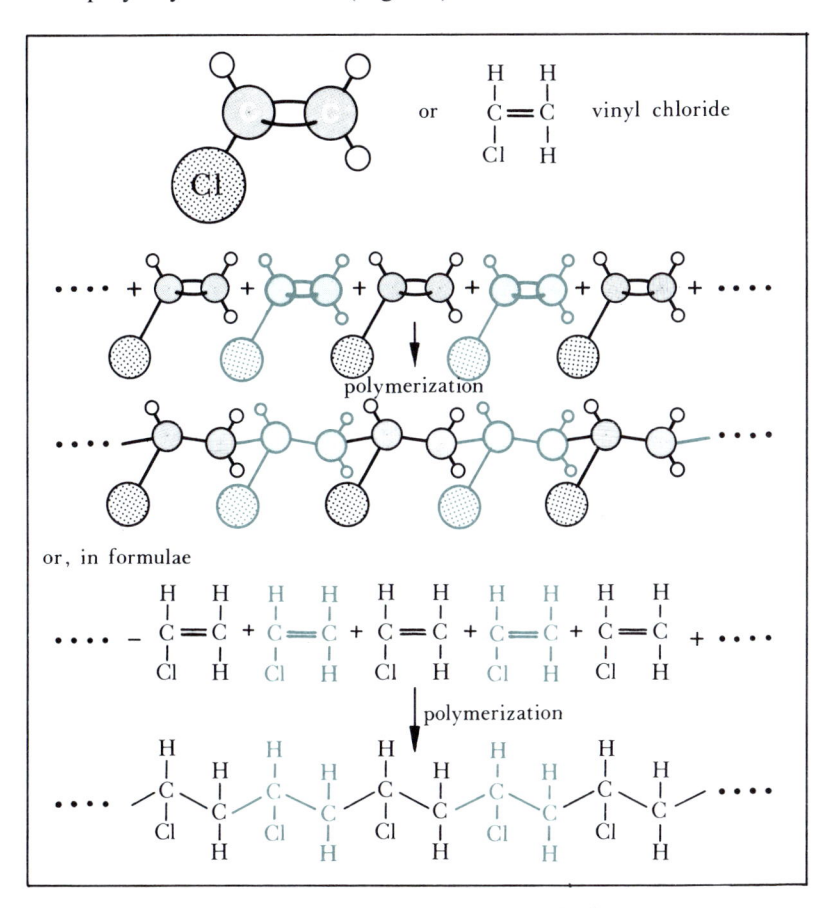

Figure 9.6 Vinyl chloride polymerizes to polyvinyl chloride, PVC

Polyvinyl chloride is denser, burns less readily, and is much more rigid than polythene. Clothing made of PVC does not contain pure PVC but has substances called **plasticizers** added to it to make it more supple. These substances act like lubricants between the long polyvinyl chloride chains, and enable the chains to slide over each other more easily.

Substituting a C_6H_5— group for one of the hydrogen atoms in ethylene produces styrene, the monomer from which polystyrene is made.

Polystyrene is a rigid glass-like material. A piece of polystyrene produces an almost metallic ringing noise when dropped on to wood. It can be used in its transparent form to make sandwich boxes, or it can be coloured by the addition of pigments of any colour. Many plastic toys are made of polystyrene. The expanded polystyrene used for ceiling tiles and as a packing material is made by blowing many tiny bubbles in polystyrene as it sets.

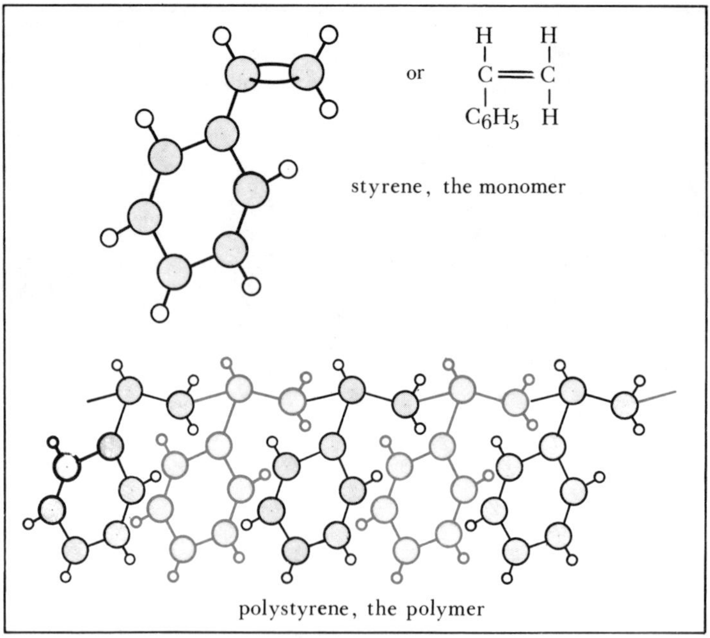

styrene, the monomer

$$\begin{array}{cc} H & H \\ | & | \\ C = C \\ | & | \\ C_6H_5 & H \end{array}$$

polystyrene, the polymer

Figure 9.7 **Formation of polystyrene**

The three polymers polythene, polyvinyl chloride, and polystyrene all have monomers containing double bonds, and all form polymers by addition. They differ by the side groups occurring on the long chain which makes up the backbone of the polymer molecule. The bigger the side group is, the more the side groups of various molecules get intermeshed, so large side chains make a polymer that is more rigid. Rigid polymers such as polystyrene crack or break when struck whereas flexible polymers such as polythene are tough and merely bend.

Condensation polymerization

Demonstration experiment 9.3 *Making nylon thread and chips*

Dissolve 1 cm^3 sebacoyl chloride in 25 cm^3 carbon tetrachloride and put this into a 100 cm^3 beaker. Dissolve 1 g of hexamethylene diamine (1.6 diaminohexane) in 25 cm^3 water, add 5 cm^3 dilute sodium hydroxide solution, and pour this second solution carefully down the beaker wall, so that it floats on top of the denser carbon tetrachloride layer without mixing. Cover the beaker with a watch-glass and warm it by standing it for 5 minutes in a large beaker containing water initially at 60°C. Where the layers touch a reaction takes place between the sebacoyl chloride and the hexamethylene diamine, and a skin of nylon is formed. Lift this slowly out of the beaker with tweezers, forming a thread, which may be wound on to a glass rod or test-tube. Test the thread by pulling gently to see if it is elastic.

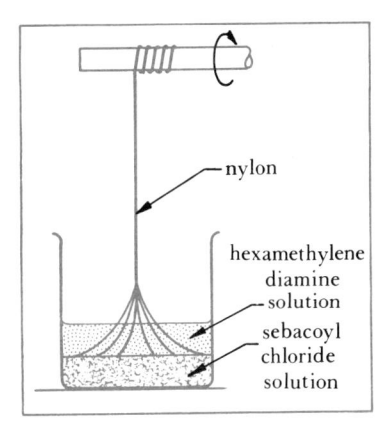

Figure 9.8 Making nylon thread

When you have produced some thread, stir the contents of the beaker so that the solution is mixed. Filter the mass produced, wash it by pouring water through the funnel, then squeeze the lump with a test-tube to remove some of the water it contains and allow it to stand overnight in a desiccator. Examine the solid chip of nylon produced, then touch it with the tip of a heated nail, and draw the nail away to produce a fibre.

Experiment 9.3 is an example of a condensation polymerization. This differs from addition polymerization in that when the two monomers react a hydrogen atom is squeezed out from the —NH_2 part of the hexamethylene diamine and a chlorine atom is squeezed out from the sebacoyl chloride. This leaves an unused bond at the end of each monomer, and these unused bonds link, joining the two monomer molecules. Since both monomers are double-ended, the reaction takes place at both ends of each monomer, so that a chain is formed. The hydrogen and chlorine which were squeezed out from the monomer molecules react forming hydrogen chloride. The type of polymerization, in which a substance such as hydrogen chloride is produced along with the polymer, is called **condensation polymerization**.

Representing hexamethylene diamine by H(hex)H and sebacoyl chloride

Cl(seb)Cl we can write the equation as:

$$H(hex)H + Cl(seb)Cl + H(hex)H + Cl(seb)Cl + \ldots$$
$$\downarrow$$
$$\text{polymerization}$$
$$\downarrow$$
$$H(hex)\underset{+HCl}{\rule{1cm}{0.4pt}}(seb)\underset{+HCl}{\rule{1cm}{0.4pt}}(hex)\underset{+HCl}{\rule{1cm}{0.4pt}}(seb)\rule{0.4cm}{0.4pt}\ldots$$

Nylon is most familiar as a yarn woven into fabrics—stockings and tights, socks, shirts, and sheets. A continuous filament is made by squeezing melted nylon through fine holes and then cooling it so that it sets into a fine fibre. The fibre is stretched, and then several fibres are twisted together to produce the yarn. For some purposes the continuous filament is chopped into short lengths which are then spun into nylon yarn just as raw cotton is spun into cotton thread. This type of yarn is called spun yarn or staple fibre yarn, and is warmer and softer to the touch than continuous filament yarn. Either sort of yarn may be woven into fabric. Nylon fabrics need little or no ironing, are strong, wear out slowly, and dry easily because nylon absorbs very little water. This non-absorbency can make nylon clammy and damp to wear in some circumstances.

As the experiment with the hot nail showed, nylon is thermoplastic. This means that it can be moulded into solid articles such as zips, curtain hooks, hinges, gear wheels, door fasteners, and drawer runners. Solid nylon is a strong milky-white solid which does not corrode, is slippery so needs no lubrication, and is quiet in use.

The properties of nylon depend on the structure of the polymer molecules and their arrangement. The nylon polymer molecules are long, thin chains and this helps nylon to form long, thin threads with the molecules lying along the length of the threads. The chains tangle and are attracted towards each other, but are not joined by chemical bonds. The possibility of movement of one molecule relative to another explains the elasticity and flexibility of nylon. On heating the polymer, the molecules move about more vigorously and the nylon softens and melts; it sets again on cooling and can therefore be moulded.

Since nylon and polythene both consist of long chain molecules whose chains are tangled together but not chemically linked, their physical properties are similar. In fact, all thermoplastics are of this nature and have similar physical properties. (Terylene, made by condensation of **ter**ephthalic acid and eth**ylene** glycol, also has tangled long-chain molecules and is thermoplastic.) The main differences between the various thermoplastics are in their resistance to chemical attack, e.g., by burning, the prolonged action of air and water, or concentrated nitric acid. Since the polythene chain contains carbon and hydrogen only and the nylon chain contains short lengths of

PLASTICS

carbon and hydrogen chain linked by

$$\begin{array}{cc} H & O \\ | & \| \\ -N- & C- \end{array}$$

groups, it is not surprising that the chemical reactions of the two differ, since the group containing carbon, nitrogen, oxygen, and hydrogen can be attacked by various chemical agents. Thermoplastics also differ in their degree of chain tangling, and interference caused by side groups. This affects their softening point, their flexibility, and solubility in solvents.

Thermosetting plastics

Demonstration experiment 9.4   *The production of Bakelite, a phenol-formaldehyde plastic*

(*a*) Reflux 25 g phenol, 50 cm³ 40% formaldehyde solution (formalin) and 3 cm³ bench sodium hydroxide solution until an orange or red viscous resin is formed. This takes about an hour.
(*b*) Pour off the watery layer above the resin and bake the resin for 6 hours in an oven at 50°C to complete the preparation.
(*c*) Test the hardness of the product by scraping it with your thumbnail and a knife-blade, then put a piece of the Bakelite in boiling water for 2 minutes and hold a second piece in a bunsen flame.

Bakelite, the first fully synthetic plastic produced, is made in a two-stage process:

(*a*) Phenol (carbolic acid) and formaldehyde solution (formalin) are boiled with sodium hydroxide solution, and a viscous orange or red liquid resin is formed. This resin has a long-chain structure.

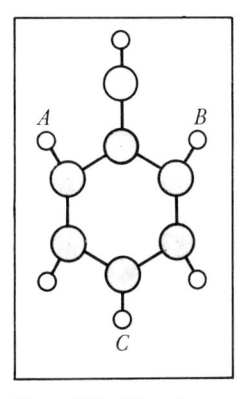

Figure 9.9 Phenol

CHEMISTRY

The phenol molecule C_6H_5OH may be represented as in Fig. 9.9 and the formaldehyde molecule CH_2O as in Fig. 9.10.

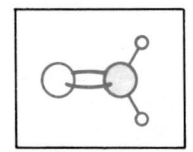

Figure 9.10 Formaldehyde

The resin production may then be represented as shown in Fig. 9.11.

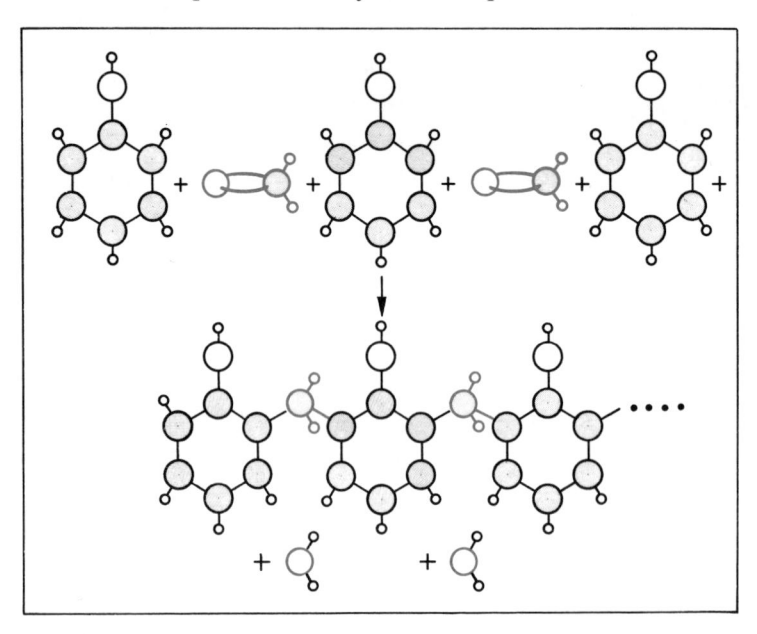

Figure 9.11 A condensation polymerization forming a long-chain resin

Linkages of the phenol molecule take place at positions A and B and water is eliminated. So far the reaction is similar to the production of nylon, where two monomers join together and produce long chains by condensation.

(b) When the long-chain resin is heated for several hours, new linkages form at some of the points marked C in Fig. 9.9. These new links join the chains into a rigid structure which extends into three dimensions, so the finished Bakelite is a hard solid (Fig. 9.12).

The chains are held in a network structure once the cross-links are made, so the material stays rigid; heating during the second stage sets the plastic permanently, so the plastic is called a thermoset or thermosetting plastic.

Moderate heat has no effect on Bakelite, whereas strong heat decomposes it completely.

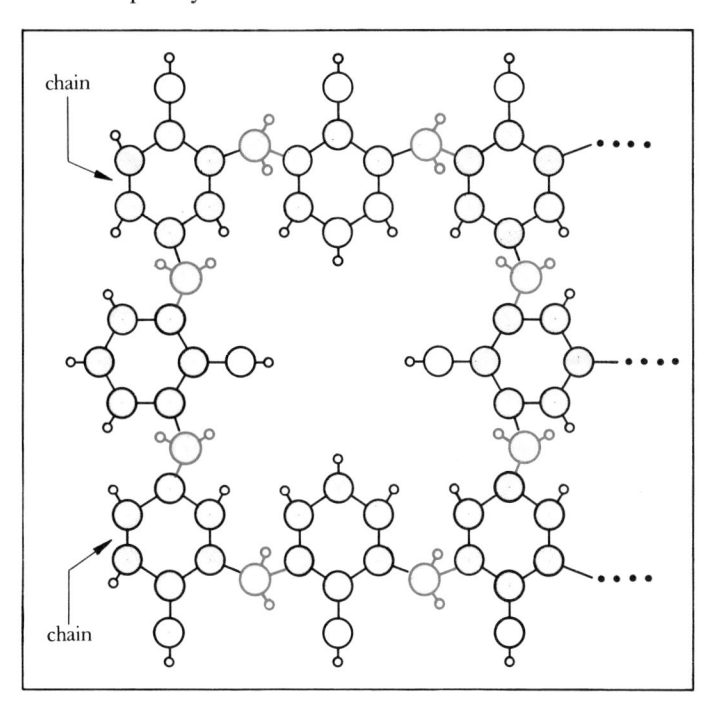

Figure 9.12 Cross links form and a rigid thermosetting plastic results

Bakelite is a dark-brown solid, hard but brittle. Up to 50 per cent of a filler such as asbestos fibres, or a very fine sawdust called wood-flour, is often mixed with Bakelite to increase its strength and toughness. It is used to make articles such as ashtrays, electric light fittings and switches, plug tops and sockets, screw-on bottle caps, buttons, furniture knobs and handles, motor car instrument panels, and handles for pans and electric irons.

Bakelite is not expensive, can be moulded accurately, has good resistance to chemical attack, does not deteriorate when exposed to light and air, and is cheap, a list of properties which reveals why it is used so extensively. Its main drawback is its unlovely dark-brown colour which cannot be altered except to black.

After the discovery of Bakelite chemists searched for other materials which would polymerize and cross-link in a similar way, without giving a final product which was brown. Modern white or brightly coloured plastic light switches and fittings, plug tops and sockets, and rigid plastic tableware show that the search was successful. Just as there is a family of close relatives of polythene, so there is another family of plastics based on condensation reactions with phenol-formaldehyde. The commonest examples are the urea-formaldehyde plastics, which use urea

$$H_2N-\underset{\underset{O}{\|}}{C}-NH_2$$

rather than phenol, and the melamine-formaldehyde plastics using melamine

$$\begin{array}{c} NH_2 \\ | \\ C \\ \diagup \ \diagdown \\ N \quad\ \ N \\ \| \quad\quad\ | \\ C \quad\ \ C \\ \diagup \quad \diagdown \ \diagup \quad \diagdown \\ H_2N \quad\ \ N \quad\ \ NH_2 \end{array}$$

in place of phenol. Note that in each case the molecule used instead of phenol has three points at which linkage can take place. Two of these points are used to build long chains containing the residues of alternate urea (or melamine) and formaldehyde molecules, and the third point is used to form cross-linkages between chains.

Experiment 9.5 *Making a urea-formaldehyde long chain resin*

Dissolve 1 g urea in the minimum possible volume of dilute hydrochloric acid in a boiling tube. Add 2 cm^3 formaldehyde solution, and shake the tube.

Examine the colour of the precipitate and feel the tube to determine if any temperature change has taken place.

Experiment 9.5 demonstrates the production of a white precipitate of a long-chain urea-formaldehyde resin. The reaction takes place readily on mixing and is exothermic, i.e., heat is evolved.

Both urea-formaldehyde and melamine-formaldehyde plastics are produced first as long-chain polymers and these are then cross-linked by heating or using a hardening catalyst (often dilute sulphuric acid). They are both milky-white in colour and the addition of pigments can produce any desired shade. They also are used with fillers, and, like Bakelite, can be used to produce laminates in which several layers of cloth are impregnated with plastic to produce strong flat sheets of the material when the resin hardens. A very similar application is the use of these plastics as glues, e.g., in the manufacture of plywood. The word 'plastic' means 'able to be moulded'. Thermoplastics always remain mouldable if heated, but thermosets cannot be moulded once the cross-links have been made. They are nevertheless described as plastics because they could be moulded at some stage of their manufacture.

PLASTICS

Familiar brand names

Alkathene is polythene—an addition thermoplastic.

Fablon is PVC—an addition thermoplastic.

Fluon, Teflon, and PTFE are polytetrafluoroethylene—an addition thermoplastic.

Bri-nylon, Celon, Blue C, and Enkalon are nylons—condensation thermoplastics.

Formica and Warerite are melamine-formaldehyde laminates—condensation thermosets.

Melaware is a melamine-formaldehyde condensation thermoset.

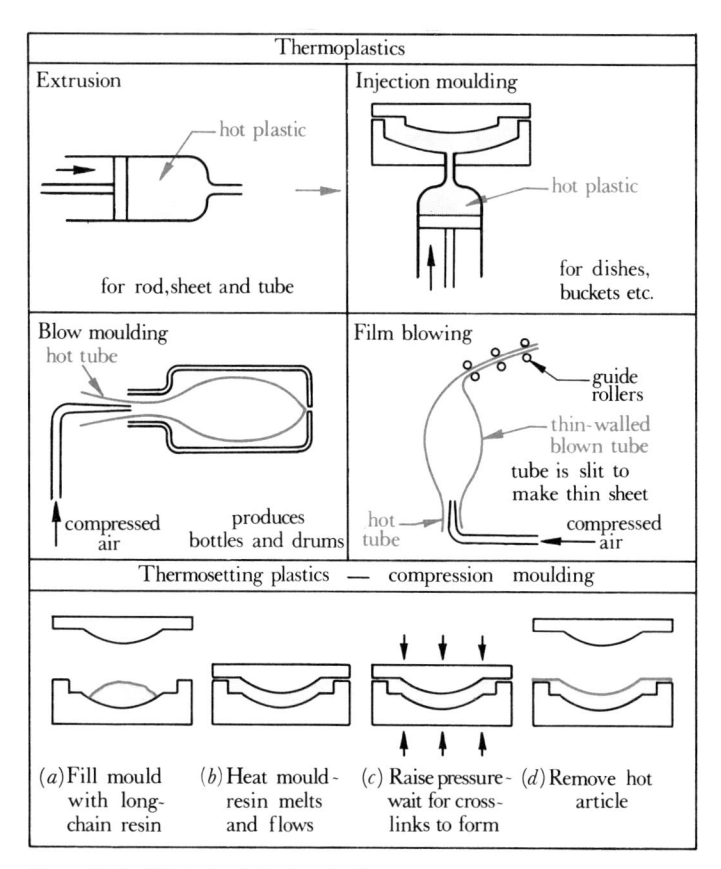

Figure 9.13 **Methods of shaping plastics**

CHEMISTRY

Summary of structures of thermoplastics and thermosets

Molecules of monomers are represented as M and N.

Thermoplastics

(a) Addition type—M contains a double bond

$$M + M + M + M + \ldots \longrightarrow M—M—M—M—\ldots$$

Examples—polythene, polyvinyl chloride, polystyrene.

(b) Condensation type—End-groups of M and N react.

$$M + N + M + N + M + \ldots \longrightarrow M—N—M—N—M—\ldots$$

(HCl or H_2O also made).

Examples—nylon, Terylene.

Thermosets

Condensation type—End-groups form chains and then mid-groups link the chains

$$\begin{array}{c} M + N + M + N + \ldots \\ M + N + M + N + \ldots \end{array} \longrightarrow \begin{array}{c} | \\ —M—N—M—N—M—N— \\ | \quad\quad\quad | \\ —M—N—M—N—M—N— \\ | \end{array}$$

Examples—phenol-formaldehyde (Bakelite), melamine-formaldehyde and urea-formaldehyde plastics.

Natural polymers

Many natural substances have long-chain molecules which can be described as polymers, although these substances are not all plastic (i.e., able to be moulded). The linking together of the molecules in a natural polymer to form a long chain is part of the natural life process of the plant or animal concerned. Among the natural polymers are resins, cellulose, starch, proteins, and rubber.

Resins

Substances which ooze out of cuts and cracks in trees sometimes, on standing, form thermoplastics called natural resins. These have been of immense importance for medical purposes, waterproofing and varnishing, but are now being replaced by cheaper synthetic products. Large amounts of the resin 'chicle' are, however, still used in the manufacture of chewing gum.

Cellulose

A plant is able to polymerize glucose, a ring-shaped molecule of formula $C_6H_{12}O_6$, by a condensation method. During polymerization each monomer molecule loses H from one side, and OH from the other side of the ring, so the formula for cellulose is

$$—(C_6H_{10}O_5)—(C_6H_{10}O_5)—(C_6H_{10}O_5)—\ldots$$

PLASTICS

The length of a chain varies, as with all polymers, and the formula of cellulose is usually written $(C_6H_{10}O_5)_n$, where n represents a number between 1000 and 3000. The long-chain molecule suggests that cellulose might form fibres. This is so—cotton, grass, hemp, and flax fibres are largely made of cellulose. The paper this book is printed on is made of cellulose.

Animals such as cattle and sheep are able to live on a diet consisting largely of cellulose because they have micro-organisms in their digestive systems which split up the cellulose, reforming glucose, which the animal then uses in the normal way. Human beings and many other animals need starch rather than cellulose, which they cannot digest.

Starch

Starch is a long-chain polymer which, like cellulose, is made from glucose monomer units by a condensation mechanism. The linkages between the monomer units differ from those in cellulose, and human beings are able to digest starch. Because starchy foods are relatively easy to grow, starches are cheap, and starch in wheat and other cereals, rice, and potatoes provides about 70 per cent of the world's food supply. Catalysts called enzymes act on the starch during digestion, depolymerizing it into smaller molecules, which are absorbed into the body and used to produce energy or fresh tissue for growth or to replace old tissues.

Proteins

Your muscles and cartilages, hair and finger-nails, your haemoglobin, and the enzymes now helping to depolymerize the starches and fats of your last meal are all proteins. Many types of protein are known, and all are polymers consisting of long chains of various monomers. These monomers are all amino-acids, and have an acid group at one part of the molecule, and an alkaline (amino) group at another part. The acid group of one molecule condenses with the amino group of another and so a long chain is built up. Proteins are so complex that few have been made artificially. In common with most long-chain polymers protein can form fibres. Silk and wool are familiar protein fibres.

Rubber

Rubber is a natural polymer, polyisoprene, consisting of long chains of isoprene molecules. The formula of the polymer is

$$\ldots -(CH_2-\underset{\underset{CH_3}{|}}{C}=CH-CH_2)-(CH_2-\underset{\underset{CH_3}{|}}{C}=CH-CH_2)- \ldots$$

The number of units in the chain varies but is usually several thousand, the majority being about eleven thousand. The tree produces the polymer in the form of latex, a milky liquid containing about one-third rubber and two-thirds water. If the water is extracted and the rubber heated with between 1 and 3 per cent sulphur (vulcanization), the sulphur joins on to the double bonds in the polymer, forming cross-links. These sulphur bridges act like the cross-links in Bakelite and other thermosetting materials, and the rubber becomes harder and less elastic.

The chains of rubber are not straight but twisted, and they tangle with each other. When rubber is stretched by a small amount the chains untwist slightly and become longer. When the tension is released the chains take up their former length and the rubber resumes its former shape and size. If the pull has been so hard that one molecule has slipped over the next and does not go back when the tension is released, a permanent stretch has taken place and the elasticity decreases, as in overstrained elastic or polythene (experiment 9.1(b)).

Chapter summary

Small molecules called monomers can be made to combine and form long-chain molecules called polymers. Plants and animals do this, producing natural polymers such as starch, cellulose, proteins, and rubber. Plastics are man-made polymers and are produced by addition or condensation methods. Thermoplastics such as polythene and nylon can be remelted, but in thermosetting plastics (thermosets) such as Bakelite, the polymer cannot be remelted. Thermosets contain permanent cross-links between the polymer chains.

Questions

1. You are designing a metal teapot, and are deciding whether to make the handle of stainless steel, polythene (a thermoplastic), or Bakelite (a thermoset). Mention one advantage and one disadvantage of each material.

2. Explain clearly the meaning of (a) polymerization, (b) thermosetting, (c) a thermoplastic.

3. Describe in general terms the differences between the structure of a thermoplastic material and a thermosetting material.

4. Draw up a table showing the formula of each of these materials, the name, type, and typical use of a plastic made from it: phenol, urea, ethylene, hexamethylene diamine, vinyl chloride, terephthalic acid.

5. Why is raw rubber much more elastic than rubber which has been vulcanized by heating with sulphur?

6. What tests would you conduct on a plastic beaker to see whether it would stand up to use in a school laboratory? What advantages and disadvantages would a polythene beaker have compared to a glass one?

10

Nitrogen, sulphur, and chlorine

Nitrogen

Air is almost four-fifths nitrogen by volume. The removal of the oxygen by phosphorus, alkaline pyrogallol, or hot steel wool gives a gas (atmospheric nitrogen) which is nearly all nitrogen but contains just over 1 per cent of the inert gas argon (for experimental details see experiment 3.1). Nitrogen is obtained industrially by cooling dry air until liquid air forms, then letting the very cold liquid air warm slightly so that the nitrogen boils off, leaving oxygen behind (see Fig. 3.14).

Nitrogen is a fairly dull non-metallic element, with few reactions which can be seen in a school laboratory. It does not react with damp red or blue litmus paper, sodium hydroxide solution, or dilute sulphuric acid. It puts out a lighted or glowing splint, has no smell, and is only very slightly soluble in water.

Many of its industrial uses depend on the fact that it is chemically unreactive at ordinary temperatures. Nitrogen is sometimes used in gas-filled electric lamps because any oxygen would oxidize the thin tungsten filament. Nitrogen is used to fill aircraft fuel tanks as the fuel is used, because if air got into the tanks an explosive mixture would form. Much nitrogen is used in the Haber Process for the synthesis (building up from elements) of ammonia.

$$N_2 + 3H_2 \rightleftharpoons 2NH_3$$

Nitrogen and hydrogen at a high temperature and pressure (e.g., 500°C and 250 atmospheres) are passed over a finely divided catalyst of iron, and some of the mixture combines forming ammonia. The ammonia is removed from the mixture by dissolving it in water, or liquefying it by cooling, and the uncombined gases are passed over the catalyst again.

CHEMISTRY

Ammonia NH_3

Demonstration experiment 10.1   *Preparation and properties of ammonia*

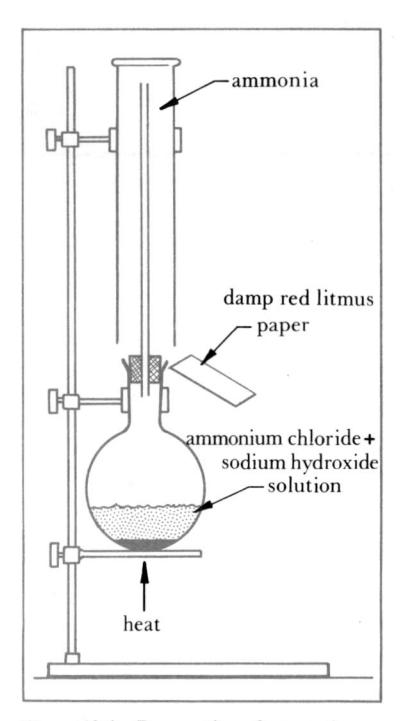

Figure 10.1 Preparation of ammonia

(*a*) Heat gently in the flask a mixture of ammonium chloride and sodium hydroxide solution. When the litmus held at the mouth of the gas jar turns blue, ammonia has filled the jar, so replace that jar with another. Collect two jars full, then fill a flask for part (*c*), using a fresh piece of litmus each time.
(*b*) Remove the top from one gas jar and quickly put it mouth downwards into a large trough containing water and methyl orange coloured red by the addition of a little acid.
(*c*) Fill a large (500 cm^3 or larger) round-bottomed flask with ammonia, put in a rubber bung containing a glass jet as shown in Fig. 10.2, and put the end of the tube into a large trough containing red methyl orange solution.
(*d*) Drop four drops of concentrated hydrochloric acid into a gas jar of ammonia and put the top on again.

Ammonia, NH_3, is a colourless tear-producing poisonous gas with a characteristic smell. It is made by heating a mixture of ammonium chloride

NITROGEN, SULPHUR, AND CHLORINE

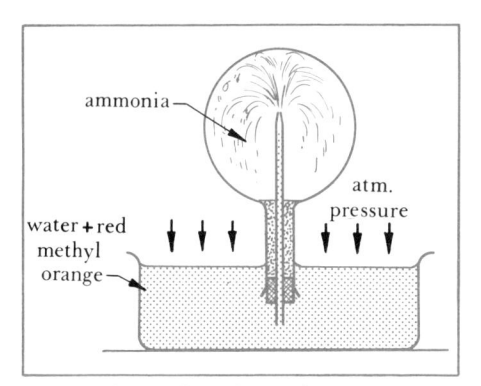

Figure 10.2 The fountain experiment

with an alkali such as sodium hydroxide solution or calcium hydroxide powder.

$$NH_4Cl + NaOH \longrightarrow NaCl + H_2O + NH_3$$
or
$$2NH_4Cl + Ca(OH)_2 \longrightarrow CaCl_2 + 2H_2O + 2NH_3$$

Ammonia can be collected by upward delivery and it is therefore less dense than air.

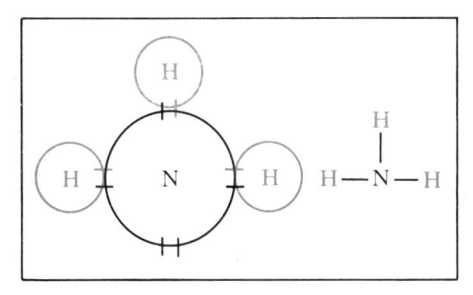

Figure 10.3 Ammonia, having a small covalent molecule, is a gas at room temperature

As the fountain experiment shows, ammonia dissolves very readily in water, forming a solution which is alkaline and turns litmus blue, or methyl orange yellow. Ammonia gas itself will turn damp red litmus paper blue, and so is described as an alkaline gas.

Ammonia reacts immediately with hydrogen chloride gas forming a dense white smoke which consists of small particles of ammonium chloride.

$$NH_3 + HCl \longrightarrow NH_4Cl$$

Because concentrated hydrochloric acid gives off hydrogen chloride gas this reaction takes place if concentrated hydrochloric acid is dropped into a gas jar of ammonia.

Ammonia is used in industrial refrigeration plants, and as a starting material for the manufacture of nitric acid, ammonium salts for fertilizers, and urea, which is used as a fertilizer and for making plastics.

Ammonium chloride NH_4Cl

The ammonium radical NH_4^+ forms salts in which it acts like a metal with valency one. Ammonium chloride is a typical ammonium salt; it is a white solid which is made by direct combination of ammonia with hydrogen chloride, or by neutralizing a solution of hydrochloric acid with ammonia solution, and then crystallizing the solid. (See Fig. 2.7 for solubility graph.)

$$NH_3 + HCl \longrightarrow NH_4Cl$$

Experiment 10.2   Heating ammonium chloride

Put ammonium chloride in a test-tube to a depth of $\frac{1}{2}$ cm, hold the tube at an angle of 45° to the horizontal, and use a small flame to heat the ammonium chloride.

When ammonium chloride is heated it appears to sublime (change directly from solid to vapour without melting), but in fact it is dissociating to ammonia and hydrogen chloride gas in the hot part of the test-tube. As these are both colourless gases there is no sign of any solid immediately above the ammonium chloride, but the gases recombine and deposit white ammonium chloride on the cool upper part of the test-tube.

$$NH_4Cl \rightleftharpoons NH_3 + HCl$$

A reaction in which a substance decomposes, then recombines when the conditions are changed is called a **dissociation** reaction.

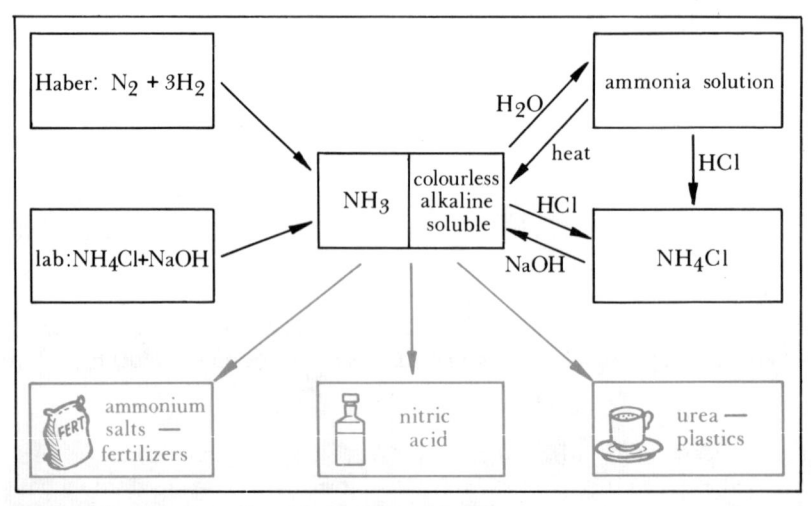

Figure 10.4   Some properties and uses of ammonia NH_3

NITROGEN, SULPHUR, AND CHLORINE

The nitrogen cycle

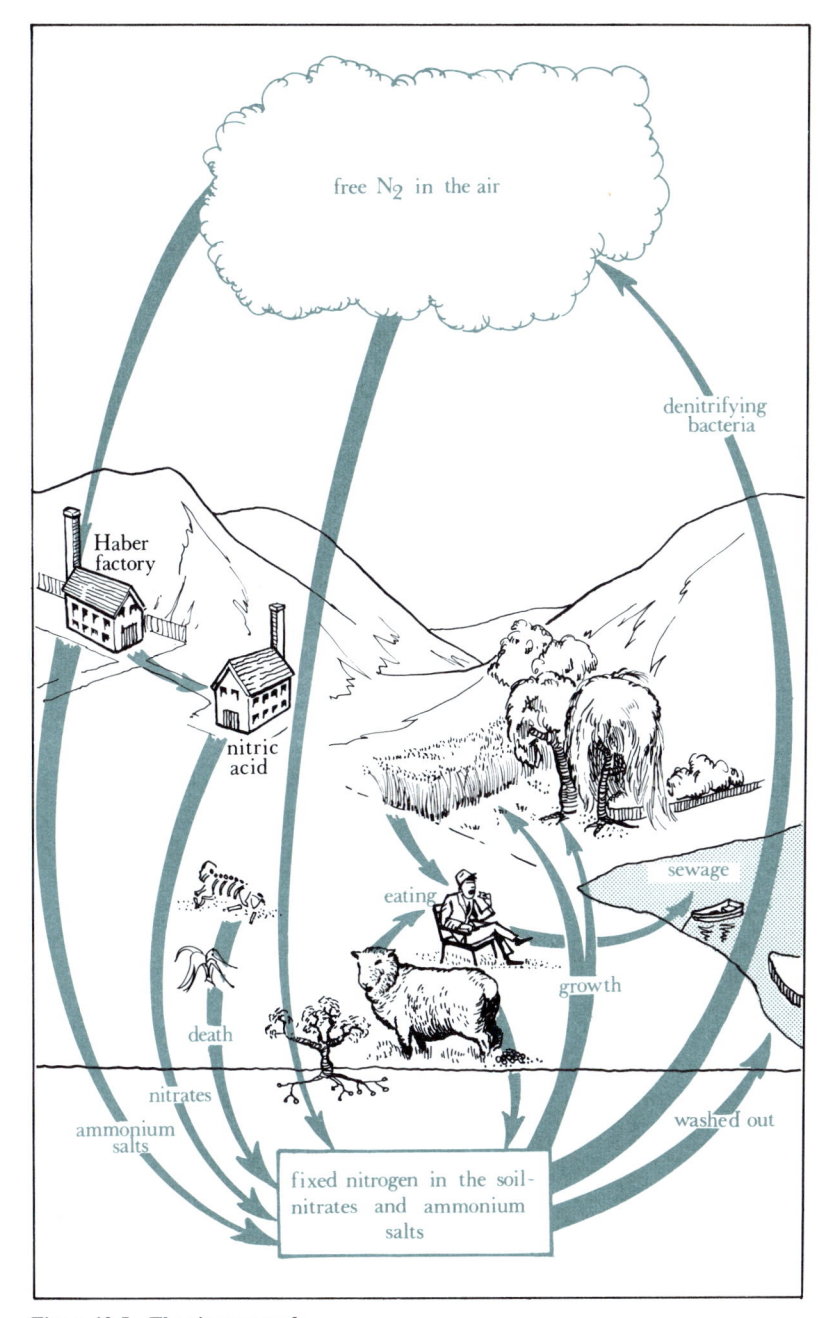

Figure 10.5 The nitrogen cycle

Some twenty of the hundred or so elements known seem to be essential to plant and animal life as we know it. These elements do not get used up because they are recirculated constantly, as we have seen with hydrogen and oxygen in the water cycle, and carbon and oxygen in the carbon cycle. The four most abundant elements in living material are oxygen, carbon, hydrogen, and nitrogen, and, as with oxygen, carbon, and hydrogen, there is a nitrogen cycle.

Plants cannot use directly the immense quantity of free nitrogen in the atmosphere; they absorb nitrogen through their roots in the form of solutions of nitrates. Nitrogen in the form of nitrates or of ammonium salts is called **fixed nitrogen**. The plants would soon use the supply of nitrates in the soil if further nitrates were not frequently provided. Nitrates, which are all soluble, are also removed from the soil by rainwater which washes them into rivers and lakes. The decay of dead plants and animals, and excretion via droppings and urine, return some fixed nitrogen to the soil in the form of ammonium compounds and compounds related to ammonia, and soil bacteria convert these to nitrates again. Other bacteria, which are found in lumps on the roots of certain plants such as beans and clover, are able to fix the free nitrogen found in air spaces in the soil, and these bacteria provide a second natural source of fixed nitrogen.

Intensive modern farming soon exhausts the fixed nitrogen in the soil, and this must be replaced more quickly than the natural methods allow if fresh crops are to be grown, so artificial fertilizers, among them ammonium salts and nitrates are applied. The fixed nitrogen in artificial fertilizers is, as the figure shows, originally taken from the nitrogen in the atmosphere via the Haber Process, which synthesizes ammonia from nitrogen and hydrogen.

Table 10.1 Oxides of nitrogen

Name and preparation	Properties
dinitrogen oxide, nitrous oxide N_2O heat ammonium nitrate (*care!*) $NH_4NO_3 \rightarrow N_2O + 2H_2O$	colourless sweet-smelling gas an anaesthetic—dentists' laughing gas neutral oxide
nitrogen monoxide, nitric oxide NO 50% nitric acid on copper $3Cu + 8HNO_3 \rightarrow 3Cu(NO_3)_2 + 4H_2O + 2NO$	colourless gas reacts with oxygen at room temperature forming NO_2 ($2NO + O_2 \rightarrow 2NO_2$) neutral oxide
nitrogen dioxide, NO_2 (a) conc. nitric acid on copper (Exp. 7.3) (b) heat lead, zinc or copper nitrate $2Pb(NO_3)_2 \rightarrow 2PbO + 4NO_2 + O_2$ zinc and copper nitrate equations are similar	brown, choking, dense gas an acidic oxide—reacts with water making acids $2NO_2 + H_2O \rightarrow HNO_2 + HNO_3$ gas contains some double molecules N_2O_4 $2NO_2 \underset{\text{heat}}{\overset{\text{cool}}{\rightleftharpoons}} N_2O_4$

NITROGEN, SULPHUR, AND CHLORINE

Artificial fertilizers contain other necessary elements as well as nitrogen—calcium, phosphorus, and potassium compounds are most commonly added.

Sulphur

Sulphur is found uncombined in various parts of the world, the most notable supplies occurring in Texas and Louisiana. These supplies are unfortunately some 150 metres underground and normal mining techniques are impossible because there is quicksand between the surface and the sulphur.

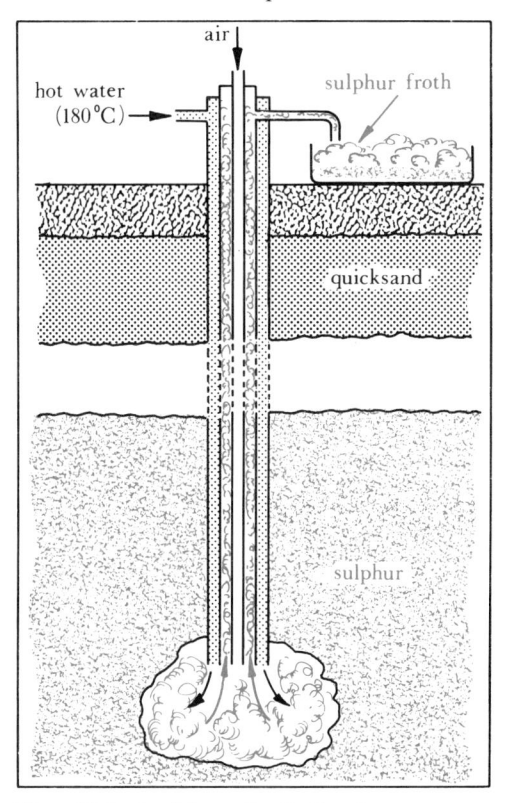

Figure 10.6 A sulphur well—the Frasch process

The ingenious Frasch Process melts the sulphur underground using water superheated under pressure, and then compressed air pumps up the sulphur in the form of a froth of melted sulphur, water, and air. At the top the air escapes and the water evaporates, leaving 99·5 per cent pure sulphur. Useful sulphur compounds are also extracted from crude natural gas and other petroleum products, in which sulphides occur, from industrial waste gases which often contain sulphur dioxide, and from coal gas and coke ovens, and these supplies supplement the free sulphur.

CHEMISTRY

The physical forms of sulphur

Experiment 10.3   *Crystalline and amorphous sulphur*

(*a*) (Demonstration)
Pour carbon disulphide into a corked test-tube to a depth of 2 cm, add a piece of roll sulphur about as big as a pea, recork the tube and shake it to dissolve the sulphur. When no more sulphur will dissolve, filter the solution on to a watch-glass, cover it with an upturned petri dish or beaker to slow evaporation, and set the apparatus aside, preferably in a fume cupboard.

(*b*) Fill a test-tube to a depth of about 3 cm with pieces of roll sulphur about the size of a pea, and heat very gently, holding the test-tube above a small flame. The sulphur should melt to a pale yellow liquid; if the liquid starts to become orange-coloured while there is still some solid sulphur left in the tube, you are heating too strongly. When all the sulphur has melted to a yellow or very pale amber liquid, warm the side of the test-tube and pour the liquid down the warm side into a dry, folded filter paper in a funnel. Let the liquid cool until enough sulphur has turned solid to form a crust right across the top of the sulphur, then open the filter paper and examine the sulphur remaining inside.

(*c*) Fill a test-tube with sulphur to a depth of 2 cm and melt it slowly as described in part (*b*). When all the sulphur has melted, tilt the tube to discover whether the liquid is free-flowing (mobile) or thick and treacly (viscous). Carry on heating until the liquid boils, observing colour changes and whether the liquid is more or less viscous at various stages of the experiment.

(*d*) Pour a thin stream of boiling sulphur from part (*c*) into a beaker half full of cold water. After 1 minute for cooling remove the product from the water, examine its colour, and pinch it to feel its texture.

Table 10.2   **The allotropes of sulphur**

Name	Appearance	Preparation
Crystalline rhombic sulphur	small plate-like crystals	crystallization from cold solution of sulphur in carbon disulphide
monoclinic or prismatic sulphur	long needle-like crystals	crystallization from hot molten sulphur or hot sulphur solution in toluene
Amorphous flowers of sulphur	powder	sublimation of sulphur vapour
roll sulphur	solid	slow cooling of liquid sulphur
plastic sulphur	brownish-yellow putty-like	rapid cooling of molten sulphur at or near its boiling point

NITROGEN, SULPHUR, AND CHLORINE

The various types of sulphur contain sulphur atoms only, and the differences between them are the results of differing arrangements of sulphur atoms within molecules, or the differing arrangement of molecules within crystals. The crystalline forms of sulphur (rhombic and monoclinic) consist

from hot liquid sulphur	from cold sulphur in CS_2
you see	you see
monoclinic — ideal form if crystals were perfect	rhombic — ideal form if crystals were perfect

Figure 10.7 Crystallization of sulphur

of buckled rings each containing eight sulphur atoms, and these rings are regularly arranged within the crystal. Roll sulphur consists of small crystals less regularly arranged. The pale yellow mobile liquid formed when sulphur melts (119°C) also contains S_8 rings, but as the temperature rises the rings shake themselves to pieces by increased thermal motion, and short chains of sulphur atoms form. The colour darkens as more chains form and join (polymerize) to form long, twisted, tangled chains, so the mixture, which contains chains of varying lengths, becomes more viscous. At 180°C the

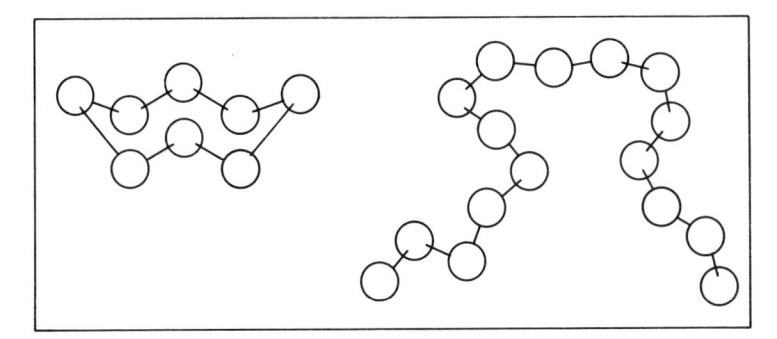

Figure 10.8 Ring and chain forms of sulphur

sulphur is dark red and so viscous that it will not pour out of the tube when this is held upside down. As the temperature increases, the chains in their turn break into smaller fragments and the viscosity decreases again. Eventually the sulphur boils (445°C) giving sulphur vapour, which contains various very short chains—S_2, S_4, etc. On slow cooling the change is reversed, the mixture becomes viscous, then lighter and more mobile. When the sulphur sets solid it is usually dark, but the yellow colour returns after a few days. If liquid sulphur is cooled very quickly there is no time for the change to short chains and rings to take place, so the long chains are left and the plastic form of sulphur is made. The long chains slowly reform rings on standing, so plastic sulphur gradually changes to a hard mass containing minute crystals of the stable rhombic allotrope.

Chemical properties of sulphur

The different forms of sulphur all have similar chemical properties. Although sulphur consists of molecules containing varying numbers of atoms and we should really write it as S_x, it is more convenient to use the single symbol S.

Sulphur burns with a blue flame in air or oxygen giving off sulphur dioxide (experiment 3.4).

$$S + O_2 \longrightarrow SO_2 + \text{heat}$$

When sulphur is mixed with iron filings and heated, a red glow spreads through the mixture, indicating that an exothermic reaction is taking place, and a black mass of iron(II) sulphide (ferrous sulphide) FeS is formed (experiment 1.9).

$$Fe + S \longrightarrow FeS + \text{heat}$$

Uses of sulphur

Large amounts of sulphur are used in the manufacture of sulphuric acid by the contact process (S → SO_2 → SO_3 → H_2SO_4, chapter 6), and for making sulphur-containing bleaches which are extensively used in the paper-making industry. Smaller amounts are used in the process of vulcanization to form the cross-links between polymer chains and so toughen the rubber (chapter 9), for making viscose rayon, matches (chapter 11), gunpowder (chapter 5), and for burning in sulphur candles to form sulphur dioxide, which is a useful fumigating agent.

Sulphur dioxide SO_2

Experiment 10.4 *Preparation and properties of sulphur dioxide*

(*a*) Cover pieces of copper in a boiling tube with concentrated sulphuric acid to a depth of 2 cm. Warm the mixture until the gas bubbles off, and observe the colour of the gas. Be careful not to boil or spill the concentrated sulphuric acid.

(*b*) Very cautiously wave some of the gas towards your nose—do not put your nose close to the mouth of the tube and sniff.

(*c*) Hold a piece of damp blue litmus paper in the gas.

NITROGEN, SULPHUR, AND CHLORINE

(*d*) Hold in the gas a piece of filter paper which has been dipped into an orange-coloured solution of potassium dichromate containing a little dilute sulphuric acid.

(*e*) Hold in the gas flower petals of various colours.

(*f*) When the mixture left in the boiling tube has cooled to room temperature note its colour, then pour it into a beaker half full of water and filter. Note the colour of the filtrate.

(*g*) Demonstration.

The fountain experiment, experiment 10.1(*c*), may be repeated using sulphur dioxide in place of ammonia, if a larger scale supply of sulphur dioxide is available. Fill the flask in a fume cupboard and make the water in the trough alkaline.

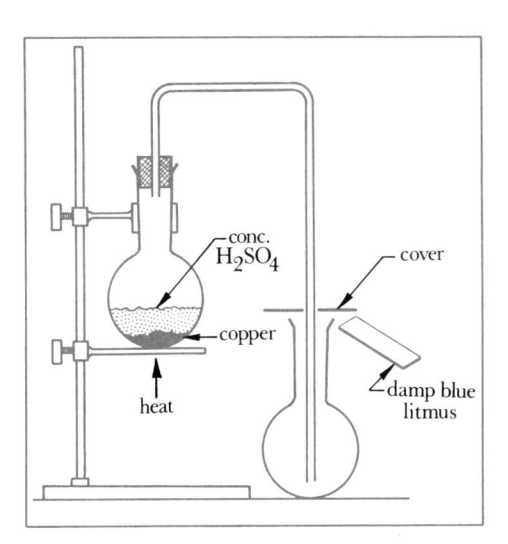

Figure 10.9 Preparation of sulphur dioxide, SO_2

Experiment 10.4 shows that sulphur dioxide is a colourless choking gas with a characteristic smell. It is made by heating copper with concentrated sulphuric acid.

$$Cu + 2H_2SO_4 \longrightarrow CuSO_4 + SO_2 + 2H_2O$$

As part (*f*) reveals, the mixture left in the test-tube is black rather than the blue that might have been expected. Other substances are made as well as copper sulphate, and the blue of the copper sulphate solution is seen only after the dark solids have been removed by filtration. Reactions which make products other than the main substances shown in the equation are called **side reactions**. Black sulphides of copper are produced by side reactions in experiment 10.4.

Sulphur dioxide, the oxide of a non-metal, turns damp blue litmus red, so it must be an acidic oxide. The gas reacts with water and forms sulphurous acid H_2SO_3.

$$H_2O + SO_2 \longrightarrow H_2SO_3$$

The gas is very soluble and a fountain experiment can be done using sulphur dioxide. As it is an acidic oxide, sulphur dioxide can also react directly with solutions of alkalis forming sulphites or hydrogen sulphites, which are used in paper making. For example,

$$Ca(OH)_2 + SO_2 \longrightarrow CaSO_3 + H_2O$$
or
$$Ca(OH)_2 + 2SO_2 \longrightarrow Ca(HSO_3)_2$$

Sulphur dioxide reacts with an orange solution of acidified potassium dichromate forming a green solution containing chromium sulphate. This reaction is sometimes used as a test for sulphur dioxide. Sulphur dioxide is acting here as a reducing agent; because it is a reducing agent it can have a mild bleaching action. Some pigments, those in certain flowers for example, are made colourless by the removal of oxygen by sulphur dioxide.

Sulphur dioxide is used in the manufacture of sulphuric acid, for direct bleaching and making sulphite and hydrogen sulphite bleaches, and for fumigation, particularly of greenhouses. It is produced by the burning of sulphur and because many fuels, particularly oils, contain sulphur, atmospheric pollution by sulphur dioxide is common. The gas is particularly harmful to elderly or asthmatic people. Rain falling through air polluted by sulphur dioxide becomes acidic because it contains sulphurous acid, some of which reacts with oxygen in the air to give sulphuric acid. This acidic rainwater attacks metals and stone in industrial areas (see Fig. 3.5). Wind can carry sulphur dioxide pollution a considerable distance from its source, e.g., Scandinavians complain of sulphur dioxide pollution originating in Germany and Great Britain.

Sulphur trioxide SO_3

Demonstration experiment 10.5   *Properties of sulphur trioxide*

Use a glass rod to put one drop of concentrated sulphuric acid on the red-hot corner of a wire gauze. Observe the product and test it with damp blue litmus paper. Do not inhale the fumes.

Sulphur trioxide is a white solid at room temperature. An intensely irritating white cloud of small particles of sulphur trioxide is made when concentrated sulphuric acid is decomposed by heating. The fumes are strongly acidic because they react immediately with water, reforming sulphuric acid.

$$SO_3 + H_2O \longrightarrow H_2SO_4$$

NITROGEN, SULPHUR, AND CHLORINE

The industrial preparation of sulphur trioxide (in the Contact Process for the manufacture of sulphuric acid) is by passing sulphur dioxide and air at a temperature of 450°C over an oxide of vanadium.

$$2SO_2 + O_2 \longrightarrow 2SO_3$$

Hydrogen sulphide H_2S

Demonstration experiment 10.6 *Preparation and properties of hydrogen sulphide*

This experiment should be done in a fume cupboard.

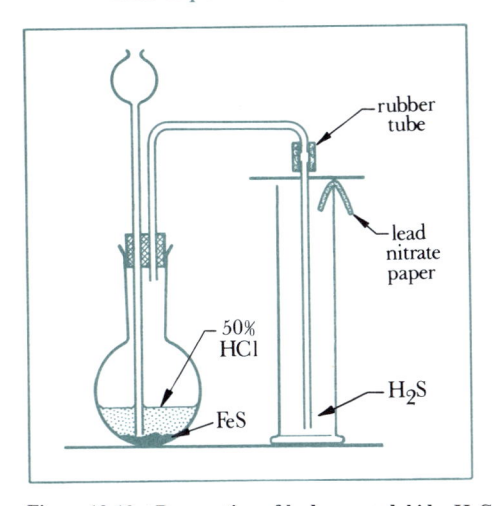

Figure 10.10 Preparation of hydrogen sulphide, H_2S

(*a*) Using the apparatus shown in Fig. 10.10, cover the bottom of the flask with pieces of iron(II) sulphide (ferrous sulphide) FeS, and add a mixture which is half concentrated hydrochloric acid and half water. Test by holding a piece of filter paper soaked in lead nitrate solution near the mouth of the gas jar, and when the paper blackens rapidly put the cover on the jar. Collect two jars full of hydrogen sulphide.

(*b*) Changing or washing the delivery tube after each experiment, bubble hydrogen sulphide through solutions of copper sulphate, cadmium sulphate and lead nitrate.

(*c*) Apply a light to a jar full of hydrogen sulphide.

(*d*) Put closed jars of chlorine and hydrogen sulphide mouth to mouth, chlorine above, slide out the cover slips, and observe the reaction.

Hydrogen sulphide is a colourless gas with an extremely strong smell which is rather like rotten eggs. It is denser than air and can be collected by downward delivery. Hydrogen sulphide is poisonous in moderate doses. Although the intense smell gives warning of the presence of hydrogen sulphide and few people are actually poisoned by it, small doses produce headaches, dizziness, and vomiting, so escapes of the gas should not be treated as a joke.

Hydrogen sulphide burns with a pale blue flame, forming a very pale yellow deposit of sulphur on the sides of the gas jar.

$$2H_2S + O_2 \longrightarrow 2H_2O + 2S$$

(O / R)

Hydrogen sulphide is oxidized on contact with chlorine giving a very pale yellow deposit of sulphur and producing hydrogen chloride gas.

$$H_2S + Cl_2 \longrightarrow 2HCl + S$$

(O / R)

This is oxidation by removal of hydrogen, and it is also correct to say that the hydrogen sulphide is acting as a reducing agent.

When hydrogen sulphide is passed through solutions of salts, sulphides are often formed. Most metallic sulphides are insoluble in water and therefore form precipitates; these precipitates are often intensely coloured. For example,

$$CuSO_4 + H_2S \longrightarrow \underset{\text{black}}{CuS} + H_2SO_4$$

$$CdSO_4 + H_2S \longrightarrow \underset{\text{yellow}}{CdS} + H_2SO_4$$

$$Pb(NO_3)_2 + H_2S \longrightarrow \underset{\text{black}}{PbS} + 2HNO_3$$

The formation by this method of a black precipitate of lead sulphide (which often has a silvery gleam) is used as a test for the presence of hydrogen sulphide. The black tarnish which appears on silver is silver sulphide produced by the action on silver of the hydrogen sulphide which is present in industrial atmospheres.

Summary of sulphur

Sulphur exists as S_8 rings in the two crystalline allotropes, but viscous melted sulphur contains tangled long-chain molecules. Sulphur is a typical non-metallic element forming two acidic oxides, sulphur dioxide, and sulphur

NITROGEN, SULPHUR, AND CHLORINE

trioxide. Sulphur dioxide (a reducing bleach and fumigant) is made when sulphur burns, and it reacts with water, producing sulphurous acid. Sulphur dioxide is oxidized to sulphur trioxide in the contact process. The action of hydrochloric acid on iron(II) sulphide makes hydrogen sulphide, a smelly poisonous gas which precipitates sulphides from many salt solutions.

Chlorine

Experiment 10.7 *Small-scale preparation and properties of chlorine*

(*a*) Put 0·5 cm depth of potassium permanganate crystals in a test-tube and add concentrated hydrochloric acid to a depth of 2 cm. Cork the top loosely. Hold the tube against a background of white paper to observe the colour of the chlorine made.
(*b*) Remove the cork and with great caution wave some of the chlorine towards your nose. Do not take a big sniff.
(*c*) Hold a piece of damp blue litmus paper in the chlorine.
(*d*) Hold in the chlorine some grass, flower petals, and coloured scraps of damp fabric. Before doing this put a little of each aside so that you can compare their colours before and after the treatment.
(*e*) Dip a strip of filter paper in potassium iodide solution and hold it in the chlorine.
(*f*) Fill with hydrogen sulphide a test-tube similar in size to that being used to generate the chlorine. Hold the two tubes mouth to mouth and observe the reaction.

$MnO_2 + 4HCl \rightarrow MnCl_2 + Cl_2 + 2H_2O$

oxidation of conc. HCl by $KMnO_4$

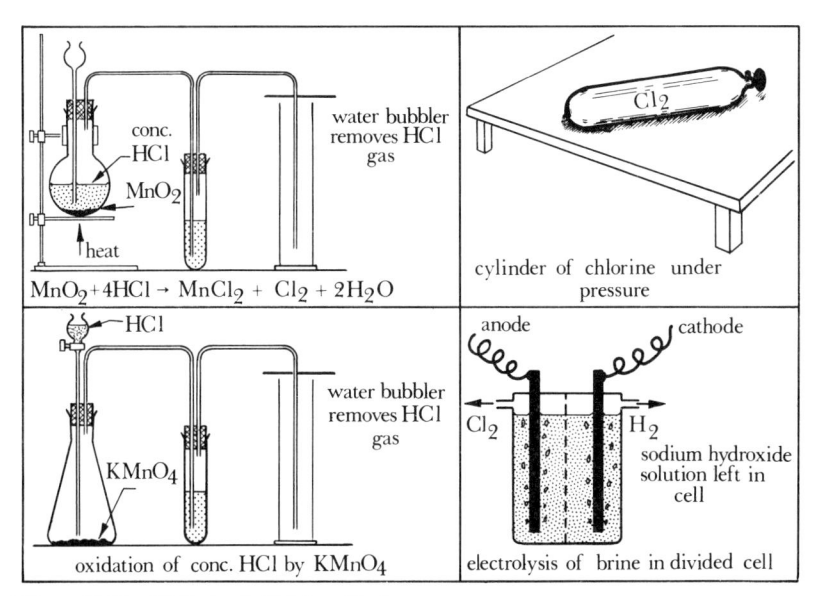

electrolysis of brine in divided cell

Figure 10.11 Methods of obtaining chlorine

Chlorine, a choking green gas which is denser than air, is made by the oxidation of cold concentrated hydrochloric acid by potassium permanganate.

Chlorine turns damp blue litmus red and then bleaches it white; it will bleach many substances—inks, dyes on cloth, grass, and flower petals—by oxidizing their dyes. If chlorine is mixed with potassium iodide solution a brown colour appears because iodine is made and dissolves in the solution.

$$Cl_2 + 2KI \longrightarrow 2KCl + I_2$$

This is a displacement or replacement reaction, similar to a replacement of a metal from its salt by another more active metal. Just as zinc displaces copper from copper sulphate solution, so chlorine displaces the less active non-metallic element iodine from potassium iodide solution. A similar reaction takes place with potassium bromide solution, which turns reddish brown when chlorine is passed through it because bromine is formed.

$$Cl_2 + 2KBr \longrightarrow 2KCl + Br_2$$

When chlorine is mixed with hydrogen sulphide a very pale yellow precipitate of sulphur forms on the sides of the jar or tube, because the chlorine oxidizes the hydrogen sulphide to sulphur by removal of hydrogen.

$$H_2S + Cl_2 \longrightarrow 2HCl + S$$

If chlorine is passed into iron(II) sulphate (ferrous sulphate) $FeSO_4$ solution acidified with dilute sulphuric acid, the chlorine oxidizes the iron(II) sulphate to iron(III) sulphate (ferric sulphate) $Fe_2(SO_4)_3$.

$$2FeSO_4 + Cl_2 + H_2SO_4 \longrightarrow Fe_2(SO_4)_3 + 2HCl$$

or

$$2Fe^{++} + Cl_2 \longrightarrow 2Fe^{+++} + 2Cl^-$$

This is oxidation by increase of the valency of the iron from two to three, and as it takes place the solution changes from pale green to brown, the colour of iron(III) sulphate solution.

If a lighted candle is lowered on a deflagrating spoon into a jar of chlorine the flame turns red and continues to burn, forming clouds of black carbon. The chlorine oxidizes the hydrocarbons in the candle by the removal of hydrogen. For example,

$$C_{16}H_{34} + 17Cl_2 \longrightarrow 16C + 34HCl$$

Chlorine also oxidizes hydrogen to hydrogen chloride.

$$H_2 + Cl_2 \longrightarrow 2HCl$$

A violent explosion occurs if the gases are mixed and lit, but they combine smoothly if passed over a catalyst of activated charcoal, as in the industrial preparation of hydrogen chloride, which is then dissolved in water to make hydrochloric acid.

Uses of chlorine

Chlorine dissolves readily in water and all drinking water supplies in the United Kingdom are sterilized by the addition of a small amount of chlorine to the filtered water; chlorine kills the bacteria not removed by the filter beds. During epidemics the amount of chlorine in the water is increased and it can often be tasted. The use of chlorine in swimming baths is similar although the amount of chlorine put in the water is greater than that used in drinking water.

Chlorine gas is used as a bleaching agent for substances such as grey cotton cloth and wood pulp. Some of its compounds which readily decompose giving chlorine are also used as bleaches. One of these is bleaching powder, which is made by the action of chlorine on calcium hydroxide.

$$Cl_2 + Ca(OH)_2 \longrightarrow CaOCl_2 + H_2O$$

Bleaching powder releases chlorine by reaction with any dilute acid; for example with nitric acid.

$$CaOCl_2 + 2HNO_3 \longrightarrow Ca(NO_3)_2 + H_2O + Cl_2$$

In the liquid commercial bleach commonly used in the home, sodium hypochlorite NaClO is the active bleaching agent. Sodium hypochlorite is made by the action of chlorine on cold dilute sodium hydroxide solution.

$$Cl_2 + 2NaOH \longrightarrow NaCl + NaOCl + H_2O$$

Chlorine is also used to make many chlorides, e.g., hydrochloric acid, carbon tetrachloride, and many organic chlorides.

Summary of chlorine

Chlorine, which is produced by the oxidation of concentrated hydrochloric acid by potassium permanganate or manganese dioxide, or by the electrolysis of a melted or dissolved chloride, is a dense, green, choking gas. Chlorine oxidizes hydrogen sulphide to sulphur, iron(II) to iron(III) compounds, hydrocarbons to carbon (e.g., burning wax), and hydrogen to hydrogen chloride. Its bleaching (litmus, flowers, fabrics) and sterilizing actions depend on its oxidizing power.

We shall now consider two typical chlorides, those of carbon and sodium.

Carbon tetrachloride CCl_4

Carbon tetrachloride, which is also called tetrachloromethane, is a colourless volatile liquid at room temperature. It is much used as a solvent, especially for oils, fats, and greases; many preparations sold for removing grease spots from clothes contain carbon tetrachloride. The vapour is an efficient fire extinguisher; liquid carbon tetrachloride is pumped in a jet on to the fire from a small hand extinguisher, and the dense vapour formed puts out a small fire by the exclusion of air. Because carbon tetrachloride vapour is anaesthetic, and poisonous in large doses, its use in fire extinguishers is declining.

Carbon tetrachloride is a covalent compound, its bonds being formed by the sharing of electrons in the outer shells of carbon and chlorine (Fig. 10.12).

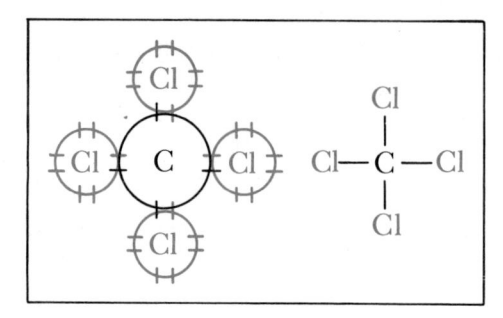

Figure 10.12 Covalent (sharing) bonds in carbon tetrachloride

Sodium chloride NaCl

At room temperature sodium chloride is a white solid consisting of small cube-shaped crystals. Sodium chloride occurs in the sea, from which it may be extracted by evaporation. The large deposits of solid salt in Cheshire, Siberia, Utah, and other parts of the world are the remains of seas which have dried up.

Sodium chloride reacts with concentrated sulphuric acid, evolving hydrogen chloride gas and leaving a residue of sodium hydrogen sulphate (experiment 6.8).

$$NaCl + H_2SO_4 \longrightarrow HCl + NaHSO_4$$

Sodium chloride solution forms a white precipitate of silver chloride when mixed with silver nitrate solution (experiment 7.1).

$$NaCl + AgNO_3 \longrightarrow NaNO_3 + AgCl$$

The electrolysis of melted sodium chloride forms sodium and chlorine, while the electrolysis of sodium chloride solution in the special Nelson cell (see Fig. 10.11 and also Appendix 4), forms hydrogen, chlorine, and sodium hydroxide solution.

Sodium chloride is ionic, so no NaCl molecules exist. Although we often find it convenient to write the formula as NaCl, Na^+Cl^- gives a better idea of the structure. A crystal of sodium chloride consists of a large orderly array of sodium ions Na^+ and chloride ions Cl^-, which is held together by

NITROGEN, SULPHUR, AND CHLORINE

the forces of electrostatic attraction. A small part of such a crystal is shown diagrammatically in Fig. 4.22, page 74.

The halogens

We have read in this chapter a little about bromine and iodine, as well as a lot about chlorine. These three elements are part of the family of five elements known as the halogens (salt formers).

Look at the Periodic Table at the back of this book to discover where the family occurs in the table, and what symbols are given for the other halogens.

Table 10.3 Properties of the halogen family of elements

Name	Symbol	Atomic Weight	Atomic number	Electrons in outer shell	Appearance at room temperature
fluorine	F	19	9	7	pale yellow gas
chlorine	Cl	35·5	17	7	green gas
bromine	Br	80	35	7	dark brown liquid
iodine	I	127	53	7	black solid
astatine	At	211	85	7	black solid

These elements are similar because they all have an electronic structure containing seven electrons in their outer shell. For example, they are all non-metals exerting a valency of one and forming anions with a charge of -1. Their properties are not identical because, as the atomic numbers and atomic weights show, the atoms gradually get larger as we read down the family from fluorine to astatine. The colours darken, the physical state at room temperature changes from gaseous, through liquid, to solid, and the reactivity changes as we examine the members of the series in order. Fluorine is the most active non-metallic element known, chlorine is a very reactive element, bromine reasonably active, and iodine and astatine are not very reactive elements.

The Periodic Table contains many other families (vertical groups) of elements, and more advanced chemistry involves close study of the reasons for the similarities and differences within families of elements such as

carbon, silicon, germanium, tin, and lead,
and copper, silver, and gold.

Fluorine itself is extremely active and harmful to flesh. It forms compounds called fluorides and some of these help to make teeth resistant to decay. Fluorides in water help children to form teeth which are strong all through, but fluoride toothpaste, which usually contains tin(II) fluoride (stannous fluoride) SnF_2, forms a decay-resistant coating on the outside of the teeth.

CHEMISTRY

It is important not confuse the element fluorine F_2 with fluorides such as sodium fluoride NaF. The difference between these two is comparable to the difference between chlorine Cl_2, a poisonous gas, and sodium chloride NaCl, a white crystalline solid essential to the human diet.

Iodine is a black solid which sublimes forming a purple vapour when heated (experiment 1.5). The antiseptic solution often called simply 'iodine', is properly named 'tincture of iodine', and consists of a solution of iodine in potassium iodide, ethanol, and water.

Chapter summary

The non-metallic elements nitrogen, sulphur, and chlorine are found with the other non-metals in the top right-hand corner of the periodic table. Nitrogen, sulphur, and chlorine are gases or solids with comparatively low melting points, because they form small covalent molecules. They have acidic oxides (SO_2, SO_3, NO_2), and could be remembered as acid-forming elements, e.g., HNO_3, H_2SO_3, H_2SO_4, and HCl. Nitrogen is not a very active element, but chlorine is: it is an oxidizing and bleaching agent and it displaces bromine from bromides and iodine from iodides. Sulphur exists in crystalline (rhombic, monoclinic) and amorphous (roll, flowers, plastic) forms.

Questions

1. Name and give the formula of: (a) an ammonium compound which dissociates on heating, (b) an alkaline gas, (c) a neutral oxide of nitrogen, (d) an allotropic element, (e) a very soluble acidic gas, (f) an insoluble sulphide, (g) a covalent chloride.

2. A gas A dissolves in water forming a solution B which turns blue litmus red. B reacts with a black oxide C forming a green gas D. D reacts with potassium iodide solution forming a brown solution of E. Name A, B, C, D, and E, and give the word and formula equation for the reaction between B and C.

3. State the conditions under which chlorine reacts with (a) hydrogen, (b) hydrogen sulphide, (c) slaked lime, and name the products. In reaction (b) state what is oxidized and why you consider it to be oxidized.

4. Name two liquids in which sulphur will dissolve and name and sketch the crystals which can be made from each solution. What happens when very hot water is mixed with sulphur, and what use is made of this process?

5. How would you decide which of two bottles of commercial bleach, on offer at the same price, was the better value?

6. Describe the part played in the nitrogen cycle by (a) the Haber Process, (b) artificial fertilizers containing fixed nitrogen.

11

Chemistry all around us

We tend to think of a chemical as something in a bottle, and chemistry as what goes on in laboratories, but this is only a small part of the story. Chemistry is everywhere; the paper, ink, and dyes of this book are chemicals, so are air, your blood, bones, tissues, and brain, the natural or synthetic fibres of your clothes, and the food of your last meal. Chemical reactions such as the oxidation of carbon to carbon dioxide, and the depolymerization (breaking down) of long-chain protein molecules into smaller molecules are taking place in your body now. Elsewhere steel is rusting, stonework is crumbling, and bacteria in sewage works are using atmospheric oxygen to oxidize noxious substances and make the liquid sewage fit for discharge into rivers. Where there is change, there is usually chemistry. Many common materials are very complex chemically and consist of mixtures with variable composition, but some of the simpler everyday substances are dealt with in this chapter.

Materials used in building

Stone

Limestone, chalk, and marble consist largely of calcium carbonate, although close examination often reveals specks of other materials. These stones (and also egg shells) can be shown to be carbonates by adding dilute hydrochloric acid and proving that carbon dioxide is evolved, while the presence of calcium can be demonstrated by a flame test as described in Appendix 2.

Other building materials include sandstones of various types—e.g., Cotswold stone, millstone grit, and similar grey stones used for building in the North and Midlands. These contain sand, whose sharp grains may often be seen among the cementing material holding the sand particles together. Many **igneous rocks**, formed by the cooling of molten materials from the interior of the Earth, are obviously crystalline. Their formation may be compared with the growth of monoclinic crystals of sulphur when molten sulphur was

CHEMISTRY

cooled in experiment 10.3(*b*). These igneous rocks are often complex mixtures of various salts and oxides, and are classified as acidic or basic rocks according to the chemical nature of the oxides present. Acidic igneous rocks contain large amounts of silicon dioxide (silica) SiO_2, which acts as an acidic oxide.

> Look at the Periodic Table to find silicon. Which element forming a well-known acidic oxide is next to silicon?

Granite is a very hard insoluble acidic rock consisting of silicon dioxide together with the silicates of aluminium, potassium, and calcium. Basic igneous rocks such as basalt contain large amounts of basic oxides such as magnesium oxide and iron(III) oxide (ferric oxide).

Clays

Clays are the basis of many building materials. Just as there are many substances which may be called plastics, so there are many clays with different compositions and hence different properties. The china clay mined in Devon and Cornwall consists almost entirely of hydrated aluminium silicate, but most clays contain, among other materials, silicon dioxide, copper, magnesium and potassium carbonates, and iron(III) oxide (ferric oxide), which accounts for the usual reddish-brown colour of clay. Clay which has been baked forms bricks and roofing tiles. Special bricks, such as the firebricks used for lining furnaces, are made from clays with particular compositions. A brick with very good resistance to high temperatures may be desired, or a brick containing the basic oxides calcium oxide and magnesium oxide may be used to remove acidic impurities from the molten contents of a furnace.

Pottery and china are made by baking clay in two stages. The first firing removes water and leaves a dry fragile article, which is then coated with colouring and glazing substances and refired at a very high temperature. The clay becomes hard and less brittle, while the glazing substances form glass-like materials on the surface.

Sand

Sand is an impure form of silicon dioxide (silica SiO_2). It is a very hard insoluble substance which has a giant molecule covalent structure extending, like that of diamond, into three dimensions. Pure silicon dioxide is a white powder which melts at almost 1700°C and forms a glassy solid on cooling. Sands are usually brown because the surface of their grains is stained with iron(III) oxide (ferric oxide) Fe_2O_3. Silver sand is almost white because it contains only a very small amount of iron. Sand from the sea usually has rounded grains because the waves have rolled it about a lot, knocking the corners off the crystals. Grains of sharp sand, which is mined inland, are more angular in shape.

Cement

Cement is a fine grey powder made by heating powdered clay and limestone in a long revolving tube-shaped cement kiln which slopes down from one end. A suspension of limestone and clay in water is sprayed into the kiln at the upper end, and flames of gas, oil, or powdered coal enter the tube at the other end. The raw materials dry and are mixed by the rotation of the furnace while being heated to 600°C, which causes them to combine forming a complex mixture of calcium silicate and calcium aluminate. This mixture falls out of the lower end, is cooled, and ground to a very fine powder. Cement is used by mixing it with water and leaving the mixture to set. The setting process is known to involve the formation of hydrated crystals which interlock and bind the mass into a hard rock-like material. Concrete is cement plus various proportions of sand and gravel. It is used for making roads, paths, building blocks, paving slabs, beams, and cast-on-site walls and floors for buildings.

Mortar

The mixture used to make joints between bricks and stones contains water, one part of cement, one part of calcium hydroxide, and six parts of sand. The sand dilutes and cheapens the binding mixture of cement and calcium hydroxide. The setting of mortar involves initially the drying out of moisture and then chemical reactions of the cement (see above) and calcium hydroxide. The calcium hydroxide, which is known to builders as hydrated lime, slowly absorbs carbon dioxide from the air and becomes converted to a hard stone-like mass of calcium carbonate.

$$Ca(OH)_2 + CO_2 \longrightarrow CaCO_3 + H_2O$$

This is an acidic oxide plus base reaction, and the water evolved as it slowly takes place contributes to the dampness of a new house. Chemically it is the same reaction as that of carbon dioxide with lime-water.

Plaster

Experiment 11.1 *Setting of plaster of Paris*

Make a stiff mixture of plaster of Paris with water and put it into a small mould. Suitable moulds are a cube cut out of stiff paper and stuck together with sticky tape, or a plasticine impression of a greased coin or medal. Compare the hardness of the original plaster of Paris, the mixture with water and the set article.

Plaster of Paris is made by heating gypsum, a mineral of formula $CaSO_4 \cdot 2H_2O$

$$2CaSO_4 \cdot 2H_2O + \text{heat} \longrightarrow (2CaSO_4) \cdot H_2O + 3H_2O$$

As with most hydrated salts, heating removes water of crystallization, but if this heating is done carefully the process can be stopped when only three-quarters of the water has gone. This leaves calcium sulphate hemihydrate which can be written either as $CaSO_4 \cdot \frac{1}{2}H_2O$ or $(2CaSO_4) \cdot H_2O$. On addition of water this process reverses, heat is evolved, and needle-shaped interlocking crystals of calcium sulphate dihydrate form, producing a hard solid. The solid is used for holding broken limbs still while the bones heal, or for plastering the internal walls of houses. Plasterboard, which is commonly used to make ceilings, consists of chopped-up plant fibres which are mixed with plaster and allowed to set. By heating calcium sulphate dihydrate to a higher temperature it is possible to remove all the water and produce anhydrous calcium sulphate.

A form of $CaSO_4 \cdot 2H_2O$ is used as blackboard chalk.

Glass

Experiment 11.2 *Heating glass*

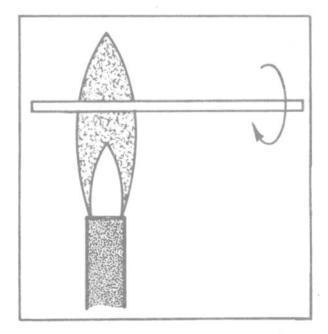

Figure 11.1 **Turn the glass steadily in the flame**

Take a piece of soda-glass rod or tube about 20 cm long and hold it horizontally in a moderate bunsen flame, turning it continuously, as shown in Fig. 11.1. Does the flame become coloured? Does the glass melt sharply or soften gradually? When the glass is very soft take it from the flame, let one end go, and observe what happens.

Repeat the experiment using Pyrex or some other resistant glass.

Of the many types of glass known, ordinary bottle or window glass, which is called soda-glass in the trade, is made by heating together a mixture of silicon dioxide SiO_2, sodium carbonate Na_2CO_3, and calcium carbonate

$CaCO_3$. The involatile silicon dioxide replaces carbon dioxide in the carbonates, forming a mixture of sodium silicate Na_2SiO_3 and calcium silicate $CaSiO_3$. For example,

$$SiO_2 + Na_2CO_3 \longrightarrow Na_2SiO_3 + CO_2$$

This mixture of sodium and calcium silicates, together with some free silicon dioxide which is left from the mixture, forms soda-glass. Glass of this composition is almost colourless, but looking through a large thickness of it (for example, through the edge of a sheet) often reveals a faint greenish tinge produced by a small amount of a silicate of iron. Coloured glasses incorporate small amounts of oxides of other elements—cobalt oxide gives a blue colour, copper a red or green, and iron a brown or green colour.

Glass is best regarded as a liquid which has been cooled below its solidifying temperature (freezing point), becoming very viscous in the process. The particles in the glass (ions and molecules) have therefore not been able to reach the exact places which would have made a regular pattern and produced a crystalline substance, so the glass has stayed non-crystalline. It is described as a **super-cooled liquid**, and does flow, but very, very slowly. Very old window glass is thicker at the bottom of the pane than at the top.

Soda-glass colours a flame yellow when it is heated because a small quantity of the sodium enters the flame and produces the characteristic yellow sodium flame colour. Glass softens slowly when heated because it is a viscous liquid whose viscosity is decreasing, rather than a solid which is melting.

Many types of glass used for special purposes have compositions which differ from that of ordinary soda-glass. Lead crystal glass contains lead and potassium compounds in place of some of the calcium and sodium compounds; it has a very high refractive index and so is used to make cut-glass ware as it sparkles. Heat-resisting glasses, which have high softening temperatures and coefficients of expansion about one-third that of ordinary soda-glass, contain some boron compounds instead of calcium and sodium compounds. Pyrex is a typical example of these boro-silicate glasses. Very many special sorts of glass are made for casting and polishing into lenses and prisms.

Glass is sealed into window frames by putty, which is made from linseed oil and a filler such as powdered chalk. On exposure to air linseed oil reacts with oxygen, and so the putty forms a hard mass.

Chemicals in the kitchen

Matches

Both safety matches and strike-anywhere matches use a fuel and an oxidizing agent. The fuel is lit by friction and the oxidizing agent helps the fuel to burn vigorously enough to light the wood or paper of the match. The stick of a match is impregnated with ammonium phosphate or a similar fire-retarding substance to ensure that the used match does not go on glowing once the flame has gone out, and some matches are coated thinly with wax, which can be seen melting as the flame burns.

Strike-anywhere matches have a head containing potassium chlorate $KClO_3$ and other oxidizing agents, a sulphide of phosphorus P_4S_3, an inert material such as zinc oxide which decreases sensitivity and regulates the burning rate of the head, glue, and a dye which is traditionally red. Friction readily ignites the phosphorus sulphide fuel, which burns using oxygen from the potassium chlorate.

Safety matches have heads containing potassium chlorate $KClO_3$ which acts as an oxidizing agent, manganese dioxide MnO_2 which catalyses the release of oxygen from the potassium chlorate, inert fillers such as powdered silica, glass, or asbestos, a water-soluble glue derived from animal bones and hides, and sulphur to act as a fuel. The brown band on the box contains red phosphorus plus inert fillers stuck on with a gum. Contact between the red phosphorus on the box and the potassium chlorate on the match head starts a local reaction which fires the head. The burning sulphur lights the wood or paper of the match.

Sodium hydrogen carbonate (sodium bicarbonate) $NaHCO_3$

Sodium hydrogen carbonate, the white powder often known simply as 'bicarb', can be made in the laboratory by passing a large volume of carbon dioxide into sodium hydroxide solution.

$$NaOH + CO_2 \longrightarrow NaHCO_3$$

Experiment 11.3   *Properties of sodium hydrogen carbonate*

(*a*) Heat the test-tube *A* containing dry sodium hydrogen carbonate to a depth of about 2 cm, passing any product into the cool dry test-tube *B* (Fig. 11.2).
Test any liquid collected in *B* with universal indicator paper, and then with white anhydrous copper sulphate.
(*b*) When the apparatus has cooled, use a dropper and a small volume of lime-water (as in experiment 6.6) to test some of the gas remaining in *A* to see if it contains carbon dioxide.
(*c*) Put some dilute hydrochloric acid on to a little solid sodium hydrogen carbonate in the bottom of a test-tube. Test any gas given off until you have found out what it is.
(*d*) Dissolve a little sodium hydrogen carbonate in water and test the solution with universal indicator.

CHEMISTRY ALL AROUND US

Sodium hydrogen carbonate (sodium bicarbonate) decomposes when heated, giving off steam and carbon dioxide, and leaving a white residue of sodium carbonate.

$$2NaHCO_3 \longrightarrow Na_2CO_3 + CO_2 + H_2O$$

Steam can often be detected as water droplets, which turn white anhydrous copper sulphate blue.

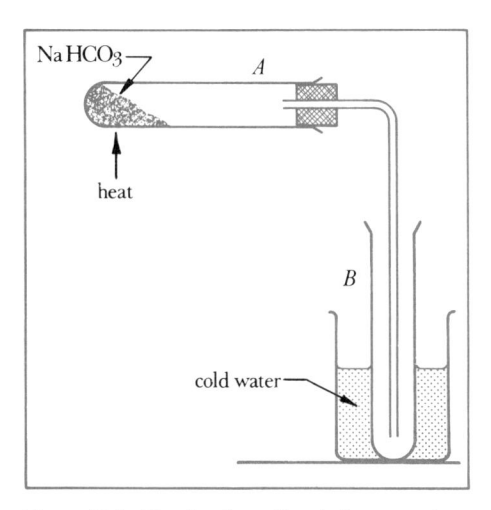

Figure 11.2 Heating dry sodium hydrogen carbonate, $NaHCO_3$

Dilute hydrochloric acid reacts with sodium hydrogen carbonate, causing fizzing as carbon dioxide escapes and leaving a colourless solution of sodium chloride.

$$NaHCO_3 + HCl \longrightarrow NaCl + H_2O + CO_2$$

The action of an acid on sodium hydrogen carbonate provides carbon dioxide pressure to squirt the water stream of a soda-acid fire extinguisher (see Fig. 6.3). Other acids react in a similar way and the reactions can be summarized as

$$acid + carbonate \longrightarrow salt + water + carbon\ dioxide$$

Sodium hydrogen carbonate solution is alkaline, and can thus be used to react with and therefore neutralize acids. This property explains its use in certain indigestion preparations, which neutralize excess stomach acid.

Baking powders use the reaction between sodium hydrogen carbonate and an acid. Many powders contain sodium hydrogen carbonate and tartaric acid, a white solid which has no reaction with dry sodium hydrogen carbonate. When the baking powder is moistened with water or milk, the acid and

229

sodium hydrogen carbonate start to react, giving off carbon dioxide which blows bubbles in the mixture thus causing cakes, scones, etc., to rise.

Health salts contain a mixture of sodium hydrogen carbonate with solid acids such as tartaric acid and citric acid. The acids react with the sodium hydrogen carbonate when dissolved in water, and the carbon dioxide produced causes fizzing. Sherbet is made from a mixture similar to health salts, with added sugar and flavouring.

Sodium carbonate decahydrate (washing soda) $Na_2CO_3.10H_2O$

The colourless translucent crystals of sodium carbonate decahydrate lose water of crystallization to the atmosphere if left in dry air, and fall to a powder of sodium carbonate monohydrate $Na_2CO_3.H_2O$. This giving up of water of crystallization to the atmosphere with the resulting destruction of the crystal is called **efflorescence**.

Sodium carbonate decahydrate is known as washing soda because it is used to soften both temporarily and permanently hard water. It does this by forming precipitates of calcium carbonate with the calcium salts which make the water hard.

thw $\quad Na_2CO_3 + Ca(HCO_3)_2 \longrightarrow 2NaHCO_3 + CaCO_3$
phw $\quad Na_2CO_3 + CaSO_4 \longrightarrow Na_2SO_4 + CaCO_3$

These reactions are both examples of the change of chemical partners which is called **double decomposition**.

Sodium carbonate reacts with dilute mineral acids giving off carbon dioxide and forming a salt plus water, as do all carbonates and bicarbonates (see experiment 6.6). For example,

$$H_2SO_4 + Na_2CO_3 \longrightarrow Na_2SO_4 + H_2O + CO_2$$

When the crystalline decahydrate is heated, water vapour is given off and a white residue of anhydrous sodium carbonate powder is left. This anhydrous sodium carbonate cannot be decomposed at the temperatures reached by a bunsen burner flame. Anhydrous sodium carbonate, which is known as soda ash, is the form commonly used in industry, for example, for the manufacture of soda-glass.

Silicones

Experiment 11.4 *Some properties of silicones*

(*a*) Take three corked glass tubes each containing a liquid silicone together with an air bubble. Hold one tube vertical so that the bubble is at the top, then invert it quickly but smoothly, and measure the time the bubble takes to get to the top again. Repeat this with the other two tubes.

CHEMISTRY ALL AROUND US

(*b*) Take two or three drops of a liquid silicone and use one finger to smear it on part of the surface of some coarse-textured non-shiny cardboard. Use a dropper to put one drop of water on the silicone-treated part of the card and one on the non-treated part.

(*c*) Smear some liquid silicone on to an area of a postcard about 2cm wide by 10 cm long. Fix strips of adhesive tape (e.g., Sellotape) about 10 cm long to two 5p pieces, then press one strip of tape on to the untreated area of the postcard and one on to the treated area as shown in Fig. 11.3. Raise the postcard slowly towards a vertical position and watch to see if the weight of the coins pulls the tapes from the card.

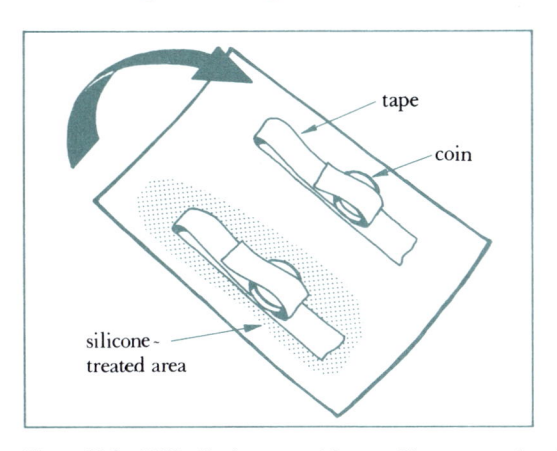

Figure 11.3 Will adhesive tape stick to a silicone-treated surface?

Silicon, which occurs near carbon in the Periodic Table, has, like carbon, the ability to form long chains. The chains consist of alternate silicon and oxygen atoms, so in this way the chains are unlike those of carbon, which are all carbon atoms. The chains are molecules of silicones, and a typical structure is shown in Fig. 11.4. This type of silicone, a long-chain polymer, would

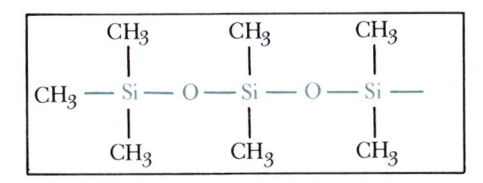

Figure 11.4 A typical silicone chain

be a free-flowing oil if the chain were short, a viscous oil or grease if the chain were of medium length, but a rubber-like material if the chain were very long.

Silicones do not occur naturally, they are man-made (synthetic) compounds which have many remarkable and useful properties. As experiment

11.4(b) shows, silicones repel water. Silicone treatment produces shower-resistant finishes on cloth used in outerwear, and on leather for shoes, and silicones are also put in polishes for outdoor use such as car polishes.

Silicones are slippery and are therefore useful for coating things which must not stick together. Experiment 11.4(c) shows that sticky tape sticks very poorly to silicone-treated surfaces, and examples of the use of silicones as non-stick surfaces include silicone-treated pans, baking tins for cakes and loaves, and moulds used for making car tyres. As silicones contain no ions or free electrons they are good electrical insulators, so solid silicones can be used in radio and electrical mechanisms.

Foods

The chemistry of foods is complex and difficult, but in chapter 9 we have already met some of the important groups of compounds useful in our diet —carbohydrates, proteins, and fats.

Carbohydrates are, as the name suggests, compounds containing carbon, hydrogen, and oxygen. There are two main types of carbohydrate: sugars, and long-chain polymers such as starch or cellulose. All sugars contain ring-shaped molecules which usually have five or six atoms in the ring. Glucose $C_6H_{12}O_6$ has one such ring, and sucrose (ordinary cane or beet sugar) $C_{12}H_{22}O_{11}$ has two rings joined together. Starch and cellulose are long-chain polymers made from large numbers of these rings; one molecule may contain as many as three thousand small rings. When a carbohydrate of either type is heated strongly, water vapour is evolved and a black mass of carbon is left—a reaction familiar to anyone who has ever burned the toast. Flour, rice, and potatoes are common sources of long-chain carbohydrates as they all contain starch, and the stems of most plants contain cellulose.

Proteins are long-chain polymers but their monomers are short-chain molecules rather than rings as in carbohydrates, and the resulting protein polymer contains nitrogen as well as carbon and hydrogen. All living things can build up proteins, but we rely on foods such as meat, cheese, and eggs which contain a high proportion of proteins to add to those which our body builds up. Not all proteins are edible; leather, hair, and silk, for example, are largely made of proteins.

Fats are compounds containing glycerol (glycerine) which has reacted with long-chain organic acids called fatty acids. Oils are fats which are liquid at room temperature. Both fats and oils are insoluble in water, but generally dissolve in solvents such as carbon tetrachloride, benzene, and petrol. In a given fat (for example, mutton fat) the fatty acids attached to the glycerol are not all the same so the fat molecules differ from each other. Thus a fat is not a pure substance but a mixture of various substances, and therefore it has no fixed, sharp melting point, but softens gradually as it is heated. This can be observed when chip pan fat melts.

CHEMISTRY ALL AROUND US

Edible fats are digested slowly so they provide a supply of energy over a period of several hours, whereas carbohydrates, which also give energy, are comparatively soon burned up.

A complete diet must contain salts (for example, sodium and potassium chloride and iodide, and calcium, magnesium, iron, and cobalt compounds), water, and vitamins as well as carbohydrates, proteins, and fats. Vitamins are chemicals of many different types which are now known to be essential to human and animal health. Many vitamins act as catalysts for important bodily processes.

Table 11.1 Food analyses

Food	Carbohydrate	Protein	Fat	kjoules per g	kcals per oz
white bread	60%	8%	1%	10	67
bacon	0	13%	50%	17	115
milk	5%	3%	4%	3	20
chocolate	59%	5%	33%	23	156
peanuts	9%	29%	50%	26	176

Note: Figures do not total 100% as water and mineral salts have been omitted.

Table 11.2 Summary of foods

	Carbohydrate	Protein	Fat	Vitamins
chemical nature	compounds of C, H, and O; sugars or long-chain molecules	polymers containing N links	compounds of glycerol	many various types
main function	supply energy	replace worn tissue	slow energy supply	catalysts

Chemicals in the bathroom

Many chemical preparations such as toothpastes, shampoos, bath preparations, and cosmetics are sold for use in the bathroom. These are often made from comparatively simple and cheap chemicals, but the market is competitive, so large sums are spent on advertising and packaging and the products are then sold at high prices.

Hair shampoos

Experiment 11.5   *Hair shampoos—soap or synthetic detergent?*

Add two or three drops of hair shampoo to 2 cm depth of distilled water in a test-tube. Shake the tube until a lather is formed, add a few drops of a dilute acid and note whether or not the lather is spoiled by the acid.

Repeat the experiment using a minute scrap of soap or a soapflake.

Experiment 11.5 shows that hair shampoo contains synthetic detergent, which does not react with a dilute acid, rather than traditional soap which will not lather in the presence of an acid. As well as the synthetic detergents, hair shampoos contain water, perfume, a little dye, and other additives.

The scalp secretes grease, and therefore hair becomes greasy, which allows dirt to stick to the hair and encourages it to hang together giving a rat-tail effect. As experiment 8.3 shows, synthetic detergents are superior to soap in hard water areas because they do not produce a sticky scum which would adhere to hair. The purpose of shampoo is to clean the hair by removing grease, and the addition of such things as lanolin, beer, egg, cream, and champagne has little or no detectable effect. Cheap shampoos are just as effective as expensive ones.

Toothpastes

The purpose of toothpaste is to help in the removal of particles of food which lodge round the teeth and gums, to remove stains from the teeth, and to neutralize acids formed in the mouth by the decayed food. Thus toothpaste contains a soap to produce froth in which food particles dislodged by brushing become suspended, and a mild abrasive such as calcium carbonate (powdered chalk) which gently scours the teeth. Calcium carbonate also helps to neutralize acids. Colouring, flavouring, and mild bleaching agents such as peroxides may also be added, and water and glycerol (glycerine) help to bind the powders into a paste. Tooth powders may contain similar substances but no water or glycerine, or they may be based on the use of salt as an abrasive.

Bath preparations

Bath salts and bath cubes consist partly of sodium carbonate crystals. These act in two ways: they soften the water, as described earlier in this chapter, and, as they are mildly alkaline, they react with fats in the skin forming soap. Bath salts have colouring and perfume added to them before sale. Bubble bath liquid consists of synthetic detergents, with colouring and perfume. The rush of water into the bath traps air in the bubbles, which are not formed by a chemical reaction.

Cosmetics

Cosmetic creams are emulsions containing oils or fats in which there are droplets of water. As oils and water do not mix alone, a substance called an **emulsifying agent** must be added to promote mixing. A common example of the use of an emulsifying agent is the addition of washing-up liquid to greasy washing-up water. The liquid helps to wrap up the grease particles so that they are emulsified, and appear to dissolve in the water (see Fig. 8.2). An emulsion is not a solution in the sense that salt or sugar in water is a solution. True solutions such as those of salt and sugar contain individual molecules or ions, whereas in a grease-in-water emulsion the grease is in clumps containing thousands of molecules. The grease clumps are much larger than individual molecules or ions, but not large enough to be seen or to settle out by sedimentation. Cosmetic creams are similar to washing-up water in reverse, as they are emulsions of water droplets in fat. When the cream is rubbed on to the skin the emulsion breaks down and the water evaporates, producing a cooling effect: hence the name cold cream. The oils and fats then sink into the skin, lubricating it and helping to prevent cracking.

Lipsticks contain a mixture of several fats, waxes and oils, colouring and perfume. The greasy substances are mixed to produce the consistency needed; if the product is too soft it smears, and if too hard it is difficult and unpleasant to apply. Some types of eye shadow are similar to lipstick.

Perfumes consist of a solution in ethanol (ethyl alcohol or alcohol) of small quantities of scented ingredients known as **essential oils**. Some of these oils are synthetic but others are obtained from plants. Many parts of plants are used as sources of natural essential oils; flowers, fruits, leaves, seeds, stems, bark, and roots are all common starting materials. The natural essential oils are expensive because they are only present in minute quantities in the plant materials. Some are extracted by mixing the raw material with water and then distilling the mixture. In another useful extraction process the starting material is warmed with ethanol, benzene, or a similar organic solvent and the solvent is then gently evaporated leaving the essential oil. Alternatively, the plant tissue may be allowed to stand in contact with warm fat. The essential oils dissolve in the fat from which they are later extracted.

The perfume chemist makes a careful choice of ingredients for a perfume —sometimes as many as fifty different essential oils are mixed with ethanol to make an expensive product. After a small-scale trial has produced a successful blend, larger quantities are then mixed, stored to mature, and sold. When perfume is used a process of fractional distillation takes place (see experiment 1.4). The alcohol evaporates fairly rapidly producing a cooling effect, and then the other substances evaporate slowly, producing the scent. A really good perfume is blended so that the ingredients evaporate at approximately equal rates, and thus the smell does not change as time elapses, only the intensity of the smell changes. Cheaper perfumes, blended from cheaper ingredients with less care, change their character as they evaporate because some of the essential oils distil off before others have done so.

Conclusion

You have now read something of the vast scope of chemistry and how it influences our lives in many ways; our clothes, knives and forks, food, cars, aeroplanes and buses, medicines, sports and pastimes are all affected by the materials chemists have discovered or invented. Some of the discoveries, (for example, nerve gases, napalm) have been put to evil uses, some have had undesirable side-effects (thalidomide, DDT), but most of them have made life pleasanter. The good effects range from minor items such as easier washing-up and wear-resistant socks, to major ones such as penicillin and antiseptic surgery, and there is every reason to suppose that chemists will continue to improve the quality of our life in the future.

Questions

1. Describe experiments which would show that set mortar contains some calcium carbonate.

2. Describe briefly (two to three lines each) the essential scientific processes which take place when (*a*) cement sets, (*b*) a match is struck, (*c*) baking powder is mixed with water, (*d*) washing soda crystals fall to powder.

3. Invent an experiment to compare the amounts of carbon dioxide made when two brands of health salts are mixed with water.

4. State what is meant by, and in each case give an example of (*a*) igneous rock, (*b*) a supercooled liquid, (*c*) efflorescence, (*d*) double decomposition, (*e*) a carbohydrate, (*f*) an emulsifying agent.

5. Explain how the processes of dissolving and fractional distillation are involved in the manufacture and use of perfumes.

6. A certain brand of bath crystals is said to 'soften the hardest water until it is as soft as rain'. How would you try to check this statement?

Miscellaneous questions

1. Make a table showing, for each of the following compounds, its chemical name, formula, appearance, and how it reacts with dilute hydrochloric acid: (*a*) bicarbonate of soda, (*b*) limestone, (*c*) washing soda, (*d*) caustic potash, (*e*) magnesia.

2. A pure acid A dehydrates sugar forming a black solid B, and when A is diluted and mixed with barium chloride solution a white precipitate C is formed. What are A, B, and C? (Give reasons for your answers).

3. Name (*a*) three mixtures which may be separated by fractional distillation, (*b*) three reducing agents, (*c*) three drying agents, (*d*) three acidic gases, (*e*) two metals which react with water, (*f*) three thermoplastics.

4. State: (*a*) two advantages of heating by natural gas compared to coal, (*b*) two advantages of natural gas compared to coal gas, (*c*) the essential difference between the molecules present in petrol and those in natural gas, (*d*) the chemical elements present in coal.

MISCELLANEOUS QUESTIONS

5. What is a mordant? Describe how you would decide whether alum was a good mordant for a certain dye.

6. Without repeating yourself, name and give a formula or equation for (*a*) four gaseous elements, (*b*) two naturally occurring gaseous compounds, (*c*) two solid non-metallic elements, (*d*) a chemical reaction which occurs naturally, (*e*) a metal extracted by electrolysis.

7. Classify into solids which react with water, solids which do not react with water, gases which react with water, gases which do not react with water: H_2, CaO, CH_4, NO_2, Na, NaCl, NH_4Cl, H_2S, K, SO_2, HCl gas, S.
Give the word equations for the solids which react with water.

8. What weight of potassium nitrate must be heated to make 4 g oxygen, if the equation is

$$2KNO_3 \longrightarrow 2KNO_2 + O_2$$

9. Name two different catalysts used in the laboratory, and one used in industry. In each case state also the names of the reactants and products of the reaction.

10. Explain what is meant by (*a*) an ionic bond, (*b*) a covalent bond, and draw an electronic diagram to illustrate each type of bond.

11. Explain the difference between (*a*) a solution and a suspension, (*b*) a thermoplastic and a thermoset, (*c*) temporarily and permanently hard water, (*d*) reduction and dehydration, (*e*) an alkali and a base, (*f*) CO and Co, (*g*) graphite and diamond.

12. Describe the action of three types of fire extinguisher, giving formulae for all chemicals mentioned.

13. Describe briefly three different laboratory examples of electrolysis, explaining the changes in each example under the headings, 'ions present', and 'reactions at electrodes'.

14. Draw sketches and write equations to show how, starting from ammonium chloride, you would prepare (*a*) hydrogen chloride gas, (*b*) ammonia gas.

15. Four drops of ethyl alcohol (ethanol) are put on to a ball-point pen stain on a tablecloth. The stain spreads and forms concentric rings coloured brown, dark blue, and red. Explain what this shows, name the method of analysis based on experiments like this, and mention two other substances which can be separated in a similar manner.

Answers to numerical examples

Ch. 2 No. 7 (*a*) 80 g per 100 g, (*b*) 35°C, (*c*) unsaturated—saturated solution contains 140 g per 1000 g
Ch. 6 No. 8 (*a*) 16, (*b*) 63, (*c*) 71, (*d*) 84, (*e*) 132, (*f*) 174, (*g*) 60
No. 9 (*a*) 25%, (*b*) 40%, (*c*) 60%, (*d*) 12·5%
No. 10 (*a*) 28 g, (*b*) 5·6 g, (*c*) 2·8 g, (*d*) 21·25 g
Misc. No. 8 12·6 g

Appendix 1

Common and chemical names

Common name	Formula	Chemical name(s)
alcohol	C_2H_5OH	ethanol, ethyl alcohol
alumina	Al_2O_3	aluminium oxide
anhydrite	$CaSO_4$	calcium sulphate
bicarbonate of soda	$NaHCO_3$	sodium hydrogen carbonate, sodium bicarbonate
caustic potash	KOH	potassium hydroxide
caustic soda	$NaOH$	sodium hydroxide
chalk	$CaCO_3$	calcium carbonate
gypsum	$CaSO_4 \cdot 2H_2O$	calcium sulphate dihydrate
hydrated lime	$Ca(OH)_2$	calcium hydroxide
lime, limestone	$CaCO_3$	calcium carbonate
limewater	$Ca(OH)_2$ soln	calcium hydroxide solution
litharge	PbO	lead(II) oxide, lead monoxide
magnesia	MgO	magnesium oxide
marble	$CaCO_3$	calcium carbonate
natural gas	CH_4	methane (mainly)
plaster of Paris	$(CaSO_4)_2 \cdot H_2O$	calcium sulphate hemihydrate
quicklime	CaO	calcium oxide
quicksilver	Hg	mercury
red lead	Pb_3O_4	dilead(II) oxide lead(IV) oxide triplumbic tetroxide
slaked lime	$Ca(OH)_2$	calcium hydroxide
vitriol (oil of vitriol)	H_2SO_4	(conc.) sulphuric acid
washing soda	$Na_2CO_3 \cdot 10H_2O$	sodium carbonate decahydrate

Appendix 2

Qualitative analysis

Finding out 'What have we got here?' is one of the jobs chemists do. A forensic chemist might analyse blood stains or dust found on a suspect's clothes, a control chemist might determine the purity of a medicine or a petrol sample, and a geochemist the contents of an ore specimen. Some analyses tell us what is present, others tell us how much of each ingredient there is. Some simple qualitative tests, which tell us what metals and radicals are present in a compound, are described here.

In these instructions the substance being analysed is written as X.

Tests for metals

Flame tests

Take a piece of platinum wire and clean it by dipping it into some concentrated hydrochloric acid on a watch-glass (*not* in the bottle), and then holding the wire in the hottest part of a bunsen flame (i.e., just above the tip of the blue cone). When the flame is no longer coloured by the substances on the wire, dip the wire into the hydrochloric acid again, then into some X on a watch-glass, and put it into the flame. Observe the colour directly, or through a direct-vision spectroscope (e.g., the Griffin pocket spectroscope) if one is available.

> Potassium compounds give a lilac flame, visible through blue glass
> Calcium compounds give a red flame
> Copper compounds give a blue/green flame with an occasional flash of yellow
> Sodium compounds give an intense orange/yellow flame.

The sodium colour is so strong that a small amount of sodium as an impurity in, for example, an ammonium compound is sometimes misleading.

CHEMISTRY

Test for ammonium compounds

Put some X in a wide test-tube and add about 2 cm depth of sodium hydroxide solution. Warm the tube gently, being careful not to point it at anyone. Wave some of the gas evolved towards your nose, and if it smells of ammonia, put a piece of damp red litmus paper near the mouth of the test-tube. If it turns blue this confirms that ammonia is given off so X must be an ammonium compound. (Do not boil the solution or you will form caustic soda spray which will affect the litmus.)

Hydrogen sulphide tests

Do these tests in a fume cupboard if possible.

Use a clean delivery tube to pass hydrogen sulphide into a solution of X in water.

A black precipitate of copper sulphide from a blue solution shows that X is a copper compound.

A black precipitate of lead sulphide from a colourless solution shows that X is a lead compound.

A white precipitate of zinc sulphide from a colourless solution shows that X is a zinc compound.

Tests for radicals (non-metallic groups)

Test for carbonates

Put some X in a test-tube and add dilute hydrochloric acid to a depth of 2 cm. If fizzing takes place use a dropper to bubble some of the gas through a little limewater in an ignition tube, as in experiment 6.6. If the limewater turns turbid (cloudy), carbon dioxide is being given off, therefore X is a carbonate.

Test for chlorides

Dissolve some X in distilled water and to the solution add some dilute nitric acid and two or three drops of silver nitrate solution. A white precipitate of silver chloride shows that X is a chloride.

The dilute nitric acid is to prevent the formation of precipitates other than silver chloride.

Test for sulphates

Dissolve some X in water and add to the solution some dilute hydrochloric acid and barium chloride solution. A white precipitate of barium sulphate shows that X is a sulphate.

APPENDIX 2

The dilute hydrochloric acid is to prevent the formation of precipitates other than barium sulphate.

Test for nitrates—the brown ring test

Dissolve a little X in 1 cm depth of water in a test-tube and add to it an equal volume of cold, freshly made iron(II) sulphate (ferrous sulphate) solution. Hold the test-tube at an angle of 45° to the horizontal, and pour concentrated sulphuric acid carefully down the inside wall of the tube. The dense acid slips to the bottom of the tube. If a brown ring forms at the junction of the acid and water layers, X is a nitrate.

Chromatography

The formation of rings when coloured inks dry on blotting paper is a simple example of chromatography, which is used to separate coloured substances, or substances which can easily be made coloured. It depends on the different rates of diffusion of solutions creeping along a porous material such as filter paper or a stick of chalk.

Separation of ink pigments

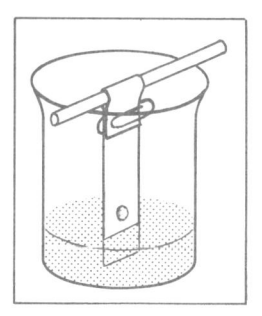

Figure A.2.1 Paper chromatography

Cut a strip of filter paper about 2 cm × 15 cm and, about 2 cm from one end, make a large spot of coloured ink on it. It is convenient to use a water-based, felt-tipped pen for this. Suspend the strip in a large beaker as shown in Fig. A.2.1, making sure the spot is above the level of the water in the beaker. Observe the effect as the water climbs up the strip by capillary action. When the water reaches the folded-over part of the strip, or when it stops climbing, hang the strip in a warm place to dry the chromatogram.

CHEMISTRY

Chromatography of grass pigments

Grind some grass with 2 or 3 cm^3 ethanol (ethyl alcohol) in a mortar and decant (pour off) the green pigment solution. Put several spots of the green liquid close to the end of a strip of filter paper 2 cm × 15 cm letting each dry before adding another, and repeat the method described above, using ethanol in place of the water in the beaker. Cover the beaker to slow evaporation.

Appendix 3

Revision notes

To pass examinations you must revise intelligently. Most pupils can concentrate on a book for about 10 to 15 minutes only before their attention wanders, so never simply sit and stare at your notes or textbook. Have a pencil and paper at hand, and, as you read, make the briefest possible notes on the topic. Doing a lot of writing is little help, and straightforward copying out is a waste of time. Aim to condense a page into about fifteen or twenty words. Abbreviating, using formulae instead of names, quick diagrams, and writing reaction schemes all help to make the work short.

An example of some such notes might be:

'Sulphur—melt underground.

monoclinic (needles, hot) and rhombic (pyramids, cold CS_2) are both S_8 rings

melting: yellow $\longrightarrow$ red viscous long chains $\longrightarrow$ black short chains . . .'

When you have made notes on a piece of work a page or two long, read through the notes to make sure you understand them, shut your eyes, try to remember as much of them as possible, then check by looking at the notes again. Now go on and do the next portion. Keep your brief notes and read through them all once more before you stop work. This method has two advantages: trying to condense the work to a minimum helps you to pick out the important general points, and the variation of activity—reading, writing, remembering, checking—helps you to concentrate instead of dreaming, or reading in a useless mechanical way.

The summaries in the book are useful for revision, but not as much use as those you make yourself. Learning equations off by heart is of little use. If you learn a lot you will muddle them up, and there are not many marks given for equations anyway. It is better and easier to learn properties, similarities, reasons, methods, and principles rather than details like equations. If you know the outline of the chemistry this will help you to recall details, and you can often make up the equations during the examination.

Do not imagine that revising a month or so in advance is useless because you will then forget everything before the examination. You will not forget it all, and the parts you do forget you will relearn quickly and easily. Finally, remember that learning chemistry is easier than learning most other subjects, because the same reaction appears in different sections; the reaction between magnesium and oxygen is a property of magnesium, a property of oxygen, and the preparation of a basic oxide, so if you revise thoroughly you will meet it three times.

Appendix 4

Ionic interpretation of reactions

Ionic substances such as sodium chloride and hydrochloric acid have ionic (electrovalent) bonds formed by electron robbery, and are composed of ions, for example, Na^+Cl^- and H^+Cl^-. Although it is often convenient to write these two compounds as NaCl and HCl, it is sometimes useful to consider their ions, which actually exist and undergo reactions. For example, in

$$HCl + NaOH \longrightarrow NaCl + H_2O$$

the acid, alkali, and salt formed are all ionic, but the water is covalent, so the reaction is really

$$H^+ + Cl^- + Na^+ + OH^- \longrightarrow Na^+ + Cl^- + H_2O$$

The ions printed in blue do not react. They are spectator ions and may be omitted from the ionic equation, which becomes

$$H^+ + OH^- \longrightarrow H_2O$$

This is the ionic equation for the reaction between hydrochloric acid and sodium hydroxide, and you should be able to show that the reactions of nitric acid with potassium hydroxide, and sulphuric acid with sodium hydroxide also produce the same ionic equation.

As well as having the same number of atoms of each sort on the two sides of the equation, an ionic equation should balance electrically. This means that the charge totals on the two sides of the equation should be equal.

Remembering that acids, bases (alkalis and metal oxides), and salts are usually ionic, and that gases are covalent, other ionic equations may be constructed. For example,

$$Ca(OH)_2 + CO_2 \longrightarrow CaCO_3 + H_2O$$
$$Ca^{++} + 2OH^- + CO_2 \longrightarrow Ca^{++} + CO_3^{--} + H_2O$$
$$\text{i.e.,} \quad 2OH^- + CO_2 \longrightarrow CO_3^{--} + H_2O$$

Note that this ionic equation, which has two negative charges on either side, balances electrically; it is not necessary for the charges on each side to total zero.

$$H_2SO_4 + Na_2CO_3 \longrightarrow Na_2SO_4 + H_2O + CO_2$$
$$2H^+ + SO_4^{--} + 2Na^+ + CO_3^{--} \longrightarrow 2Na^+ + SO_4^{--} + H_2O + CO_2$$
i.e., $$2H^+ + CO_3^{--} \longrightarrow H_2O + CO_2$$

Using ionic equations, reactions such as the neutralization of an acid by various bases, whose molecular equations look different, can be shown to have fundamental similarities. For example,

$$2HCl + CaCO_3 \longrightarrow CaCl_2 + H_2O + CO_2$$

reduces to

$$2H^+ + CO_3^{--} \longrightarrow H_2O + CO_2$$

which is identical with the equation for the action of sulphuric acid on sodium carbonate. The reactions of acids usually involve the H^+ ion, which all acids contain in solution. Remembering that a metal is not ionic, but that most of its compounds are, we can write ionic equations for reactions such as

$$Zn + H_2SO_4 \longrightarrow ZnSO_4 + H_2$$
$$Zn + 2H^+ \longrightarrow Zn^{++} + H_2$$

and

$$Zn + CuSO_4 \longrightarrow ZnSO_4 + Cu$$
$$Zn + Cu^{++} \longrightarrow Zn^{++} + Cu$$

In this last equation it is obvious that the copper has won the contest for electrons, because it has removed two electrons from the zinc atom, turning it into a zinc ion Zn^{++}.

Electrolysis

It is often useful to consider electrolysis in terms of the ions present, their movement to the electrodes, and their reactions, rather than look at the overall equation.

In the electrolysis of very dilute sulphuric acid (acidulated water):

Ions present are H^+, SO_4^{--}, and OH^- (+ more H^+ from the water)
Movement H^+ to cathode
OH^- and SO_4^{--} to anode
Reactions Cathode: $H^+ + e^- \longrightarrow H$
then $2H \longrightarrow H_2$
Anode: $4OH^- \longrightarrow 2H_2O + O_2 + 4e^-$

The four electrons given up at the anode are pushed round the external circuit by the source of electrical energy (battery, transformer, etc.,) and react with $4H^+$, forming $2H_2$ at the cathode. Thus the overall equation is

$$2H_2O \longrightarrow 2H_2 + O_2$$

Note that the SO_4^{--} ion does not react.

In the electrolysis of molten sodium chloride:

Ions present are	Na^+, Cl^-
Movement	Na^+ to cathode
	Cl^- to anode
Reactions	Cathode: $2Na^+ + 2e^- \longrightarrow 2Na$
	Anode: $2Cl^- \longrightarrow 2Cl + 2e^-$
	then $2Cl \longrightarrow Cl_2$

i.e., overall $2Na^+Cl^- \longrightarrow 2Na + Cl_2$

In the electrolysis of sodium chloride solution:

Ions present are	Na^+, Cl^-, H^+, OH^-
Movement	Na^+ and H^+ to cathode
	OH^- and Cl^- to anode
Reactions	Cathode: $H^+ + e^- \longrightarrow H$
	then $2H \longrightarrow H_2$
	Anode: $Cl^- \longrightarrow Cl + e^-$
	then $2Cl \longrightarrow Cl_2$

i.e., hydrogen and chlorine are made and Na^+ and OH^- left in solution. The solution therefore contains sodium hydroxide and some unchanged sodium chloride. The chlorine sometimes reacts with the sodium hydroxide solution before it has a chance to bubble off, but in some special cells (e.g., see Fig. 10.11) they are kept apart by a diaphragm and the process is used to make sodium hydroxide solution, hydrogen, and chlorine from sodium chloride solution, so that the overall equation is

$$2Na^+Cl^- + 2H_2O \longrightarrow 2Na^+OH^- + H_2 + Cl_2$$

Appendix 5

Data sheets

Elements, symbols, and approximate atomic weights

Element	Symbol	Approx at. wt.	Element	Symbol	Approx at. wt.
aluminium	Al	27	manganese	Mn	55
barium	Ba	137	mercury	Hg	201
calcium	Ca	40	nitrogen	N	14
carbon	C	12	oxygen	O	16
chlorine	Cl	35·5	phosphorus	P	31
copper	Cu	64	potassium	K	39
gold	Au	197	silicon	Si	28
hydrogen	H	1	silver	Ag	108
iron	Fe	56	sodium	Na	23
lead	Pb	207	sulphur	S	32
magnesium	Mg	24	zinc	Zn	65

Valencies

silver	Ag^+	calcium	Ca^{++}	aluminium	Al^{+++}
sodium	Na^+	copper	Cu^{++}	iron(III) or ferric	Fe^{+++}
potassium	K^+	iron(II) or ferrous	Fe^{++}		
hydrogen	H^+	magnesium	Mg^{++}		
		zinc	Zn^{++}		
hydrogen carbonate or bicarbonate		(HCO_3^-)		carbonate	(CO_3^{--})
chloride		Cl^-		oxide	O^{--}
hydroxide		(OH^-)		sulphate	(SO_4^{--})
nitrate		(NO_3^-)		sulphide	S^{--}

Index

Acetic acid, 121, 122
Acetylene, 52, 53, 143
Acids, 123
Activity series, 167–169
Addition polymerization, 187, 189
Air:
  in water, 43, 44
  percentage oxygen in, 39–41
  substances present in, 41, 42
Alcohol, ethyl (ethanol), 6, 7, 98, 99, 242
Allotropy, 79, 210
Alloy, 133, 136, 138, 139, 150, 160
Aluminium:
  properties and uses of, 147, 160, 161
  sulphate, 162
Alums, 162
Amalgams, 150
Ammonia:
  oxidation of, 119
  preparation of, 203, 204
  properties and uses of, 205, 206
  solution, 113
Ammonium:
  chloride, 206
  dichromate, 4
  test for, 240
Anion, 71
Anode, 135, 246, 247
Anodizing, 160
Argon, 41, 69
Atmosphere, 39
Atomic:
  number, 70
  structure, 65–69
  weight, 70, 124, 125, 248
Atoms, 12, 13, 65–69

Bakelite, 195–197
Baking powder, 229, 230
Bases, 123
Bath salts, 234
Biro, Lazslo, 3
Blast Furnace, 139–141
Bleaching, 214, 218, 219

Bond:
  covalent, 72–75
  double, 187
  electrovalent (ionic), 70–72
Brass, 136
Bromine, 218, 221
Bronze, 136
Brown ring test, 241
Brownian movement, 36
Bunsen burner, 93
Butane, 97, 186

Calcium:
  carbonate, 85, 155, 156, 223
  hydrogen carbonate, 177–183
  hydroxide, 87, 156, 157, 225
  oxide, 155, 156
  properties of, 29, 30, 155
  sulphate, 177–183, 225, 226
Calgon, 180
Calor gas, 97
Carbohydrates, 232, 233
Carbolic acid, 1, 195
Carbon:
  black (lamp black), 82
  cycle, 89, 90
  dioxide,
    preparation of, 85, 86, 88, 89
    properties of, 87, 88
    test for, 87
    uses of, 87, 88
  monoxide, 84, 139
  tetrachloride, 219, 220
Carbonate, test for, 240
Carbonic acid, 120, 121
Catalysis, 46, 47, 106, 119
Cathode, 135, 246, 247
Cation, 71
Cellulose, 200, 201
Cement, 225
Chalk, 156, 223, 226
Charcoal, 4, 81, 82
Chemical change, 30, 31
Chlorides, test for, 240

249

Chlorine:
  preparation and properties of, 217, 218
  uses of, 219
Chromatography, 241, 242
Clays, 224
Coal and coke, 90–93
Coal gas, 92–94
Combustion, 50
Condensation polymerization, 193
Conservation of matter, 15, 16
Constant Composition, Law of, 15
Contact process, 106
Copper:
  alloys of, 136
  heat treatment of, 166
  oxide, 136, 137
  purification of, 134, 135
  reactions of, 134–136
  sulphate, 32, 109, 137, 138
Corrosion, 41, 42
Cosmetics, 234, 235
Covalent bonding, 72–75, 187
Cracking, 97, 187
Crystals, 27–29
Crystallization, 27–29, 210, 211
  water of, 29

DDT, 3
Dehydration, 32, 107
Deliquescent, 153
Densities, table of, 21
Detergent, synthetic:
  action of, 171–175
  comparison with soap, 177
  preparation of, 175
Diamond, 79, 80
Diffusion, 58, 59
Displacement, 137, 168, 169, 218
Dissociation, 206
Distillation:
  fractional, 6–8
  liquid air, 51, 52
  petroleum, 95, 96
  simple, 5, 6
Double decomposition, 230
Drying, 21
Dunlop, John, 1

Efflorescence, 230
Electric Arc Furnace, 141, 142
Electrochemical series, 167–169
Electrolysis:
  ionic equations for, 246, 247
  of sodium chloride solution, 217, 247
  of water, 56
Electrons, 65–67

Electroplating:
  of copper, 135
  of zinc, 151, 152
Electrovalent bonding, 70–72
Elements:
  definition of, 13
  families of, 221
  list of, 248
Emulsion, 174, 234, 235
Endothermic reaction, 94
Energy, 101, 102
Enzymes: 98
  digestive, 201
  in synthetic detergents, 173
Equations, 47–49
  ionic, 245, 246
Essential oil, 235
Ethyl alcohol (ethanol), 6, 7, 98, 99, 242
Ethylene (ethene), 187, 190, 191
Exothermic reaction, 94
Explosions, 100, 101

Fats, 174, 232, 233
Fatty acid, 174, 175
Fermentation, 98
Ferric compounds (*see* Iron(III) compounds)
Ferrous compounds (*see* Iron(II) compounds)
Fertilizers, 112, 120, 208, 209
Filtrate, 9
Filtration, 8, 9, 32, 33
Fire extinguisher, 87, 88, 111, 162, 219, 220
Flames, 99, 100
Flame tests, 239
Fleming, Sir Alexander, 2
Fluorine, 221, 222
Foods, 232, 233
Formaldehyde, 195–198
Formula weight, 125–127
Furnace:
  blast, 139–141
  electric arc, 141, 142
  open hearth, 141, 142

Gas carbon, 83, 84
Galvanizing, 112, 150
Glass, 138, 226, 227
Glucose, 200, 201
Glycerine (glycerol), 174, 175, 234
Gold, 132–134
Graphite, 80
Gunpowder, 82

Haber process, 203
Halogens, 221
Hard water:
  causes of, 177, 178
  properties of, 178, 179
  softening of, 180–182

Health Salts, 230
Helium, 41, 66
Hydrochloric acid:
  preparation of, 112, 113
  properties of, 113–116
  uses of, 116
Hydrocarbons, 97, 186
Hydrogen:
  burning of, 59–61
  chloride, 112, 205
  covalent bonding in, 72
  peroxide, 46, 47, 48, 146
  preparation of, 55–57
  properties of, 57–62
  as reducing agent, 61–62
  sulphide, 215, 216, 240
  uses of, 62, 63
Hydrogenation, 63
Hydrolysis, 174, 175
Hygroscopic, 107

Igneous rock, 223
Indicators, 105, 122, 123
Inert gases, 41
Initiator, 187
Iodine, 9, 10, 218, 221
Ion exchange resin, 180–183
Ionic bonding, 70–72
Iron:
  compounds of,
    iron(III) oxide (ferric oxide), 139, 144, 147
    iron(II) sulphate (ferrous sulphate), 146, 241
    iron(II) sulphide (ferrous sulphide), 14, 15, 215
  conversion to steel, 141–143
  extraction from ore, 139–141
  pig, 141
  reactions of, 144
  rusting of, 144–146

Kinetic theory, 34–36

Lamp black, 83
Lead:
  nitrate, 149
  oxides of, 4, 147, 149
  properties and uses of, 147–149
  sulphide, 216
Lime slaking, 156
Limestone, 223
Lime-water, 87, 156, 157
Lister, Joseph, 1

Magnesium:
  oxide, 159
  properties and uses of, 157–159
Manganese dioxide (manganese(IV) oxide), 46, 47, 65, 116
Marble, 155, 156, 185, 186, 223
Matches, 228
Mercury, 150
Metalloids, 131
Metals:
  and non-metals, 130, 131
  chemical reactivity of, 167–169
  hardening and softening of, 166–167
  physical properties of, 165
  prices and uses of, 163, 164
  structure of, 165
  tests for, 239, 240
Methane, 94, 95
Micelle, 173
Mixtures, 14, 15
Molecular structure, 70–75
Molecules, 13
Monomers, 190
Mordants, 162
Mortar, 225

Natural gas, 94, 95
Neon, 41, 68
Neutralization, 108, 114, 245
Neutrons, 67
Nitrates, test for, 241
Nitric acid:
  preparation of, 116–118
  properties of, 118, 119
  uses of, 120
Nitrogen:
  from the atmosphere, 203
  cycle, 207, 208
  fixed, 208
  oxides of, 208
  properties and uses of, 203
Nylon, 2, 192–194

Oil, 95–98
Open hearth furnace, 141, 142
Optical bleach, 176
Organic Chemistry, 99
Oxidation, 63–65, 146, 216, 218
Oxides, types of, 104, 105
  of nitrogen, 208
Oxygen:
  extraction from air, 51, 52
  percentage in air, 39–41
  preparation of, 44–46
  properties of, 49–51
  uses of, 52, 53

Particles in matter, 11, 12
Penicillin, 2
Percentage composition, 126
Perfumes, 235
Periodic Table, 132, 221, end paper
Petrol, 96–98
pH, 122, 123
Phenol, 195–197
Phosphorus, 51, 227, 228
Photosynthesis, 89
Physical Change, 30, 31
Pig iron, 141
Plaster of Paris, 225, 226
Plasticizers, 191
Plastics:
   advantages of, 186
   definition of, 198
   types of, 189, 190
Pollution, 42, 97, 214
Polymers, 190
Polymerization:
   addition, 187, 189
   condensation, 193
Polystyrene, 191, 192
Polythene, 186–189
Polyvinyl chloride (PVC), 191
Potassium:
   chlorate, 48, 49, 227
   permanganate, 115, 116
Precipitate, 87
Pressure cooker, 18, 19
Producer gas, 94
Propane, 97
Proteins, 201, 232, 233
Protons, 67
Putty, 227
PVC, 191
Pyrogallol, 40

Qualitative analysis, 239–241
Quicklime, 156

Radical, 76, 240
Reacting weights, 126–128
Reduction:
   by carbon monoxide, 139
   by charcoal, 4, 81
   by hydrogen, 61, 62, 63, 64
Replacement, 168, 169, 218
Resin:
   Bakelite, 195, 196
   ion-exchange, 180–183
   natural, 200
Rubber, 201, 202
Rusting, 144–146

Salts, 123
Sand, 224
Saponification, 174
Shampoos, 233, 234
Side reactions, 213
Silica, 224
Silicon, 224, 231
Silicones, 230–232
Silver and silver compounds, 132–134
Slag, 140
Soap:
   action of, 172–174
   comparison with synthetic detergent, 177
   preparation of, 174, 175
   reaction with hard water, 179
Soda water, 120
Sodium:
   carbonate, 230
   chloride, 220, 221
   hydrogen carbonate, 228–230
   hydroxide, 29, 30, 108, 109, 153, 154
   nitrate, 154
   properties and uses of, 29, 30, 152, 153
Solubility:
   effect of temperature on, 25, 26, 43, 44
   graphs, 26
   in various solvents, 22, 23
   in water, 22
Solute, 23
Solution, saturated, 25, 26
Solvent, 23
Stalactites and stalagmites, 184
Starch, 201, 232
Steel:
   hardening and tempering of, 166, 167
   production from iron, 141–143
   stainless, 3, 143
   uses of, 143
Sublimation, 9, 10, 88
Sugar, 98, 107, 232
Sulphates, test for, 240
Sulphur:
   allotropes of, 210–212
   chemical properties of, 212
   dioxide, 212–214
   extraction of, 209
   trioxide, 106, 214, 215
   uses of, 202, 212
Sulphuric acid:
   manufacture of, 106
   properties of, 107–111
   uses of, 111, 112
Supercooled liquid, 227
Synthesis, 60

Terylene, 1, 2, 194
Thermal decomposition, 137

Thermit reaction, 147, 161
Thermoplastics, 189, 190
Thermoset, 189, 190, 195–200
Tin, 138
Toothpaste, 234

Urea, 198

Valency, 75–77, 248
Vinegar, 121, 122
Vulcanization, 202

Water:
    air in, 43, 44
    boiling point of, 18–20
    cycle, 33, 34
    evaporation of, 20
    fluoridation of, 221
    freezing point of, 20
    gas, 94
    hard, 177–183
    made from hydrogen, 59, 60
    of crystallization, 29
    origins of, 18
    reactions of, 29–31
    supply, 32–34, 219
    test for, 32
    vapour, 20, 21
Wood charcoal, 81, 82

Yeast, 98

Zinc, 150–152

Teacher's notes

Contents

		PAGE
Preface		2
CHAPTER		2
1	How chemists work	3
2	Water	5
3	Oxygen and burning	6
4	The simplest atom—hydrogen—and others	9
5	Carbon, fuels, flames and energy	13
6	Acids, bases and salts	15
7	Metals old and new	19
8	Detergents	21
9	Plastics	23
10	Nitrogen, sulphur, and chlorine	26
11	Chemistry all around us	
APPENDIX		28
2	Qualitative analysis	29
4	Ionic interpretation of equations	

CHEMISTRY

Preface to the teacher's notes

These notes are meant to be read in conjunction with the text, and they contain a variety of material. Some of this will undoubtedly be familiar to many readers, but I hope everyone will find parts of it useful. The notes contain straightforward hints, tips, and information on topics such as the concentration of reagents, first aid, setting up of apparatus, sources of experimental error, answers to numerical examples, and the like. There are suggestions for further practical work and for projects. Some examining boards ask each candidate to submit a report on a project, by which they mean a semi-independent practical investigation which has involved several hours' laboratory work, but in addition to ideas for this type of work, I have included some suggestions for 'library projects' which will involve the use of reference books. Where simplifications have been made these are noted, and sometimes discussed. Although the book as it stands is a possible teaching route, it will not suit everyone, and alternative orders are suggested in some places. Finally, there are more than a dozen boards setting CSE chemistry examinations, all with differing syllabuses, and a volume vastly larger than this would be needed to cover all the topics set by all the boards—the Teacher's Notes indicate some of the omissions.

A book usually reveals a great deal about its author, and this one is no exception. It will be apparent to anyone looking through the text and these notes that I believe chemical theory, however enlightening and elegant this might be to the initiated, to be less appropriate to CSE work than are simple descriptive matter clearly explained and the relationship of chemistry to everyday life.

Chapter 1

PAGE

1. A possible homework would be making a list of things made from new materials. Parental or grandparental help would be essential.
3. You could discuss DDT as an aspect of pollution. It has done immense good in malarial areas.
4. As a spectacular variation of experiment 1.1 heat the ammonium dichromate in a corked hard-glass test-tube. The reaction is

$$(NH_4)_2Cr_2O_7 \longrightarrow N_2 + 4H_2O + Cr_2O_3$$

and the gases produced shoot the cork out of the tube.
In experiment 1.2 asbestos paper tape may be used instead of the tin lid.
5. In experiment 1.3(*a*) and (*c*), use a small volume of ink in the test-tubes.
8. Experiment 1.4, fractional distillation, always leaves a little water in the alcohol, but there is no need to mention this at this level, unless the question is raised by the class. The alternative names ethanol, methylated spirits, industrial spirit are introduced in chapter 2. In the case of oil distillation there are dozens of chemicals in the crude oil rather than two, and the cut-off points between the fractions are fixed as convenient to the users of the finished products.
8. As the use of natural gas increases, and less coal is gasified there will be less coal tar to distil. Some coal-tar distillation plants are being converted for recovery

TEACHER'S NOTES

PAGE

      of industrial waste, e.g. contaminated solvents, thus using spare capacity and reducing a possible source of pollution by industrial waste.

8   You can parallel this problem, or discovery, method in class by discussing experiments and inviting suggestions from the class rather than simply producing an experimental recipe to follow.

9   Ammonium chloride is often used to demonstrate sublimation although this reaction is strictly a thermal dissociation. The iodine experiment is more spectacular and the expensive iodine can be returned to the bottle afterwards.

11   One or two drops of ether or perfume may be used instead of H_2S in experiment 1.7.

11   The Whitley Bay Smoke Cell produced by various manufacturers for the Nuffield Foundation is easy to use and produces good results using about seventy magnifications.

14   The testing of the Fe and S mixture and the FeS with a magnet is often unconvincing because it is hard to prepare FeS free from uncombined iron, and the whole mass sticks to the magnet.

15   In the interest of simplicity two departures from truth are made in discussing experiment 1.9. The iron(II) sulphide is largely ionic, so does not contain molecules, and it belongs to a class of substances prone to lattice defects, so it does not obey strictly the law of constant composition. Teachers with keen scientific consciences should use the formation of, for example, water to discuss molecule formation and constant composition. The iron(II) sulphide nomenclature is not used in the text until the work on valency has been done in chapter 4.

16   An experiment to show no weight change on reaction (e.g., that between potassium iodide and lead nitrate solutions) could be introduced here.

Chapter 2

18   As in many places in a CSE Chemistry course, a reference to pollution problems arises from the work here. Plenty of water falls on the UK, we just do not use it correctly, because letting dirt (industrial waste, sewage effluent, dissolved-out fertilizers) into our rivers is a cheap way of moving the problem out of the immediate vicinity. Of the rain falling in this country, only 0·0001 per cent, i.e., one-millionth, finds its way into our piped water system.

19   A hand pump, e.g., a Geryk, or a filter pump will demonstrate the experiment with warm water (e.g., 45°C).

20   An extended investigation on the effects on speed of evaporation could be done here. Factors investigated could include surface area of water, influence of a solute, temperature, wind speed (using a three-speed fan, or fan convector heater). To vary temperature, put containers of water at varying distances from a source of heat. Evaporation rate can be measured by weight or volume decrease, or by time for a single drop of standard size to evaporate.

21   The units in the table are purposely given in grammes to make comparison between substances easier.

22   To obtain equal heaps of the substances for experiment 2.2 use a wooden splint with a pencil mark 1 cm from the end as a spatula. Pupils could filter the liquid, evaporate to dryness, and look for a residue from this experiment.

22   The spelling of soluble frequently presents difficulty. The word can be compared with solution, and if the correct pronunciation is emphasized this also helps the

PAGE

       spelling. A project on the influence of state of substances, temperature, and stirring on solution rate could be done here.

23 Alcohol is a term in frequent use, but strictly represents a class of similar compounds of which ethanol (ethyl alcohol C_2H_5OH) is one. Industrial spirit contains ethanol, methanol, and water. Methylated spirits has a purple dye, and petrol and pyridine in it to make it unpalatable.

23 A project on stain removal is easy for the class to devise. Similar stains (e.g., fruit juice, grass, grease, oil plus carbon black) on white cloth can be tested with, for example, water, steam, washing-up liquid, acetone, benzene, ethanol, and various commercial products. Time taken and ease of removal on a four-point scale such as untouched/slightly removed/almost all removed/completely removed can be tabulated.

27 Lead iodide, PbI_2, made by mixing very dilute solutions of lead nitrate and potassium iodide, makes a good demonstration of crystallization. A 250 cm^3 beaker of colourless hot lead iodide solution turns to a yellow mass of tiny sparkling crystals on cooling. If the lead iodide does not all dissolve when the solution is boiled, dilute it.

29 A project on crystal growing is possible here. The usual methods can be supplemented by growth on a microscope slide, on an overhead projector stage, or in a microprojector. Reference: *Crystals and Crystal Growing*, Holden and Singer, published by Heineman.

29 As monovalent copper is not met in this book, copper sulphate is used throughout in preference to Cu(II) sulphate.

29 The percentage of water in copper sulphate crystals can be determined as a class experiment if you have enough balances of a suitable type (e.g., top-pan direct readout, or torsion balances).

29 The hydrogen released in experiment 2.13 can be caught by using a sodium spoon, weighting the sodium with gauze so that it sinks, or by holding oiled sodium in crucible tongs, and plunging it into water as shown in Fig. TN.2.1. A

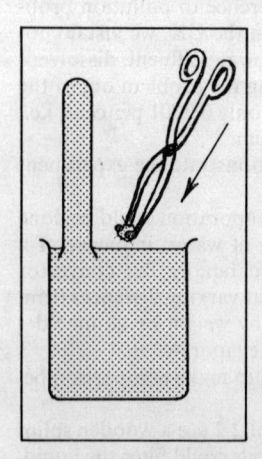

Figure TN.2.1 Collecting hydrogen from the sodium/water reaction

       quick decisive movement gets the sodium under the test-tube before the water attacks it. A face-mask or goggles are advisable for this technique.

TEACHER'S NOTES

PAGE

32 Experiment 2.14 could be done with anhydrous cobalt chloride instead of anhydrous copper sulphate. An extended version of experiment 2.14 would be to distil copper sulphate crystals, collect the distillate, find its boiling point, then pour the distillate on to the anhydrous residue.

33 The strong form of words in the fluoridation paragraph is used deliberately to provoke discussion of a moral problem. The toxicity of fluorides in small dosage is still a matter of dispute, although the benefits to teeth are undeniable.

Chapter 3

39 There are many methods of estimating the approximate percentage of oxygen in the air. Figure 7.9 uses the rusting of steel wool. White phosphorus may be used to absorb oxygen in a graduated tube. In experiment 3.1(a) the glass rod prevents the wool from moving, acts as a dust filter, cools the hot gas and reduces dead volume in the apparatus. In experiment 3.1(b) the liquid levels inside and outside the tube should be equalized if a more accurate result is required. Burning a candle under a bell jar is not a reliable method as the candle often goes out when there is still 10 per cent oxygen left.

42 Dirt can be extracted from air using a handkerchief as a filter on the inlet of a suction-type vacuum cleaner. Suck air through for, say, 15 minutes at various places, in various weather conditions and compare the condition of the filter. Make sure the air exit is as far as possible from the intake.

43 Work on the percentage of gases in water could be extended to include lake, pond, well, sea, river, and rainwater, and soda-waters of various brands. CO_2 dissolves slowly in water, and could be collected in a gas syringe.

44 The dissolving of a solid in water is sometimes a chemical change.

45 20 vol. H_2O_2 yields 20 vol. of oxygen from 1 vol. solution, but an old solution, which has decomposed in the bottle, may only give 5 vol. of oxygen or even less. Store the peroxide in a cool dark place.

46 Cylinders of oxygen may be bought or hired from The British Oxygen Company, who will supply a safety booklet on request. There is no need to have a cylinder with dials—a reducing valve, which is much cheaper, is all you need.

46 From experiment 3.3 onwards this chapter contains three main themes: making oxygen, catalysis, and burning. If you do not wish to teach catalysis here, the oxygen can be made by heating potassium permanganate, or obtained from a cylinder.

46 Experiments with various catalysts and H_2O_2 can be done using a gas syringe and a test-tube with side arm (Fig. TN.3.1).

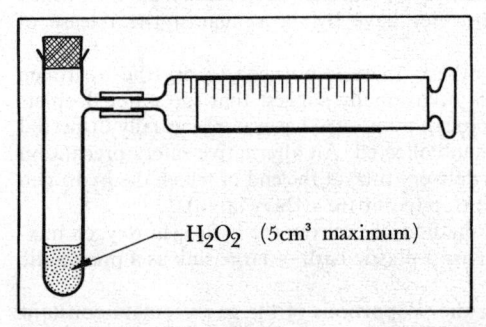

Figure TN.3.1 Measuring the oxygen obtained from hydrogen peroxide

CHEMISTRY

PAGE

Plot the volume of O_2 against time after adding, e.g., MnO_2, CuO, PbO, Pb_3O_4, Fe_2O_3, brick dust or sand.

47 There are two types of catalyst. One provides a surface on which the reaction takes place—MnO_2 acts thus on H_2O_2. The second type combines with one of the reactants to make an intermediate compound, which then decomposes giving back the catalyst—MnO_2 in $KClO_3$ is this type.

49 The oxygen made from $KClO_3$ often has a faint 'chemical' smell, probably because it contains a little ozone as impurity.

49 The products of combustion could be tested with indicators here, rather than in experiment 6.1, if desired.

49 To dispose of phosphorus residues from experiment 3.4, mix them with water, filter, then support the filter paper on a gauze and heat it strongly in a fume cupboard.

51 Benzene burns to C, CO, or CO_2 according to oxygen supply, but one equation only is shown. Sulphur often forms a little SO_3 (white fumes) when burnt in oxygen, as well as SO_2. The white solid, formerly called phosphorus pentoxide P_2O_5, is now known to be P_4O_{10} and is so named in the results table.

52 The 8 mm cassette film CFN 04374, 'Liquid Air Fractionation', produced for the Nuffield Foundation, is useful at this point.

Chapter 4

55 In experiment 4.1 the copper catalyst is formed on the surface of the zinc by displacement

$$CuSO_4 + Zn \longrightarrow ZnSO_4 + Cu$$

The safety precaution is strongly recommended; omitting it once I blew a rubber bung and part of a delivery tube up to the laboratory ceiling. Collection by upward delivery (sometimes downward displacement of air) is not recommended as air usually mixes with the hydrogen.

56 The electrolysis of water can be used to demonstrate its volume composition.

57 An alternative method of demonstrating the low density of hydrogen is to suspend two 1000 cm^3 beakers bottom up from the arms of a balance and counterpoise them with pieces of Plasticine on the lighter one, then put a hydrogen delivery tube under one—it will rise and then fall as the hydrogen diffuses out.

58 The cotton wool in the experiments using bubbles or balloons to demonstrate the low density of hydrogen has the effect of arresting acid spray. A useful contrast to a bubble or balloon full of hydrogen is one full of carbon dioxide, which falls quickly. Some local authorities have bye-laws against the release of hydrogen-filled balloons.

59 In experiment 4.4 on water synthesis there is no need to dry the hydrogen if this is from a cylinder. Pupils occasionally suggest that the water droplets might come from the air, but you can point out that water is usually dispersed into the air by heating rather than collected. An alternative safety precaution is to put some wire gauze in the delivery tube at the end of which the hydrogen burns. The gauze acts as a flame trap (compare a Davy lamp).

60 In experiment 4.5 a convenient method of pouring the hydrogen/oxygen mixture into a detergent bottle is to use a plastic bath or large sink as a pneumatic trough. (Fig. TN.4.1.)

Pre-mixing is advisable because the proportions of the gases remain constant if some gas bubbles miss the bottle. Enthusiasts for explosions can explode a

TEACHER'S NOTES

mixture consisting of two-sevenths oxygen and five-sevenths acetylene in the same way, obtaining a much louder bang—cotton wool in the ears, and a long taper for lighting are advised. This experiment together with experiments 3.4 and 4.4 are useful for discussing energy changes in chemical reactions. A small plastic bottle of hydrogen/oxygen mixture may be exploded if clamped in a retort stand. A translucent bottle shows the flame produced—see experiment 5.9(*b*) The flame travels upwards—Keep clear!

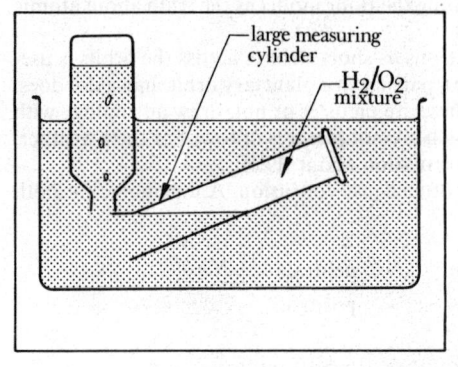

Figure TN.4.1 Filling a plastic bottle with a 2:1 mixture of hydrogen and oxygen

61   The reduction in experiment 4.6 can be done using coal gas or carbon monoxide in place of hydrogen. The reduction is seldom quantitative in the hands of pupils and usually gives disastrous results if used in experiments involving weighing. If **dry** hydrogen is used, water collecting in cool parts of the tube is significant.

62   The test for hydrogen given (burning in a dry tube and looking for a blue flame and a mist of water droplets) is not specific to hydrogen. Methane and other flammable hydrogen-containing compounds burn forming steam, but they also form carbon dioxide if there is enough oxygen available for full combustion.

63   Oxidation by increase of valency is not dealt with here, but is mentioned in chapter 7 when iron compounds are discussed.

65   Pupils often find it hard to accept that an optical microscope, however good, can never show us an atom. This analogy sometimes helps:

A wave coming in from the sea washes over a single grain of sand, ignoring it. The sand does not deflect the wave, so looking at the wave would not tell us whether the sand grain was there. A sand-hill, made of many millions of grains, does deflect the wave, because the wave and the hill are roughly equal in size. Similarly, we cannot see one carbon atom, but can see, e.g., a grain of carbon composed of millions of atoms of carbon.

The problem of atomic structure is probably the most difficult a chemistry teacher has to face. The Bohr model is specified in many syllabuses, but it has defects as a model, and also presents teaching difficulties. It is represented in the text as a counting device in which electrons are placed in groups according to their energies. It counts electrons and explains formulae, e.g., $NaCl$, $CuCl_2$, NH_3, and CH_4, but will not explain molecular shapes, and causes further difficulty when covalent bond formation is taught. If pupils ask about other models, you could mention the bee and flower model in which the electron moves irregularly near the nucleus, and the charge-cloud or orbital model, in which the electron is smeared out in space. It does not help to answer, 'You don't understand what a model is', when someone asks, 'Which is really true?', and the best answer to this question is, 'The charge-cloud model, as far as we know, but it is much too difficult for you to understand'. There is an element of sophistry in this, of course: although we point out the defects of the Bohr model, we go on to use something very like it, and the distinction between a model and the truth is clear in our minds rather than the pupils'. This is unavoidable, but it is probably preferable to presenting the Bohr model as the truth about atomic structure.

The device of representing electrons as short strokes across the orbits is useful because a stroke looks less like a particle in a planetary orbit than a dot does.

If pupils worry as to whether these are pictures or not, draw an analogy with maps and temperature charts, which are not pictures of towns or their weather, but nevertheless give valuable information about them.

67 Spellings of neutron and nucleus often cause confusion. A mnemonic for both spelling and charge is:

neutron	**neu**tral
proton	**p**ositive

69 The series of structures stops at calcium, before the start of the transitional series in which the third shell expands from temporary fullness at eight electrons to permanent fullness at eighteen electrons.

70 The examples show that atomic number and relative atomic mass (atomic weight) increase together. The inversion of argon (atomic number 18, relative atomic mass 40) and potassium (atomic number 19, relative atomic mass 39) is not stressed, nor is the occurrence of isotopes. The topics of radioactivity and isotopy could be introduced at any time after the material on atomic structure has been digested.

70 The topics of molecular structure and valency are difficult, and it is often helpful to explain this to the class before starting.

70 Pupils sometimes ask, 'Why is sodium 2.8.1 and not 2.9?' or, 'Why does the one electron leave the sodium for the chlorine and not the seven move from the chlorine to the sodium?' Fundamentally, science does not answer 'Why?' questions, but tries to describe in general terms what actually happens. This is a more satisfying answer than, 'It just is'. 'Why?' questions invariably lead in the end to a non-science such as metaphysics. For example, 'Why does an apple fall?' 'Gravitational forces.' 'Why are there gravitational forces?' There is no final scientific answer to the second question. We simply find gravitational forces the best available description of one aspect of the universe as we see it.

70 In this section the words electrovalent and ionic are used interchangeably as pupils should know both terms.

70 For the purpose of simplicity an isolated chlorine atom has been shown in Fig. 4.17 rather than a chlorine molecule, but this does not affect the description of the sodium chloride structure. It is essential to emphasize that atoms are not different colours and that all electrons are alike, the two colours being used for clarity only.

71 The doubly charged magnesium ion is written Mg^{++} rather than Mg^{2+} for a more graphic effect.

TEACHER'S NOTES

PAGE

72 For clarification, or for problems for pupils, you could use as further examples of ionic bonding calcium oxide, potassium chloride, sodium oxide, magnesium chloride, or aluminium oxide.

72 At the start of the section isolated hydrogen and chlorine atoms are shown rather than molecules. This makes the explanation simpler and does not affect the description of the hydrogen chloride molecule. The greatest weakness of the Bohr model is that it is difficult to imagine the two shared (i.e., bonding) electrons going round both atoms at once. If pupils raise this difficulty honesty is the best policy—admit it is a defect of the model. In the charge-cloud model this difficulty does not arise; the charge density build-up between the two atoms forms the bond. In the bee and flower model the electrons spend more time between the atoms than elsewhere.

74 The examples given are all small covalent molecules. Very large covalent molecules such as diamond, silicon dioxide, and silicon carbide exist. These have very strong bonds within their molecules, and since a solid specimen of one of these substances may be one giant molecule, they are among the hardest, highest melting point substances known. Plastic substances also consist of covalent molecules which are large but not the giant size of diamond, silicon dioxide, and silicon carbide. For extra examples or problems you could ask for the structure of hydrogen chloride, hydrogen sulphide, and carbon tetrachloride.

75 Pupils dislike the rote learning aspect of valency. The unpleasantness is decreased if valency is presented as a labour-saving device in which the learning of twenty items allows a pupil to construct ninety-six formulae. I see no harm in allowing pupils to use formulae as shorthand, and this too can be an incentive to learning valencies.

The use of plus and minus signs on the symbols is probably better than hooks or roman figures which cross-multiply for unstated reasons, and has the advantage that the later use of ionic formulae and equations, if desired, is greatly facilitated. The automatic use for two-atom ions of brackets which are omitted if not needed is much easier than remembering to put in brackets where they are needed. The treatment of valency as a recipe to be followed for the deduction of formulae, with a partial explanation given afterwards, allows teachers to use valencies before electronic structure is covered.

76 The method of using valencies gives correct formulae even when the compound formed is covalent (e.g., H_2O, $FeCl_3$). This is because one negative charge represents one filled space in an outer shell. This space could be filled by a shared electron rather than a stolen electron. The shared electron together with one other electron from the receiving atom forms one covalent bond. This gives a one-to-one compound, just as would be the case if one electron were transferred to form an ionic bond.

Chapter 5

79 In this chapter some formula equations are used without a preceding word equation, if all the substances have been named in the text.

79 Diamonds, which generate interest in both boys and girls, can stimulate a library project in their own right, or part of a larger project on jewels in general. Items on formation (natural and synthetic), density, hardness, structure, colour, and composition, and famous stones and their stories are possible. *The History and Use of Diamond*, by S. Tolansky (Methuen, 1962), *Jewels*, by P. J. Fisher

CHEMISTRY

PAGE

(Batsford, 1965), and parts of *Crystals, Diamonds and Transistors*, by L. W. Marrison (Pelican, 1968), are useful books.

79 Hardness has various meanings—resistance to abrasion, to indentation, to scratching, and rebound hardness. Diamond is harder in some crystal directions than others. Modern synthetic materials such as boron nitride ('borazon') are as hard as the softer directions in diamond, but diamond still qualifies as the hardest substance known.

80 The electrical conductivity of graphite is easily shown using a short length of thick, soft propelling-pencil lead.

81 The beads of lead produced by the reduction are soft enough to mark paper. Lead was once used for writing, hence 'lead' pencil.

82 If any colour remains in the filtered solution, reboil with more charcoal. Sugar as extracted from canes is brown, and is decolorized by charcoal.

82 Removal of poisonous gases may be simulated by this experiment. *A* contains bromine water, *B* lumps of charcoal which have been degassed in a vacuum, and *C* water. Bromine is seen only in the left-hand limb of the U-tube and none appears in *C* (Fig. TN.5.1).

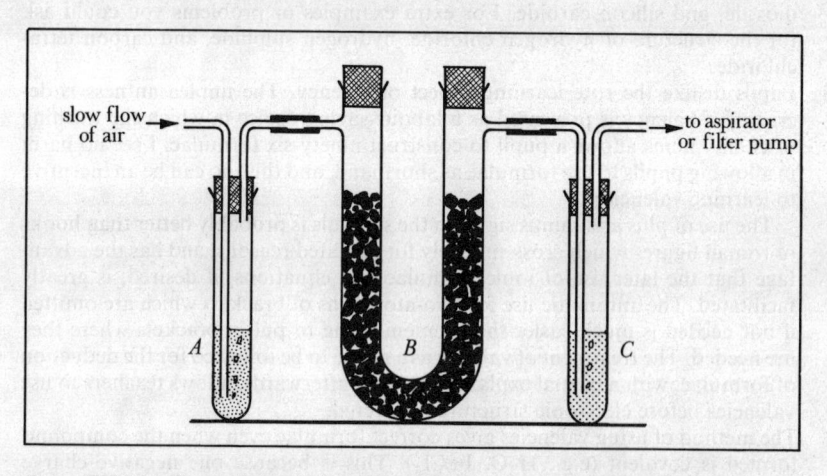

Figure TN.5.1 Charcoal absorbs bromine vapour

82 The volume of benzene used is so small that if the tube cracks the fire will be confined to the sand tray. Toluene may be used instead of benzene. Don't produce too much carbon black by this method—the rain of black smuts readily distracts classes.

83 Other forms of carbon include coke, animal charcoal (bone black), and sugar charcoal. Coke is about 98 per cent carbon. Animal charcoal is made by heating bones—a most obnoxious experiment—to produce a mixture of carbon with calcium phosphate, which is removed by dilute hydrochloric acid. Sugar charcoal is spectacularly made by the dehydration of damp sugar by concentrated sulphuric acid, and subsequent washing to remove the acid (experiment 6.2(*c*)).

TEACHER'S NOTES

PAGE

84 Carbon monoxide is produced when concentrated sulphuric acid reacts on sodium formate. The mixture froths and the carbon monoxide may be burnt at the mouth of the test-tube.

84 Less complete burning of petrol also produces carbon in car engines, which need decarbonizing periodically.

85 Add concentrated hydrochloric acid if the production of carbon dioxide slows and there is calcium carbonate left in the flask. The carbon dioxide collected contains traces of air, water, and hydrogen chloride, and sometimes smoke from the spill. It is possible to collect carbon dioxide over water, but some examining boards disallow this.

85 Carbon dioxide may also be obtained from cylinders.

85 The density of carbon dioxide is dramatically shown by direct weighing. Balance two 1000 cm^3 beakers on the pans of a balance, then put a carbon dioxide delivery tube into one, which goes down. As the carbon dioxide diffuses out, balance is restored.

86 Gas syringes may be used to show the solubility of carbon dioxide in water and alkalis. When discussing soda-water it is wise to emphasize that we do not taste laboratory chemicals.

86 There are in fact two possible reactions:

excess NaOH: $2NaOH + CO_2 \longrightarrow Na_2CO_3 + H_2O$

excess CO_2: $NaOH + CO_2 \longrightarrow NaHCO_3$

87 Stored-pressure (e.g., Nu-Swift) extinguishers use carbon dioxide pressure to squirt a water-jet on to the fire. The carbon dioxide takes no part in extinguishing the flames.

88 Old mortar will often fizz and give a positive lime-water test when reacted with dilute hydrochloric acid.

89 The average person, at rest, uses only about one-fifth of the inhaled oxygen, so exhaled air still contains 16 per cent oxygen.

89 A stuffy atmosphere in a room is caused by high humidity and temperature rather than shortage of oxygen.

90 As coal consumption declines oil consumption increases; it increased sevenfold in the twenty years between 1946 and 1966 in the United Kingdom.

91 Coal is a good subject for a project. The divisions of coal are not absolute; e.g., semi-anthracites are known.

91 NO CASH reminds the pupils that coal contains nitrogen, oxygen, carbon, ash, sulphur, and hydrogen.

91 Smog particles are water-drops on a dirt nucleus.

92 Pupils can detect ammonium compounds in the distillate and H_2S in the crude gas of experiment 5.5.

94 The 10 per cent other gases in coal gas include nitrogen and oxygen from air leaks, ethylene, some higher hydrocarbons, and enough carbon dioxide to turn lime-water turbid.

94 Producer gas buses ran during the Second World War when oil was scarce. A trailer contained a gas generator full of hot coke, and the guard stoked up from time to time. The buses were very slow on hills.

94 A typical analysis of natural gas is 95 per cent methane, 3 per cent higher hydrocarbons, and 2 per cent nitrogen.

94 Methane is also present in marsh gas, firedamp in mines, and bio-gas from silage and chicken manure decay.

CHEMISTRY

PAGE

95   The Petroleum Information Bureau, 4, Brook Street, Hanover Square, London W1, is a valuable source of information and visual aids on oil products.

97   The hydrocarbons in oil contain rings and branched chains of carbon atoms as well as straight chains. Crude oil also contains sulphur compounds, some of which are not removed during refining.

97   The use of ball-and-spring molecular models of methane, ethane, propane, butane, and octane helps the explanation of refining, and a model of a large molecule is useful if cracking is under discussion. Cracking gives an opportunity for the introduction of unsaturated compounds and addition polymerization if this is desired. Medicinal paraffin may be thermally cracked by passing over heated broken pot, and the resulting gases shown to decolorize bromine water. Use of models to demonstrate a possible reaction can then introduce ethylene and other unsaturated hydrocarbons, the raw materials for addition polymerization.

97   The octane number of a fuel is a measure of its resistance to pre-ignition, which causes engine knock (pinking). 90 octane fuel has the same resistance as a mixture containing 90 per cent iso-octane and 10 per cent n-heptane.

97   $C_{14}H_{30}$ is tetradecane; $C_{16}H_{34}$ is hexadecane.

98   Lead compounds from burned petrol are another example of atmospheric pollution.

98   The proof number of an alcoholic mixture gives the concentration of solution. 100 per cent proof spirit is approximately 50 per cent alcohol. 160 per cent proof, or 60 per cent over proof (60 OP), is 160 per cent of 50 per cent, i.e., about 80 per cent alcohol.

Ethyl alcohol is made industrially by the hydration of ethylene derived from oil cracking.

$$C_2H_4 + H_2O \longrightarrow C_2H_5OH$$

The size of the traditional container decreases as the concentration of alcohol in the drink increases: beers in tankards, wine in wine-glasses, spirits in tots, liqueurs in thimble-sized glasses.

99   Figure 1.1, which shows old and new products, could be used to drive home the organic/inorganic distinction.

100   Hydrochloric acid is used because chlorides are usually readily volatile and colour the flame well. A selection of salts of each metal (e.g., $NaCl$, Na_2CO_3, $NaHCO_3$) may be used. A simple spectroscope splits the coloured light from the tinted flame, producing coloured lines, and can be used to illustrate how we know what elements are present in stars.

100   Do not stand the tin under a light fitting. If you have collected the gas over water, check before lighting that both holes are free from films of water. Cricketers may sometimes obtain a round of applause by catching the tin on its way down. The bang with natural gas is not very loud. A gas mixture has an upper (gas-rich) and a lower (air-rich) explosive limit; all mixtures between these ranges explode. For methane/air mixtures the upper limit is 15 per cent methane and the lower limit is 6 per cent methane.

101   High explosives burn faster because the oxygen is in the same molecule as the fuel. This creates a much more intimate mixture than having fuel in one particle and oxidizer in the next.

101   Classes should be warned about the dangers of home-made explosives, and explosives taken from dissected fireworks. The main dangers arise on mixing,

TEACHER'S NOTES

PAGE

and if powders are stored in screw top jars. Many boys know that weed-killer and sugar make an explosive mixture, so witholding the recipe is not much use as a safety precaution. I urge boys not to make explosives, tell a story of a boy I taught who lost a finger, and say, 'If you must make explosives, make very small quantities by pouring the mixture from one paper to another **never** by stirring.'

A good library project arises from explosives—gunpowder, Nobel, dynamite, nitroglycerine, TNT, guncotton, mechanical explosions including Krakatoa, nuclear explosions, rockets, guns, and use in petrol and diesel engines.

101 In 1970 the energy consumed in Western Europe was 55 per cent derived from oil, 34 per cent coal, 7 per cent natural gas, 4 per cent hydroelectric, and 1 per cent nuclear. The respective 1960 figures are 30 per cent, 65 per cent, 2 per cent, 3 per cent, less than $\frac{1}{2}$ per cent. In 1970 proven oil reserves were only twenty-six times annual consumption.

Pupils need telling that electricity is a convenient form in which power is used, not a source of power.

Chapter 6

104 Samples of the oxides may be made by burning sulphur or phosphorus in gas jars of air, burning magnesium in air over a watch glass, and heating strongly a marble chip perched on the edge of a gauze. Universal indicator may be used instead of litmus. The sulphur dioxide exerts a mild bleaching action on the litmus.

105 Amphoteric oxides have been omitted from this classification. The oxides of e.g., aluminium, chromium, zinc, and lead can act either as acidic (equation 1) or basic (equation 2) oxides.

$$Al_2O_3 + 2NaOH \longrightarrow 2NaAlO_2 + H_2O \qquad \text{Equation 1}$$
$$6HCl + Al_2O_3 \longrightarrow 2AlCl_3 + 3H_2O \qquad \text{Equation 2}$$

These metals thus form both aluminates and aluminium salts, chromates, dichromates, and chromium salts, zincates and zinc salts, plumbates, plumbites, and lead salts.

105 Screened methyl orange contains a blue dye and it changes from purple to green, which is more distinct than red to yellow. The juice of red cabbage and pigments of many flower petals can act as indicators. The Nuffield 'O' level chemistry scheme, Stage I, gives details of some experiments.

106 For reactions of acids with indicators, bases, alkalis, carbonates, and metals the technical or commercial quality acid is adequate. It should not be used for acid radical tests, however, as the impurities sometimes interfere with the results. (See Appendix 2.)

The quantities of concentrated acid needed for a litre of dilute acid are H_2SO_4, 55 cm^3; HNO_3, 135 cm^3; HCl, 180 cm^3. Add the acid to tap water, stirring the while, and make the final volume up to 1 litre.

106 The lead chamber process is obsolescent in this country—no new chambers have been built for many years.

107 In my laboratory concentrated sulphuric in an open measuring cylinder clamped in a retort stand quadrupled its volume in three years. The dehydrating action

of concentrated sulphuric can also be shown on bandage. Writing done with dilute sulphuric acid and allowed to dry is invisible, but appears as black letters when the paper is warmed over a bunsen.

107 Nevertheless, flood concentrated sulphuric on flesh with water, because a quick stream of water has a cooling effect. Similarly wash out with a copious stream of water glassware which has contained concentrated sulphuric. Always beware of a dense layer of sulphuric acid below water, ready for sudden violent mixing.

108 Crystallization may be shown using a petri dish in an overhead projector, or a cavity slide in a microprojector.

109 Sulphuric acid starts to react with marble chips, but the insoluble calcium sulphate layer formed soon stops the reaction.

110 The hydrogen made from iron often smells of hydrocarbons produced from the carbon in the iron, and pupils sometimes think the smell is hydrogen sulphide. The hydrogen may be collected in a test-tube inverted over the reaction tube.

111 A foam fire extinguisher contains sodium hydrogen carbonate solution, aluminium sulphate solution which acts as an acid, and a foaming agent (see Fig. 7.20). If aluminium sulphate solution or dilute sulphuric acid is poured into a measuring cylinder containing sodium hydrogen carbonate solution and a liquid detergent, an impressive volume of foam is produced. It is advisable to stand the measuring cylinder in a trough.

112 A common error is to suppose the sulphuric acid is itself used as a fertilizer.

112 For brighter pupils the uses can be linked with the properties:
fire extinguisher—acid/carbonate reaction,
ammonium sulphate—acid/alkali reaction using ammonia solution.

113 The liquid in the beaker may be tested for a chloride if you have done this test. In the beaker the covalent HCl gas reacts with the water forming Cl^- ions and H_3O^+ (i.e. hydrated H^+) ions.

113 The fumes are droplets of concentrated HCl.

113 This gives an opportunity to revise the terms synthesis and synthetic.

114 Since the solubility of sodium chloride falls only slightly between boiling point and room temperature, only a small fraction (8 per cent) of the solid in a saturated solution crystallizes, and the rest must be obtained by evaporation.

115 The similarity of the zinc, magnesium, and iron equations gives an opportunity for some valency revision.

115 A piece of iron(II) sulphide about as big as a capital O in this text is suitable for experiment 6.9(f). If the reaction is very slow use 50 per cent HCl.

117 After experiment 6.11 allow the residue in the flask to solidify then wash with a large volume of water. A retort, or ground glass joint apparatus, is suitable for this experiment. The oxidizing power of nitric acid may be demonstrated using the very concentrated acid produced.

119 The reaction of dilute nitric acid on copper produces nitrogen monoxide (nitric oxide). As the concentrated acid of experiment 6.13 becomes diluted during the reaction, this gas is produced in increasing quantity.

119 A trace of oxides of nitrogen often comes off with the hydrogen in experiment 6.14(e).

120 The term dissociation may be used for the loss of carbon dioxide from carbonic acid.

Rainwater contains carbonic acid, but industrial pollution introduces other substances which affect the pH.

TEACHER'S NOTES

PAGE

To emphasize the origins of the substances it is sometimes preferable to write the equation for calcium hydrogen carbonate formation as

$$CaCO_3 + H_2O + CO_2 \longrightarrow Ca(HCO_3)_2$$

The actual reaction is ionic

$$CO_3^{--} + H^+ \longrightarrow HCO_3^-$$

121 The molecule shown is not ionized. In solution some of the hydrogen atoms ionize from the —OH leaving acetate ions CH_3COO^-.

121 An acid containing 10 per cent acetic acid by volume is suitable for experiment 6.15. Pure acetic acid, freezing point 17°C, is often solid in winter, and is called glacial acetic acid. The formation of acetates from acetic acid is another example of the rule that an -ic acid gives an -ate salt. (Hydrochloric acid is an exception to the rule.)

121 A project on acids in our lives would reveal the extent to which we depend on these chemicals.

122 pH is a logarithmic scale, and a tenfold increase in acid concentration produces an increase of 1 in pH. Molar hydrochloric acid (36·5 g in 1000 cm³ of solution) has a pH of 0, and more concentrated solutions have a negative pH, i.e., the pH scale extends beyond 0. Similarly, any solution of sodium hydroxide more concentrated than 40 g in 1000 cm³ has a pH greater than 14.

123 The concentration of indicator solution needed is often specified on the bottle. More dilute solutions can be used but the colour changes are harder to see.

123 The pH values of the various materials will vary with the dilution of the solutions made.

123 Salts are not dealt with in detail and a suitable homework would be the listing of the name, formula, colour, and action of heat on various salts. This information appears in various sections of this book.

124 I have used the word 'weight' in the text instead of the more correct 'mass', and omitted the adjective 'relative'. Thus 'relative atomic mass' and 'relative molecular mass' are simplified to 'atomic weight' and 'formula weight'. I feel that the conceptual and verbal simplification justifies the departure from strict accuracy for work at this level.

125 Many types of mass spectrometer exist. Deflection may be electrostatic or magnetic, and detection electrostatic, or photographic. As in the chapter on atomic structure, the topic of isotopes has been omitted. It could be introduced here when the value 35.5 is assigned to chlorine, which is 75 per cent ^{35}Cl and 25 per cent ^{37}Cl.

126 Two significant figures only are justifiable in most of the calculations, but a third has been left in where rounding-off might produce a puzzling answer (e.g., 130 for problem (c)).

127 We assume in this section that all reactions go to completion.

128 No overall summary is provided as there are seven summaries within the chapter.

Chapter 7

130 This chapter emphasizes the relationship between the properties of a metal and its uses, and the fact that energy must be supplied to extract a metal from its ore. Details of electrolytic manufacturing are not given, but some are indicated in these notes for use if desired. The metals are taken in the order in which they

PAGE

were used by man, which is shown at the end of the chapter to be related to the electrochemical series. The work on the general properties of metals could be advanced from the end of the chapter to follow zinc (i.e., before any of the 'new' electrically-extracted metals).

The instruction 'Observe . . .' replaces direct questioning after experiments in this and later chapters.

131 Malleability can be related to the word 'mallet'.
132 Typical groupings of the objects might be: living/not, valuable/not, used in cooking/not, able to contain something/not, round/not.
132 The Periodic Table is based on atomic number, but this, through its effect on electronic arrangement, controls chemical behaviour, including metallic and non-metallic characteristics and ionic charge, so these are all related. Catalytic activity and coloured oxides are characteristic properties of transitional elements.
134 As with many reactions in this chapter, an ionic equation is appropriate here; but as many pupils find these difficult and off-putting, they are not usually in the main text.

$$Ag^+ + Cl^- \longrightarrow Ag^+Cl^-(c)$$

The nitric acid prevents precipitation of silver carbonate, and of silver oxide in alkaline solutions.

134 Silver, gold, and platinum are intrinsically interesting, especially to girls, and are good subjects for projects.
134 Most articles described as 'real gold' are rolled gold and contain very little gold.
135 As monovalent copper is not mentioned the compounds have been called 'copper' and not 'copper(II)'. The ore Cu_2S is not named, and the extraction process has been considerably simplified.
135 The electrodes in experiment 7.2 may be weighed before and after the electrolysis.
135 Ionic equations may be used with the diagram of copper purification (in which the concentration of Cu^{++} in the cell remains constant).
136 Good conductivity is a disadvantage in hot water cylinders, but copper is easy to bend and join, and bimetallic corrosion is avoided if cylinder and pipes are both copper.
136 If adequate fume cupboards are available copper oxide may be made from copper via copper nitrate as a class experiment.
137 Experiment 7.4 is extended in experiment 7.17.
138 Bronze was probably discovered when mixed copper/tin ores were used in charcoal-fired pottery kilns with forced blast.
138 The world's supply of tin is rapidly being spread over rubbish dumps and incorporated into scrap steel. The price of tin has increased sixfold in twenty years.
138 The lead in experiment 7.5 oxidizes as it melts and forms a crust. With larger quantities in crucibles the sharp melting of the metals can be contrasted with the pasty stage of the alloy.
139 Before smelting, the ore is crushed and sintered to improve gas flow in the stack. The treatment is simplified—the coke does some reducing and there is phosphate in the slag. Slag formation is essentially an acid plus base reaction.
141 Like water and type metal, cast iron expands on solidification, thus forcing its way into all the corners of a mould.

Most liquids (compare candle-wax setting in a specimen tube or crucible) contract on freezing.

TEACHER'S NOTES

PAGE

The British Steel Corporation Information Office, 33, Grosvenor Place, London SW1, supplies useful booklets on iron and steel.

144 This is a suitable place for some revision of valencies, including the use of brackets.

144 The action of hot iron on steam may be demonstrated using the wet asbestos method and steel wool.

144 I have seen a brightly polished piece of steel strip start to rust within a double lesson.

145 The diagram of steel wool rusting shows a method similar to experiment 3.1(*b*). Levelling and constant temperature are needed to estimate the percentage of oxygen in the air. Degrease the steel wool by shaking with acetone and dry it over a radiator.

146 Starting from iron and dilute sulphuric acid pupils could prepare iron(II) sulphate, crystallize it, and then heat the crystals.

147 Equal volumes of aluminium and iron(III) oxide are used. A little potassium nitrate or barium peroxide sprinkled round the magnesium fuse is useful. I have never had a failure after warming the mixture before lighting.

147 Some pupils find blow-pipes difficult to use—they could heat the oxide mixed with charcoal on asbestos paper tape. It is advisable to tell the class never to suck when using a blow-pipe. An attempt to produce iron on a block is instructive; the experiment sometimes succeeds, but the larger energy needed is obvious. Let the blocks cool thoroughly, or douse them with water before storing.

149 Lead (IV) oxide, lead dioxide, PbO_2 is omitted. A lead cycle involving PbO, Pb, $Pb(NO_3)_2$ makes an interesting practical.

150 Mercury poisoning is now regarded more seriously than it was. It leads to insanity and death through brain damage. (Felt-makers used mercury—hence 'as mad as a hatter'.) Inaccessible spilled mercury should be treated with a wash of sulphur and slaked lime. Organic mercury compounds used as seed dressings are more dangerous than inorganic, as they are eliminated from the body over months rather than days.

150 Zinc was not known in the ancient world. Although furnaces attained the smelting temperature of 1400°C, the zinc vaporized and then burned. Mentioning the distillation of zinc and mercury confirms that this process is not confined to aqueous and oily substances. Burning zinc needs very strong heating but is worthwhile as the flame and wisps of oxide (philosopher's wool) are both spectacular.

151 Experiments 7.9(*b*) and (*c*) are conveniently explained ionically. For example,

$$Zn_{(c)} + 2H^+_{(aq)} \longrightarrow Zn^{++}_{(aq)} + H_{2(g)}$$

152 A strip of steel about 1 cm wide is convenient for this experiment. A greasy thumb print on the polished metal shows in the plating. The plated iron would make a fourth tube in experiment 7.6. This is a convenient place to introduce the mnemonic POLECAT for *po*sitive ions *le*ave the solution at the *cat*hode.

152 Pupils often confuse sodium and potassium with white phosphorus, and say they are kept under water.

Sodium carbonate monohydrate is the eventual product of sodium left in moist air.

153 The electrolytic manufacture of sodium hydroxide is complex. Chloride ions

	discharge at the anode, giving chlorine, and hydrogen ions at the cathode. Sodium ions and hydroxyl ions (from water) are left.
154	Sodium hydroxide solution bumps badly, and great care is needed if it is boiled. There are two possible products when it reacts with dibasic acids, e.g., $NaHSO_4$, and Na_2SO_4; $NaHCO_3$, and Na_2CO_3. Appropriate choice of indicator, or of quantities, can be used to obtain the desired product.
154	Rain would dissolve the deposits of sodium nitrate and wash them into the sea. Pupils could heat sodium nitrate and test for oxygen.
156	The expressions 'limes', and 'in the limelight' are relevant. Calcium oxide harms eyes and skin—it is used by farmers to dispose of diseased animal corpses, and (allegedly) by murderers.
156	Calcium hydroxide is also called hydrated lime. The lime-water test is often produced like a rabbit out of a hat in first-year work. It can be justified by testing lime-water with a series of gases—O_2, N_2, H_2S, Cl_2, CO_2, etc., as available—and with indicator paper.
158	Freshly cleaned magnesium reacts very slowly with water.
159	Do not inhale asbestos dust before or after the experiment. Good contact between the magnesium and the tube helps ignition, so make the snake of magnesium a good fit in the test-tube. Keep the steam flowing during burning. The tube often cracks during the experiment, but if it does not, beware of sucking back. This method can be used for zinc and iron also, and is suitable for class practical.
160	While his courtiers ate from mere gold plates, Napoleon III ate from an aluminium plate.
160	The current passes almost entirely through the aluminium, steel having a high resistance to AC.
160	An experiment on plain and coloured anodizing is described in *Colourful Chemistry*, by F. C. Brown (EUP). The book is available with chemicals in a Griffin & George kit.
162	The Al^{+++} ion discharges negatively charged colloids in sewage, which then coagulate and precipitate.
162	Alums are sometimes written in the form $K_2SO_4.Al_2(SO_4)_3.24H_2O$. Not all fabrics, or all dyes, need mordants.
163	The prices are for small quantities of the cheapest form of the metal in 1971.
165	Do not allow the class to think that metal atoms **want** to give away electrons; the electrons must be taken, but a relatively small amount of energy is needed for this compared with removing an electron from a non-metal. A model of metallic structure can be made if several pupils (representing metal ions) pull on a piece of wood (representing an electron); they are all bound together in a mass.
167	The ordering of reactivity can be done by memory and discussion, or by looking up the facts in the text.
168	The electrochemical series can be extended to include non-metals as well. Preparations of hydrogen by metal/acid methods can be discussed as replacement reactions if hydrogen is put in the series.
168	Experiment 7.17 is hard for pupils to appreciate as there are many reactions. Labelling the tubes is essential. All the reactions are ionic. For example,

$$Zn_{(c)} + Cu^{++}_{(aq)} \longrightarrow Cu_{(c)} + Zn^{++}_{(aq)}$$

TEACHER'S NOTES

PAGE

After the experiment the class could predict various reactions and then try them. $AgNO_3/Zn$, $Pb/MgSO_4$ are suitable.

Chapter 8

172 This chapter involves considerable simplification in that it deals mainly with anionic synthetic detergents, ignoring cationic and non-ionic types. Detergent marketing is sophisticated and competitive and the products are consequently complex. A booklet suitable for teachers is 'Detergents', free from Unilever Education Section, Unilever House, Blackfriars, London EC4.

The *Which* reports for March 1969 (Shampoo), May 1969 (Soap), and September 1969 (Synthetic detergents) are also useful. Detergents are described in the text as molecules, not ions.

172 The terms 'syndet' and 'surfactant' have been proposed for synthetic detergents.

174 An emulsion contains colloidal droplets, i.e., droplets about 10^{-6} cm diameter. These are below visible size but bigger than individual atoms or ions. The detergent heads are outward-facing, so the surface of the droplet is negatively charged, and has positive ions surrounding it. Similarity of charge prevents droplets from coalescing and precipitating. Figure 8.2 shows only the actual detergent molecules, not the additives.

174 Experiment 8.1 is quick because the fat and alkali both dissolve in the ethanol. A soapy smell is very quickly apparent. A suitable quantity of alkali consists of 40 pellets of sodium hydroxide, which take a long time to dissolve, in 10 cm^3 water. The soap produced contains free alkali and a large volume of water. Pupils could add hard water to this soap and look for a precipitate.

Saponification is related to the French 'le savon'—soap.

Oils and fats are both esters made from glycerol which has reacted with three molecules of fatty acid. These molecules are usually different, e.g., a stearate, an oleate, and a palmitate, but have been shown as similar. Oils are liquid at room temperature, fats are solid.

174 Palmolive and Castille soaps give clues to the origins of some oils. The finished soap is ionic, $C_{17}H_{35}COO^-Na^+$. This is not stated in the text.

Toilet soaps are still made by boiling in soap kettles as a higher quality product results. Toilet and laundry soaps are sodium salts; potassium soaps are softer and are used for shaving and shampooing, and will lather with sea water. Machinery greases contain hydrocarbons plus lithium or aluminium soaps.

175 If the product of experiment 8.2 is too viscous to pour out, wash it in the tube.

176 A typical powder detergent might contain solid sodium n-dodecylbenzene sulphonate, which is $C_{12}H_{25}$—C_6H_4—SO_3^- Na^+, the sodium salt of an alkyl ($C_{12}H_{25}$) aryl (C_6H_4) sulphonate (SO_3^-). The detergent part carries a negative charge and so is anionic.

176 A liquid detergent might contain substances such as sodium n-dodecyl sulphonate $C_{12}H_{25}SO_3^-$ Na^+, an alkyl sulphonate salt, also anionic. (Sulphonates are now commoner than sulphates.) Some compounds of this type have branched chains in their tails, and cause trouble in sewage works as they are biologically hard (not broken down easily by bacteria). Hard detergents are not now generally available in the UK. There are also non-ionic types, often having chains of ethylene oxide —(O—CH$_2$—CH$_2$)— groups, and these may be mixed with the anionic type. There are also cationic detergents, some of which are low-foaming, or good germ killers, so are used in dishwashing

19

PAGE	
	machines or hospitals. The percentage of water in proprietary products may be determined by evaporating a weighed amount of the liquid to constant weight in an oven at 105°, or in a desiccator. Foam stabilizers, and solubilizer (to stabilize the emulsion), are added to liquid detergents for dishwashing.
176	The *New Scientist* for 15th October 1970 has points for and against enzyme detergents, put by a manufacturer's writer and the Consumers' Association; the Association concluded that the advantages of enzymes were marginal.
176	Optical bleaches act similarly to Day-Glo poster colours and the bright reflective arm-bands and jackets worn by workers on busy roads.
177	Measured volumes of water are not necessary for experiments 8.3 and 8.6. It is convenient to fill each tube to a standard depth, e.g., to the height of a test-tube rack. For 8.3(*b*) dilute the liquid synthetic detergent until one drop produces about 1 cm depth of foam. A soap flake may be picked up with a damped finger or wooden splint.
177	Much interesting project work can be done on soaps and synthetic detergents, perhaps with the Home Economics Department. A booklet, 'Experiments in Detergency', is available from The Shell Centre, London SE1 7NA. Past volumes of *Which* suggest many lines of enquiry. Volumes of washing-up liquid needed to emulsify a standard volume of oil may be found. A standard stain can be made from thick oil and carbon black to compare washing efficiency. The Griffin & George Cosmetics Kit contains experiments on shampoos, shaving creams, and bath preparations.
177	Tap water and sea water (real or made using sea-water tablets from suppliers) may be evaporated in experiment 8.4.
177	Temporary, temporarily, permanent, and permanently cause spelling troubles. Very clear pronunciation helps the class. Make temporarily hard water by diluting lime-water with its own volume of water, then passing a stream of CO_2 bubbles (an aquarium diffuser is ideal) through the lime-water contained in a tall narrow vessel such as a gas jar or measuring cylinder. Clearing is lengthy, and the last remnants of solid may be filtered to save time. The preparation can be demonstrated. The finished solution deteriorates on keeping. Permanent hardness is caused by Ca^{++} from saturated calcium sulphate solution, and may be simulated by a 1 g per litre solution of calcium chloride. Tap water may contain both types of hardness. Your local Water Board engineer will probably provide an analysis. All water contains some dissolved solid. Areas with hard rock of low solubility (e.g., Aberdeen, Lake District, Malvern) have as little as 15 parts per million solids. Under 50 ppm is regarded as soft, 300 ppm fairly hard. There is immense variation from place to place (for example, Ipswich water is fifteen times harder than Liverpool) and at an individual place from season to season (river supplies are harder when flowing slowly in summer).
178	If kettle fur is available you could add dilute hydrochloric acid to it and test for carbon dioxide.
179	Two pupils, one of whom has hands covered with blackboard chalk, which is plaster of Paris $CaSO_4.2H_2O$, washing their hands simultaneously is a telling demonstration. Although hardness has been discussed relative to calcium compounds, the corresponding magnesium ones exist and react similarly.
180	For experiment 8.6 a lather may be defined as a complete film of bubbles which lasts 30 seconds. Pupils often mistake a thick scum for a lather. Calgon is a

TEACHER'S NOTES

PAGE	
	polymetaphosphate $(NaPO_3)_6$. Washing soda effloresces on standing, losing water to form powdery $Na_2CO_3.H_2O$. Its solution is feebly alkaline, and when used in bath salts reacts with fats in the skin, producing soap. Sodium sesquicarbonate is $Na_2CO_3.NaHCO_3.2H_2O$.
182	Alumino-silicates (zeolites) have now been superseded in domestic water softeners by cross-linked polystyrene resins with side-chains which exchange cations or anions, e.g., replace Ca^{++} in the water by Na^+. Other resins replace Ca^{++} by H^+, or SO_4^{--} by OH^-. Zeocarb 225, sodium form, is suitable for experiment 8.6(c). Using x cm³ of resin, pass through $x/5$ cm³ hard water per minute. To regenerate the column pass $5x$ cm³ 10 per cent HCl in 30 minutes, then $1.2x$ cm³ 5 per cent NaOH, and rinse with distilled water. Running the column dry makes channels in the bed. The column will also decolorize 0.6 g per litre $CuSO_4.5H_2O$ solution by removal of Cu^{++}.
182	For clarity, Fig. 8.7 has the inlet tube turned through 90° in a horizontal plane. Regeneration may be nightly in a large hotel or hospital, or three monthly in a domestic softener where water-use and hardness are small.
184	As the drop percolates through the ceiling, release of hydrostatic pressure helps decomposition of the calcium hydrogen carbonate solution. Stalactites form under old bridges as water percolates through mortar. Quick evaporation of the hanging drop speeds the growth.

Chapter 9

186	The topic presents difficulties, but plastics are so common and important that their study is essential. The general aim of the chapter is to induce a feeling for the relation between structure and properties, without discouraging pupils by an indigestible mass of impenetrable formulae. The treatment is by no means exhaustive; polypropylene, Perspex, rayons, and the epoxy resins and polyurethanes are not mentioned. Much project work is possible, and useful material is found in *Projects in Chemistry*, by M. Hayes (Batsford), *Your Book of Plastics*, by J. G. Cook (Watford, Merrow), *A Handbook of Textiles*, by A. M. Collier (Pergamon Press).
	Experiments in Polymer Chemistry, by H. S. Finlay, is available free from The Shell Centre, Downstream Building, London, SE1, and the Shell Plastics Kit (£2) contains specimens, a background booklet, and a simple identification scheme for some plastics.
	The Griffin Polymer Kit contains chemicals for eleven polymer experiments.
186	If at all possible demonstrate the cracking of butane using molecular models.
187	Work on ethylene could be done here or in chapter 5. Small quantities are conveniently made by the 'wet asbestos' method (experiment 7.14), using ethanol in the asbestos and dehydrating it with heated broken plant pot fragments farther up the tube. The ethylene is collected over water. It may be burned, and its double-bonded (unsaturated) nature shown by its reaction with bromine water.
187	Small amounts of polythene were made by ICI in 1935. The shortage of rubber and the needs of radar during the Seond World War encouraged large-scale production. Differing catalysts produce products having densities between 0.91 and 0.97 g cm⁻³ and differing flexibilities. Some low density specimens have short side-chains.
188	If the polythene specimen fits tightly in the measuring cylinder, twist it in the direction of its spiral for removal.

CHEMISTRY

PAGE
- 189 Polythene containers cause pollution, as do many other plastics, because they resist attack by air and water.
- 189 Suitable sources of thermoplastics are ballpoint pen inner and some outer tubes, insulation from wire, and cream and yoghourt cartons. Old radio knobs, rigid screw-on bottle tops, plug tops, and electric fittings are usually thermosets. The distinction between melting and decomposing can be used to revise chemical and physical change.
- 191 The use of plasticizers is not confined to PVC.
- 192 Other relatives of polythene include polypropylene (Propathene), polytetrafluoroethylene (PTFE, Fluon, Teflon), and polymethyl methacrylate (Perspex, Lucite) whose monomers are:

$$\begin{array}{ccc} H\ \ CH_3 & F\ \ F & H\ \ CH_3 \\ |\ \ | & |\ \ | & |\ \ | \\ C\!=\!C & C\!=\!C & C\!=\!C \\ |\ \ | & |\ \ | & |\ \ | \\ H\ \ H & F\ \ F & H\ \ COOCH_3 \end{array}$$

- 192 Hexamethylene diamine (1.6 diaminohexane) should not be touched or inhaled as dust, and is also expensive. The reaction is:

$$H_2\!-\!N\!-\!(CH_2)_6\!-\!N\!-\!\underline{H + Cl}\!-\!\overset{O}{\overset{\|}{C}}\!-\!(CH_2)_8\!-\!\overset{O}{\overset{\|}{C}}\!-\!\underline{Cl + H}\!-\!N\ldots$$

$$\downarrow$$

$$H_2\!-\!N\!-\!(CH_2)_6\!-\!N\!\underset{+HCl}{\rule{1cm}{0.4pt}}\overset{O}{\overset{\|}{C}}\!-\!(CH_2)_8\!-\!\overset{O}{\overset{\|}{C}}\underset{+HCl}{\rule{1cm}{0.4pt}}N\ldots$$

This is part of a molecule of nylon 6.10, the numbers being the number of carbons between the nitrogen atoms of the

$$\begin{array}{c} O\ \ H \\ \|\ \ | \\ -C\!-\!N- \end{array}$$

(amide) groups. BriNylon is nylon 6.6.

- 194 Enkalon, nylon 6, is made from $HOOC.(CH_2)_6.NH_2$. All nylons have similar, but not identical properties. They are polyamide fibres (compare Terylene, polyester). The first nylon was produced by the du Pont Corporation in 1935, and the name was derived from the words New York and London.

  When nylon is stretched the chains become approximately aligned, providing maximum interchain attraction and greater strength. High tenacity yarns are stretched more than normal yarns. The alignment makes nylon more nearly crystalline and improves the lustre.

  Experiment 9.1 may be repeated with nylon, using fabric.

  Nylon is more readily attacked than polythene, for which no solvent is known at room temperature.

- 195 In experiment 9.4 the phenol is caustic, and noxious fumes are evolved. The experiment may be done with small quantities in a test-tube, using a very small

TEACHER'S NOTES

PAGE

flame. Break the tube to remove the baked product. The chemical bonds holding Bakelite chains in a network should now be contrasted with the weaker attractions between the polymer molecules of thermoplastics.

Bakelite was invented by Dr Baekeland, a Belgian working in the US in 1907. Modified natural materials such as ebonite, and the artificial silks, now called rayons, had been used earlier. Rayons, which now constitute 60 per cent of the world's man-made fibre production, are based on natural cellulose molecules, and have been made since 1884.

198 Urea formaldehyde resin is produced according to:

$$+ H_2N-CO-NH_2 + CH_2O + H_2N-CO-NH_2 +$$
$$\downarrow$$
$$-NH-CO-NH-----CO-NH-CO-NH-$$
$$+ H_2O \quad + H_2O$$

200 Allyl compounds, containing two double bonds, produce thermosets by addition. One double bond builds long chains, then the other forms cross-links.

201 Proteins in foods are digested by enzymes which are also proteins, but of different types. Insulin is a fairly simple protein containing only fifty-one amino-acid units. The peptide link in proteins is

$$\begin{array}{cc} O & H \\ \| & | \\ -C-N- \end{array} \quad \text{(compare nylon)}$$

201 Isoprene is:

$$\begin{array}{c} H_2C=C---C=CH_2 \\ | \quad | \\ CH_3 \quad H \end{array}$$

Chapter 10

203 There is 78 per cent nitrogen by volume in dry air. The boiling points of the main constituents are O_2 $-183°C$, Ar $-186°C$, N_2 $-196°C$, and there is sometimes some argon in liquid oxygen.

203 Nitrogen can be made by heating a solution of sodium nitrite and ammonium chloride, and collected over water, if you wish to demonstrate its inertness.

204 It is advisable to distinguish carefully between ammonia, ammonium, and ammonia solution (a more correct name for ammonium hydroxide).

204 In experiment 10.1(a) and (c) do not boil the solutions so that steam condenses in the gas jar or flask. The ammonia evolved is wet, but all the experiments work well with it, even the fountain experiment. Ammonia may be dried by passing through lump quicklime in a tube or tower. To start the fountain in experiments 10.1(c) or 10.4(g), put the flask horizontally in the water; the small head required and the cooling effect usually do the trick.

205 As ammonia dissolves in water the water molecules are forced apart by extensive hydrogen bonding, and the density actually decreases. The most concentrated solution possible has a density of 0.880 g cm^{-3}.

206 The reaction between ammonia and hydrogen chloride is effectively demonstrated by putting their solutions in neighbouring watch-glasses and blowing across them. Plugs of cotton wool, soaked in the solutions and pushed into the ends of a horizontal glass tube 1 cm in diameter and 20 cm long, form a ring of

PAGE

ammonium chloride approximately one-third of the way from the acid end, demonstrating diffusion speeds.

208 After O, C, H, and N, the next most abundant elements are Ca, P, Cl, and F.

208 Some sewage is made into compost, and the nitrogen from the rest is partly returned via fish used as food. There is some fixation of nitrogen by lightning, which forms oxides of nitrogen and eventually dilute nitric acid, which falls in rain.

208 It has been estimated that without the Haber Process:
(*a*) widespread famines would have started in the 'thirties as Chilean nitrates became exhausted,
(*b*) the German war effort would have stopped in 1917 for lack of foods and explosives.
Lack of fixed nitrogen is a factor in creating dust bowls. Crop rotation, and lying fallow were early methods of conserving fixed nitrogen.

208 The gas mixture is 80 per cent N_2O_4 at room temperature, reducing to 0 per cent at 180°C. NO_2 is brown, N_2O_4 colourless, so the colour darkens as the temperature of the gas is raised to 180°.

209 There is no overall summary for nitrogen, but separate summaries are provided for ammonia and nitric acid (chapter 6).

209 Sulphur has been used for fumigation since 1000 BC. Native sulphur is visible and the smell of sulphur dioxide is apparent in volcanic craters. The production of sulphur in Sicily is not so important now because one Frasch well can produce 400 tonnes of sulphur per day.

210 The allotropy of sulphur is fully treated as it is a good example of the effect of structure on properties. Pupils should be told that the name is roll sulphur, not rolled. The whole of experiment 10.3 works better with roll than flowers of sulphur. Carbon disulphide is volatile, flammable, poisonous, explosive when mixed with certain proportions of air, and has a smell reminiscent of decaying cabbages, so it should be handled with care. Excellent monoclinic crystals can be made by cooling a hot saturated solution of roll sulphur in toluene or xylene. Make the solution by refluxing the solvent and dropping in small pieces of sulphur until no more dissolves—the solution may be re-used if kept in a well-stoppered bottle.

The forms of sulphur may be remembered by the mnemonic 'clinic-needle'.
If the sulphur vapour catches fire it can be smothered or blown out.
When the liquid is poured out the vapour sometimes sublimes, forming flowers of sulphur on the surface of the water.

211 Models of the buckled S_8 ring may be made from molecular model kits or from polystyrene spheres.

212 Sulphur dioxide may be obtained from small cylinders or flagons, or by the action of a warm dilute acid on a sulphite, metabisulphite, or hydrogen sulphite. The black mixture formed in experiment 10.4 contains CuS and Cu_2S. Good ventilation is essential during sulphur dioxide experiments.

213 The bleaching action is explained by:

$$\text{dye} + H_2SO_3 \longrightarrow (\text{dye less oxygen}) + H_2SO_4$$

Sometimes the bleached dye re-absorbs oxygen from the air and becomes coloured again.

214 Atmospheric sulphur dioxide attacks garden fungi, so that roses in towns seldom suffer from black spot, a rather marginal advantage for pollution.

TEACHER'S NOTES

PAGE

215 The properties of hydrogen sulphide can be demonstrated using small-scale apparatus, or a test-tube and dropper. Always empty an H_2S apparatus in the fume cupboard. After the H_2S/Cl_2 reaction the presence of HCl gas can be demonstrated by putting a little concentrated ammonia solution in the gas jar.

216 The yellow cadmium sulphide is used as a pigment, e.g., in car headlamp bulbs. Ionic equations could be used for these precipitations.

217 Chlorine preparation was mentioned in experiment 6.10. The permanganate equation is:

$$2KMnO_4 + 16HCl \longrightarrow 2KCl + 2MnCl_2 + 8H_2O + 5Cl_2$$

Take special care to keep chlorine away from asthmatic children, but in any case use a well-ventilated laboratory.

218 The electronic structure of Cl_2 could be revised here.

218 Multicoloured fabrics such as flower prints often bleach interestingly.

218 The iodine can be extracted by carbon tetrachloride, forming a purple solution (compare vapour).
With abler children the ionic approach will permit a fuller explanation of the difference between electrolyzing fused NaCl and a solution of NaCl (see also Appendix 4). If the products of electrolysis of brine are allowed to mix they react, producing a solution containing sodium chloride and hypochlorite:

$$2NaOH + Cl_2 \longrightarrow NaCl + NaClO + H_2O$$

218 The sulphur formed in experiment 10.7(f) is often so pale as to look almost white, because it is very finely divided. A finely divided substance often differs in colour from a massive specimen; compare finely powdered $CuSO_4.5H_2O$ with a large crystal. Metals such as Mg, Na, and Fe wire burn in chlorine synthesizing their chlorides. This could be used to illustrate an extended definition of oxidation, i.e., $Mg \longrightarrow Mg^{++}$.

218 The specks of carbon produced when wax burns in chlorine progressively absorb the blue end of the spectrum, and the flame reddens—compare a red sunrise.

219 Bleaching powder is a complex substance, and $CaOCl_2$ is an approximation to the formula.

219 A modern replacement of the carbon tetrachloride fire extinguisher is the BCF extinguisher, containing bromochlorodifluoromethane, $CBrClF_2$, a volatile liquid which is propelled to the fire by a charge of nitrogen at 10 atmospheres pressure. Do not use carbon tetrachloride on burning metals.

220 Sea water contains, among others, the ions Na^+, K^+, Mg^{++}, Ca^{++}, Cl^-, Br^-, SO_4^{--}, CO_3^{--}. On evaporation small amounts of $CaCO_3$ and $CaSO_4$ deposit first, followed by NaCl. The subsequent order of deposition depends on the temperature of evaporation. (See Fowles, *School Science Review*, **143**, November 1959.) After mentioning that sodium chloride is ionic it is convenient to compare the structures and properties of Na^+Cl^- and CCl_4, using models if available.

221 The influence of fluorides on tooth decay was discovered during a survey initiated by sweet manufacturers in the USA. Fluorine is not the only trace element influencing tooth formation, e.g., molybdenum appears to be necessary for healthy teeth.

CHEMISTRY

Chapter 11

PAGE

223 Project work, often involving physics and biology as well as chemistry, can arise naturally from any of the sixteen main topics dealt with in this section.

224 Silicon dioxide, silica, occurs as quartz, flint, and kieselguhr (the absorbent in dynamite), as well as in sand. Silver sand is almost white, and flows readily as it has rounded grains. It was much used in hour glasses. Sharp sand does not flow, and is used to make moulds for metal casting. A model of the silica structure is useful.

225 Various mixes such as 1:1, 2:1, 3:1 sand and cement can be cast into bars about 2 cm square and 15 cm long, and their breaking strains compared with that of a pure cement bar. Lengthwise reinforcement by galvanized wire, bent at 90° near the ends to anchor them, increases the tensile strength considerably. Moulds are made by nailing parallel wooden strips on to a base board and filling in with Plasticene the ends of the troughs so created.

225 Before 1939 most mortar was made from $Ca(OH)_2$ without cement. The grey colour came from ground-up coke and old brick used as filler in addition to sand. Set mortar gives off CO_2 with dilute HCl.

225 Plaster of Paris was originally made for artists in Montmartre. The heat evolution on setting is noticeable when a large quantity sets. Modern wall plasters may contain cement as well as plaster. The rough, scored base-coat plasters are similar to mortar. The yellow-coated dustless chalk is made from calcium carbonate (whiting) bound together with oily material; it evolves CO_2 with dilute HCl.

225 Glass is an excellent topic for a project: its history, manufacture, etching and shaping by blowing, blow-moulding, extrusion, pulling, and casting are all interesting. The Griffin Technical Study Kit 'Glassmaking' describes experiments on making, colouring, and investigating glass.

227 Supercooling is quite a common phenomenon; the unusual aspect of supercooled glass is its stability under all sorts of varied conditions. Very occasionally glass crystallizes or devitrifies. Thin glass fibres are flexible, but even a medicine bottle bends. Prove this by putting a bung carrying a length of capillary tube into a medicine bottle full of coloured water. Squeezing the bottle alters the level of liquid in the tube. Try squeezing the long and then the short sides for a surprising result.

227 Dyestuffs are hard to treat meaningfully and briefly, and are omitted from the chapter, but are good for project work. Orange-peel, mosses, tree-bark, onion skins, coffee, fruit juices, and plant roots macerated in water plus a little ethanol provide natural dyes. Using cotton, wool, and synthetic fabrics with and without aluminium sulphate or alum as a mordant, and dyeing for differing times at various temperatures, provides a starting point. (Mordant by boiling the fabric in the mordant solution before dyeing.) The Griffin kit 'Dyes and Dyeing' provides chemicals and ideas for further work on natural and synthetic dyes.

228 The history and chemistry of firemaking and fire extinguishing is a good project.

228 Of the two reactions between sodium hydroxide solution and carbon dioxide, only the second is mentioned in the pupils' book.

excess NaOH: $\quad 2NaOH + CO_2 \longrightarrow Na_2CO_3 + H_2O$

excess CO_2: $\quad\quad NaOH + CO_2 \longrightarrow NaHCO_3$

TEACHER'S NOTES

PAGE

228 The industrial process is the Solvay (ammonia-soda) Process, summarized by

$$NH_3 + CO_2 + NaCl + H_2O \longrightarrow NaHCO_3 + NH_4Cl$$

228 In experiment 11.3(c) gases which could be tested for are H_2, CO, CO_2, O_2, Cl_2. It is instructive to heat sodium carbonate also.

229 A flask fitted with a delivery tube and charged with sodium hydrogen carbonate solution and a capsizable test-tube of concentrated sulphuric acid makes a model soda-acid fire extinguisher.

229 There are two types of baking powder, quick-acting (sodium bicarbonate with tartaric acid or potassium hydrogen tartrate $KHC_4H_4O_6$) and slow-acting (sodium hydrogen carbonate with disodium dihydrogen pyrophosphate, $Na_2H_2P_2O_7$). The quick-acting gives CO_2 on moistening, the slow-acting gives an appreciable supply only on heating. Domestic powders are usually a mixture of both types with starch or flour.

230 Andrews Liver Salt contains sodium hydrogen carbonate, tartaric and citric acids, sugar, and magnesium sulphate. The latter has a purgative effect.

230 Silicones can contain rings as well as chains, and the analogy with carbon plastics is completed by the existence of hard infusible cross-linked silicones. An experiment on preparation of silicones appears in H. S. Finlay's booklet on plastics mentioned in the notes to chapter 9.

Tubes about 1 cm bore and 50 cm long are suitable for experiment 11.4. Silicones are expensive but a bottle costing just over £1 will last for years.

Silicones suitable for experiment 11.4(a) are Hopkin & Williams, Freshwater Road, Chadwell Heath, Essex. nos. MS 200/3 cs, MS 200/100 cs, and MS 200/100 000 cs. The MS 200/100 cs may be used for parts (b) and (c).

232 Some non-stick pans are coated with silicones, some with polytetrafluoroethylene (PTFE, Fluon, Teflon).

232 Glucose, containing one ring, is a monosaccharide; sucrose, which consists of a glucose ring joined to a fructose one, is a disaccharide.

232 Candle wax, although chemically different from animal fats, is a good example of the gradual softening of a mixture when heated.

233 Simple food tests are:
    starches—the starch-iodine test
    fats—rubbing on paper to produce a stain
    protein—yellowing with concentrated nitric acid or the biuret test.
Pupils given these reagents and specimens of the three food-types can sort out which method tests for which type, and then use the tests on foods of unknown composition.

233 The amount of water in shampoos can be determined by weighing then evaporating at 105° or in a desiccator. *Which*, November 1959 and March 1969, contain reports on shampoos.

234 Sodium sesquicarbonate $Na_2CO_3.NaHCO_3.2H_2O$ is commonly used in bath salts.

234 The Griffin Cosmetic Science Kit contains chemicals and instructions for the preparation of fifteen types of cosmetic.

235 Some work on the colloidal state could be done here. An emulsion is a colloidal suspension of a liquid in a liquid, foams are gas in liquid, aerosols (mists) are liquid in gas, and gels are liquid in solid. All these types of colloid are used in cosmetics. The upper and lower limits to colloidal particle size are roughly

CHEMISTRY

PAGE

10^{-5} cm and 10^{-7} cm diameter, so not all the parts of a foam or the so-called aerosol from a pressurized spray pack are truly colloidal.

235 This chapter contains only a small selection of the chemistry relevant to everyday life. Other topics suitable for project work include chemistry in the garden, adhesives, dyes, paints and pigments, and fuels. *Projects in Chemistry*, by M. Hayes (Batsford), contains many valuable suggestions.

Appendix 2

239 The tests may be introduced by discovery method; e.g., give initially a selection of named salts for flame testing, so that pupils observe the colours. The dependence on metal can be emphasized by testing sodium chloride, carbonate, sulphate, nitrate, etc.

239 Alternatives to platinum wire are:
   nichrome wire (cut off the end after use)
   a charred match stick
   a pencil lead
   a roll of charred filter paper

Flame colouration has been met in experiment 5.8(c). Spectroscopic methods akin to flame tests are used in industrial analysis, and in astronomy for analysing the composition of stars.

239 For tests other than flame tests pupils should be taught to use about 2 cm depth of any liquid reagent and a pile of solid which would cover the last $\frac{1}{2}$ cm of a wooden splint.

240 Many other sulphides precipitate with hydrogen sulphide, e.g., HgS, Ag_2S, and FeS (all black), SnS_2 (yellow), SnS (brown), and CdS (yellow).

240 The distinction between carbonates and hydrogen carbonates is not made, as pupils will meet only $NaHCO_3$ and $KHCO_3$. These hydrogen carbonates evolve carbon dioxide and steam when heated, and there is a further evolution when acids are added to the residue.

240 In the chloride, sulphate, and nitrate tests the acid added contains the same radical as the test reagent, e.g., if using silver nitrate solution add dilute nitric acid.

241 Spurious results can arise in qualitative analysis unless a complete scheme is used. Lead nitrate, for example, forms a precipitate in the sulphate test, but this is lead chloride rather than barium sulphate. Similarly bromides or iodides can form a brown ring. Such wrong results can be avoided if salts for analysis by this scheme are selected from:
   sodium carbonate, chloride, sulphate, and nitrate
   potassium carbonate, chloride, sulphate, and nitrate
   ammonium carbonate, chloride, sulphate, and nitrate
   copper carbonate, chloride, sulphate, and nitrate
   zinc chloride, sulphate, and nitrate
   calcium carbonate, chloride, and nitrate.

Pupils should do the tests in the order described in Appendix 2. Pupils' results are conveniently presented in a table containing three columns: Experiment, Observation, Conclusion.

Many other tests could be based on the chemistry in this book, e.g., displacement by chlorine water or a solution of chloramine T for iodides and bromides, warming with concentrated sulphuric acid for chlorides and nitrates, hydroxide

TEACHER'S NOTES

PAGE

precipitation by ammonia solution or sodium hydroxide solution, or heating the dry solid to test for nitrates and some carbonates.

241 Spirit-based inks need ethanol for chromatographic separation. Colours such as black, brown, purple, and orange provide interesting results. A strip of paper handkerchief provides a good column. A. V. Jones, *School Science Review*, 179, **47**, 299, 1970, describes many variants of these basic experiments.

242 The green colour from grass is a mixture of chlorophylls *a* and *b* which cannot be separated by this simple method, while the yellow marking contains xanthophyll.

Appendix 4

245 Two simplifications have been made in the treatment of this topic: acids have been regarded as containing H^+ rather than H_3O^+, and the subscripts denoting physical state have been omitted.

246 The activity series dealt with in chapter 7 could now be reconsidered ionically. Similarly the metals which evolve hydrogen with dilute acids can be shown to be those from which H^+ can win an electron, and hydrogen evolution discussed as an example of a displacement reaction.

Periodic T...

			H hydrogen					

Li lithium	Be beryllium							
Na sodium	Mg magnesium							
K potassium	Ca calcium	Sc scandium	Ti titanium	V vanadium	Cr chromium	Mn manganese	Fe iron	Co cobalt
Rb rubidium	Sr strontium	Y yttrium	Zr zirconium	Nb niobium	Mo molybdenum	Tc technetium	Ru ruthenium	Rh rhodium
Cs caesium	Ba barium	La lanth-anum	Hf hafnium	Ta tantalum	W tungsten	Re rhenium	Os osmium	Ir iridium
Fr francium	Ra radium	Ac actinium	Ku kurchatovium	105	Spaces available for artifici...			

Key
Metals
Non-metals
Metalloids
Inert Gases

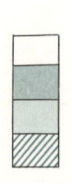

Ce cerium	Pr praesodimium	Nd neodimium	Pm promethium	Sm samarium
Th thorium	Pa protoactinium	U uranium	Np neptunium	Pu plutonium